Get More and Do More

Get Smart at Dummies.com

Las Vegas
FOR
DUMMIES®
6TH EDITION

by Rick Garman

WILEY

Wiley Publishing, Inc.

Las Vegas For Dummies, 6th Edition

Published by
Wiley Publishing, Inc.
111 River St.
Hoboken, NJ 07030-5774
www.wiley.com

Copyright © 2011 by Wiley Publishing, Inc., Indianapolis, Indiana

Published simultaneously in Canada

For general information on our other products and services, please contact our Customer Care Department within the U.S. at 877-762-2974, outside the U.S. at 317-572-3993, or fax 317-572-4002.

For technical support, please visit www.wiley.com/techsupport.

Wiley also publishes its books in a variety of electronic formats. Some content that appears in print may not be available in electronic books.

ISBN: 978-0-470-64375-4

Manufactured in the United States of America

10 9 8 7 6 5 4 3 2 1

WILEY

About the Author

Rick Garman has been writing about Las Vegas since 1997 when he and best friend Mary Herczog began writing the *Frommer's Las Vegas* guide book. His Web site, Vegas4Visitors.com, is one of the most respected Las Vegas travel resources on the Web. When not gambling away every penny he earns writing about the city he loves, Rick lives in Los Angeles and works in the entertainment industry.

A Note from the Author

Mary Herczog wrote this book (and a great many others) for a decade or so, about half as long as we were best friends. It was not long after we began our Vegas writing careers in 1997 that Mary was first diagnosed with breast cancer. Over the next dozen years, Mary faced her recurring illness with a kind of aplomb that most people found either inspiring or confounding; as she chose to focus less on whatever treatment she was undergoing and more on what fantastic meal she was going to get to eat on her next trip to Vegas. She wrote about what she called her "tribulations" in a series of articles for The Los Angeles Times and later on her Web site CancerChick.com as a way of demystifying the process, hoping that it might make it a little less scary for anyone else who might be going through the same thing. Through it all, she continued to write her guide books to Vegas and New Orleans and other destinations, which she loved doing partly out of her adoration of travel in general and partly out of her incredible knack for being able to tell people what to do and usually be right.

Mary Herczog died on February 16, 2010, surrounded by her family, her friends, and her dogs, exactly as she wanted it to be . . . if it had to be at all. About a week earlier, she asked me to take over the *Las Vegas For Dummies* guide book, and I am both humbled and honored to do so. Even though my name is on the title page, this is and always will be her book. Viva Las Vegas, Mary . . . the city will not be the same without you.

Publisher's Acknowledgments

We're proud of this book; please send us your comments through our Dummies online registration form located at www.dummies.com/register/.

Some of the people who helped bring this book to market include the following:

Editorial

Editors: Lindsay Conner, Production Editor; Jennifer Moore and Jamie Ehrlich, Development Editors

Copy Editor: Elizabeth Kuball

Cartographer: Liz Puhl

Editorial Assistant: Andrea Kahn

Senior Photo Editor: Richard Fox

Cover Photos:

Front cover: Close-up of dice on game table © Comstock Images / AGE Fotostock, Inc.
Back cover: The Fountain Show at the Bellagio Resort © Kerrick James / Alamy Images

Cartoons: Rich Tennant (www.the5thwave.com)

Composition Services

Project Coordinator: Sheree Montgomery

Layout and Graphics: Julie Trippetti

Proofreaders: Cara L. Buitron, Rebecca Denoncour

Indexer: Slivoskey Indexing Services

Publishing and Editorial for Consumer Dummies

Diane Graves Steele, Vice President and Publisher, Consumer Dummies

Kristin Ferguson-Wagstaffe, Product Development Director, Consumer Dummies

Kelly Regan, Editorial Director, Travel

Publishing for Technology Dummies

Andy Cummings, Vice President and Publisher, Dummies Technology/ General User

Composition Services

Gerry Fahey, Vice President of Production Services

Debbie Stailey, Director of Composition Services

Contents at a Glance

Maps at a Glance

Table of Contents

Introduction

....

*W*elcome to Las Vegas, a truly original city, where all the greatest landmarks are reproductions and the name of the game is gambling. This neon jungle is, at turns, classy, tacky, cheesy, and sleazy, but it's always entertaining. If there's one sure bet in this town, it's that you'll never be bored — even if you don't pull a single slot handle.

But navigating your way through the sensory overload that is Sin City without exhausting yourself should be a priority; you are, after all, on vacation. All you need to ensure an enjoyable trip to Las Vegas is some patience, some advance planning, and a little luck. (Hitting it big can do wonders for one's mood.)

About This Book

Pay full price? Read the fine print? Do it their way?

Excuse me? There's no need for any of that.

You picked this book because you know the *For Dummies* brand and you want to go to Las Vegas. You also probably know how much you want to spend, the pace you want to keep, and the amount of planning you can stomach. You may not want to tend to every little detail, yet you don't trust just anyone to make your plans for you.

In this book, we give you the lowdown on Las Vegas, which challenges Orlando as the number-one tourist destination in the United States. Rising from its modest beginning as a small, old-time gambling town, the city has more hotel rooms than any other. And for sheer spectacle, it's hard to beat Vegas. Here you can watch a volcano explode, see a pirate ship sink, stroll by the Eiffel Tower, and cross the Brooklyn Bridge. And did we mention that you can gamble?

To say that taking it all in can be overwhelming and exhausting would be a massive understatement. No need to worry. As Vegas veterans with years of experience, we've scoured the city from the Strip to downtown to find the best deals around. In this book, we guide you through Las Vegas in a clear, easy-to-understand way, allowing you to find the best hotels, restaurants, and attractions without having to read the book like a novel — cover to cover (although you *can* read this book cover to cover if you choose). With this book, you can find the best and most essential ingredients for a winning vacation.

Please be advised that travel information is subject to change at any time — and this is especially true of prices. Therefore, we suggest that you write or call ahead for confirmation when making your travel plans. The authors, editors, and publisher cannot be held responsible for the experiences of readers while traveling. Your safety is important to us, however, so we encourage you to stay alert and be aware of your surroundings. Keep a close eye on cameras, purses, and wallets, all favorite targets of thieves and pickpockets.

Conventions Used in This Book

In this book, we've included lists of hotels, restaurants, and attractions. As we describe each, we often include abbreviations for commonly accepted credit cards. Here are the abbreviations of each:

AE: American Express

DC: Diners Club

DISC: Discover

MC: MasterCard

V: Visa

We've divided the hotels into two categories — our personal favorites and those that don't quite make our preferred list but still get our hearty seal of approval. Don't be shy about considering these "runner-up" hotels, if you're unable to get a room at one of our favorites or if your preferences differ from ours. The amenities that the runners up offer and the services that each provides make all these accommodations good choices to consider as you determine where to rest your head at night.

We also include some general pricing information to help you as you decide where to unpack your bags or dine on the local cuisine. We've used a system of dollar signs to show a range of costs for one night in a hotel (the price refers to a double-occupancy room) or a meal at a restaurant (included in the cost of each meal is a soup or salad, an entree, a dessert, and a nonalcoholic drink). Check out the following table to decipher the dollar signs:

Cost	Hotel	Restaurant
$	$74 or less	$9 or less
$$	$75–$99	$10–$19
$$$	$100–$149	$20–29
$$$$	$150–$249	$30–$34
$$$$$	$250 or more	$35 or more

Foolish Assumptions

As we wrote this book, we made some assumptions about you and what your needs may be as a traveler:

- ✔ You may be an experienced traveler who hasn't had much time to explore Las Vegas and wants expert advice when you finally do get a chance to enjoy that particular locale.

- ✔ You may be an inexperienced traveler looking for guidance when determining whether to take a trip to Las Vegas and how to plan for it.

- ✔ You're not looking for a book that provides all the information available about Las Vegas or that lists every hotel, restaurant, or attraction available to you. Instead, you're looking for a book that focuses on the places that will give you the best or most unique experience in Las Vegas.

If you fit any of these criteria, then *Las Vegas For Dummies,* 6th Edition, gives you the information you're looking for!

How This Book Is Organized

Las Vegas For Dummies, 6th Edition, is divided into six parts. Each chapter is written so that you don't have to read what came before or after, though we sometimes refer you to other areas of the book for more information.

Part 1: Introducing Las Vegas

Think of this part as the hors d'oeuvres. In these chapters, we tempt you with the best experiences, hotels, restaurants, and attractions in Las Vegas. We also cover the city's historic highlights and throw in a weather forecast and a look at special events to help you decide when to visit.

Part 11: Planning Your Trip to Las Vegas

How much money should you budget? Should you use a travel agent? How about buying a package tour? Where can you find the best airfare? We answer those questions and then talk about booking tips and online sources. We also talk about travel insurance and renting a car, and provide special tips and resources for families, seniors, travelers with disabilities, and gay and lesbian travelers.

Part 111: Settling Into Las Vegas

Here we introduce you to the neighborhoods and explore some of the *modus transporto* (buses, taxis, and so on). We also give you a menu of area hotels and motels, and review local restaurants and buffets.

Part IV: Exploring Las Vegas

Jackpot! In this part, we take you on a stroll through Sin City, enabling you to do your best at adding to the coffers of the casinos. We take a thorough look at the attractions, entertainment (and yes, some people consider getting married at a drive-thru window entertaining!), shopping, and recreational opportunities in the city. Oh, and if you've managed to miss this until now, there's a lot of gambling. Because you probably want to press your luck at least once, we include everything you need to know to play the most popular games and find the best casinos. We even provide a few helpful itineraries to help you cruise Vegas's hot spots in the most efficient manner, and give you a couple day-trip options in case you want to get away from all the glitz.

Part V: Living It Up After Dark: Las Vegas Nightlife

An adult playground, Las Vegas really heats up after the sun sets, offering numerous opportunities to party all night long. In this part, we explore the city's life after dark, from big, splashy production shows, such as Cirque du Soleil, to some of the hottest dance clubs in town.

Part VI: The Parts of Tens

Every *For Dummies* book offers the delightful Parts of Tens. Finding this part is as certain as the casino coming out ahead at the gambling tables. In this part, we serve up a bunch of cool facts about Las Vegas and salute some of the city's past greats. We share the top ten Vegas values, and we end the part with a return to nature: an introduction to ten Nevada desert dwellers, in case you manage to pull yourself away from the bright lights.

Quick Concierge

In back of this book, we include an appendix — your Quick Concierge — containing lots of handy information you may need when traveling in Las Vegas, such as phone numbers and addresses of emergency personnel or area hospitals and pharmacies, lists of local newspapers and magazines, protocol for sending mail or finding taxis, and more. Check out this appendix when searching for answers to lots of little questions that may come up as you travel. You can find the Quick Concierge easily, because it's printed on yellow paper.

Icons Used in This Book

You find several icons scattered throughout the margins of this book. Consider them your road map for finding the information you need.

Keep an eye out for the Bargain Alert icon as you seek out money-saving tips and/or great deals.

 The Best of the Best icon highlights the best Vegas has to offer in all categories — hotels, restaurants, attractions, activities, shopping, and nightlife.

 Watch for the Heads Up icon to identify annoying or potentially dangerous situations such as tourist traps, unsafe neighborhoods, and budgetary rip-offs.

 You find useful advice on things to do and ways to schedule your time when you see the Tip icon.

 Look to the Kid Friendly icon for attractions, hotels, restaurants, and activities that are particularly hospitable to children or people traveling with kids. Keep in mind that Las Vegas is not that receptive to small fries, so it's not the ideal spot for a family vacation, regardless of what it once claimed.

 Because you're likely to press your luck at some point during your stay in Las Vegas, look to the Gambling Tip icon for a little guidance on maximizing your chances and minimizing your losses.

Where to Go from Here

We've briefed you on what to expect from this book, so roll the dice and start reading. You have lots to do before you arrive, from arranging a place to snatch a few hours' sleep between poker sessions to finding the best places to spend your winnings. Like the Boy Scouts' creed, the successful Vegas traveler needs to "be prepared"; follow the advice in this book, and the odds of your having a great vacation will be hard to beat. And, last but not least, have fun — the city is designed to entertain you, so open your mind and enjoy it!

Part I
Introducing Las Vegas

The 5th Wave   By Rich Tennant

"Welcome to 'Jungle Jungle,' Las Vegas' newest theme hotel. You're in treehouse 709. The vines are around the corner to your left. I'll have a monkey bring up your luggage."

In this part . . .

To get the most enjoyment out of a vacation with the least amount of hassles, it helps to know what's awaiting you in your chosen paradise before the landing gear lowers. If you want your Las Vegas vacation to pay off in spades, you need to plan it as far in advance as possible.

In this part, we highlight the joys of a trip to Sin City and help you sort out the logistics of planning your trip, from choosing the best times to go to determining your vacation budget. But before we get into the nitty-gritty details, we take a look at some of the best things Las Vegas has to offer.

Chapter 1

Discovering the Best of Las Vegas

In This Chapter
▶ Enjoying the best Las Vegas experiences
▶ Finding the best places to stay and dine
▶ Seeing the best shows

"*I*t's Vegas, baby!" is the catchphrase from the independent hit movie *Swingers* — and that's all you need to know.

Okay, maybe you need to know a little more. But if a city exists that has its heart — and all sorts of other body parts — right on its sleeve, and all its goods in the shop window (which is, by the way, subtly outlined in blazing bright neon), it's Las Vegas. This isn't a coy metropolis or an unassuming city. Vegas is a gaudy monstrosity of delight — a city designed solely to take your money and break your heart while making you love it and beg for more. And people do keep coming — Las Vegas is one of the most popular tourist destinations in the world. Don't come here looking for culture and self-improvement, but do come here looking for a whale of a good time. You're sure to have it.

The following are our picks for the best of Las Vegas.

Best Vegas Experiences

From hitting the big jackpot to hanging out with dolphins, here are some of the best experiences Vegas has to offer.

✔ **Best most-Vegas moment:** Seeing the Strip at night, when it's coated in lights. Everything gleams, shimmers, shimmies, and beckons. The sight is sinful and delicious. Even a cynic's jaw drops, and even the purest of the pure get a little bit giddy. It's a testament to the philosophy that anything is possible — there's both hope and horror in that.

Las Vegas at a Glance

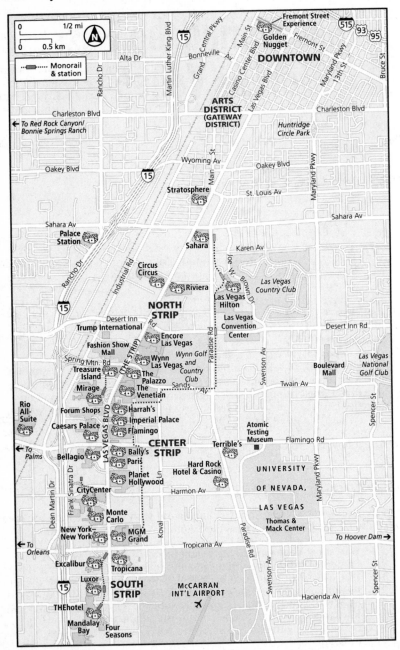

✔ **Best hoped-for Vegas moment:** Hitting that million-dollar jackpot with one pull of a handle. Good luck to you.

✔ **Best free show:** The Fountains of Bellagio. Sounds silly, until you see those giant spouts of water dance and leap to everything from opera arias to Sinatra. Try to not grin at least once. We dare you.

✔ **Best non-Vegas moment:** Hanging out with the coolest water mammals around in the Mirage's **Dolphin Habitat.** The trainers, who have the best job in the city, have them jump periodically (all natural movements they would do for fun anyway). The dolphins love it. You will, too.

✔ **Best cheapskate-Vegas fun:** Playing penny slots. C'mon, live a little!

Best Vegas Hotels

See Chapter 9 for complete reviews of the hotels that follow.

✔ **Best drop-dead hotel: Aria Las Vegas** is eye candy for the masses; a reinvention of what a Las Vegas casino hotel can (and maybe should) be. With an ostentatious, dramatic, modern design (inside and out) and more things to do than you'll have time for, it is the blueprint for the future of Sin City.

✔ **Best hotel for the well-heeled: The Four Seasons,** naturally. It has a reputation for a reason. All is comfort, all is class. And honestly, it probably isn't any more expensive than some of the other high-end hotels on the Strip.

✔ **Best resort hotel: Red Rock Resort** is on the border between the city and the wildlife of Red Rock Canyon and offers the best of both worlds.

✔ **Best totally Vegas hotel:** It's not really as it once was, but although **Caesars Palace** has stripped away some of its cheese, it still ranks as the archetype for all Vegas hotels. There's the theme, typified by the Roman soldiers strolling the property and the talking Roman statues in the Rome-themed shopping mall. There's the sense of luxury. There's Celine and Cher. And there's the size. Some think it romantic, some think it a hoot — just like Vegas itself.

✔ **Best theme hotel: New York–New York,** where the entire NYC skyline is built into the hotel's structure and major Manhattan landmarks are a part of the hotel's public spaces.

✔ **Best swimming pool: Mandalay Bay's** water area, with a wave pool, a beach, a lazy river, several other basic pools, and even an outdoor casino, is so fabulous it has to check room keys to keep nonguests away. We also like the tropical wonderland around the **Mirage's** amorphous pool; and **Caesars Palace** has its Garden of the Gods with eight (!) separate pools, each with its own atmosphere.

✔ **Best bathrooms:** THEhotel has a sunken tub so deep, the water comes up to your chin, plus a flat-screen TV. The rest of it is marble and big. We were tempted to write this entire book from there.

✔ **Best downtown hotel:** It's a tie between the **Golden Nugget,** the overall sharpest and most together hotel, with rooms comparable to the Mirage, and the cheaper and oddly sweet **Main Street Station.**

Best Vegas Restaurants

See Chapter 10 for complete reviews of the following restaurants.

✔ **Best celebrity-chef restaurants:** If money is no object, you have to eat at **Joël Robuchon** at the Mansion (in the MGM Grand), where the master chef continues his sterling reputation. (Truth be told, Robuchon isn't in the kitchen all the time, but many of his employees from his famous establishments are in charge, and they execute their duties flawlessly.) Considerably less dear is **Picasso** (in the Bellagio) where Julian Serrano, late of San Francisco's Masa, actually holds court most nights. Otherwise, you probably can rely on the fact that someone is paying careful attention to Emeril's **Table 10** (in the Palazzo), Thomas Keller's **Bouchon** (in the Venetian), and Charlie Palmer's **Aureole.** If these chefs themselves aren't wielding the utensils, they've made darn sure someone reliable — and maybe even on their way to their own celebrity-chef fame — is.

✔ **Best non-celebrity-chef restaurants: Rosemary's** is run by two chefs who cut their teeth on noted restaurants in New Orleans before coming to Vegas to help open up Emeril's Seafood at the MGM Grand. **Alize** (in the Palms) is another venture from Andre (of Andre's in Monte Carlo, also highly recommended). Then there's **Raku Grill,** with its deliriously delicious robata-grill small plates. We've had some of our best meals in Vegas at these restaurants. The chefs may not be household names, but they ought to be.

✔ **Best new restaurant:** Speaking of celebrity chefs, Todd English has expanded his Vegas empire with the moderately priced but highly enjoyable **Todd English P.U.B.**

✔ **Best budget meal:** The submarine sandwiches at **Capriotti's** are so big, not to mention so delicious, that three people could probably feel well fed off one large sandwich — which costs around $9.

✔ **Best buffet:** The days of cheap Vegas buffets are over — if you want food that's more than just fuel, at least. If you don't mind spending a bit (but still probably less overall than you might at any moderately priced restaurant), spend it on the range of French regional-inspired dishes at **Paris, Le Village Buffet** (in the Paris hotel) or the less thematically oriented, but still terrific **Wynn Las**

Vegas Buffet. Otherwise, of the more moderately priced (but still not all that pricey) buffets, **Main Street Station** has the freshest and nicest one.

✔ **Best red meat:** We love the prime rib at **Lawry's,** but if you want other cuts of cow, try the pepper-rubbed delicacies at **Strip House.** The latter a little too pricey? Locals love what they do to meat at **Austins Steakhouse.**

Best Vegas Entertainment

See Chapters 16 and 17 for reviews of these and other nightlife options:

✔ **Best production shows:** We have tears in our eyes when we watch **Cirque de Soleil's O,** as they perform feats of skill and beauty in, over, across, above, and around a tank of water like no other. And for sheer audacity of mechanics, plus an actual plot, Cirque may have topped itself with **KÀ.**

✔ **Best headliner show:** For two hours, you get **Garth Brooks** and his guitar, and it's one of the most transcendent musical experiences you'll ever see. You don't even have to like country music to enjoy it!

✔ **Best smart guys: Penn & Teller** ostensibly do magic, but it's basically an excuse for hip, intelligent, social commentary. Vegas doesn't deserve them. Probably no one does. Go and show your appreciation.

✔ **Best classic Vegas revue:** The nipple-tastic, topless *Jubilee!* is everything you could want in a Vegas revue: pointless sketches about Samson and Delilah and the sinking of the *Titanic;* lip-syncing, topless show girls; and giant Bob Mackie headdresses. It's absurd — and the best of an endangered species.

Chapter 2

Digging Deeper into Las Vegas

*V*egas is simple: Gamble and gawk. Repeat as needed. Okay, so there may be a *little* more to the town than that — or, rather, perhaps there is more detail to those two activities than that.

History 101: The Main Events

There has rarely been a time in Vegas's post-Bugsy history when the city wasn't booming, but it's amazing what a little global economic meltdown can do to a city. Development hasn't stopped — there are new hotels, casino, attractions, restaurants, and general hubbub to see and do all the time — but the boom is certainly not quite as big these days as it has been in the past.

The 1930s: The Eighth Wonder of the World

For many years after its creation, Las Vegas was a mere whistle-stop town, a desert hellhole. That all changed in 1928 when Congress authorized the building of nearby Boulder Dam (later renamed Hoover Dam), bringing thousands of workers to the area. It's probably just a coincidence that in 1931, after the city was flooded with all kinds of bored, tired men with disposable income, gambling once again became legal in Nevada. Upon the dam's completion, the workers left, and the Las Vegas Chamber of Commerce worked hard to lure the hordes of tourists who came to see the engineering marvel (it was called "the Eighth Wonder of the World") to its casinos. But it wasn't until the early years of World War II that visionary entrepreneurs figured out how to sprinkle the glitter on Vegas and its future.

The 1940s: Las Vegas goes south

Contrary to popular lore, developer Bugsy "My First Name Is Benjamin, Dammit!" Siegel didn't actually stake a claim in the middle of nowhere — he just built a few blocks south of already-existing properties.

In 1941, El Rancho Vegas, ultraluxurious for its time, was built on a remote stretch of highway (across the street from where the Sahara now stands). Scores of Hollywood celebrities were invited to the grand opening, and El Rancho Vegas soon became the hotel of choice for visiting film stars.

Other properties followed, with each new property trying to outdo existing hotels in luxurious amenities and thematic splendor — a trend that continues today. Las Vegas was on its way to becoming the entertainment capital of the world. Throughout the decade, the city was Hollywood's celebrity playground. The Hollywood connection gave the town glamour in the public's mind. So did the mob connection (something Las Vegas has spent decades trying to live down), which became clear when, in 1946, notorious underworld gangster Bugsy Siegel began construction on the fabulous Flamingo, a tropical paradise and "a real class joint."

A steady stream of name entertainers came to Las Vegas. In 1947, Jimmy Durante opened the showroom at the Flamingo. Other headliners of the 1940s included Dean Martin and Jerry Lewis, tap-dancing legend Bill "Bojangles" Robinson, the Mills Brothers, skater Sonja Henie, and Frankie Laine. Future Las Vegas legend Sammy Davis, Jr., debuted at El Rancho Vegas in 1945.

While the Strip was expanding, the downtown area kept pace with such new hotels as the El Cortez and the Golden Nugget. By the end of the decade, Fremont Street was known as "Glitter Gulch," its profusion of neon signs proclaiming round-the-clock gaming and entertainment.

The 1950s: Building booms and A-bombs

Las Vegas entered the new decade as a city (no longer a frontier town) with a population of about 50,000. Hotel growth was phenomenal, and that laid the groundwork for the Vegas of today. (Who says this town has no tradition?) The Desert Inn, which opened in 1950 with headliners Edgar Bergen and Charlie McCarthy, brought country-club elegance (including an 18-hole golf course and tennis courts) to the Strip.

In 1951, the Eldorado Club Downtown became Benny Binion's Horseshoe Club, which would gain fame as the home of the annual World Series of Poker. In 1954, the Showboat sailed into a new area east of downtown. The Showboat not only introduced buffet meals, but also offered round-the-clock bingo and a bowling alley (106 lanes to date).

In 1955 the Côte d'Azur–themed Riviera became the ninth big hotel to open on the Strip. Breaking the ranch-style mode, it was, at nine stories, the Strip's first high-rise. Liberace, one of the hottest names in show business, was paid the unprecedented sum of $50,000 a week to dazzle audiences in the Riviera's posh Clover Room.

Elvis appeared at the New Frontier in 1956 but wasn't a huge success; his fans were too young to fit the Las Vegas tourist mold. In 1958, the $10-million, 1,065-room Stardust upped the spectacular stakes by importing the famed *Lido de Paris* spectacle from the French capital. It became one of the longest-running shows ever to play Las Vegas.

Throughout the 1950s, most of the Vegas hotels competed for performers whose followers spent freely in the casinos. The advent of big-name Strip entertainment tolled a death knell for glamorous nightclubs in the United States; owners simply couldn't compete with the astronomical salaries paid to Las Vegas headliners. Two performers whose names have been linked to Las Vegas ever since — Frank Sinatra and Wayne Newton — made their debuts there. Mae West not only performed in Las Vegas, but also cleverly bought up a half-mile of desolate Strip frontage between the Dunes and the Tropicana.

Competition for the tourist dollar also brought nationally televised sporting events such as the PGA's Tournament of Champions. In the 1950s, the wedding industry helped make Las Vegas one of the nation's most popular venues for goin' to the chapel. Celebrity weddings of the 1950s that sparked the trend included singer Dick Haymes and Rita Hayworth, Joan Crawford and Pepsi chairman Alfred Steele, Carol Channing and TV exec Charles Lowe, and Paul Newman and Joanne Woodward.

On a grimmer note, the '50s also heralded the atomic age in Nevada, with nuclear testing taking place just 65 miles northwest of Las Vegas. A chilling 1951 photograph shows a mushroom-shaped cloud from an atomic bomb test visible over the Fremont Street horizon. Throughout the decade, about one bomb a month was detonated in the nearby desert (an event, interestingly enough, that often attracted loads of tourists).

The 1960s: The Rat Pack and a pack rat

The very first month of the new decade made entertainment history when the Sands hosted a three-week "Summit Meeting" in the Copa Room that was presided over by "Chairman of the Board" Frank Sinatra with Rat Pack cronies Dean Martin; Sammy Davis, Jr.; Peter Lawford; and Joey Bishop — all of whom happened to be in town filming the original *Ocean's Eleven.*

The building boom of the '50s took a brief respite. Most of the Strip's first property, El Rancho Vegas, burned down in 1960. And the first new hotel of the decade, the first to be built in nine years, was the exotic Aladdin in 1966.

During the '60s, negative attention focused on mob influence in Las Vegas. Of the 11 major casino hotels that opened in the previous decade, 10 were believed to have been financed with mob money. Then, like a knight in shining armor, Howard Hughes rode into town and embarked on a $300-million hotel- and property-buying spree, which included the Desert Inn (in 1967). Hughes was as "bugsy" as Benjamin Siegel any day, but his pristine reputation helped bring respectability to the desert city and lessen its gangland stigma.

Las Vegas became a family destination in 1968, when Circus Circus burst onto the scene with the world's largest permanent circus and a "junior casino" that featured dozens of carnival midway games on its mezzanine level. In 1969, Elvis made a triumphant return to Las Vegas at the International's showroom and went on to become one of the city's all-time legendary performers. His fans had come of age.

Hoping to establish Las Vegas as "the Broadway of the West," the Thunderbird Hotel presented Rodgers and Hammerstein's _Flower Drum Song_. It was a smash hit. Soon the Riviera picked up _Bye Bye Birdie,_ and, as the decade progressed, _Mame_ and _The Odd Couple_ played at Caesars Palace. While Broadway played the Strip, production shows such as the Dunes' _Casino de Paris_ became ever more lavish, expensive, and technically innovative.

The 1970s: Merv and magic

In 1971, the 500-room Union Plaza opened at the head of Fremont Street on the site of the old Union Pacific Station. It had what, at the time, was the world's largest casino, and its showroom specialized in Broadway productions. The same year, talk-show host Merv Griffin began taping at Caesars Palace, taking advantage of a ready supply of local headliner guests. He helped popularize Las Vegas even more by bringing it into America's living rooms every afternoon.

The year 1973 was eventful: Over at the Tropicana, illusionists extraordinaire Siegfried & Roy began turning women into tigers and themselves into legends in the _Folies Bergère._

Two major disasters hit Las Vegas in the 1970s. First, a flash flood devastated the Strip, causing more than $1 million in damage. Second, gambling was legalized in Atlantic City. Las Vegas's hotel business slumped as fickle tourists decided to check out the new East Coast gambling mecca.

As the decade drew to a close, an international arrivals building opened at McCarran International Airport, and dollar slot machines caused a sensation in the casinos.

The 1980s: The city erupts

As the '80s began, Las Vegas was booming once again. McCarran Airport began a 20-year, $785-million expansion program.

Siegfried & Roy were no longer just the star segment of various stage spectaculars. Their own show, _Beyond Belief,_ ran for six years at the Frontier, playing a record-breaking 3,538 performances to sellout audiences every night. It became the most successful attraction in the city's history.

In 1989, Steve Wynn made Las Vegas sit up and take notice. His gleaming white-and-gold hotel, the Mirage, was fronted by five-story waterfalls, lagoons, and lush tropical foliage — not to mention a 50-foot volcano that dramatically and regularly erupted! Wynn gave world-renowned illusionists Siegfried & Roy carte blanche (and more than $30 million) to create the most spellbinding show Las Vegas had ever seen.

The 1990s: King Arthur, King Tut, King Suite

The 1990s began with a blare of trumpets heralding the rise of a turreted medieval castle fronted by a moated drawbridge and staffed by jousting knights and fair damsels. Excalibur reflected the '90s marketing trend to promote Las Vegas as a family vacation destination.

More sensational mega-hotels followed on the Strip, including the *new* MGM Grand, backed by a full theme park (it ended Excalibur's brief reign as the world's largest resort), Luxor Las Vegas, and Steve Wynn's Treasure Island. And from this point to the present, hotels would open, close, implode, and be rebuilt to dizzying new heights, over and over, in a constant cycle of death and rebirth — Vegas-style.

In 1993, a unique, pink-domed, 5-acre indoor amusement park, Grand Slam Canyon, became part of the Circus Circus hotel. In 1995, the Fremont Street Experience was completed, revitalizing downtown Las Vegas. Closer to the Strip, rock restaurant magnate Peter Morton opened the Hard Rock Hotel, billed as "the world's first rock 'n' roll hotel and casino." The year 1996 saw the advent of the French Riviera–themed Monte Carlo and the Stratosphere Casino Hotel & Tower, its 1,149-foot tower the highest building west of the Mississippi. The unbelievable New York–New York arrived in 1997.

But it all paled compared to what was to come in 1998–99. As Vegas hastily repositioned itself from "family destination" to "luxury resort," several new hotels, once again eclipsing anything that had come before, opened. Bellagio was the latest from Vegas visionary Steve Wynn, an attempt to bring grand European style to the desert, while at the far southern end of the Strip, Mandalay Bay charmed. As if this weren't enough, the Venetian's ambitious detailed re-creation of everyone's favorite Italian city came along in May 1999. It was followed in short order by the opening of Paris Las Vegas in the fall of 1999.

The 2000s: Reimagining the city once again

The 21st century began with a bang as the Aladdin blew itself up and gave itself a from-the-ground-up makeover — and then yet another makeover into Planet Hollywood in 2006 — while Steve Wynn blew up the Desert Inn to make room for a new showstopper, Wynn Las Vegas, which opened in 2005. Every place has expanded, with first the Luxor, then Caesars, Mandalay Bay, Venetian, and Bellagio all adding new towers and hundreds more rooms each. Both Wynn and the Venetian added enormous expansions called Encore and Palazzo, respectively. If they aren't doing that, they're redoing rooms that just got makeovers a couple years ago. Moguls keep bragging: Their hotel will be the biggest, most expensive, most amazing ever seen.

The catchphrase these days is *luxury resort.* Not content to simply reverse the ill-considered "family destination" branding, the casino hotels have, as much as possible, systematically stripped themselves of their cartoonish themes. Public spaces and rooms gradually have turned sleek and modern — handsome for sure, but also increasingly generic. Each tries to outdo its neighbor with high-end shopping; luxurious spas; fancy beds; and gourmet, celebrity-chef-driven restaurants.

The $9-billion CityCenter complex of hotels, casino, shopping, and entertainment took this paradigm to its logical conclusion, creating a city within the city, distinctly cutting edge in a way that makes everything else around it look almost stodgy — a remarkable feat considering its eye-popping neighbors.

But it almost didn't come to fruition. The global recession nearly drove its parent company into bankruptcy, a fate that befell several other in-development megaresorts. Although a couple projects still are under construction or in development, the 2010s will likely produce fewer grand openings than Vegas has seen in a long time.

Of course, a turn of luck — an improvement of fortune — could change all that in a heartbeat for Vegas. Clearly, no one can rest on his laurels here, for this is not only a city that never sleeps, but one in which the wheels of progress never stop turning, even for a heartbeat.

Building Blocks: Local Architecture

You don't exactly get architecture in Vegas — more like set design. If you're a Frank Lloyd Wright aficionado, you may be appalled, but for the rest of us, Vegas has a number of buildings that make your eyes bug out. Las Vegas may well be the only city in the world where the skyline is made up of other cities, and even countries. New York, Egypt, Paris, Venice — all are represented in the facades of extraordinary hotel-resort complexes, behemoths of more than 3,000 rooms. And their themes span the globe and the ages. Visit the Sphinx at **Luxor,** watch sexy pirates battle at **Treasure Island,** ride a gondola through the **Venetian,** take in a joust at **Excalibur,** ride a Coney Island roller coaster at **New York–New York,** or climb the Eiffel Tower in **Paris Las Vegas.** Even the nonthemed hotels are architectural wonders. Consider the sleek bronze curves of **Wynn Las Vegas** and **Encore,** or the sinewy glass-and-steel skyscrapers at **CityCenter.** In other cities, the hotels are built near the tourist attractions. In Vegas, they *are* the tourist attractions. Makes things simple, doesn't it? And as awesome as the scene is in the daytime, it's even more spectacular at night, when the eye-popping lights assault your senses and seem to turn night into day.

We discuss hotels in more detail in Chapter 9.

Hail to the Chef

Vegas used to have a terrible reputation, which was richly deserved, for really crappy food. No one minded that much, however, because the prices were so cheap. The good news is, the quality has skyrocketed; the bad news is, so have many of the prices. Vegas now has a restaurant from many (if not most) of the celebrity chefs and name-brand eateries in the United States, and it can stand proudly alongside more tradition-ally lauded culinary cities. When food critics from the *New York Times* and the *Los Angeles Times* fall all over themselves to salute a Vegas res-taurant (specifically, multiple-Michelin-starred Joël Robuchon's ventures at the MGM Grand), you know something serious is up.

Meanwhile, Thomas Keller, of French Laundry (Napa Valley) and Per Se (New York City) fame, has a branch of his French bistro **Bouchon**, while Alain Ducasse has opened up shop in town, too. Too high-falutin? How about that Emeril guy from the Food Network? Bam! He has two restau-rants in Vegas. You figure it's too hard to get into **Spago** in Los Angeles? Vegas has one of its own. Feast on innovative Italian cuisine at Mario Batali's **B&B Ristorante**, dine under the works of the master at **Picasso**, or down vodka and caviar with abandon at **Red Square**.

But if all you care about is stuffing yourself — and hey, we're right there with you — the famous Vegas buffets are still in action, presenting each and every diner with enough food to feed a small country, or at least several very hungry football teams. And if you crave a Big Mac in the middle of the night, you can find it, and about a billion (okay, maybe we're exaggerating a little — but not by much) other fast-food joints, spread all over town.

Check out Chapter 10 for more information on finding good eats, what-ever your budget.

Oh, Craps!

You may have heard a vague rumor stating that there is gambling in Vegas. Boy, is there ever. Get off the plane, and you see slot machines right there in the airport, just waiting for you to lay your eager hands on them. But don't — the gambling odds at the airport are notoriously bad. Try to control yourself. If we make one absolute promise to you in this book, it's that you'll have ample time and opportunity to lose your money — casinos beckon with numerous games of chance, from black-jack to poker to roulette.

Don't kid yourself: Vegas has presented itself as many things over the years (from adult playground to family destination and back again), and it will come up with still more personas in years to come. But this desert oasis was built for one purpose and one purpose only: to part you from your money. Luckily, spending a little money can be a very enjoyable thing, if you, er, play your cards right. (And with some luck and a peek at Chapter 11 for gambling tips, we hope that you do.)

Ditching the Glitz

Las Vegas is designed to make visitors forget about the outside world and such mundane matters as their bank balances. And it does its designers proud. Nevertheless, you may find yourself yearning for something a little less artificial after a few days of sensory overload. And ditching town for a bit probably won't hurt that bank balance either.

None of Las Vegas's monumental hotels would exist without the modern marvel that is **Hoover Dam.** Just 30 miles outside the city, this feat of engineering provides the juice that keeps Las Vegas's cash cows running.

If you want to keep your body up and running, numerous recreational opportunities — from swimming to hiking — await you at **Lake Mead.** And for sheer natural beauty, you can't beat the almost otherworldly terrain of **Red Rock Canyon** and **Valley of Fire State Park.**

A day trip out of town doesn't mean that you run out of spectacles to see, but natural wonders tend to be more restful than blinking lights and feathered showgirls (for most people anyway).

If you want to schedule your hiatus from the hype right away, head over to Chapter 15.

Crooners, Giggles, and Jiggles

Frank Sinatra and his Rat Pack buddies made Vegas the hot destination. By the time Elvis established himself as a regular performer, Vegas shows were legendary. Although those glamour days are somewhat in the past, top performers still consider Vegas a must-stop. At any given time, you can see a number of big-production shows, ranging from the exquisite artistry of **Cirque du Soleil** to the high-kicking showgirls of *Jubilee!* and a host of other options — renowned magicians, big-name headliners, comedians, and free lounge singers and bands. And yes, the topless revues, though no longer the main attraction, still have their place. If you want to dig right in and find out what shows are waiting for you, jump to Chapter 16.

And if sweating it out on the dance floor is more to your taste, Las Vegas's club scene will more than satisfy your appetite. Sashay your way into the city's appropriately snooty rendition of the legendary **Studio 54,** down almost any kind of rum concoction you can imagine as you dance the night away at **rumjungle,** rub elbows with the beautiful and the size zeroes at **Tao,** see and be seen at mega-clubs **Pure** or **XS.** Or see if any of the "ultralounges" (featuring such tantalizing names as **Tabu** and **Blush**) really are all that sinfully fun. If we can offer one sure bet when it comes to Sin City's after-dark action, it's that you'll find at least one club that caters to your demographic. If you want to delve further into the club-and-bar scene, check out Chapter 17.

Sin City Celebrated: Recommended Movies and Books

Vegas is used as the backdrop, and even supporting player, in many a movie. The most famous is that Rat Pack platform, *Ocean's Eleven,* and while lacking that same zing, the quite successful remake with Brad Pitt and George Clooney (with 2007's *Ocean's Thirteen* sequel returning to Vegas). But who could forget Robert Redford's various, surely not civic-supported, shenanigans as he tries to win Demi Moore in *Indecent Proposal* and steal a horse in *The Electric Horseman?* Vegas movies rarely provide good role models, from the bad craziness in *Fear and Loathing in Las Vegas,* to the mobster activity in *Bugsy* and *Casino,* and to Nicolas Cage's attempts to drink himself to death in the company of a hooker in *Leaving Las Vegas.* But nothing beats the sheer misery and delight of that bomb of bombshells, *Showgirls.* Let's counter all that with some Vegas good times, like the Flying Elvii of *Honeymoon in Vegas,* the Griswold family antics in *Vegas Vacation,* the mystical beauty of the entirely soundstage-built Vegas of Coppola's *One From the Heart,* or the "what happens in Vegas stays in Vegas" insanity of Golden Globe winner *The Hangover.*

With Vegas in literature, it used to be that you needn't go any farther than *Fear and Loathing in Las Vegas,* in which Hunter S. Thompson and his lawyer go gonzo and take on the town. (The town didn't stand a chance.) But recently, a spate of excellent nonfiction books about the town has been published. Veteran reporter Marc Cooper examines Las Vegas and his own fascination with it in *The Last Honest Place in America.* In *Bringing Down the House,* author Ben Mezrich gives a riveting account of how six MIT students figured out how to beat blackjack — and made off with millions before they got caught. In *Positively Fifth Street,* author James McManus came to report on the World Series of Poker, stayed to play, and nearly won. Author Andres Martinez didn't, but that wasn't his goal — he wanted to spend his entire $50,000 book advance gambling, and he did, and wrote about it in *24/7: Living It Up and Doubling Down.*

Chapter 3

Deciding When to Go

In This Chapter

▶ Considering the pros and cons of each season

▶ Checking out a calendar of special events

*B*y most standards, Las Vegas remains a busy town throughout the year, but certain seasons hold advantages over others. Deciding when to take your trip may affect how much you pay, what you're able to see, and how crowded the gambling tables will be. In this chapter, we analyze the advantages and disadvantages of visiting during various times of the year so that you can decide on the time of year that works best for you. You also can turn to Chapter 9 to find some handy resources to help you discover what's going on and when.

Revealing the Secrets of the Seasons

Las Vegas is a year-round city. Although the weather can be tricky and strange, you aren't going to get blizzards or tons of rain or other fun-dampening problems. Sure, it can get hot — oh, man, can it! — but that's why they invented swimming pools and air-conditioning, both of which are found in Vegas in abundance (see Table 3-1 for average temperatures in Las Vegas). But, because it's a year-round city, you may find that when it's off season for other popular tourist destinations, Vegas's hotel rooms are full, thanks to conventions, a highly publicized boxing match, or some other crowd-drawing event.

 Do remember that weekdays here are considerably less crowded than weekends, which means that you're likely to find the best hotel rates on weekdays.

Table 3-1 gives you the lowdown on the average temperatures in Las Vegas. Remember, though, that these are only averages. You may want to pack an outfit or two for cooler or warmer weather, depending on when you plan to travel.

Table 3-1					Las Vegas Average Temperatures							
	Jan	**Feb**	**Mar**	**Apr**	**May**	**June**	**July**	**Aug**	**Sept**	**Oct**	**Nov**	**Dec**
Average (°F)	44	50	57	66	74	84	91	88	81	67	54	47
Average (°C)	7	10	14	19	23	29	33	31	27	19	12	8
Avg. High (°F)	55	62	69	79	88	99	105	103	96	82	67	58
Avg. High (°C)	13	17	21	26	31	37	41	39	36	28	19	14
Avg. Low (°F)	33	39	44	53	60	68	76	74	65	53	41	36
Avg. Low (°C)	1	4	7	12	16	20	24	23	18	12	5	2

Flip to the section "Checking Out the Calendar of Events," at the end of this chapter, to find out how you can plan for — or around — all the festivities throughout the year.

Spending springtime in Vegas

Spring is a popular vacation time for most travelers, many of whom make Vegas their destination. Some of the best reasons to go to Vegas in the springtime follow:

- ✔ It's not hot yet!

- ✔ Kids are still in school, so adults have the run of this most adult of destinations.

- ✔ It's a good time to go hiking in **Red Rock Canyon,** where the wildflowers will be blooming. (To find out more about out-of-town excursions, turn to Chapter 15.)

But keep in mind the following springtime pitfalls:

- ✔ Just because it's not hot doesn't mean that the weather is necessarily nice. Strong winds can blow, making lying by the pool a nasty adventure and producing cold nights. And it can rain. (One year, a heavy downpour put so much water on the Strip that people were using rowboats!)

- ✔ Some production shows take time off during the spring to rest up. (See Chapter 16 for more information on finding schedules for these events.)

Heating up with the summer scene

Another popular travel time is summer. Ahhh, summer. The lazy days and quiet nights. . . . Well, not in Vegas! Vegas is a bustling metropolis throughout the year, and summer is no different. Here are some points to consider:

- It may be hot, but at least it's not humid. Yes, dry heat really does feel less stifling!

- June and July are traditionally among the slowest times of the year, meaning smaller crowds and often much better hotel rates.

- All those wonderful hotel pools are fully open and operational, as is the city's water park.

But keep in mind the following:

- It gets really stinkin' hot in the summer (refer to Table 3-1 for average temperatures in Las Vegas).

- Between conventions, family vacations, and savvy travelers, summer is rapidly becoming as popular a time to go as any other.

- Did we mention that it gets really hot in the summer?

- Because of the heat, everyone is at the pool (even though it's probably too hot to stay outside for long), making the pool areas less peaceful and more party-hearty.

- School is out, and the Strip is swarming with kids who don't have that much to keep them occupied.

Wild weather

Las Vegas rests in the middle of a desert, so how wacky can the weather possibly get? A lot crazier than you think. Although Las Vegas's location results in broiling-hot temperatures in the summer, many people tend to forget that deserts get cold and rainy; wind is another a potential hazard.

Winter temperatures in Las Vegas have been known to dip below 30°F, and when you toss in 40-mph winds, it adds up to a very chilly stroll on the Strip. And snow is not an unheard-of occurrence. Most years see a flurry or two falling on Las Vegas, and, since 1949, a total of 12 "storms" have resulted in accumulations of 2 inches or greater, with the largest storm dumping 9 inches onto the Strip in January 1949. In December 2003, parts of Las Vegas got 6 inches of the white stuff, and although it didn't stick around too long on the Strip, the sight of the famous welcome to fabulous las vegas sign in the middle of a driving blizzard was quite a spectacle. And, more recently (the winter of 2008–09), Vegas received nearly 3 inches of snow on the Strip itself, with nearly 10 inches accumulating in other areas of town. Locals usually find the snow a charming addition to the city (and the stuff melts completely in a day or two, so they don't have to shovel it — lucky them).

But although snow is a novel quirk that many Vegas residents and visitors welcome, rain isn't always as well received. The soil in Las Vegas is parched most of the year, making it difficult for the land to absorb large amounts of water coming down in a short time. Between June and August, when most of the area's rainfall takes place due to the southwest's monsoon season, there is a good possibility of flash flooding.

(continued)

(continued)

At times, the skies open up and don't shut down, resulting in flooding that wreaks havoc on Sin City. On July 9, 1999, Mother Nature unleashed more than 3 inches of rain in just a few hours on a city that averages about 4 inches of rain per year. The deluge killed two people, swamped hundreds of cars, and destroyed millions of dollars in property. As the Strip turned into a raging river, tourists took refuge in the hotels, but at least one resort — Caesars Palace — had to close its casino and shopping arcade because of flooding.

The topography of the Las Vegas region also makes it prone to high, often damaging winds. Situated at the bottom of a bowl ringed by mountains, 15- to 20-mph steady winds are not uncommon, and gusts of 70 to 80 mph have been recorded. In 1994, a brief windstorm knocked down the massive sign at the Las Vegas Hilton, and in 2010 a storm blew through that tore apart the Cloud 9 balloon, billed as the largest tethered helium balloon in the world.

Enjoying fall in the desert

In our opinion, fall is a beautiful time of year — no matter where you are. Here are some autumn bonuses for the Las Vegas scene:

- ✔ You get the best weather in the fall — still warm enough to swim, but not so hot that you want to shrivel up and die.
- ✔ The kids are back in school, and adults have the city to themselves again.

Some things to look out for, however:

- ✔ Several major trade shows and events bring out the convention types, so watch out for limited room availability and high rates.
- ✔ Beware of unpredictable September or October Indian-summer heat waves. (Don't forget the summer duds and sunscreen — just in case!)

Wintering in the West

Winter brings visions of softly falling snowflakes (and slick roads and salt trucks) to most travelers. But that's not often the case in Las Vegas. Here are some reasons you may want to plan a winter vacation in Vegas:

- ✔ Next to June and July, the week before Christmas and the week after New Year's are the two slowest times of the year. In fact, December generally isn't a bad month for crowds.

- ✔ Hotel prices sink during the slowest weeks of the winter, making it much easier to get a good room at a great rate.

Winter does have its downside, however. Consider the following:

✔ Tourists are quickly catching on to the fact that winter travel is slower in Vegas, so eventually those cold months may become as crowded as any other.

✔ Desert winters can get surprisingly cold — some years, you may even see snowfall! (As recently as 2007, they did. Ah, the snowfall on the Eiffel Tower. . . .)

✔ Because the weather is nippy, hotels (assuming fewer people want to swim) may close part or all their pool areas for maintenance purposes.

✔ It's the other time of year (along with springtime) when shows can close for a week. Hey, performers need vacations, too.

✔ New Year's Eve crowds in Vegas are starting to rival those in New York's Times Square, and Valentine's Day brings waves of people to town looking for a romantic quickie wedding.

✔ The biggest convention to hit town, the **Consumer Electronics Show,** is held during this season.

✔ And don't forget the **Super Bowl,** the NCAA's **March Madness,** and the **NASCAR Nextel Championship,** all of which bring out the sports-book gamblers (see the next section for details).

Checking Out the Calendar of Events

Following is a sampling of the events that showcase the best that Vegas has to offer. To get a more detailed listing of convention and event dates, call the **Las Vegas Visitor Information Center** (☎ 877-847-4858; www.visitlasvegas.com) and ask them to send you their brochures on these topics.

Note that two big events — June's **CineVegas International Film Festival** (www.cinevegas.com) and November's **Comedy Festival** (www.thecomedyfestival.com) — were cancelled for 2010 but may return in 2011. Check the Web sites for up-to-date information.

You need to order tickets for most events through the hotel or organization sponsoring the affair. Keep in mind that hotel prices and crowds soar when special events and conventions take place, so either avoid coming to town during those times of the year or be prepared to pay the price — in spades.

January

The **Consumer Electronics Show** (☎ 866-233-7968; www.cesweb.org) is a major convention with attendance of nearly 120,000. Usually second week in January.

Sports fans galore flock to Vegas every January to wager on the **Super Bowl** (www.superbowl.com). Usually last Sunday in January.

February

Valentine's Day, the special Hallmark-approved day of romance, lures any number of optimistic couples to Vegas chapels, seeking legal verification of their love. February 14 and closest weekend.

March

Nearly 200,000 race fans descend on Vegas for the **NASCAR Nextel Cup** (www.nascar.com) at the Las Vegas Motor Speedway (☎ 800-644-4444; www.lvms.com) just north of town. *Note:* This event usually is held in March, but double-check before you make plans.

The Strip turns into a hotbed of hoops betting action during **March Madness** (www.ncaasports.com), the NCAA's basketball championship. Late March through early April.

Those crazy kids are increasingly foregoing the beach and heading to the desert for **spring break.** Expect crowds of people significantly younger and buffer than you are. Second and third weeks of March.

May

The **Gay & Lesbian Pride Celebration** (☎ 702-615-9429; www.lasvegas pride.org) is held every year and features a pride parade and festival. Several smaller parties and events take place all week long. Usually first week in May.

June

The famed **World Series of Poker** (www.worldseriesofpoker.com) starts in June, with high-stakes gamblers and show-biz personalities competing for six- and seven-figure purses. Events take place daily, with entry stakes ranging from $500 to $50,000. The whole thing takes a four-month break and then winds up in November with the No-Limit Hold'em Championship, otherwise known as the Main Event. Players must put up $10,000 for a shot at winning multimillions but it costs nothing to go watch the action. It was formerly held at Binion's Horseshoe Casino, but Binion's was sold, and both the Horseshoe name and the World Series of Poker are now owned by Harrah's. These days, the events, and a major poker convention, are held at the **Rio** (☎ 888-752-9746; www.riolas vegas.com). Starts in June.

September

Oktoberfest is celebrated at the **Mount Charleston Resort** (☎ 800-955-1314 or 702-872-5408; www.mtcharlestonlodge.com), with music, folk dancers, sing-alongs around a roaring fire, special decorations, and Bavarian cookouts. Mid-September through end of October.

November

At **Thanksgiving,** loads of people take advantage of the four-day weekend and come to town — and yes, the hotel buffets serve turkey. Fourth Thursday of the month.

December

The biggest rodeo event in the country, the **National Finals Rodeo** (www.nfrexperience.com), has 170,000 attendees each year. The top 15 male rodeo stars compete in six different events: calf roping, steer wrestling, bull riding, team roping, saddle bronco riding, and bareback riding. The top 15 women compete in barrel racing. Order tickets as far in advance as possible. For information, visit the Web site or contact the **Las Vegas Events ticket office** (☎ 702-260-8605). First two weeks of the month.

On **New Year's Eve,** more than 300,000 visitors jam the city to count down to the new year. The Las Vegas Strip is closed off to accommodate all those revelers, rivaling the attendance in Times Square! You need to book your room well in advance to enjoy this party. December 31.

Part II

Planning Your Trip to Las Vegas

The 5th Wave By Rich Tennant

"...and do you promise to love, honor, and always place maximum bets on the dollar slots?"

In this part . . .

Okay, it's nitty-gritty time. We open this part of the book by chatting a little about travel agents, package tours, and getting the best airfare. Then it's time to find a place to rest your weary bones. We help you shuffle through the neighborhoods of Las Vegas, zero in on a room that's just right for you, get it booked, and send you packing. Then we advise you on last-minute details, such as buying travel insurance, renting a car, reserving tickets for hot shows in advance, and choosing what to pack before you leave.

So, if you're ready, let's start the ball rolling!

Chapter 4

Managing Your Money

. . . .

In This Chapter

▶ Managing your dollars and cents
▶ Gathering cost-cutting tidbits
▶ Using traveler's checks, credit cards, ATMs, or cash
▶ Protecting yourself against thievery

. . . .

Once upon a time — last week, it seems to us — Las Vegas had a reputation for being a cheap vacation. The theory held that if rooms and food were cheap (if not free) and shows were bargains, then patrons would feel more comfortable spending lots of money gambling. Even if they lost their shirts, the reasoning went, they would think, "Well, but my room was free, and I ate myself into a coma at the buffet for $2, so really, the trip was a bargain!" Buoyed by such feelings of good will, a repeat visit was thus ensured.

If that is the picture you have of Vegas, wipe it from your mind. This town has massive casino-hotel resorts to pay for. See those chandeliers up there? Enjoy them — you're gonna pay for them. These days, prices have receded from the almost exclusionary highs, but it still isn't cheap to visit. Here we show you the best inexpensive and high-end options in all the important travel categories so that you can decide where you want to spend your money — and it's just fine with us if that place is the craps table.

Planning Your Budget

Budgeting your trip shouldn't be difficult — as long as you remember that Las Vegas was designed to lighten your wallet and does an excellent job of it.

Lodging

This is a tricky thing in Vegas. The same hotel room can go for $49 on one night (because, say, it's a summer weekday) and then, on the very next day, go for $350 (because a huge convention just started, or it's Super Bowl weekend). Consequently, giving you an "average" rate can be difficult, although you can figure on spending around $150 per night based on double occupancy. (Though again, if you plan your trip right and aren't too picky about where you stay, you can spend as little as half that, even on the Strip.) You can spend significantly more or less, depending on what you're looking for. The higher profile a hotel is, the more it's going to cost. So, for the fancy theme resorts, figure at least $200 for a double. If you can get into the Mirage or Aria Las Vegas, for example, for less (and, surprisingly, you often can), that's a good deal. (See Chapter 9 for a listing of great hotels.)

Transportation

We suggest that you rent a car in Vegas (see Chapter 8 for more information). Although the traffic is terrible, which can make driving a chore, it's still better than paying ridiculous taxi rates or relying on the limited public transportation. You can walk — everywhere is flat, and just about everything is in a straight line — but it's not the most pleasant activity, particularly on a hot summer day. Parking is free and ample, and nearly every hotel has free valet parking. (Tip the nice folks $2 or $3; they'll often have your air-conditioning already going when you get in.) Plan on spending about $30 a day for a rental car. Having said all that, the monorail (even though it isn't cheap and has stops that are sometimes inconveniently located) is a decent alternative to that long hot walk on the Strip.

Dining

The good news is that Vegas has had a boom in world-class restaurants.

The bad news is that this boom has happened only in the high-end restaurants. Many of the places we feel most comfortable recommending, in terms of quality, are costly — upwards of $100 per person, and that's before alcohol. You can certainly dine more cheaply; there are still a few inexpensive (under $15) all-you-can-eat buffets and "meal deals" ($8 complete steak dinners), but those don't make for particularly memorable dining experiences. We suggest trying a little of both; have one great expensive meal, and then seek out the cheaper options. Plan on spending anywhere from $50 to $70 a day per person for food. The truly frugal and those with humble tastes can do just fine on about $35 per day.

Attractions

Wonderfully, this town has a number of free attractions. The hotels themselves, of course, are the main sights of interest, and several of them (**Bellagio, CityCenter, MGM Grand,** the **Mirage, Rio, Treasure Island,** and **Wynn Las Vegas**) have free shows and attractions. And it costs nothing to watch the curiously entertaining spectacle of other people risking their cash inside the casinos.

Unfortunately, most of the other attractions in town, although not expensive in terms of actual cost, are overpriced for what they are. (For example, the **Bellagio Gallery of Fine Art** consists of just one or two rooms but costs more than the entrance fee to the bigger-than-big

Louvre in Paris!) And only a handful of these overpriced attractions are oughta-do's (see Chapter 12) — good places to scratch that "I need some relief from gambling/I need to distract the kids" itch.

Shopping

This is one area where you can save oodles on your vacation bill. Although Vegas has lots of shopping opportunities, it's mostly of the same variety you can find anywhere. Some of the major stores here are attractions in their own right — the **Forum Shops at Caesars Palace** and **Grand Canal Shoppes,** to name a couple — so they're perfect places to stroll if you'd rather browse than buy. If you're the type who can't come back from a vacation without having made a major purchase, you can find some cool places to spend your money, as well as some outlet centers that offer bargain-basement merchandise. (See Chapter 13 for shopping suggestions.)

Entertainment

Here is another place where you can stretch your budget. You don't have to spend any money on nightlife, yet you still can *have* nightlife. Most casinos offer free drinks to gamblers, even if they aren't spending much of anything; and every hotel has at least one lounge with free live music nightly.

We think that you ought to see one of the astounding **Cirque du Soleil** shows, because they're so memorable — but tickets cost from $69 to $175. You can find shows cheaper than Cirque du Soleil, ranging from about $25 to $75.

Superstars of the music world are putting down roots in Vegas with **Cher, Celine Dion,** and **Garth Brooks** amongst the biggest, but even those who need to roam still put Vegas on their tour schedules regularly, with everyone from **Madonna** to **Lady Gaga** rolling into town at venues both huge (the 15,000 seat MGM Grand Garden Arena) and intimate (a few hundred at Boulder Station's Railhead). Tickets for the big-name acts, unsurprisingly, will set you back hundreds of dollars, but you often can catch nostalgia (otherwise known as "has been") acts at smaller halls around town for under $50.

If you want to see comedy headliners, such as **Rita Rudner,** tickets will average $45 to $65. If you don't care where you get your laughs, a ticket to one of Las Vegas's many comedy clubs will set you back approximately $20 (and that may even include a few drinks).

Cover charges for the city's dance clubs range from free (**Cleopatra's Barge Nightclub,** at Caesars) to the ridiculously priced (**Bank,** at the Bellagio). Half of you will be happy to know, however, that sexism (of a sort) still reigns in Sin City; women — even at the high-priced clubs — invariably pay a cheaper cover than men (and sometimes, no cover at all). Don't forget to tack on the price of the alcohol that you may consume while partying the night away; the possible damage that too many drinks can do to your wallet (especially at expensive, hot-spot-of-the-moment clubs) should be enough to spur you to limit your alcohol intake.

Finally, if you plan to sample the city's famous (or infamous) strip clubs, you'll have to cough up a cover charge of at least $10. And if you want to get up-close-and-personal service, keep in mind that lap dances start at $20 and escalate from there. A few too many of those, and you'll strip-mine your wallet in no time.

Gambling

And then there is gambling. How much should you budget for gambling? Figure out how much you can afford to lose. That's right — assume that you're going to lose every penny; if you don't, count yourself lucky. If you come back with the same amount you brought, you're very lucky. And if you come back with more, well, break out the champagne and enjoy it, because it probably won't happen again.

When gambling, it's best to make your goal not so much to win, but to make your money last as long as possible. If you blow it all in the first hour, that's no fun at all. If you plop your last quarter in a slot at the airport on your way home, you can pat yourself on the back. Remember that gambling is entertainment, not a way to raise funds.

Table 4-1 gives you a bird's-eye view of what you're likely to pay to live it up in Las Vegas.

Table 4-1	What Things Cost in Las Vegas
Transportation	*U.S. $*
Taxi from airport to the Strip	$15–$20
Taxi from airport to downtown	$18–$25
Accommodations	*U.S. $*
Double room at Wynn Las Vegas	$259
Double room at MGM Grand	$179
Double room at Circus Circus	$79
Food and Beverages	*U.S. $*
Five-course tasting at Picasso	$115
Four-course dinner at Olives	$65–$80
Dinner buffet at the Mirage	$25
Dinner buffet at Gold Coast	$17

Attractions	U.S. $
Show tickets for Mac King	$25
Show tickets for Cirque du Soleil's *Mystère* at Treasure Island (taxes and drinks extra)	$60–$95
Show tickets for headliners at Hard Rock Hotel	$20–$200
Show tickets for headliners at Caesars Palace	$50–$275

Cutting Costs — But Not the Fun

You can conserve your cash in more than just a couple ways when you vacation in Las Vegas. Use these tips to keep your vacation costs manageable:

✔ **Go during the off season.** If you can travel at nonpeak times (notably summer), you'll find that hotel prices are significantly reduced from prices in peak months.

✔ **Travel in the middle of the week.** Airfares vary depending on the day of the week and the time of day. If you can travel on a Tuesday, Wednesday, or Thursday, you may find cheaper flights to your destination. When you inquire about airfares, ask if you can get a cheaper rate by flying on a different day or at a different time of day. Also, keep in mind that hotel rates in Las Vegas tend to be cheaper on weekdays than they are on weekends.

✔ **Try a package tour.** You can book flights, hotels, ground transportation, and even some sightseeing just by making one call to a travel agent or packager, and it may cost a lot less than if you try to put the trip together yourself. (See Chapter 5 for specific companies to call.)

✔ **Surf the Web.** Airlines and hotels often have special Internet-only rates that are appreciably cheaper than rates quoted over the phone. Also, you can find good comprehensive packages online.

✔ **Always ask for discount rates.** Membership in AAA, frequent-flier plans, trade unions, AARP, or other groups may qualify you for discounted rates on car rentals, plane tickets, hotel rooms, and even meals. Ask about everything — you may be pleasantly surprised.

✔ **Ask if your kids can stay in your room with you.** A room with two double beds usually costs the same as a room with a queen-size bed. Some hotels, though their numbers are shrinking, don't charge you the additional-person rate if the additional person is pint-size and related to you. Even if you have to pay $20 or $35 for the extra-person charge and/or a rollaway bed, you save hundreds by not taking two rooms (and you can keep a closer eye on your little scamps).

✔ **Try expensive restaurants at lunch instead of dinner.** If you want to try a top restaurant (see Chapter 10 for some of the best), consider having lunch instead of dinner. Lunch tabs are usually much cheaper, and the menu often boasts many of the same specialties.

✔ **Skip the souvenirs.** Your photographs and your memories should be the best mementos of your trip. If you're worried about money, you can do without the T-shirts, key chains, Elvis salt-and-pepper shakers, fuzzy dice, and other trinkets.

✔ **Grab every free tourist magazine that you can get your hands on.** You can find these little gems in all Las Vegas hotel rooms and in hotel lobbies. They often contain valuable coupons for restaurant and attraction savings. (Feel free to skip the X-rated ones that solicitors try to push off on you in the streets!)

✔ **Dine out.** Try to eat outside your hotel whenever possible. The giant hotel complexes figure that you're a captive audience; even when they do provide more moderately priced food, you'll usually have to wait in long lines. The usual chain suspects (fast-food joints and so on) are all over town — although the food's not terribly interesting, it's certainly more budget-minded. Many of the lower-profile hotels also offer late-night meal deals (steak dinners for $8, full breakfasts for $3, prime-rib meals for $10, and so forth). They may mean eating at strange hours, but they're worth taking advantage of.

✔ **Don't gamble your life savings away.** Really, the biggest budget pitfall for the Vegas visitor is the gambling. If you get that gleam in your eye when you're near a blackjack table and have a hard time exercising self-restraint, try leaving your ATM card at home or in your hotel room and carrying only as much cash as you're willing to lose.

Using Paper, Plastic, or Pocket Change

You can choose from a number of options to pay for your vacation (including meals, souvenirs, and so on). In this section, we explore the available options to help you determine the one that's right for you.

Relying on ATMs

One thing you can count on in Las Vegas is the ability to get ready cash. Each and every casino owner wants you to have easy access to your money so that you can hand it over to them. After all, if you run out of cash and can't use your ATM card at 3 a.m., you can't drop any more quarters in that Double Diamond slot machine that you're just sure is going to pay off big at any moment.

There are cash machines every 5 feet in Las Vegas, which is mighty convenient. However, they clip you upwards of $5 for each transaction. Also, keep in mind that many banks impose a fee every time you use your card at a different bank's ATM, and that fee can be higher for international transactions. On top of this, the bank from which you withdraw cash may charge its own fee. To compare banks' ATM fees within the U.S., use `www.bankrate.com`. Try to anticipate your cash needs to cut down on the number of trips you'll make to the ATM; it will leave you with more cash to hand over to those other one-armed bandits.

MasterCard/Cirrus (`www.mastercard.com`) and **Visa/Plus** (`www.visa.com`) are the two most popular ATM networks; check the back of your ATM card to find out what network your bank is affiliated with. (The toll-free numbers also provide ATM locations where you can withdraw money.) It's always a good idea to find out what your per-day withdrawal limit is before you leave home.

You may be in the habit of carrying cash when you're on vacation. We really can't recommend carting more than one to two days' worth of money around with you in Las Vegas. Although security in the casinos is tight, pickpocketing on the Strip is the crime of choice. When you consider how easy it is to access an ATM, there's no reason to tote a wad of cash. (Just be sure to factor in the additional charges at the machines.) If you do choose to carry cash, make sure that you never flash it around — you may attract the wrong kind of attention.

Charging up a storm

Traveling with credit cards is a safe alternative to carrying cash. Credit cards also provide you with a record of your vacation expenses after you return home. Plus, foreign travelers get a better exchange rate. You also can get cash advances with your credit cards at any bank (although you start paying interest on the advance the moment you receive the cash, and you don't receive frequent-flier miles on an airline credit card). At most banks, you don't even need to go to a teller; you can get a cash advance at the ATM if you know your personal identification number (PIN). If you forgot your PIN or didn't even know you had one, call the phone number on the back of your credit card and ask the bank to send it to you. It usually takes five to seven business days, although some banks will do it over the phone if you tell them your mother's maiden name or pass some other security hurdle.

Most casinos make it easy to get a cash advance with your credit card. Isn't that nice of them? The problem is that they charge outrageous processing fees — usually 7 percent to 10 percent of the amount you're advancing (so, $200 costs you an additional $16, on top of what your card will charge you in interest). Don't do it!

Toting traveler's checks

These days, traveler's checks are less necessary because most cities have 24-hour ATMs that allow you to withdraw small amounts of cash as needed. However, keep in mind that you'll likely be charged an ATM withdrawal fee if the bank isn't your own. If you're withdrawing money every day, you may be better off with traveler's checks — provided that you don't mind showing identification every time you want to cash one.

You can get traveler's checks at almost any bank. **American Express** offers denominations of $20, $50, $100, $500, and (for cardholders only) $1,000. You'll pay a service charge ranging from 1 percent to 4 percent. You also can get American Express traveler's checks over the phone by calling ☎ 800-221-7282; Amex gold and platinum cardholders who use this number are exempt from the 1 percent fee.

Visa offers traveler's checks at Citibank locations nationwide, as well as at several other banks. The service charge ranges between 1.5 percent and 2 percent; checks come in denominations of $20, $50, $100, $500, and $1,000. Call ☎ 800-227-6811 for information. AAA members can obtain Visa checks without a fee at most AAA offices or by calling ☎ 866-339-3378. **MasterCard** also offers traveler's checks; call ☎ 800-223-9920 for a location near you.

Keeping Your Money Safe (And What to Do If It's Stolen)

Vast amounts of money always are on display in Vegas, and crooks find lots of easy marks. Don't be one of them. Here are some tips to help you avoid this agonizing situation (or at least ease the pain if it happens anyway):

✔ Don't depend on hotel security to look out for your property. At gaming tables and slot machines, men should keep their wallets well concealed and out of the reach of pickpockets (the front pants pocket is a good place), and women should keep their purses in view (preferably on their laps) at all times. A thief can easily swipe a purse that's sitting at your feet, whether you're at a bar or a slot machine. Thieves are just waiting for you to become so entranced with your game that you let your guard down, so don't let it happen.

✔ Be careful about how and where you carry your cash. Whether inside the casinos or strolling the Strip, women should always keep their purses slung diagonally across their chests, preferably under a jacket. The best kind of purse to take is one that folds over rather than one that just has a zipper on top. Don't sling your purse or camera over your chair when you're in a restaurant. Men should use a money belt or a fanny pack to store cash, credit cards, and traveler's checks.

✔ If your hotel has an in-room safe, use it. Stash excess cash, traveler's checks, and any other valuables that you don't immediately need. If your hotel room doesn't have a safe, put your valuables and cash inside the hotel's safe-deposit box. In general, the best policy is to use an ATM and only withdraw the amount of money you'll need to cover your expenses for about two days at a time.

✔ If you do win a big jackpot in the casinos, ask the pit boss or slot person to cut you a check rather than give you your winnings in cash. The cash may look cool, but flashing it around sends the wrong signal to the wrong kind of people.

✔ Almost every credit card company has a toll-free emergency number that you can call if your cards are lost or stolen. The credit card company may be able to wire you a cash advance off your credit card immediately, and it can often get you an emergency credit card within a day or two.

The issuing bank's toll-free number usually is printed on the back of the credit card. Make note of this number before you leave on your trip and stash it somewhere other than your wallet. If you forget to write down the number, you can call ☎ 800-555-1212 — that's **toll-free directory assistance** — to get the number. **Citicorp Visa's** U.S. emergency number is ☎ **800-847-2911. American Express** cardholders should call ☎ **800-441-0519,** and traveler's-check carriers need to call ☎ **800-221-7282** for all money emergencies. **MasterCard** holders must call ☎ **800-622-7747.**

✔ Traveler's checks can be somewhat cumbersome; considering the number of ATMs in Vegas, they're probably unnecessary. Nevertheless, they're the safest way to carry large amounts of cash (although we don't recommend that). After you buy them, record the checks' serial numbers and keep that list in a separate location from the checks. It's also a good idea to leave the serial numbers with a relative back home. If your checks are stolen, call the issuer, give the serial numbers, and ask for instructions on getting your checks replaced.

✔ If, despite your best efforts, your wallet disappears, you're not likely to recover it. The police have the best of intentions, but they probably can't help. Even so, when you realize that your wallet is gone and cancel your credit cards, you should still call the police — you may need their report number for credit card or insurance purposes.

Chapter 5

Getting to Las Vegas

. . . .

In This Chapter

▶ Booking a flight

▶ Driving to Las Vegas

▶ Checking out package tours

. . . .

An oasis plopped down in the middle of a barren desert and surrounded by nothing but miles and miles of sand, Las Vegas is the most isolated metropolis in the United States.

Because there is no train service to Las Vegas, you have to either fly or drive to reach the city. Without further ado, read this chapter to find out your traveling options — somewhere out there is a roulette table with your name on it!

Flying to Las Vegas

As we discuss later in this chapter, a package tour can be just dandy for some folks. But others wouldn't dream of letting anyone else plan their trip. If you're a do-it-yourselfer, the following information can help you plot the perfect trip all on your own.

Finding an airline

The following airlines have regularly scheduled flights into Las Vegas (some of these are regional carriers, so they all may not fly from your point of origin): **AeroMexico** (☎ 800-237-6639; www.aeromexico.com), **Air Canada** (☎ 888-247-2262; www.aircanada.ca), **Alaska Airlines** (☎ 800-426-0333; www.alaskaair.com), **Allegiant Air** (☎ 702-505-8888; www.allegiantair.com), **American** (☎ 800-433-7300; www.aa.com), **British Airways** (☎ 800-247-9297; www.britishairways.com), **Continental** (☎ 800-525-0280; www.continental.com), **Delta** (☎ 800-221-1212; www.delta.com), **Frontier Airlines** (☎ 800-432-1359; www.frontierairlines.com), **Hawaiian Airlines** (☎ 800-367-5320; www.hawaiianair.com), **JetBlue** (☎ 800-538-2583; www.jetblue.com), **Mexicana Airlines** (☎ 800-531-7921; www.mexicana.com), **Midwest Airlines** (☎ 800-452-2022; www.midwestairlines.com), **Southwest** (☎ 800-435-9792; www.southwest.com), **Sun Country**

(☎ 866-359-6786; www.suncountryairlines.com), **United** (☎ 800-241-6522; www.united.com), **US Airways** (☎ 800-428-4322; www.usairways.com), and **Virgin Atlantic Airways** (☎ 800-862-8621; www.virgin-atlantic.com).

Getting the best airfare

These days, with a little know-how and advance planning, the independent traveler should have no trouble snagging a deal on airline tickets. Through the Internet alone, consumers have more options than ever before in locating the best airfares, whether from airline Web sites or online travel and booking sites (see the next section, "Booking your ticket online"). Here are some tips on how to get the best prices on airline tickets.

Competition among the major U.S. airlines is unlike that of any other industry. A coach seat is virtually the same from one carrier to another (you know: small, cramped, and basically uncomfortable), yet the difference in price may run as high as $1,000. If you're a business traveler and need the flexibility to purchase your tickets at the last minute or change your itinerary at a moment's notice, or you want to get home before the weekend, you wind up paying the premium rate (known as the *full fare*). If you don't require this level of flexibility, you can probably get a better deal. Consider the following:

- ✔ **Plan ahead.** On most flights, even the shortest hops, the full fare is close to $1,000 or more, but a 7-day or 14-day advance-purchase ticket is closer to $200 to $300. Keep an eye on Southwest: Two months or so in advance, the airline often offers one-way tickets to Vegas from Los Angeles for as little as $49 or $59.

- ✔ **Be flexible about the dates you travel.** You often can get a bargain-basement deal (usually a fraction of the full fare) if you can book your ticket far in advance; don't mind staying over Saturday night; are willing to travel on a Tuesday, Wednesday, or Thursday; or are willing to travel during less-trafficked hours.

- ✔ **Check out consolidators.** Also known as *bucket shops,* consolidators are a good place to check for the lowest fares. Their prices are much better than the fares you can get yourself and are often even lower than what your travel agent can get you. You see their ads in the small boxes at the bottom of the page in your Sunday newspaper's travel section.

Several reliable consolidators are worldwide and available on the Net. **STA Travel** (☎ **800-781-4040;** www.statravel.com), the world's leader in student travel, offers good fares for travelers of all ages. **Air Tickets Direct** (☎ **888-858-8884;** www.airticketsdirect.com) is based in Montreal and leverages the currently weak Canadian dollar for low fares.

 ✔ **Look for sales.** Don't forget that the airlines periodically lower the prices on their most popular routes. These fares have advance-purchase requirements and date-of-travel restrictions, but you can't beat the price — usually no more than $400 for a cross-country flight. To take advantage of these airline sales, watch for ads in your local newspaper and on TV and radio, and call the airlines or check out their Web sites.

These fare sales tend to take place during seasons of low travel volume. You rarely see a sale around Thanksgiving or Christmas, when people are more willing to pay a premium.

Booking your ticket online

The "big three" online travel agencies — **Expedia** (www.expedia.com), **Orbitz** (www.orbitz.com), and **Travelocity** (www.travelocity.com) — sell most of the air tickets bought on the Internet. (Canadian travelers should try www.expedia.ca and www.travelocity.ca; U.K. residents can go for www.expedia.co.uk and www.opodo.co.uk.) Each has different business deals with the airlines and may offer different fares on the same flights, so shopping around is wise. Expedia and Travelocity will also send you an **e-mail notification** when a cheap fare becomes available to your favorite destination. Of the smaller travel-agency Web sites, **SideStep** (www.sidestep.com) receives good reviews from users. It purports to "search 200 sites at once" but still only beats competitors' fares as often as other sites do.

Although not as widely available as they once were, great **last-minute deals** are available through free weekly e-mail services provided directly by the airlines. Most of these deals are announced on Tuesday or Wednesday and must be purchased online. Most are valid only for travel that weekend, but some (such as Southwest's) can be booked weeks or months in advance. Sign up for weekly e-mail alerts at airline Web sites or check megasites that compile comprehensive lists of last-minute specials, such as **Smarter Travel** (www.smartertravel.com). For last-minute trips, the aptly named **lastminute.com** often has better deals than the major-label sites.

If you're willing to give up some control over your flight details, use an *opaque fare service* such as **Priceline** (www.priceline.com) or **Hotwire** (www.hotwire.com). Both offer rock-bottom prices in exchange for travel on a "mystery airline" at a mysterious time of day, often with a mysterious change of planes en route. The mystery airlines are all major, well-known carriers — and the possibility of being sent from Philadelphia to Chicago via Tampa is remote. But your chances of getting a 6 a.m. or 11 p.m. flight are pretty high. Hotwire tells you flight prices before you buy; Priceline usually has better deals than Hotwire, but you have to play their "Name Your Own Price" game. Priceline does have a non-opaque service in which you have the option to pick exact flights, times, and airlines from a list of offers.

Hit the Road, Jack!

Getting there is often half the fun. If you're one of those folks who wants to put the pedal to the metal and the rubber to the road (even if it means a longer journey), you may enjoy driving to Vegas.

If you plan on hitting the highway, keep in mind that **AAA** (☎ **800-222-4357**; www.aaa.com) and some other automobile clubs offer free maps and optimum driving directions to their members. On the Internet, **Google Maps** (http://maps.google.com) and **MapQuest** (www.mapquest.com) provide free driving directions.

Watching the weather

Be sure to check out the weather forecast before setting out on your journey: A snowstorm approaching through the Rockies or a heat wave across the Southwest may cause you to reconsider your travel route. If your local TV station or newspaper doesn't give you enough information, check out the **Weather Channel** on cable TV or on the Web at www.weather.com. The channel also offers a 24-hour weather hot line (☎ **900-932-8437**), which costs 95¢ per minute.

Planning your route

Las Vegas is located on the southern tip of Nevada right along I-15, the major north–south route from Los Angeles to the Canadian border. I-15 actually runs through the city, past downtown, and less than a quarter-mile from the famed Vegas Strip.

Check with a reliable source before actually planning your route (unless you're in no hurry and you just want to ramble along), but the following are some good choices from some of the major U.S. regions:

- ✔ **California:** If you're coming from Northern or Central California, consider taking Highway 99 from Sacramento to Highway 58 in Bakersfield, which will take you to I-15 in Barstow. Portions of that route are still a two-lane, undivided highway, but most of the trip is freeway-style driving. From Southern California, take I-15 all the way. And remember, everyone comes back from a weekend in Vegas on Sunday afternoon or in the early evening, something you should avoid doing, if at all possible. Otherwise, pack snacks — your five-hour drive could turn into nine.

- ✔ **Upper Midwest:** If you're coming from the upper Midwest, your best bet is probably I-80, which stretches from Pennsylvania all the way to San Francisco. It may not be a particularly scenic drive, but it's the safest and fastest route to the point where it intersects with I-15 in Utah. Another option is I-70, which runs from Missouri to I-15 in Utah.

- ✔ **Northwest:** The best way to travel from the Northwest is probably I-84 running from Oregon to I-15 in Utah.

✔ **The scenic route:** If you're coming from anywhere east of Las Vegas, you may get your kicks by taking historic Route 66. Parts of this route have been replaced by interstates, but for the most part, it still meanders from Chicago to Los Angeles, offering more than 2,000 miles of beautiful Americana. You can take it all the way to Kingman, Arizona, where you hook up with Highway 93. This road takes you past the famous Hoover Dam (see Chapter 15 for more information on the Hoover Dam and other side trips) and then right into Las Vegas. You can't beat it if you have the time or a sense of wanderlust!

Choosing a Package Tour

Package tours, put simply, are a way of buying your airfare, your accommodations, and the other elements of your trip (such as car rentals, airport transfers, and sometimes even activities) in one fell swoop, and often at discounted prices. A package tour probably is a good bet for a popular destination such as Las Vegas. In many cases, you pay less for a package that includes airfare, hotel, and transportation to and from the airport than you would pay for the hotel alone if you were to book it yourself. The reasoning is simple: Packages are sold in bulk to tour operators, who resell them to the public. It's kind of like buying your vacation at Sam's Club — except the tour operator is the one who buys the 1,000-count box of garbage bags and resells them at a cost that undercuts what you'd pay at your average neighborhood supermarket.

Package tours can vary by leaps and bounds, however. Some offer a better class of hotels than others. Some offer the same hotels for lower prices. Some offer flights on scheduled airlines, while others book charters. Some even limit your choice of accommodations and travel days. The upshot here is that you can make sure you get what you want at a price you're comfortable with.

A great starting point when looking for a package deal is the travel section of your local Sunday newspaper. Also check the ads in the back of national travel magazines, such as *Travel + Leisure, National Geographic Traveler,* and *Condé Nast Traveler.* **Liberty Travel** (☎ 888-271-1584; www.libertytravel.com) is one of the biggest packagers in the Northeast; it usually boasts a full-page ad in Sunday papers. **American Express Vacations** (☎ 800-346-3607; www.americanexpress.com/travel) is another option.

Don't forget another good resource: the **airlines** themselves! They often package their flights together with accommodations. When choosing the airline, pick the one that has frequent service to your hometown and lets you accumulate frequent-flier miles. **Southwest Vacations** (☎ 800-243-8372; www.swavacations.com) recently offered a Las Vegas package out of Los Angeles that included airfare and three nights at Aria Las Vegas for just over $300 per person (based on double occupancy) for a

Highway Access to Las Vegas

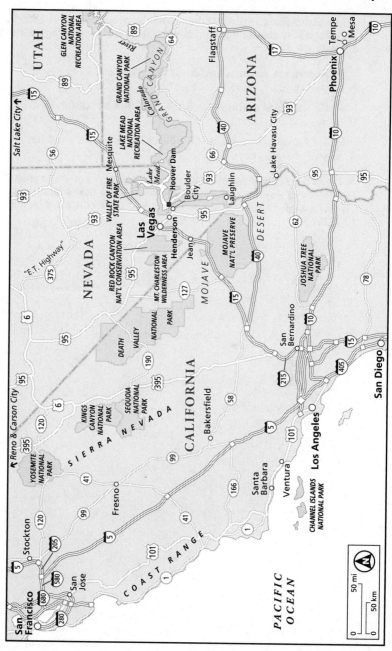

midweek stay. A package offered by **Delta Vacations** (☎ 800-654-6559; www.deltavacations.com) out of New York City included airfare, accommodations at the Flamingo, and associated fees for $820 for a couple to stay three nights midweek. Other airline packagers include the following:

- ✔ **American Airlines Vacations** (☎ 800-321-2121; www.aa vacations.com)

- ✔ **Continental Airlines Vacations** (☎ 800-301-3800; www.cool vacations.com)

- ✔ **US Airways Vacations** (☎ 800-422-3861; www.usairways vacations.com)

Some of the biggest hotels also offer packages. If you have your heart set on staying at a particular hotel, call and ask if it offers land/air packages. (We include a list of the major resorts and their contact information in Chapter 9.)

Chapter 6

Catering to Special Travel Needs or Interests

*W*orried that your kids are too young for Sin City or that you're too old to enjoy a Las Vegas show? Afraid that you may experience barriers blocking your access or lifestyle? In this chapter, we dispense a little advice for travelers with specific needs.

Traveling with the Brood: Advice for Families

Once upon a time, the Vegas masterminds decided to try to go after the family market. Family-oriented attractions, such as amusement parks, roller coasters, and arcades, sprang up to try to get parents to bring their kids along with them to the Las Vegas wonderland (instead of, say, Walt Disney World). The resorts included such family perks as hotel child-care centers. In fact, many of the hotels were initially designed with kids in mind. **MGM Grand,** for example, had a mammoth *Wizard of Oz* theme as soon as you entered the hotel, and the **Stratosphere** and **Excalibur** hotels had similar kiddie themes.

Let's just say that the plan didn't work too well.

The kid-friendly hotels have pretty much ditched all their child-appealing elements. Now there just isn't a lot for the wee ones to do. And, of course, there's that whole "What Happens in Vegas Stays in Vegas" city motto.

Regardless of the extravagant facades, the main lure of Vegas is, of course, gambling. You have to be at least 21 to even enter a casino (although most hotels allow kids to walk through the casino en route to somewhere else — after all, you usually can't get anywhere in a hotel without walking through the casino!). In other words, your little good-luck charms can't stand next to you at the craps table to blow on your dice. The upshot: If you intend to spend much time gambling (or indulging in any of the other "adult" pastimes), you have to find a safe and fun spot to leave the kids while you hit the tables. And, quite frankly, you probably wind up spending more money taking care of the kids than you win gambling. What's more, many hotels (such as the Bellagio) forbid anyone under 18 from being on the property at night, unless they're staying at the hotel. Other hotels, when contacted about kid-friendly possibilities, stated that they didn't want to be considered in any such discussion. This is clearly a 180-degree spin from the "family-friendly" marketing campaign of the past.

Don't get us wrong — with a little bit of creativity and a few extra bucks, you can bring your entire family, and everybody will have a good time. But if you have the choice, it's probably best to leave the kids at home.

The first thing to do to ensure that your family vacation doesn't end up like a *National Lampoon* nightmare is to flip through this book looking for hotels, restaurants, and attractions marked with the Kid Friendly icon.

If you're considering bringing your independent-minded older kids or teenagers with you on your trip, keep in mind that Las Vegas has a curfew law in effect. Local ordinances forbid anyone under 18 from being on the Strip without a parent after 9 p.m. Elsewhere in the county, minors can't be out without parents after 10 p.m. on school nights and midnight on the weekends.

Making Age Work for You: Tips for Seniors

People over the age of 60 are traveling more than ever before, and they're coming to Vegas in droves. Even if your idea of a good time is rubbing elbows with the "youngsters" at Studio 54 (and maybe it is!), you'll find that the tourists in Vegas come from all walks of life.

In Las Vegas, people 62 and over can get discount fares on the local bus system by obtaining a Reduced Fare Identification Card from the **Downtown Transportation Center,** 300 N. Casino Center Blvd. (☎ **702-676-1822**). You need to apply for the card in person, and you must provide proof of age.

Some theaters, museums, and other attractions offer discounts to seniors, so ask about discounts when you pay your admission fee. As always, you need to show identification with proof of age.

Another perk of having so much life experience is that most of the major domestic airlines — including **American, Continental, United,** and **US**

Airways — offer discount programs for senior travelers. Just be sure to ask about them when you book a flight.

Members of **AARP** (☎ **888-687-2277** or 202-434-2277; www.aarp.org) get discounts on hotels, airfares, and car rentals. AARP offers members a wide range of benefits, including *AARP The Magazine* and a monthly newsletter. Anyone 50 or over can join.

Many reliable agencies and organizations target the 50-plus market. **Road Scholar** (☎ **800-454-5768;** www.roadscholar.org), formerly known as Elderhostel, arranges study programs for those 55 and over (and a spouse or companion of any age) in the United States and in more than 80 countries around the world. Most courses last five to seven days in the United States (two to four weeks abroad), and many include airfare, accommodations in university dormitories or modest inns, meals, and tuition. **ElderTreks** (☎ **800-741-7956;** www.eldertreks.com) offers small-group tours to off-the-beaten-path or adventure-travel locations for travelers 50 and over.

Recommended publications offering travel resources and discounts for seniors include: the quarterly magazine *Travel 50 & Beyond* (☎ **713-974-6903;** www.travel50andbeyond.com) and *Unbelievably Good Deals and Great Adventures That You Absolutely Can't Get Unless You're Over 50,* by Joan Rattner Heilman.

Accessing Las Vegas: Advice for Travelers with Disabilities

Las Vegas is truly for everyone, and a disability shouldn't stop you from visiting and having a great time. Vegas really has gone to great lengths to accommodate individuals with special needs. All the major hotels come equipped with the basics, such as ramps and elevators, and most have rooms outfitted with the latest technology designed for accessibility.

In order to get the most out of your visit, be sure to inform your reservations agent of your requirements.

Having said that, keep in mind the vastness of the massive hotel resorts. It can be a long haul from the front entrance to your room, to the pool, or to anywhere at all. Some casinos don't have a lot of aisle space, making them hard to maneuver. And you can count on encountering a whole lot of people and a whole lot of stuff between you and your ultimate destination.

Many travel agencies offer customized tours and itineraries for travelers with disabilities. **Flying Wheels Travel** (☎ **877-451-5006** or 507-451-5005; www.flyingwheelstravel.com) offers escorted tours and cruises that emphasize sports, and private tours in minivans with lifts.

Accessible Journeys (☎ 800-846-4537 or 610-521-0339; www.accessible journeys.com) offers wheelchair travelers and their families and friends resources for travel.

Avis Rent A Car has an Avis Access program that offers such services as a dedicated 24-hour toll-free number (☎ 888-879-4273) for customers with special travel needs; special car features such as swivel seats, spinner knobs, and hand controls; and accessible bus service.

Organizations that offer assistance to travelers with disabilities include **MossRehab ResourceNet** (www.mossresourcenet.org), which is an online library of accessible-travel resources; the **Society for Accessible Travel & Hospitality** (☎ 212-447-7284; www.sath.org), which offers a wealth of travel resources for all types of disabilities and informed recommendations on destinations, access guides, travel agents, tour operators, vehicle rentals, and companion services; and the **American Foundation for the Blind** (☎ 800-232-5463; www.afb.org), a referral resource for the blind or visually impaired that includes information on traveling with Seeing Eye dogs.

For more information specifically targeted to travelers with disabilities, check out the quarterly magazine *Emerging Horizons* (www.emerging horizons.com).

Traveling Tips for Gays and Lesbians

The hotels and casinos in Las Vegas want your money — regardless of your lifestyle. Many of the mega-resorts actively advertise in gay and lesbian papers with the hopes of luring some of those disposable-income dollars away from you.

As of this writing there is only one exclusively gay hotel in Las Vegas, the **Blue Moon Resort**, 2651 Westwood Dr. (☎ 866-798-9194; www. bluemoonlv.com). The plain box motel exterior and the vaguely industrial neighborhood mask a really rather nice interior, with aesthetically pleasing and comfortable rooms, a small but luxuriously landscaped pool and grotto area, a steam room, and more.

We list a few of the best gay bars in Chapter 17. For your traveling pleasure, you also can check out the following list of some other great resources:

✔ *QVegas* (☎ 702-650-0636; www.qvegas.com): Vegas's local monthly gay and lesbian newspaper lists all the bars, restaurants, and events in town. When you arrive in Vegas, grab one for the latest information on what's happening. You often can find them in hotel lobbies, at gay bars, or in the media boxes on the streets.

✔ *EDGE Las Vegas* (www.edgelasvegas.com): This comprehensive site features information on all the gay and gay-friendly bars and restaurants, local news, events, and more.

The International Gay & Lesbian Travel Association (☎ 800-448-8550 or 954-776-2626; www.iglta.org) is the trade association for the gay and lesbian travel industry, and offers an online directory of gay- and lesbian-friendly travel businesses.

Many agencies offer tours and travel itineraries specifically for gay and lesbian travelers. **Above and Beyond Tours** (☎ 800-397-2681; www.abovebeyondtours.com) is the exclusive gay and lesbian tour operator for United Airlines. **Now, Voyager** (☎ 800-255-6951; www.nowvoyager.com) is a well-known San Francisco–based gay-owned and -operated travel service. **Olivia Travel** (☎ 800-631-6277 or 510-655-0364; www.olivia.com) charters entire resorts and ships for exclusive lesbian vacations and offers smaller group experiences for both gay and lesbian travelers.

The following travel guides are available at most travel bookstores and gay and lesbian bookstores, or you can order them from **Giovanni's Room** (☎ 215-923-2960; www.giovannisroom.com): *Spartacus International Gay Guide* (www.spartacusworld.com/gayguide) and *Odysseus,* both good, annual English-language guidebooks focused on gay men; the *Damron* guides (www.damron.com), with separate, annual books for gay men and lesbians; and *Gay Travel A to Z: The World of Gay & Lesbian Travel Options at Your Fingertips,* by Marianne Ferrari (available from Ferrari International; Box 35575, Phoenix, AZ 85069), a very good gay and lesbian guidebook.

Chapter 7

Taking Care of the Remaining Details

In This Chapter
▶ Weighing the pros and cons of renting a car
▶ Buying travel and medical insurance
▶ Making sure you stay healthy
▶ Keeping in touch while you're away from home
▶ Getting to know airline security measures

*B*efore you leave for your vacation, you probably feel that you need to do a thousand things: make reservations, put the dog in the kennel, pack your bags, and so on. Trust us: If you organize everything ahead of time, you'll save precious hours. In this chapter, we tell you how to take care of some of the pesky details such as renting a car and buying travel insurance.

Renting a Car in Vegas

Do you need to rent a car in Las Vegas? Need? No. But we really think you should consider it. Technically, everything on the Strip is within walking distance — it's roughly 3 miles from **Circus Circus** to **Mandalay Bay** — but who wants to walk that in 100°F heat (or, in winter, in near gale-force winds)? Without a car, you may be less inclined to get off the Strip and go downtown or to the **Atomic Testing Museum** (and we just can't have that). Sure, you can hail a taxi, but you could easily spend more on taxi fare than on car rental.

If you're the type of person who needs cold, hard facts, consider this: If you take a taxi from the airport to the **Riviera Hotel & Casino,** for example, you wind up paying at least $20, plus tip. And then if you want to see the pyramid-shaped **Luxor** hotel (a solid 3 miles away), that's another $20 to $25 round-trip. Suppose that, later the same evening, you want to go see the **Fremont Street Experience** downtown and then finish off the evening with a cocktail at the top of the **Stratosphere Tower:** You've just racked up at least another $30 — more if traffic is heavy. If you add everything up, you've spent $70 on taxis; for that amount, you could be cruising the Strip in your own convertible for all to see.

The walking wounded

The biggest game of chance on the Strip may be not inside the casinos, but outside on the street. Because blocks on the Strip tend to be longer than long, pedestrians often ignore crosswalks and dash across the Strip regardless of their location. When Lady Luck is with these jaywalkers, all they have to face are angry drivers swerving — while swearing — to avoid them. But, like all other gambling in Vegas, the odds for this game do not favor the player.

When traffic conditions are favorable — and sometimes even when they aren't — drivers in Las Vegas have no compunction about flooring it. And the Strip isn't very pedestrian friendly — stop signals at the crosswalks can be so short that an Olympic sprinter would have trouble getting across the street in time. When you combine these two factors, the end result is that traffic accidents are a fact of life on the Strip. In order to safeguard pedestrians, the city is increasing the number of above-ground sidewalks (notably in all four directions at the corner of Tropicana and the Strip, at the corner of Flamingo and the Strip, and Spring Mountain and the Strip).

It may take you a little longer to get where you're going, but our advice is to cross at traffic lights or use the above-ground sidewalks. Otherwise, you should ask yourself, "Are you feeling lucky today?" Those of you who have seen a Dirty Harry movie know that you won't like the answer.

And the preceding scenario doesn't take into account the time you waste standing in line for a taxi (up to an hour on weekend nights is not unheard of). With car rentals often available for as low as $25 a day (maybe a bit more for a convertible, but who's counting?), your best bet is obvious.

When you consider the freedom that having your own set of wheels gives you, and the fact that every hotel in town offers free parking to guests and nonguests, the obvious answer is, "You betcha you should rent a car."

And rent your car *before* you get into town, especially if you're arriving during a peak tourist period. You have more time to search for a good rate, and you won't have to spend precious vacation time scouring the Strip for a rental you can afford.

If, however, you decide not to rent a car, you can hop on an airport shuttle service to get to your hotel. You don't have to arrange any of this in advance (flip to Chapter 8 for more details). After you're settled in, though, you're either going to have to hail a cab or hoof it. Okay, we suppose we should mention that Vegas has a regular city **bus service,** but it gets mixed reviews for timeliness and convenience. We recommend it only for brave souls. On the other hand, the **Las Vegas Monorail** provides a reasonable alternative to a car. It travels along most of the Strip, stopping at various intervals, with a jog over to the Hilton and the

Convention Center. Unfortunately, the Atomic Testing Museum isn't on the route, darn it. Though the monorail costs at least twice as much as the bus, it's much faster and more stylish.

Finding the best rate

Car-rental rates vary even more than airline fares. The price depends on the size of the car, the length of time you keep it, where and when you pick it up and drop it off, where you take it, and a host of other factors. As with other aspects of planning your trip, using the Internet can make comparison-shopping for a car rental much easier. You can check rates at most of the major agencies' Web sites. Plus, all the major travel sites — **Expedia** (www.expedia.com), **Orbitz** (www.orbitz.com), and **Travelocity** (www.travelocity.com), for example — have search engines that can dig up discounted car-rental rates. Just enter the car size you want, the pickup and return dates, and the location, and the server returns a price. You even can make the reservation through any of these sites.

Whether you reserve online, in person, or by phone, getting answers to the following key questions may save you beaucoup bucks:

- ✔ **Are weekend rates lower than weekday rates?** If you're keeping the car five or more days, a weekly rate may be cheaper than the daily rate. Ask if the rate is the same for pickup Friday morning as it is Thursday night.

- ✔ **Are there drop-off charges?** Some companies may assess a drop-off charge, if you don't return the car to the same rental location; others, notably National, don't.

- ✔ **Are rates cheaper in town?** Some rental companies will give you a lower rate if you're willing to pick up and drop off the car at a location in town rather than at the airport.

- ✔ **Are there any age restrictions?** Many car-rental companies add on a fee for drivers under 25, and some don't rent to them at all.

- ✔ **Is that the best rate?** If you see an advertised price in your local newspaper, be sure to ask for that specific rate; otherwise you may be charged the standard (higher) rate. Don't forget to mention membership in AAA, AARP, and trade unions. These memberships usually entitle you to discounts ranging from 5 percent to 30 percent.

- ✔ **Do you offer any frequent-flier bonuses?** Check your frequent-flier accounts. Not only are your favorite (or at least most-used) airlines likely to have sent you discount coupons, but most car rentals add at least 500 miles to your account.

Adding up the cost of renting a car

On top of the standard rental prices, other optional charges apply to most car rentals. The **collision damage waiver**, which requires you to pay for damage to the car in a collision, is charged on rentals in most states but is covered by many credit card companies. Check with your credit card company before you go so that you can avoid paying this hefty fee (as much as $20 a day). Face it: An extra $20 in your pocket can mean a few extra pulls on a slot machine!

Car-rental companies also offer additional *liability insurance* (if you harm others in an accident), *personal-accident insurance* (if you harm yourself or your passengers), and *personal-effects insurance* (if your luggage is stolen from your car). Your insurance policy on your car at home probably covers most of these unlikely occurrences. However, if your own insurance doesn't cover you for rentals or if you don't have auto insurance, definitely consider the additional coverage — ask your car-rental agent for more information. Unless you're toting around the Hope diamond — and you don't want to leave that in your car trunk anyway — you can probably skip the personal-effects insurance, but driving around without liability or personal-accident coverage is never a good idea. Even if you're a good driver, other people may not be, and liability claims can be complicated.

Some companies also offer **refueling packages,** which means that you pay for an entire tank of gas upfront. The price is usually fairly competitive with local gas prices, but you don't get credit for any gas remaining in the tank when you drop off the vehicle. If you decide not to go with this option, you pay only for the gas you use, but you have to return the car with a full tank or face high charges for any shortfall. If you're worried that a stop at a gas station on the way to the airport may cause you to miss your plane, or, especially, if the rates at the rental-car place are lower than prices at the gas station (it does happen), by all means, take advantage of the fuel-purchase option.

Note: Some rental-car companies are now charging a "luxury fee" for renting a car from the airport location. Be sure that you have paperwork guaranteeing your rate.

Playing It Safe with Travel and Medical Insurance

Three kinds of travel insurance are available: trip-cancellation insurance, medical insurance, and lost-luggage insurance. The cost of travel insurance varies widely, depending on the cost and length of your trip, your age and health, and the type of trip you're taking, but expect to pay between 5 percent and 8 percent of the vacation itself. Here is our advice on all three:

- ✔ **Trip-cancellation insurance** helps you get a refund if you have to back out of a trip, if you have to go home early, or if your travel supplier goes bankrupt. Allowed reasons for cancellation can range from sickness to natural disasters to the Department of State declaring your destination unsafe for travel. (Insurers usually won't cover vague fears, though, as many travelers discovered who tried to cancel their trips after 9/11 because they were wary of flying.)

A good resource is **Travel Guard Alerts** (www.travelguard.com/customerservice/alertlist), a list of companies considered high-risk by Travel Guard International (www.travelguard.com). Protect yourself further by paying for the insurance with a credit card — by law, consumers can get their money back on goods and services not received if they report the loss within 60 days after the charge is listed on their credit card statement.

Note: Many tour operators, particularly those offering trips to remote or high-risk areas, include insurance in the cost of the trip or can arrange insurance policies through a partnering provider, a convenient and often cost-effective way for the traveler to obtain insurance. Make sure the tour company is a reputable one, however. Some experts suggest you avoid buying insurance from the tour or cruise company you're traveling with, saying it's better to buy from a third-party insurer than to put all your money in one place.

✔ For domestic travel, buying **medical insurance** for your trip doesn't make sense for most travelers. Most existing health policies cover you, if you get sick away from home — but check before you go, particularly if you're insured by an HMO.

✔ **Lost-luggage insurance** is not necessary for most travelers. On domestic flights, checked baggage is covered up to $2,500 per ticketed passenger. On international flights (including U.S. portions of international trips), baggage coverage is limited to approximately $9.05 per pound, up to approximately $635 per checked bag. If you plan to check items more valuable than the standard liability, see if your valuables are covered by your homeowner's policy or get baggage insurance as part of your comprehensive travel-insurance package. Don't buy insurance at the airport — it's usually overpriced. Be sure to take any valuables or irreplaceable items with you in your carry-on luggage — many valuables (including books, money, and electronics) aren't covered by airline policies.

If your luggage is lost, immediately file a lost-luggage claim at the airport, detailing the luggage contents. For most airlines, you must report delayed, damaged, or lost baggage within four hours of arrival. The airlines are required to deliver luggage, once found, directly to your house or destination free of charge.

For more information, contact one of the following recommended insurers: **Access America** (☎ 800-284-8300; www.accessamerica.com), **Travel Guard International** (☎ 800-826-4919; www.travelguard.com), **Travel Insured International** (☎ 800-243-3174; www.travelinsured.com), or **Travelex Insurance Services** (☎ 800-228-9792; www.travelex-insurance.com).

Staying Healthy When You Travel

Getting sick will ruin your vacation, so we *strongly* advise against it (of course, last time we checked, the bugs weren't listening to us any more than they probably listen to you).

Obviously, Vegas is not the jungle, so it's not like you're going to have to worry about malaria. But there are a few health pitfalls awaiting any visitor, and we don't just mean hangovers. Many guests forget about how strong that desert sun can be, even in the winter. You'll know their folly by their lobster-red skin. Be sure to wear sunscreen if you're going to be outdoors for more than five minutes. If you do much walking, or even sitting by the pool in the summer, drink plenty of fluids (water especially), and remember that beer dehydrates you. It's all about keeping cool, and not just at the poker table.

Anyone with breathing problems or smoke sensitivity should know that while antismoking laws have cleared the air in parts of Vegas (restaurants and the like), smoking is still legal in casinos. Consequently, you still have to pass through clouds of smoke in most hotels to get to wherever you're headed. It can be a huge shock to walk into a casino if you've forgotten what a smoky environment is like. And don't forget to request a nonsmoking room (and rental car) if you don't want to smell stale secondhand smoke.

Other health tips:

- ✔ If you have health insurance, carry your identification card in your wallet. Likewise, if you don't think that your existing policy is sufficient, purchase medical insurance for more comprehensive coverage.

- ✔ Bring all your medications with you, as well as a prescription for more if you think you may run out. If possible, bring a couple of extra days' worth, plus another day or so for the ones you drop down the sink.

- ✔ Bring an extra pair of contact lenses or glasses in case you lose your primary pair.

- ✔ Don't forget to bring over-the-counter medicines for common travelers' ailments, such as diarrhea or stomach acid. Gift shops carry these items, but you pay a premium (and you won't find a gift shop on the airplane).

- ✔ If you suffer from a chronic illness, talk to your doctor before taking your trip. For conditions such as epilepsy, diabetes, or heart disease, wear a MedicAlert identification tag to immediately alert doctors to your condition and give them access to your medical records through MedicAlert's 24-hour hot line. Participation in the MedicAlert program requires a yearly subscription. Contact the **MedicAlert Foundation** (☎ **888-633-4298;** www.medicalert.org) for more information.

If you do get sick, ask the concierge at your hotel to recommend a local doctor. This is probably a better recommendation than what you may get from a doctor's referral number. If you can't get a doctor to help you right away, try the emergency room at the local hospital. For a list of hospitals that service the Las Vegas area, see the Quick Concierge at the back of the book.

Avoiding "economy-class syndrome"

Deep-vein thrombosis (or, as it's know in the world of flying, "economy-class syndrome") is a blood clot that develops in a deep vein. It's a potentially deadly condition that can be caused by sitting in cramped conditions — such as an airplane cabin — for too long. During a flight (especially a long-haul flight), get up, walk around, and stretch your legs every 60 to 90 minutes to keep your blood flowing. Other preventive measures include frequent flexing of the legs while sitting, drinking lots of water, and avoiding alcohol and sleeping pills. If you have a history of deep-vein thrombosis, heart disease, or another condition that puts you at high risk, some experts recommend wearing compression stockings or taking anticoagulants when you fly; always ask your physician about the best course for you. Symptoms of deep-vein thrombosis include leg pain or swelling, or even shortness of breath.

Staying Connected by Cellphone or E-Mail

You shouldn't have too much trouble staying connected in Vegas. Cellphone reception in Vegas is better than in rural areas, but it can still be a little iffy. We personally get terrible reception on our cellphones in most Vegas hotels, unless we're right by a window. That may just be our lousy service provider, though. Cellphones are allowed in casinos, but good luck hearing whoever's on the other end. As always, you should be respectful of others when using cellphones in restaurants and turn them off for shows and other theatrical events.

Most Vegas hotels offer Wi-Fi access for an additional fee, and many have pricey business centers with computers.

Using a cellphone across the United States

Just because your cellphone works at home doesn't mean it works elsewhere in the country (thanks to our nation's fragmented cellphone system). It's a good bet that your phone will work in major cities. But take a look at your wireless company's coverage map on its Web site before heading out — T-Mobile, Sprint, and Nextel are particularly weak in rural areas. If you need to stay in touch at a destination where you know your phone won't work, **rent** a phone that does from **InTouch USA** (☎ **800-872-7626;** www.intouchglobal.com) or from a rental-car location, but beware that you pay $1 per minute or more for airtime.

If you're venturing deep into national parks, you may want to consider renting a **satellite phone ("satphone"),** which is different from a cellphone in that it connects to satellites rather than ground-based towers. A satphone is more costly than a cellphone but works where there's no cellular signal and no towers. Unfortunately, you pay at least $2 per minute to use the phone, and it only works where you can see the horizon (that is, usually not indoors). In North America, you can rent Iridium satellite phones from **Roadpost** (☎ **888-290-1616** or 905-272-5665; www. roadpost.com). InTouch USA offers a wider range of satphones but at higher rates. As of this writing, satphones are very expensive to buy.

If you're not from the United States, you may be appalled at the poor reach of our **Global System for Mobiles (GSM) wireless network,** which is used by much of the rest of the world. Your phone probably will work in most major U.S. cities; it definitely won't work in many rural areas. And you may or may not be able to send SMS (text messaging) home. Assume nothing — call your wireless provider and get the full scoop. In a worst-case scenario, you can always rent a phone; InTouch USA delivers to hotels.

Accessing the Internet away from home

Travelers have any number of ways to check their e-mail and access the Internet on the road. Of course, using your own laptop — or even a personal digital assistant (PDA) or electronic organizer with a modem — gives you the most flexibility.

If you're used to visiting cybercafes on your travels, keep in mind that Vegas doesn't have many cybercafes readily accessible to the average visitor. Plus, those independent businesses don't reliably *stay* in business. See what's currently open at **www.cybercaptive.com** and **www. cybercafe.com**.

Most **youth hostels** nowadays have at least one computer where you can get onto the Internet. And most **public libraries** across the world offer Internet access free or for a small charge. Avoid **hotel business centers** unless you're willing to pay exorbitant rates.

Most major airports now have **Internet kiosks** scattered throughout their gates. These kiosks, which you also see in shopping malls, hotel lobbies, and tourist information offices around the world, give you basic Web access for a per-minute fee that's usually higher than cybercafe prices. The kiosks' clunkiness and high prices mean they should be avoided whenever possible.

To retrieve your e-mail, ask your **Internet service provider (ISP)** if it has a Web-based interface tied to your existing e-mail account. If your ISP doesn't have such an interface, you can use the free **mail2web** service (www.mail2web.com) to view and reply to your home e-mail. For more flexibility, you may want to open a free, Web-based e-mail account with **Gmail** (http://mail.google.com) or **Yahoo! Mail** (http://mail. yahoo.com), if you don't already have one. (Microsoft's Hotmail is another popular option, but Hotmail has severe spam problems.) Your home ISP may be able to forward your e-mail to the Web-based account automatically.

If you need to access files on your office computer, look into a service called **GoToMyPC** (www.gotomypc.com), which provides a Web-based interface for you to access and manipulate a distant PC from anywhere — even a cybercafe — provided your "target" PC is on and has an always-on connection to the Internet (such as with Road Runner cable). The service offers top-quality security; but if you're worried about hackers, use your own laptop rather than a cybercafe computer to access the GoToMyPC system.

If you're bringing your own computer, **Wi-Fi** (wireless fidelity) is the way to go. More and more hotels, cafes, and retailers are signing on as wireless "hotspots" from which you can get a high-speed connection without cable wires, networking hardware, or a phone line. You can get Wi-Fi one of several ways. Many laptops have built-in Wi-Fi capability. Mac owners have their own networking technology, Apple AirPort. If you have an older computer, you can buy a **Wi-Fi card** (around $50) and plug it into your laptop. You sign up for wireless access service much as you do cellphone service, through a plan offered by one of several commercial companies that have made wireless service available in airports, hotel lobbies, and coffee shops, primarily in the United States (followed by the U.K. and Japan).

Starbucks serves up free Wi-Fi with its coffee nationwide; go to www.starbucks.com/coffeehouse/wireless-internet for more information. **Boingo** (www.boingo.com) has set up networks in airports and high-class hotel lobbies. **iPass** (www.ipass.com) providers also give you access to a few hundred wireless hotel-lobby setups. Best of all, you don't need to be staying at the **Four Seasons** to use the hotel's network; just set yourself up on a nice couch in the lobby.

Most Vegas hotels offer Wi-Fi, but for a daily fee that can be pretty costly. To find places that provide **free wireless networks** in Vegas and other cities around the world, go to **www.personaltelco.net/index.cgi/WirelessCommunities**.

If Wi-Fi is not available at your destination, most business-class hotels throughout the world offer dataports for laptop modems or high-speed access for a fee. You can bring your own cables, but many hotels rent them. **Call your hotel in advance** to see what your options are.

In addition, major ISPs have **local access numbers** around the world, allowing you to go online simply by placing a local call. (Local calls at hotels in Vegas usually cost about $1 for the first 30 minutes, but then go way up for each additional minute thereafter.) Check your ISP's Web site or call and ask how you can use your current account away from home and, if so, how much it'll cost.

If you're traveling outside the reach of your ISP, the **iPass** network has dial-up numbers in most of the world's countries. You have to sign up with an iPass provider, who will then tell you how to set up your computer for your destination(s). For a list of iPass providers, go to www.ipass.com and click Individual Purchase. One solid provider is **i2roam** (☎ **866-811-6209** or 920-235-0475; www.i2roam.com).

Wherever you go, bring a **connection kit** of the right power, a spare phone cord, and a spare Ethernet network cable — or find out whether your hotel supplies them to guests.

Keeping Up with Airline Security

Security procedures in the United States post-9/11 often have caused jams in the security check-in lines. Allow yourself plenty of time to go through. Generally, you're fine if you arrive at the airport **one hour** before a domestic flight and **two hours** before an international flight.

Bring a **current, government-issued photo ID** such as a driver's license or passport. Keep your ID at the ready to show at check-in, the security checkpoint, and sometimes even the gate. (Children under 18 don't need government-issued photo IDs for domestic flights, but they do for international flights to most countries.)

In 2003, the Transportation Security Administration (TSA) phased out **gate check-in** at all U.S. airports. And **E-tickets** have made paper tickets nearly obsolete. If you have an E-ticket, you can beat the ticket-counter lines by using airport **electronic kiosks** or even **online check-in** from your home computer. Online check-in involves logging on to your airline's Web site, accessing your reservation, and printing out your boarding pass — and the airline may even offer you bonus miles to do so! If you're using a kiosk at the airport, bring the credit card you used to book the ticket or your frequent-flier card. Print out your boarding pass from the kiosk and simply proceed to the security checkpoint with your pass and a photo ID. If you're checking bags or looking to snag an exit-row seat, you'll be able to do so using most airline kiosks. Even the smaller airlines are employing the kiosk system, but always call your airline to make sure these alternatives are available. **Curbside check-in** is also a good way to avoid lines, although a few airlines still ban curbside check-in; call before you go.

Security checkpoint lines often can be long. If you have trouble standing for long periods of time, tell an airline employee; the airline will provide a wheelchair. Speed up security by **not wearing metal objects** such as big belt buckles. Keep in mind that only **ticketed passengers** are allowed past security, except for folks escorting disabled passengers or children.

Travelers in the United States are allowed one carry-on bag, plus a "personal item" such as a purse, briefcase, or laptop bag. As this was written, there are strict guidelines about what can be carried onboard, particularly with regard to liquids. The TSA provides a list of **what you can carry on** and **what you can't;** for a current list of restricted items, visit www.tsa.gov. Meanwhile, many airlines are now charging for checked luggage; check your airline's Web site for its current policies.

Part III
Settling Into Las Vegas

In this part . . .

Las Vegas is truly a city that never sleeps. Navigating your way amid the haze of neon lights, mega-resorts, and the Strip's ever-present traffic can be intimidating at first. Don't worry — it's not as complicated as it looks. In this part, we walk you through the city's neighborhoods, tell you where and how to catch local transportation, show you where to get more information whenever you need it, and explore hotel and dining options with you.

Chapter 8

Arriving and Getting Oriented

*N*o matter how you get here, you'll probably be dazzled at first, particularly if you've never been to Las Vegas. It's so . . . bright. Neon.
Weird. You'll want to come back just to see if you dreamed it. Even if
you've been here before, you may be shocked at how little you recognize. Vegas is rarely idle; constant tear-downs and build-back-ups mean
that every decade or so, the landscape looks totally new. It's a mind-
blowing sight, so take it in and enjoy it.

 If you're driving, just remember to take your eyes off the buildings and
put them back on the road every so often. (We know — it's very distracting to drive past pyramids and lions and pirate ships!)

Making Your Way to Your Hotel

For general tips on making your way around town, you can refer to
"Getting Around Las Vegas," later in this chapter; but here we give you
some sound advice for getting into town and to your hotel.

Arriving by plane

McCarran International Airport is located at the southern end of the
city, at 5757 Wayne Newton Blvd. (☎ **702-261-5211;** www.mccarran.
com). You're really not too far from the action — unlike in some big
cities, where you have to cover many miles to get to your hotel from the
airport, you only have to go about a mile to get from McCarran to the
Strip. Of course, at rush hour, it may take an hour to cover that mile!

Ready, set, gamble!

As soon as you get off the plane, you learn the first rule of Las Vegas: Gambling is *everywhere*. Even in the airport. There are more than 1,300 slot machines and video-poker games right at McCarran. These banks of machines (known as carousels) are in all the satellite terminals, the main terminal, and the baggage-claim area.

Most people advise that you avoid these machines like the plague — supposedly, they offer lower winnings (known as *paybacks*) than hotel machines. Then again, we know people who have hit it big on those very machines. So, we won't blame you if you drop a few coins. After all, who can resist such a quintessential Las Vegas experience as shaking hands with a one-armed bandit while waiting for your luggage?

Not only is the location super-convenient, but so is the airport itself. It's busy, no doubt (it's the seventh-busiest airport in the world, with around 40 million people passing through annually); but it's surprisingly simple to navigate. Big, modern, and well planned, it has two terminals and more than 100 gates. And if you come back sometime around the year 2012, you'll find another 14 gates in an all-new, half-mile long third terminal.

Hitting the road

Assuming that you took our advice and rented a car (see Chapter 7), head outside past the baggage-claim area to the shuttle-bus stops and look for the rental-car buses. These will transport you to an off-site rental car facility where you find all the usual suspects: **Alamo, Avis, Budget, Enterprise, Hertz, National,** and **Thrifty,** among others. After you finish all the paperwork at the counter, follow the signs to your car in the big structure, and you're off.

When you leave the facility, take a right on Warm Springs Road and then a quick right on Las Vegas Boulevard. That's the Strip, and it's just a couple miles to the heart of the action.

Catching a cab

Just outside the doors from the baggage-claim area is the taxi stand. If a couple flights have arrived at roughly the same time, the line for a cab can be daunting, with waiting times of up to 20 minutes. Basic taxi fare is $3.30 for the first mile plus an additional $1.80 for getting picked up at the airport, $2.40 for each additional mile, plus gas surcharge, airport levies, and time penalties if you get stuck in traffic. The state governs these fares, so they should be the same for every company. An adequate tip for the cab driver is 10 percent to 15 percent; if you're sharing a fare, you should do 10 percent per person or per small group.

Going in style

If you want to try a fun alternative to cabbing it through town, why not avoid the taxi lines and consider taking a limo? You can call ahead to your hotel (most of the big ones have a limo service) and arrange to have a driver pick you up at the airport. Just give the hotel staff your flight information, and the limo driver will even be waiting at your gate, holding a little sign with your name on it. How ritzy!

Not only is it fun to pretend to be among the rich and famous, but you don't have to actually be rich to enjoy this perk: The rates can be reasonable for limos if you're traveling with a large group. As a matter of fact, it's sometimes less expensive than taking a cab, considering that you can fit more people into a limo. And the drivers are much more accommodating. Sit back and enjoy the sights (or watch the onboard TV) in style. And don't forget to tip the kind driver for his efforts.

All taxis can carry up to five passengers. While you're stuck waiting in line at the taxi stand, strike up a conversation with the other people around you to see if anyone is headed in your direction and is willing to split the fare with you. Hey, cheaper is better!

Cabs usually are lined up and waiting outside the airport and major hotels at all times. For this reason, you really should never have to call for a cab. For more information on getting around Vegas by cab and a list of the major cab companies in town, see "By taxi," under "Getting Around Las Vegas," later in this chapter.

Table 8-1 shows you a few examples of what you can expect to pay for a cab from McCarran to various parts of the city. Keep in mind that these are just estimates, so your actual fare may vary a bit depending on traffic and route taken.

Table 8-1	Cab Prices from the Airport
Where Are You Going?	*How Much Will It Cost?*
To the South Strip area	$12–$18
To the Center Strip area	$14–$21
To the North Strip area	$16–$22
To the downtown area	$22–$27
To the Paradise Road area	$9–$17

Jumping on a shuttle

If you want to take a shuttle, go to the same place in the airport where you pick up a taxi or board the rental-car buses. There you find shuttle buses that run regularly to and from the Strip and downtown. These buses are big and comfy, and they can be a bargain if you're by yourself or with one other person. Shuttle buses charge about $6.50 per person for a trip to the Strip or Paradise Road areas and $8 per person to go downtown. And they take you right to your hotel.

If you have more than two people in your group, however, you can probably take a cab for less.

Taking a shuttle is not always a piece of cake: If the people on your bus aren't going to the same hotel as you (or one close by), you end up riding and waiting through a lot of extra stops. (If you share our luck, your hotel will be the last stop on the trip.) The shuttles have luggage racks, though, which make these a better bet than a city bus.

Although several companies operate shuttle services, **Bell Trans** (☎ **702-739-7990**) is the biggest and most reliable. You usually can spot these large shuttle vans, with rates posted on the sides, cruising the airport.

Getting on the bus

We're going to be blunt here: For reasons we discuss later in this chapter (see "Getting Around Las Vegas"), the bus should be your last resort. **Citizen's Area Transit** (CAT; ☎ **702-228-7433**), runs regular service to and from the airport. The fare for a bus to the Strip is $3 for adults, $1.50 for seniors and children. Take CAT only if you have no other option. If you're lugging a heavy load, remember that even if the bus stops right in front of your hotel (which it probably won't), you may have a long walk from the bus stop to the door (distances in Vegas can be deceiving).

If you decide to take the bus (despite our advice to the contrary), remember that schedules and routes vary, so call for information. In general, though, the **no. 109** bus goes from the airport to the South Strip Transfer Terminal at Gilespie Street and Sunset Road, where you can transfer to the Gold line, which runs the Strip. Alternately, the **no. 108** bus departs from the airport and takes you to the Stratosphere, where you can transfer to the Deuce line, which stops close to most Strip- and Convention Center–area hotels.

Arriving by car

If you're driving into town (regardless of whether you're coming from the airport), you'll probably be coming in on **I-15,** the major north–south freeway that runs right through the city. The following recommendations help you determine which exit to take, depending on where you're staying:

✔ **If you're staying on the South Strip** (for example, **Mandalay Bay** or **MGM Grand**): Traveling north on **I-15,** exit at **Tropicana Avenue,** and turn right at the stoplight. The Strip is less than a half-mile to the east — trust us, you can't miss it. Southbound travelers should take the same exit but follow the signs for **Tropicana Avenue East.**

✔ **If you're staying on the Center Strip** (for example, **Bellagio** or **Harrah's**): North- or southbound drivers should take either the **Eastbound Flamingo Road** or **Spring Mountain Road** exit. The former puts you at the intersection populated by **Caesars Palace, Bellagio, Paris, Wynn Las Vegas,** and more, while the latter drops you off near **Treasure Island,** the **Mirage,** and the **Venetian.**

✔ **If you're staying on the North Strip** (for example, **Stratosphere** or **Circus Circus**): Coming from the north or south, exit at **Sahara** and head east. The Strip is about ¾ mile away.

✔ **If you're staying in the Paradise Road area** (for example, **Las Vegas Hilton** or **Hard Rock Hotel**): Take the **Flamingo Road** exit and head east. When you cross the Strip, go about another mile to **Paradise Road.** At this intersection, you'll be right around the 4000 block, with higher numbers to the south (turn right) and lower numbers to the north (turn left).

✔ **If you're staying downtown** (for example, the **Golden Nugget** or **Main Street Station**): From **I-15,** the quickest route is to take the freeway offshoot that runs past downtown. The interchange is a bit tricky (locals call it the "spaghetti bowl"), with the freeway carrying three different numbers: **515, 95,** and **93.** Whatever you want to call it, take it south and exit at **Casino Center Boulevard.** This dumps you right into the heart of downtown, with **Fremont Street** crossing two blocks ahead and **Las Vegas Boulevard** (which eventually becomes the Strip) three blocks to the left.

Figuring Out the Neighborhoods

Even though Las Vegas is a very spread-out city, the area you'll most likely be staying in is very centralized and easy to navigate.

Vegas boasts three main neighborhoods. There's the **Strip,** where all the big hotels and resorts are located; **downtown,** where you find **Glitter Gulch** and the **Fremont Street Experience;** and the **Paradise Road** area, which is home to the **Las Vegas Convention Center** and some smaller, noncasino hotels. We give you the pros and cons of basing yourself in each one in this section. We also include a few other neighborhoods that may be of some interest to you if you're staying for more than a few days or are planning future trips.

The best analogy to help you envision the layout of Las Vegas is this: Las Vegas is shaped sort of like a crooked Santa Claus cap. The **Strip** is one side of the cap, **Paradise Road** is the other, and **downtown** is the fuzzy ball on top. Chew on that one for a moment.

Las Vegas Neighborhoods

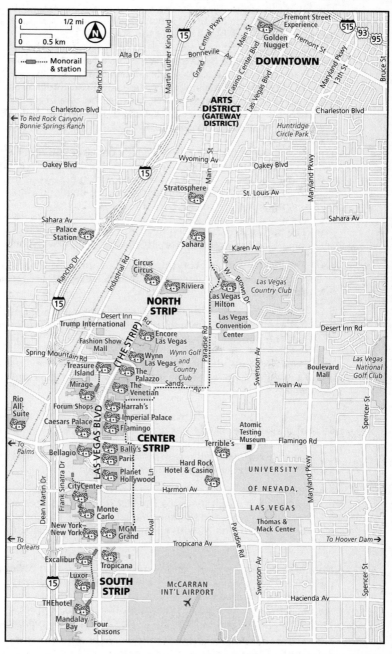

The Strip

The **Strip** (also known as **Las Vegas Boulevard South**) is the heart of Vegas. It acts as the center of town, so addresses are all measured from there (100 West is a block west of the Strip, 100 East is a block east, and so on). The southern and center parts of the Strip are the most action-packed. That's where first-time visitors generally spend most of their time, and with good reason — this 4-mile stretch of road is home to the biggest, splashiest, and (in some cases) gaudiest hotels and casinos on Earth. All the major players you've heard about are here: **Bellagio, Caesars Palace, CityCenter, MGM Grand,** the **Mirage, New York–New York,** the **Venetian,** and **Wynn Las Vegas,** to name just a few.

The Strip is very spread out. If it's a nice day and you're feeling frisky (and wearing sensible shoes), you can try walking from one end to the other. Just be sure to bring cab fare with you in case your legs give out. To make things a bit more manageable, we've divided the Strip into three sections for the purposes of this book:

- ✔ **The South Strip** runs roughly from Harmon Avenue south and includes **CityCenter, Luxor, MGM Grand,** and **New York–New York.**

- ✔ **The North Strip** is everything north of Spring Mountain/Sands up to the Stratosphere Tower — **Circus Circus, Encore, Sahara,** and **Wynn Las Vegas,** to name a few.

- ✔ **The Center Strip** is everything in between and includes **Bellagio, Caesars Palace, Flamingo,** the **Mirage, Palazzo, Treasure Island,** and the **Venetian.**

If you're a first-time visitor to Vegas and you want to be close to all the glitzy sites, the Strip is your best bet. Consider the pros and cons, however:

- ✔ **Pros:** All the megaresorts are here — many within walking distance of one another (and trust us, you want to spend time gawking at these hotels). The Strip offers a wide variety of choices, from superluxurious casino resorts to standard motels. And don't forget: This is really why you're coming to Vegas!

- ✔ **Cons:** This is why everyone comes to Vegas, so this is where the crowds are. Don't overlook the fact that most places are on the expensive side, and the few cheap hotels are cheap in every sense of the word. Finally, with so much to do on the Strip, it's easy to miss out on the rest of the city.

Note also that the extreme end of the North Strip (near **Stratosphere** in particular, but even as you get closer down toward **Sahara**) is not nearly as bustling as it once was — in fact, it's kind of desolate and creepy in spots. The closer you get to the center, the better. The South Strip, with **Excalibur, MGM Grand, New York–New York,** and **Tropicana** on four corners, is pretty happening.

The Las Vegas Strip is one of the most popular destinations in the country, and, as such, tourist traps are everywhere. Be aware that anything you buy on the Strip — a meal, film, a souvenir, or a can of shaving cream — costs more than anywhere else in town. Be careful to pack enough film and an adequate supply of all your toiletries so that you don't run out and get price-gouged. And, by all means, try to resist buying souvenirs until you're in another part of town. (For more information on shopping in Vegas, see Chapter 13.)

Downtown

Downtown is the oldest section of the city. It's located just southeast of where I-15 and the 515/95/93 freeways come together. **Las Vegas Boulevard** runs right into Fremont Street (now a pedestrian walkway with no auto traffic allowed), where most of the area's big hotels are located.

This is where the Las Vegas phenomenon began. Hotels and casinos sprang up here long before the Strip was anything more than a gleam in Bugsy Siegel's eye. The area is informally known as "Glitter Gulch" (narrower streets make the neon seem brighter here).

The bulk of the action is concentrated on and around Fremont Street between Main and Ninth (about a 5-minute drive from the north end of the Strip), putting any number of casinos within a block or two of one another. In the not-so-distant past, downtown had fallen victim to the high-profile aura surrounding the Strip. Revitalized by the **Fremont Street Experience** (see Chapter 12), downtown has been transformed from a seedy, unsafe row of low-rent hotels and strip joints to a more pleasant, friendly row of medium-rent hotels (with only the occasional strip joint). And it's all tied together by a pedestrian mall topped with a canopy that features a very fancy light show set to music. In parts, it's more like a small town than "Vegas"; but then again, it's more manageable.

 Bordering neighborhoods are questionable in terms of safety, so stick to the well-traveled, brightly lit parts.

Following are the pros and cons of downtown:

- ✔ **Pros:** Downtown is less crowded and less overwhelming than the Strip. You often get better bargains on hotels and entertainment. And if you don't want to rent a car, you save on transportation, because everything in the downtown area is within walking distance or a short (read: cheap) cab ride away.

- ✔ **Cons:** You find fewer choices of hotels and places to play than on the Strip. Again, it's more like a small town in some ways than big-wow Vegas. It's also somewhat isolated from all the really famous, big-ticket venues in town. If you're bringing kids, keep in mind that downtown is still seedy in spots and doesn't cater much to families.

Paradise Road

This area is so named because it refers to — surprise! — **Paradise Road** and the area surrounding it. The actual road is a major north–south artery that runs from **McCarran** to its intersection with the **Strip** (which parallels **Paradise Road,** for the most part, about half a mile to the west) at the **Stratosphere Tower.**

You can find a few large hotels and attractions here, but mostly it's made up of smaller noncasino hotels and a lot of restaurants. The **Las Vegas Convention Center** is located in this area, so it's a good area to base yourself in if you're attending a convention. The road runs parallel to Las Vegas Boulevard about a mile away, and most hotels and casinos are located between Harmon and Sahara avenues. (When you read the hotel reviews in Chapter 9, keep in mind that a "Paradise Road" designation does not necessarily mean that the hotel is right *on* Paradise Road but rather in the vicinity.)

Hotels here are mostly of the generic chain variety, which can take a big chunk of fun out of your Vegas experience. Many boast that they're an easy walk to the Strip, but that depends on your definition of *easy*.

Following are the pros and cons of Paradise Road:

- ✔ **Pros:** This area offers more noncasino hotels as a quiet alternative to the busy Strip and downtown. And it's within close proximity to all the action without being right in the middle of it. Thanks to the monorail, access to the Strip is easier than ever.

- ✔ **Cons:** Paradise Road has fewer hotel, entertainment, and recreation choices than either the Strip or downtown. And it isn't within true walking distance of the fun stuff. Finally, if there's a convention in town, forget it!

Between the Strip and downtown

If you take **Las Vegas Boulevard** north, you end up downtown. Most of the city's wedding chapels are located between the **Strip** and **downtown** (see Chapter 12 for more about the nuptial scene). Unless you're actually getting married, this area is really only good for its high silliness and kitsch factor ("Joan Collins was married here!"). Hey, it may be fun for something a little different.

East Las Vegas

The **East Las Vegas** area is where locals go to gamble. It's less crowded and glitzy (locals don't really need the wow factor). The odds are better, too — you can actually find a 9/6 video poker machine (see Chapter 11 for more on this) and single-deck blackjack! The table limits tend to be lower, everything is a little cheaper, and those hotels tend to go out of their way to cultivate a local — and loyal — clientele.

Several big casino hotels are located along **Boulder Highway** near Flamingo Road, including **Sam's Town Hotel & Gambling Hall,** 5111 Boulder Hwy. (☎ 800-634-6371; www.samstownlv.com). We don't recommend getting a hotel in this neighborhood, simply because most of the other places you may want to see are too far away — it's about 7 or 8 miles to the Strip. The upside is that prices often are much lower than what you'd pay on the Strip. So, if you're feeling particularly adventuresome — or tight in the wallet — it may be worth your while to check it out. Take **Flamingo Road** east from the Strip to get here.

West Las Vegas

Another predominantly suburban area, **West Las Vegas** is dotted with a few resorts of note, including **Red Rock Resort,** the JW Marriott, and the locals' favorite Suncoast. These casino hotels are even farther away than the East Las Vegas locations mentioned earlier (10 or 11 miles in usually heavy traffic), but they can be surprisingly upscale, luxurious places where you often can stay for less than what similar accommodations on the Strip cost. Take **Charleston Avenue** west from the Strip to get to the general vicinity.

Henderson

If you're looking for something a bit off the beaten path, and you want to see some fun, family-oriented attractions, check out **Henderson.** It's basically a suburb that makes up the southern part of Las Vegas from I-15 all the way over to Lake Las Vegas. Two of our favorite hotels in Vegas are here: the **Green Valley Ranch** resort and **M Resort** (both are reviewed in Chapter 9). Mostly tract homes and chain stores, Henderson is not the kind of place you wander around and explore — you go with specific destinations (like the two hotels we just mentioned) in mind.

Maryland Parkway

The **Maryland Parkway** is another major north–south artery about 2 miles west of the Strip and 1 mile west of Paradise Road. If you're looking for retailers or food chains, you can find just about every major (and minor) one on this road: **JCPenney, Sears, Toys "R" Us,** and all the big drugstores, just to mention a few.

If you need to pick up something such as shaving cream or a spiffy new bathing suit, and you don't feel like paying the exorbitant prices charged in hotel stores, this area is a good bet.

Finding Information after You Arrive

No matter how well you prepare for your trip, you may still find yourself in need of pertinent information after you arrive in Las Vegas. Check out the following resources to get the latest news and current happenings:

✔ Every **major hotel** has tourist information at its reception, show, sightseeing, or concierge desk. The friendly folks who work at these desks can tell you about special events, concerts, or shows in town that you may have missed during your research. Don't be shy about making show reservations at the big hotel's show desks. They can make reservations for you at any show in town — not just the ones in that particular hotel. (The only caveat here is that the concierge is probably prejudiced toward his personal or professional favorites, so you may not be getting an unbiased opinion.)

✔ Go to the **Las Vegas Visitor Information Center,** 3150 Paradise Rd. (☎ **877-847-4858** or 702-892-7575; www.visitlasvegas.com), to pick up packets of free information.

✔ Visit the **Las Vegas Chamber of Commerce,** 6671 Las Vegas Blvd. S., Ste. 300 (☎ **702-735-1616;** www.lvchamber.com) and ask for its *Visitor's Guide,* which contains extensive listings for accommodations, attractions, excursions, children's activities, and more. The people who work there can also answer many of your other questions (including those about quickie weddings and divorces).

✔ Check listings in the local newspapers and magazines. Las Vegas has two major newspapers on sale in the city: the *Las Vegas Review-Journal* (www.lvrj.com) and the *Las Vegas Sun* (www.lasvegassun.com); both have regular entertainment listings. You also can find free local magazine publications, such as *What's On, The Las Vegas Guide* (www.whats-on.com) and *Las Vegas Magazine* (www.lvshowbiz.com), in hotels and restaurants throughout the city.

✔ For hip and unbiased opinions regarding local sites and attractions, pick up the *Las Vegas Weekly* (www.lasvegasweekly.com), a free alternative arts, culture, and lifestyle journal that can be found all over town (particularly in bookstores or music shops).

Getting Around Las Vegas

For a city of its stature, Las Vegas doesn't have a phenomenal public transportation network. That's not a surprise, considering that the casinos want you to stay put. There are city buses but no subways or rail lines. You're likely to get around in one of four ways: driving, taking a cab, taking a bus, or hoofing it. In this section, we give you the pros and cons of each of these alternatives, plus some tips that may save you time and money.

By car

Driving is a good option for getting around in Vegas. When you consider practicality and convenience, nothing beats your own set of wheels. Although you can walk to a lot of nearby attractions, you can get the most out of the city when you're mobile and not relying on taxis, buses, or your feet to get somewhere. Of course, as practical as having a car is, there are also some drawbacks to consider. We give you the lowdown on both in this section.

Considering the pros

Renting a car provides you with added mobility and freedom that you don't get from other means of transportation. Unless you're a marathon walker, the Strip is too sprawling to walk its entire length. Anywhere else is too far away for a cheap cab ride, and bus service is ineffective at best. Cars are cheaper than taking cabs everywhere, especially if you want to get out and explore.

 Parking is not much of a concern in Vegas, because you can find lots of inexpensive (or free) garages throughout the city. As we mentioned earlier, all the major hotels have free self-parking, and most have free valet service — though be sure to tip the person delivering your car.

Dealing with the cons

Of course, driving yourself through this wonderland of a city does have its drawbacks. Las Vegas traffic is notoriously congested, and it's especially so on and around the Strip. The stoplights alone can take forever to maneuver. We once took a drive from the one of the southernmost Strip hotels, the **Luxor,** to the northernmost, the **Stratosphere.** It took almost 30 minutes to cover the 4-mile drive. That's an average of about 8 mph.

Vegas is not immune to the construction problems that you find in most major cities. In fact, you may find that Vegas is even more prone to these "improvements" because of its continual state of transition. Just be aware that the roads here always are ripped up for some project or another, which only adds to traffic problems.

 You can find lots of gas stations at the Tropicana Avenue exit just west of the freeway, but you should probably steer clear of them: Their prices are way higher than those at other places in town.

Although it may sound like fun to cruise around Las Vegas in a cool Porsche or convertible, you're better off sticking to something small and cheap. After all, it's just going to be sitting in a parking garage most of the time, and the parking attendants don't really care what you drive.

Steering clear of traffic jams

As we mention earlier in this chapter, driving in Las Vegas can be a nightmare when it comes to traffic. Because the Strip is exceptionally crowded at all times, day or night, avoid it at all costs. Over the course of our oh-so-frequent visits (we like to call it research!), however, we have found a few alternative routes that are easier on your schedule and your blood pressure.

Alternate Routes to Avoid Gridlock

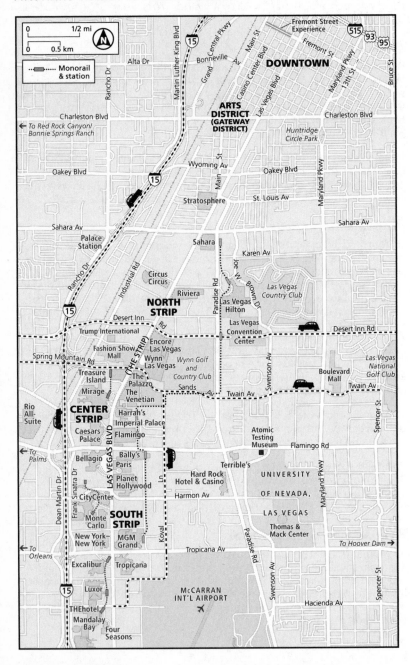

If you don't want to get stuck in bumper-to-bumper traffic on the Strip, here are some alternate routes for traveling **north–south:**

✔ **I-15:** This major interstate runs parallel to the Strip and is easily accessible from **Tropicana, Flamingo, Spring Mountain,** and **Sahara avenues.** If you need to get from one end of the Strip to the other, or especially if you're going downtown, this route is your best bet. The only exception is during morning and evening rush hours, when you can finish reading *War and Peace* in the time it takes to get from one place to another.

✔ **Dean Martin Drive/Industrial Road:** This quick-and-dirty route for getting from one Strip location to another is also a good alternative. It's located just west of the Strip, and it runs the entire length of it and beyond, with access from the northbound lanes of I-15. The smooth, four-lane minihighway has a lot less traffic and fewer stop-lights, and even though it has two names (Dean Martin south of Twain Avenue, Industrial from that spot north), it's just one road that can save you some time.

✔ **Koval Lane:** Koval runs parallel to the Strip on the east side between **Las Vegas Boulevard** and **Paradise Road.** It runs only from **Tropicana** to **Sands,** so it isn't good for end-to-end Strip runs, but short trips are a lot faster on Koval. Just be sure to avoid this route on Friday and Saturday nights; gridlocked traffic on the Strip often spills over here.

✔ **Frank Sinatra Drive:** More or less constructed as a way for hotel employees to get to and from home and work, Frank Sinatra Drive is a relatively unexplored option. It runs behind Mandalay Bay, Luxor, Excalibur, New York–New York, Monte Carlo, and Bellagio, with back entrances to several, and eventually connects to Industrial. It can get a little confusing back there. Still, if you do it right, you can get from Caesars Palace to Mandalay Bay in under five minutes.

The major **east–west** arteries, such as **Flamingo** and **Tropicana,** can get congested, too, so here are some alternatives that generally move faster:

✔ **Spring Mountain/Sands/Twain:** It's one street with three different names, depending on where you are. It crosses the Strip next to **Treasure Island** and **Paradise Road** near the **Fairfield Inn.** You find fewer stoplights and less traffic here than on other major east–west routes such as **Flamingo Road** or **Tropicana Avenue.**

✔ **Desert Inn Road:** This is another terrific project engineered by the city. This street has been changed into a six-lane divided freeway (with no traffic lights) that begins at **Paradise Road** on the east and ends at **Valley View** just west of **I-15.** It provides limited access to and from the Strip, so it's best used for getting from one side to the other without the hassle of **Las Vegas Boulevard, I-15,** or cross-walks filled with tourists.

Getting your bearings

The **Stratosphere** hotel has revolutionized driving for tourists in Las Vegas. At 110 stories, this larger-than-large structure is the tallest building west of the Mississippi River. It can be seen from just about every place in town (and from many places outside of town!). It's more than twice as tall as any other building in Las Vegas. If you get lost while driving, take a minute to scan the horizon and find the **Stratosphere Tower.** Head toward it, and you eventually arrive at the northern end of the Strip and Paradise Road, only 5 minutes from downtown.

Following the rules of the road

If you're counting on Vegas having loose speed limits and traffic laws, don't. Despite rumors about western states being lax, Las Vegas police and the Nevada Highway Patrol strictly go by the book. Here are a few general rules:

- ✔ The speed limits in Vegas are comparable to those in the rest of the United States, with 35 to 45 mph common on many major streets, 25 to 35 mph on side streets, and 55 to 70 mph on the freeways. Be sure to scope out the specific speed limits on the road you're traveling.

- ✔ Turning right on red lights is permitted in Las Vegas. If you don't follow this convention, you're likely to hear about it from the guy behind you in the Caddy with the steer-horn hood ornament.

- ✔ Most of the time, you need to wait for the green arrow if you want to make a left turn at a major intersection. Up to three lanes of traffic can turn at the same time.

- ✔ U-turns are allowed at intersections where there is no sign strictly forbidding them.

By taxi

If you plan on spending all or most of your time in one general area, using the city's taxi service is a viable option. If you plan to go very far, however, be prepared to open your wallet — wide.

You see taxis everywhere in Vegas, so finding one usually isn't a problem. You find a line of them outside most major hotels and the airport, even at 4 a.m. Although we can't vouch for every driver, car, and company, all the taxis we've taken have been clean and the drivers professional and courteous. In case you happen to wander into less-traveled territory and need to call a taxi, here's a list of some of the major cab companies in town:

ᐟ ABC (☎ 702-736-8444)

ᐟ Checker (☎ 702-873-2000)

ᐟ Desert (☎ 702-386-9102)

ᐟ Henderson (☎ 702-384-2322)

ᐟ Yellow (☎ 702-873-2000)

Our main issue with using taxis is that they're so darned expensive. Once, we were too tired to walk back from the southern end of the Strip to our hotel in the center section, so we hailed a cab. You guessed it: We immediately got stuck in nighttime traffic — and that meter kept on ticking even though we weren't moving. To go about 2 miles cost almost $15 with tip. Now, a good cabbie does his best to avoid such nonsense (even if it means making less money), but if you do take a cab, be prepared to boss the driver into the swiftest route.

Taxi fares are regulated by the state of Nevada and should be the same for all companies: $3.30 for the first mile and $2.40 for each additional mile, plus time penalties (for those times when you're stuck in traffic). Be sure that the rates are prominently displayed in the cab before letting the driver start the meter.

On foot

After you get into a centralized neighborhood (Center Strip, downtown, and so on), you won't have a problem walking from one hotel to the next. It's certainly easier than retrieving a car every time. If, however, you want to get out of one neighborhood and into another neighborhood, walking becomes a bigger deal.

Is that the Mirage or just a mirage?

Maybe it's the desert that makes distances here so deceiving, or the fact that the buildings are so darned big that it makes them seem closer than they really are. Either way, getting from point A to point B always seems to take much longer in Las Vegas than you think it will. We can't count the number of times we've said, "Here we are at the Mirage/Treasure Island/Bellagio and we have dinner/business/show tickets for next door at Caesars/the Mirage/Monte Carlo. We can leave about 15 minutes before we need to be there." Thirty-five minutes later, after negotiating the casino crowds at our hotel, trekking through to the exit, using the moving sidewalk or tram or our feet to get to the entrance next door, finding the entrance, negotiating the crowds there, and getting lost . . . we finally arrive. Barely. The moral of the story: Always give yourself extra time, even if you're just going next door.

Obviously, the biggest plus to walking is that it's free and it's a good way to burn off your steak-and-shrimp dinner. All it's going to cost you is the price of a pair of comfortable shoes. If you're okay with staying in one basic area, why not make the hike?

A major negative is the weather, which can be brutally hot during the day and exceptionally chilly at night. This is something to consider when you're looking down the street and saying, "Oh, it's not that far!" (Remember that distances are deceiving in Las Vegas, where everything is larger than life and, therefore, seems closer than it is.) Another thing to keep in mind is that the pedestrian traffic is often as congested and frustrating as the street traffic. This is especially true during peak holidays or convention times.

If you have the kids with you, keep this in mind: Sex is a big industry in Las Vegas. Many strip clubs and escort services place people on the sidewalks to hand out flyers and magazines that you may not want your children to see. (They're pretty graphic.) You can just say "no," but remember that many people take the brochures and then discard them on the ground where anyone, including your little angel, can get an eye-popping peek at them. Of course, the brochures are nothing compared to those multistory-high, nearly bare bottoms adorning various casino hotels in the name of promoting some in-house show or other — and the billboards are harder to ignore.

If you do decide on hoofin' it, remember the following:

✔ For comfort's sake, be sure to bring some good walking shoes to Las Vegas — even if you have a rental car, you'll be doing a lot of walking. If you opt for sandals, don't forget to put sunscreen on your feet, and watch out for sidewalks cluttered with trash and broken glass.

✔ When walking long distances in Vegas, carry plenty of water. Buy yours at a convenience store — it's cheaper than the bottles sold in casinos, and the casinos allow you to bring water in.

✔ If you get a bit tired, several of the casino hotels have free monorail systems or moving sidewalks to help you rest your sore feet (and to guide you, lemminglike, to their casinos). See the following section for details on these transportation options.

By monorail, trams, and moving sidewalks

When you're dead tired, and you don't feel like you can move another inch, take heart. Vegas is full of monorails, trams, and moving sidewalks to help you get from one spot to another without moving a muscle. Naturally, these conveniences are there to lure you into the hotels that operate them, but one tends to overlook that sort of thing when the alternative means adding a few blisters to already sore feet.

- **Las Vegas Monorail:** This monorail (☎ 702-699-8200; www.lvmono rail.com) is the biggest, grandest people mover in Vegas yet, despite several delays in the opening (and post-opening) of the system that made us want to compare it to a certain *Simpsons* episode. The $650-million system whisks you from the MGM Grand at the south end of the Strip to the Sahara at the north end in about 15 minutes, with stops at Bally's and Paris, the Flamingo and Caesars Palace, Harrah's, the Convention Center, and the Las Vegas Hilton along the way. The cost is $5 per person per one-way trip, or you can get multiride or multiday passes if you plan on using it a lot. Be advised that sometimes the stops themselves aren't right at the hotel in question, and there may be an additional block or two of walking before you truly arrive. A 2009 bankruptcy has not stopped the trains from running, but it has probably stopped the line from getting extended to downtown or the airport, as was originally planned.

- **Tram from Treasure Island to the Mirage:** Even though these two hotels are right next to each other, you won't find a quicker way to get from one to the other. Pick up the tram at the back of Treasure Island between the hotel and its parking deck, and it delivers you practically to the front door of the Mirage — or vice versa. Convenient, huh?

- **Mandalay Bay/Luxor/Excalibur monorail and people movers:** A high-capacity monorail takes you from the corner of Tropicana and the Strip south to Mandalay Bay. The northbound trip features stops at Luxor and Excalibur. An air-conditioned moving sidewalk covers the same journey between Luxor and Excalibur, and a new indoor mall bridges the gap between Luxor and Mandalay Bay.

- **CityCenter monorail:** This new (as of 2009) monorail takes you from Bellagio to Monte Carlo in just a few minutes, with a stop at the Crystals mall at CityCenter (next to Aria Las Vegas) in between. The stations are not in the most convenient places, but it still beats walking.

By bus

Citizen's Area Transit (CAT; ☎ 702-228-7433) is the city bus service, and it gets really mixed reviews. You shouldn't rely on it as your major source of transportation, because the service is unreliable — like most bus services, schedules are an abstract concept — and the routes don't always make sense. Of course, many people rely on the bus services, and the bus can be so jam-packed that you have to stand through much of your endless journey.

Nevertheless, the city bus service is cheap. Buses on the Strip run $3 for adults and $1.50 for seniors and kids, so it's a pretty good bargain. The **Deuce** is a double-decker bus that trolls the Strip and downtown for that $3 fare or a remarkable $7 for the entire day (get on and off as much as you like); it suffers from the same kind of overcrowding as the regular buses and gets stuck in the same traffic, but at least the views are a little better while you're sitting in gridlock.

Chapter 9

Checking In at Las Vegas's Best Hotels

. . . .

In This Chapter

▶ Discovering a hotel room that meets your needs
▶ Choosing the right neighborhood
▶ Finding the best room at the best rate
▶ Arriving without a reservation
▶ Getting the scoop on the best hotels in Las Vegas

. . . .

*H*ave you ever dreamed of seeing the pyramids of Egypt? Wanted to swan about the banks of the canals of Venice? Is hanging out in Times Square your kind of fun? What about going to a circus, complete with acrobats and trapeze artists? You can do all this and more in Las Vegas.

It's natural to think of a hotel stay in terms of amenities and ambience. But you need to readjust your thinking before you arrive in Vegas. In most other cities, hotels are built *near* the attractions. In Vegas, the hotels *are* the attractions, going way beyond mere room service and a swimming pool. We're talking roller coasters, wildlife, castles, clowns, and slot machines out the wazoo. It's not exactly your everyday choice between a Marriott and a Motel 6, although there are some of those, too.

You don't need to feel overwhelmed by the Vegas scene, because in this chapter we tell you what you need to know to make the choices that are right for you. Trust us — you'll walk into this glittering city with a firm grasp on where you want to go.

Getting to Know Your Options

Even after you know what kind of price range you can afford (see Chapter 4) and what neighborhood you'd like to stay in (see Chapter 8), you still need to consider a few things.

Stay where you play — or not

This is a big decision. Don't kid yourself: Gambling is a major Vegas activity, so you won't lack for casino action. If you're itching to spin the roulette wheel, it may be nice to have immediate access to one 24 hours a day. If you don't consider it a high priority, you may feel differently. Regardless of your preference, here's what you need to know:

- ✔ **Casino hotels:** If you opt for a casino hotel, you're in for round-the-clock entertainment, dining, and action. Casino hotels are often loud, crowded, enormous places that actively discourage relaxing (it hinders your gambling, don't you know). They can be confusing and difficult to navigate. On the other hand, you can gamble or have a steak dinner at 3:30 a.m.

- ✔ **Non-casino hotels:** Most non-casino hotels provide you with a room, a pool (maybe), a parking space, and not a lot more. But they also can offer a quiet getaway from the hustle and bustle of this happening town. On the other hand, if they have extras (such as a workout room), unlike the casino hotels, you probably won't have to pay for them.

In the end, only you can decide whether you'd rather stay in the middle of the fray or slip away for a little peace and quiet at the end of the day.

One popular misconception is that non-casino hotels offer cheaper rooms. That's not necessarily true. You may find a good deal occasionally, but most non-casino hotels have to make up for a lack of gaming revenue by charging higher room rates.

The big and the small of it

There really is no such thing as a small hotel in Las Vegas. So, your options are not really big versus small — they're gargantuan versus big. (For the sake of this argument, however, we call it big versus small.)

- ✔ **Small fries:** On one hand, you have the small hotels, which often give more personalized service. These are the places where you don't need to leave a trail of bread crumbs to find your room, and you don't get stuck for an eternity in a line at the front desk. However, the smaller hotels usually offer less in the way of amenities such as pools, health clubs, and restaurants.

- ✔ **Big cheeses:** These cities unto themselves have spared no expense in keeping you entertained and pampered (and they're full of gambling action and boutiques). In the biggest hotels, you're given a map when you check in (no kidding). Consider a 15-minute walk from your room to the spa or pool — in your workout clothes *or bathing suit* — right through the middle of a crowded casino. Scary thought.

We give you the rundown on the relative size of each hotel. This size comparison has to do with more than just the number of rooms and how many people can fit into the main dining room; it's about the sprawl, or how far you have to walk from the elevator to the front door, and how easily you can negotiate the place. When you make your final decision, consider whether you prefer convenience and personal service or having every conceivable amenity and amusement available without ever having to smell the desert air.

To theme or not to theme

What's the deal? Everyone knows Vegas is all about the wacky theme — look at that castle! Or at that pyramid! And yet the powers that be have decided that you, their desired guest, are no longer lured by pharaoh heads on your bedspread or other kitschy details. To this end, hotels have been systematically removing much of the silliness in favor of a more generic "luxury resort" look. But they can't change the outsides — well, they can, but most don't go that radical route — and so you still have the option of staying in a place that smacks of Venice or Paris, in a big giant castle, or a cartoon version of the New York skyline. Just know that many of the theme hotels fall into the "gargantuan" category.

Into everybody's life a little chain must fall

Every high-profile chain has a spot in Vegas: **Holiday Inn, Marriott, Westin,** and so on. Now, normally we like to tout Mom and Pop over Big Business, but Vegas has few of the former, hotel-wise. Sure, hard-core travelers may snort at your lack of adventure, but there's nothing wrong with choosing the reliability and the certain quality assurance of a chain. Truth be told, rooms in many of the major Strip places often aren't much different from the dull standard hotel comforts found in a generic chain, though the accommodations are often larger. So, don't fret if the Strip hotels are booked.

After all, these days even the big hotels have more than a whiff of chain about them. **Harrah's** is a famous casino-hotel line all by itself, and that's before you add such Las Vegas stalwarts as **Bally's, Caesars Palace, Flamingo,** and **Paris** to their portfolio. **Circus Circus, CityCenter, Bellagio, Excalibur, Luxor, Mandalay Bay, MGM Grand,** the **Mirage, Monte Carlo,** and **New York–New York** are all owned by one giant corporation that controls roughly 75 percent of the rooms on the Strip.

Family fun or adult action

When we say "adult hotels," we don't mean sleazy décor and mirrors everywhere. We simply mean that some places aim for the grown-up market by deliberately leaving out the things that appeal to kids, such as video arcades and water rides. Others simply have a more adult, sophisticated ambience, which may even include such grown-ups-only touches as "European-style" (topless) pools. In some cases, they actively discourage guests from bringing kids. **Bellagio** actually bars kids who aren't staying at the hotel from entering after 6 p.m. — and yes, the staff does check room keys. Some hotels even ask publications that write about Vegas for families not to include them in any relevant articles or books — that says a lot.

 If you have kids who will be joining you on your vacation, look for the Kid Friendly icon when you read the hotel reviews. These icons highlight the (increasingly few) places that cater to families.

Finding the Best Room at the Best Rate

Pricing a hotel is a tricky thing in Vegas; the same room that you can have for $49 on one night can be as much as $350 the following night. Maybe that's an exaggeration, but not by much. (We just checked a big-name hotel: $309 one night, $159 two nights later.) In theory, the more you pay, the plusher the furnishings and the linens, the faster the service and the posher the place. But again, come to Vegas on a busy weekend, and you'll probably pay $200 or more for a very basic hotel room.

Rooms are expensive here, there's just no getting around that. But these days, it's a little easier to find bargains if you hunt for them. The downturn in the economy caused a downturn in tourism, and that translates into more empty hotel rooms. That, in turn, can mean cheaper prices and better deals.

Keep in mind, however, that old maxim "you get what you pay for." Vegas has remade itself as a "luxury resort" adult vacation destination, one not conducive to budget travel. Most of the higher-profile hotels — **Bellagio, Four Seasons, Mandalay Bay,** the **Venetian** — and the deliberately styled "luxury resort" hotels — **Palazzo, THEhotel** at Mandalay Bay, **Venezia Tower** at the Venetian, **Wynn Las Vegas** — have prices that generally start high and go higher. So, although you may find rooms at these places for less than you would've paid during more flush economic times, you're still going to pay more than you would at a budget motel off the Strip — a lot more.

Finding the best room and getting the best rate seems like a tall order — unless you're armed with some great tips and general guidelines. Allow us to make the task a little less stressful for you.

Uncovering the truth about rack rates

The *rack rate* is the maximum rate that a hotel charges for a room. It's the rate you get if you walk in off the street and ask for a room for the night. You sometimes see the rate printed on the emergency-exit diagrams posted on the back of the hotel-room door.

Hotels are happy to charge you the rack rate, but you don't have to pay it. Hardly anybody does. The best way to avoid paying the rack rate is surprisingly simple: Just ask for a cheaper or discounted rate. You may be pleasantly surprised.

A rack rate is kind of like a full-fare ticket on an airplane. The only people who end up paying full price are the ones who didn't plan in advance, don't care what they're paying, or have inflexible travel dates.

Hotels make no money on empty rooms, so they compete with each other to fill up vacancies. When occupancy rates drop even more during off-season lulls, the big resorts aggressively court travelers with discounted room rates.

Although we've done our best to give you the most accurate hotel rates, the fact is that most Vegas hotels are just making them up. The prices we list here may not reflect the price that you're offered when you try to book. Some of the cheap prices in this chapter could well be available only midweek during a blue moon in leap year, while the hotels with outrageously high prices routinely offer room specials for half that. Not surprisingly for Vegas, it's a crapshoot. The tips in this section should help you make some sense of the whole mess, or at least provide you the best deal you can at any given time.

Snagging a great room rate

For those who don't have an unlimited vacation budget (face it, very few of us do), here are some hints for navigating the labyrinth of Vegas hotel rates. All are invaluable ways to cut room costs, but your best bet may be to book directly on the Internet (see "Surfing the Web for hotel deals," later in this chapter). If you decide to book directly with the hotel, try these tips:

- ✔ **Travel with a group.** If you're traveling with your family or a group of friends who are willing to share a room, you can save big bucks. Be sure to ask the reservations agent at each hotel about the policy on occupancy. Most room rates are based on *double occupancy* (two people), and charges for extra guests vary wildly. Some hotels let small children stay for free in their parents' rooms but charge anybody else up to $35 a night extra; other hotels allow up to four people to a room at no extra charge.

- ✔ **Check the Internet.** Most hotels in Las Vegas offer their lowest rates via the Web. It's simple economics: If you book it yourself through the hotel's Web site, it doesn't have to pay a person to talk to you. Many hotels even offer Internet-only specials. The moral of the story is, get thee to a computer!

- ✔ **Call both the local and the toll-free numbers.** Reserving a room through the hotel's toll-free number may result in a lower rate than if you call the hotel directly. On the other hand, the central reservations number may not know about discount rates at specific locations. (Local franchises may offer a special group rate for a wedding or a family reunion, for example, but may neglect to tell the central booking line.) So, your best bet is to call both the local number and the toll-free number to see which one gives you a better deal.

Some of the major hotels in Las Vegas are now charging a *telephone convenience fee* (an extra $10 or so that they'll tack onto your bill just for the privilege of talking to a real, live human being). If you call, ask before you book if you're going to get penalized for dialing instead of booking online.

✔ **Time your reservation and be flexible with your dates.** Unless your boss is dictating your vacation schedule, try to think in year-round terms. Room rates change with the season and as occupancy rates rise and fall. As you would probably expect, you can get the best bargains during off-peak times (Sun–Thurs, the slower summer months, and the weeks in Dec leading up to Christmas are good times). If a hotel is close to full, it'll be less likely to extend discount rates; if it's close to empty, it may be willing to negotiate. Resorts are most crowded on weekends, so they usually offer discounted rates for midweek stays.

The reverse is true for business and convention hotels, most of which are crowded during the week. See Chapter 3 for a list of dates for the biggest Vegas conventions and special events; try to avoid these expensive dates if you can.

✔ **Put your membership to use.** Be sure to mention your membership in AAA, AARP, frequent-flier programs, and any other corporate rewards program when you make your reservation. You never know when it may be worth a few dollars (sometimes more) off your room rate.

✔ **Go low-key.** The boom in "luxury resort hotels" has meant a corresponding boom in hotel prices. But here's a promising side effect: The older hotels, finding it hard to compete with their newer, flashier brethren on the "gee whiz" level, are making up for it by lowering their prices. They do this in an attempt to lure the savvy — that's you, of course! — over to their side. Sure, you may have to give up a spiffier room and service, but if you save as much as $100 a night, it's worth it!

The hotels in Las Vegas *are* the tourist attractions, so you don't have to actually stay in the biggest and brightest to experience most of what it has to offer. Unless you have your heart set on a spa or you plan to do a lot of relaxing at a fabulous pool at your own hotel, it doesn't matter where you sleep, right? Consider checking in to a cheaper, more out-of-the-way hotel. You can drop your luggage off and then explore.

✔ **Try a package tour.** Package tours combine airfare and accommodations in one purchase. Because package-tour companies buy in bulk, they can pass major savings along to you. Just be sure that you understand their restrictions and can live with the terms. (For more information on package tours to Las Vegas, see Chapter 5.)

A word about smoking

All Las Vegas hotels have at least some nonsmoking rooms; most have entire floors set aside for those who eschew the habit. As far as the rest of the hotel is concerned, it depends. Smoking is not allowed in restaurants and certain bars, but it is allowed on casino floors. Because the casino floor dominates pretty much every part of a casino hotel, you may have a problem if you're sensitive to smoke. If you're a nonsmoker, it's important to request a smoke-free room when you make your reservations. Keep in mind that at most hotels, special requests can't be guaranteed, especially during ultra-busy times. (If you're allergic to smoke, definitely let the reservations agent know — you may have more luck getting them to guarantee a nonsmoking room for you.)

We talk a lot in this chapter about landing great deals, but be careful when shopping for a bargain. Make sure that you aren't getting stuck in an older section of the hotel that isn't as nice as the rest. Ask hotel reservation agents for details on amenities and conditions (is this a recently renovated/redecorated room, for example), and tell them that you're writing it down. If your room doesn't match the description when you get there, don't be afraid to speak up.

Surfing the Web for hotel deals

The major travel-booking sites (**Expedia, Orbitz,** and **Travelocity;** see Chapter 5 for details) offer hotel booking, but if you use a site devoted primarily to lodging you may find properties that aren't listed on the more general online travel agencies. Some lodging sites specialize in particular types of accommodations, such as bed-and-breakfasts, which you won't find on the more mainstream booking services. Others offer weekend deals on major chain properties that cater to business travelers and have more empty rooms on weekends.

Check out the following resources when trying to book online:

- **allhotels** (www.allhotels.com): Although the name is something of a misnomer, the site does have tens of thousands of listings from throughout the world. Bear in mind, however, that each hotel has paid a small fee to be listed, so it's less an objective list and more a book of online brochures.

- **PlacesToStay** (www.placestostay.com): This site lists one-of-a-kind places in the United States that you may not find in other directories, with a focus on resort accommodations. Again, the listing is selective — this isn't a comprehensive directory, but it can give you a sense of what's available at different destinations.

✔ **Other sites:** You can find a number of other good Vegas-specific reservations sites on the Web, including www.lasvegashotel.com, www.lasvegasreservations.com, and www.lasvegasrooms.com. All these sites offer discounted rooms at the major hotels and at some cheaper properties.

Reserving the best room

Here are some of our strategies for getting a great room:

✔ **Always ask for a corner room.** They're usually larger, quieter, and closer to the elevator. They often have more windows and light than standard rooms, and they don't always cost more.

✔ **Steer clear of construction zones.** Be sure to ask if the hotel is renovating; if it is, request a room away from the renovation work. The noise and activity may be a bit more than you want to deal with on your vacation.

✔ **Request your smoking preference.** Be sure to ask for either a smoking or nonsmoking room if you have a preference. Otherwise, you're likely to get stuck with a room that doesn't meet your needs.

✔ **Inquire about the location of the restaurants, bars, and discos.** If you have a disability that prevents you from venturing too far, you may have a problem in Vegas, where the rooms can be the equivalent of a city block away from the hotel's entertainment and dining options. Ask about handicap facilities and hotel layout. You may have to seriously consider which hotel you stay at. (See Chapter 6 for more information about getting around town if you have a disability.)

✔ **Ask for a room with a view.** Ask for a room that overlooks the Strip if you're staying in a hotel situated in that part of town; otherwise, the only view you may get is of the parking garage. Rooms with Strip views usually don't cost more, although some hotels do charge for the privilege of soaking in the Las Vegas skyline from the privacy of your room. For example, Paris charges more for a room with a view of Bellagio's fountain show across the street.

If you're booking your room through a travel agent, ask the agent to note your room preferences on your reservation. When you check in at your hotel, your preferences pop up when the reception desk pulls your reservation. Special requests can't be guaranteed, but making them in advance can't hurt.

Remember: If you aren't happy with your room when you arrive, talk to the front-desk staff. If they have another room, they should be happy to accommodate you, within reason.

Arriving without a Reservation

Okay, so you're standing in the bookstore in the Las Vegas airport, having just arrived in town on a last-minute whim. Now you realize that you don't have hotel reservations, and the prospect of sleeping at the bus station looms large. What do you do? Well, whip out your cell phone (or find a payphone if you don't have one).

Most of the hotels in this book have local numbers listed in addition to their toll-free numbers (which usually don't work in Las Vegas). This may sound obvious at first, but stick with us: Start by calling a few and seeing if they have any vacancies. If they do, you can relax and take your time in selecting a hotel that fits your needs and budget. If you get nothing but "Sorry, sold out," read on.

You can go through the phone book and call numbers at random, but you risk getting stuck in a bad neighborhood or overpriced dump. Instead, try a hotel reservations service that can find and book a room for you — without charging a service fee — like the one offered by the **Las Vegas Visitor Information Center** (☎ **877-847-4858** or 702-892-7575), open daily from 7 a.m. to 7 p.m. But keep in mind that these services usually are tied to specific businesses, so they try to steer you toward a place where they collect a commission instead of help you find another option that may suit you better. We recommend using reservations services only if you're having no luck finding a vacancy.

If you still have no luck finding a room, you'll have to do some real work: Go get a rental car (you can't do what we have in mind on foot or by taxi) and start driving. (For information on renting a car, see Chapter 8.) Begin with the many little hotels near the airport. If you strike out there, head to the **Strip** — that's where most of the rooms in Las Vegas are located. Even if you got a "sold out" on the phone, try the front desk anyway, in case there has been a last-minute cancellation.

Your next hunting ground should be **Paradise Road** and the streets crossing it, such as **Flamingo, Convention Center,** and **Harmon.** This area has a lot of nice but generic chain hotels. These hotels may not be a top pick in this book or be included in the reservations systems, but they're fine in a pinch.

Also, don't forget that many of the hotels (such as **Circus Circus, Excalibur,** and **Luxor**) are owned by the same companies. Throw yourself on the mercy of the front-desk clerk and ask if any "sister" hotels have vacancies.

Finally, go **downtown,** but be careful — some areas are not very safe.

Avoiding hidden costs

Vegas hotels are full of unexpected little budget busters. The most obvious are gym/spa fees. Most of the major hotels have health clubs with machines, steam rooms, and the like. Although you may expect to pay extra for a massage and other spa services, you may not expect to pay to use the treadmill. But just about all Strip hotels charge any-where from $15 to $30 a day for you to do so. The Four Seasons is a lone exception on the Strip. Most of the chains don't charge spa fees, though their workout rooms are, by and large, inferior to the ones at the costly Strip lodgings.

Savvy travelers generally know not to use the phone in the room, where local calls cost anywhere from $1 to $1.50 each. Long distance is even worse; nearly all the hotels use some outrageous long distance carrier, and the results can be $30 for a 15-minute call. Another telephonic pitfall is dial-up Internet access; many hotels begin to charge even local calls after 30 minutes. At as much as 30¢ a minute, it adds up fast. Even high-speed Internet access can come with a hefty fee.

Lately, some enterprising hotels have started charging what they call a "resort fee" or "facilities fee," which tacks anywhere from $5 to $20 a day onto your bill. What this covers depends on where you stay, but it may include such items as gym and spa usage, parking, shuttles, telephones, and assorted miscellanea (daily shoeshine?). Be sure to ask when making your reservations if the hotel you're investigating has such a fee.

The moral of this story? If money is a concern, unless you know for sure that something is free, ask.

Pricing the Competition

We provide a dollar rating for each hotel listing in this chapter. Check out Table 9-1 for how the symbols break down.

Table 9-1	Key to Hotel Dollar Signs	
Dollar Signs	*Category*	*Price Range*
$	Unbelievably cheap	$74 or less per night
$$	Inexpensive	$75–$99 per night
$$$	Moderate	$100–$149 per night
$$$$	Expensive	$150–$249 per night
$$$$$	Very expensive	$250 or more per night

We base the ratings on what you can expect to pay, on average, for a standard room with single or double occupancy. The ratings don't necessarily correspond with the rack rates that are printed with the listing, because, in Vegas, the rack rates are often listed at the low-water mark, representing rates that are rarely offered; in reality, the average rate is usually higher.

To give you a slightly better idea of what you get for your money in Vegas, here's a more detailed description of our price categories. Don't forget, though, that thanks to ricocheting prices, there can be a lot of overlap between categories. Check normally higher-priced hotels just in case they have specials going on, and don't be too surprised if even a normally lower-priced hotel ends up going for much more than predicted.

- ✔ **$ ($74 or less):** Don't expect to readily find a good room in this category unless you stay at a so-called "locals" hotel, which can be as much as 20 minutes off the Strip, or in an older, no-frills downtown location. Even then, your stay pretty much has to be midweek or otherwise off-peak. (Having said that, some higher-profile Strip and downtown hotels can offer special deals that drop their rooms into this category, so it's worth checking just in case.) The good news is that even at the low end, the "locals" hotels can offer not just very basic, motel-like rooms, but also all kinds of entertainment options such as movie theaters and bowling alleys.

- ✔ **$$ ($75–$99):** The rooms in this category are split: Some can be pretty plain, but others, especially in the higher-end "locals" hotels, can be rather stylish. You can count on a TV (possibly even a flatscreen) and probably a moderately (if not inexpensively) priced buffet.

- ✔ **$$$ ($100–$149):** Figure on more and nicer amenities (hair dryers, robes, better bathroom supplies), health clubs, bigger TVs, and larger rooms and bathrooms. There will likely be Wi-Fi, but you'll have to pay for it. Room service may or may not be standard. The second-tier mega-resorts on the Strip and some of the non-casino hotels fall into this category.

- ✔ **$$$$ ($150–$249):** Besides a large, well-decorated room, you can count on a larger-than-a-closet bathroom with ample towels. In a casino hotel, you can expect to find several restaurants, a health club, a show or two, and several thousand rooms. Non-casino hotels usually have business centers.

- ✔ **$$$$$ ($250 or more):** You're paying for the prestigious name, location, and/or service. Expect round-the-clock concierge service, sumptuous lobbies, elegant décor, and beautiful room furnishings. You find a full range of amenities, multiple phones (some people like this; we travel to get away from phones), probably multiple TVs, and fancy beds and linens. Rooms may actually be junior suites. There will be one or more restaurants for fine dining, a bar and/or lobby cocktail lounge, nightclubs, and an excellent and expensive spa/health club.

Having said all that, it's important to note that hotel prices in Vegas are fluid at best, and a hotel with an "unbelievably cheap" designation may charge over $250 on the night you happen to be visiting while one with a "very expensive" designation may charge $100. Use the dollar signs as guidelines, but don't take them as gospel.

The Best Hotels in Las Vegas

In this section, we deliberately don't include every single hotel in town. That would defeat the purpose of giving you some helpful advice, now wouldn't it? Because price is such a big factor for most travelers, we note rack rates in the listings and precede each listing with dollar signs to make them easy to reference. Remember, however, that the prices listed here are the "official" rack rates; they're rarely what you're going to wind up paying. If one of these hotels sounds good to you but appears to be out of your price range, don't give up too quickly. It may be having a special promotion or a slow week that will get you in for a lower rate than normal — call to find out.

Almost all the hotels listed have free parking for guests (usually self-parking and valet), unless otherwise noted.

Aria Las Vegas
$$$$ South Strip

The main hotel in the $9 billion (yes, really) CityCenter complex is a game-changer for Las Vegas. It's not that it offers anything significantly different from most Las Vegas hotels — there are rooms, of course (4,000 of them); multiple restaurants; shopping; pools; a spa; a big casino; and more. But it's the way that all of it is presented that makes the difference. Done in a cutting-edge, modern design, the look and feel of the hotel is spectacular — luxurious without feeling pretentious, comfortable without feeling low-rent, and more eye candy than you'll know what to do with. From a design perspective, this is the most beautiful hotel in the city, filled with texture (stone, wood, fabric, metal, and on and on), light, and energy. But beyond the pretty, you get a solid package of amenities. Rooms are plenty roomy and deliriously high-tech, with control panels that operate everything from the drapes and lights to the entertainment system. More than a dozen restaurants, including a buffet, serve up just about every cuisine you can imagine (although none of it is terribly cheap). The casino, one of the biggest in the city, offers all your gaming favorites from slots to blackjack and beyond. We hit one big jackpot here, but the rest of the time we may as well have been throwing our money on the floor — but the casino sure is purty to look at while you're doing it. Or maybe you could go spend your money on the latest Cirque du Soleil show, *Viva Elvis,* featuring the music of Elvis Presley. This hotel is not the least expensive in Vegas, but it certainly isn't the most expensive either — it gives you a lot of bang for your buck.

See maps p. 96 and p. 98. 3720 Las Vegas Blvd. S. (at Harmon Avenue). ☎ **866-359-7757** *or 702-590-7757. Fax: 702-531-3887.* www.arialasvegas.com. *Rack rates: $159 and up double. AE, DC, DISC, MC, V.*

Las Vegas Accommodations Overview

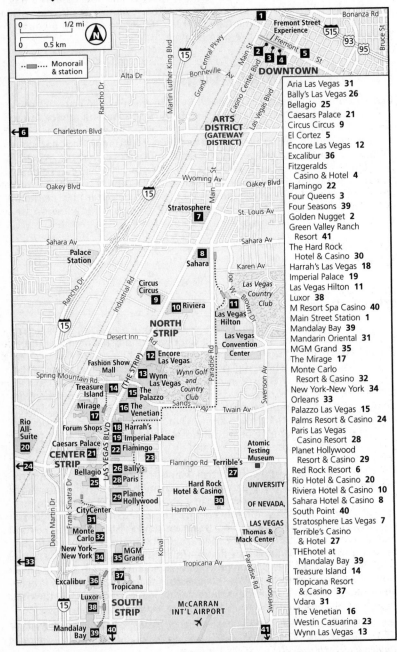

Aria Las Vegas **31**
Bally's Las Vegas **26**
Bellagio **25**
Caesars Palace **21**
Circus Circus **9**
El Cortez **5**
Encore Las Vegas **12**
Excalibur **36**
Fitzgeralds
  Casino & Hotel **4**
Flamingo **22**
Four Queens **3**
Four Seasons **39**
Golden Nugget **2**
Green Valley Ranch
  Resort **41**
The Hard Rock
  Hotel & Casino **30**
Harrah's Las Vegas **18**
Imperial Palace **19**
Las Vegas Hilton **11**
Luxor **38**
M Resort Spa Casino **40**
Main Street Station **1**
Mandalay Bay **39**
Mandarin Oriental **31**
MGM Grand **35**
The Mirage **17**
Monte Carlo
  Resort & Casino **32**
New York-New York **34**
Orleans **33**
Palazzo Las Vegas **15**
Palms Resort & Casino **24**
Paris Las Vegas
  Casino Resort **28**
Planet Hollywood
  Resort & Casino **29**
Red Rock Resort **6**
Rio Hotel & Casino **20**
Riviera Hotel & Casino **10**
Sahara Hotel & Casino **8**
South Point **40**
Stratosphere Las Vegas **7**
Terrible's Casino
  & Hotel **27**
THEhotel at
  Mandalay Bay **39**
Treasure Island **14**
Tropicana Resort
  & Casino **37**
Vdara **31**
The Venetian **16**
Westin Casuarina **23**
Wynn Las Vegas **13**

Bally's Las Vegas
$$$ Center Strip

Poor Bally's. Here it is, the very epitome of a Las Vegas hotel, all glitzy glamour and neon (not to mention home to the best topless show in town), but more and more, it just gets overlooked. It's too upscale to have a theme, so it lacks that cartoon appeal, but it isn't upscale enough to compete with the new luxe wonders on the Strip. It's even upstaged by its very own **Paris Las Vegas,** right next door. The hotel is centrally located, and you enter from the Strip via moving sidewalks that pass through muted neon-light pillars, waterfalls, and lush landscaping. Bright and cheerful marble, wood, and crystal are the rule throughout. The oversized rooms contain a sofa — a rarity in Las Vegas. The hotel is not huge in comparison with other Vegas hotels, but it does have more than 2,800 rooms (which you often can get at cheaper prices than anything nearby), an airy casino, a noteworthy spa and fitness center, tennis and basketball, a handsome Olympic-size swimming pool, and a whole range of restaurants. It's connected to Paris via a nice walkway, a funny transition from gaudy older Vegas to "classy" faux-theme Vegas.

See maps p. 96 and p. 99. 3645 Las Vegas Blvd. S. (at Flamingo Road). ☎ **800-634-3434** *or 702-739-4111. Fax: 702-967-3890.* `www.ballyslv.com`. *Rack rates: $99 and up double. AE, DC, MC, V.*

Bellagio
$$$$$ Center Strip

Although today a billion dollars is a drop in the bucket, back in the '90s, it bought you a lot of hotel. Bellagio is determined to show you what a grown-up experience Las Vegas can be — so much so, that it doesn't want nonguests under 18 to even enter the property, at least at night. The result is this enormous, gorgeous, and slightly intimidating resort. Bellagio has everything the other hotels have, and then some — just more sophisticated. It has an art gallery (in Vegas, no less!); some of the best restaurants in town (including one with Picassos hanging casually on the walls); a conservatory full of fresh flowers and plants that are changed almost monthly to reflect the seasons; a 12-acre lake out front that hosts a water fountain ballet (the coolest and least-cheesy free show in town); a neoclassical pool area right out of an Italian villa; plush rooms full of nifty amenities; and big, gleaming bathrooms.

Oh, it's grand — grand, we tell you! (Though at 4,000 rooms, it is honestly just a little too big to provide the kind of intimate service you get at most hotels in the same class and price range — not that it doesn't try hard.) What it isn't is cheap. After all, Bellagio wants to lure the sort of well-heeled folk who are used to dining with Picassos looking over their shoulders. But just because your own walls may not be graced by Pablo, nothing prevents you from living the Bellagio life for a couple days, particularly because you sometimes can catch the hotel's normally sky-high rates in an affordable mood.

See maps p. 96 and p. 99. 3600 Las Vegas Blvd. S. (at Flamingo Road). ☎ **888-987-6667** *or 702-693-7111. Fax: 702-693-8546.* `www.bellagio.com`. *Rack rates: $169 and up double. AE, DC, DISC, MC, V.*

South Strip Accommodations

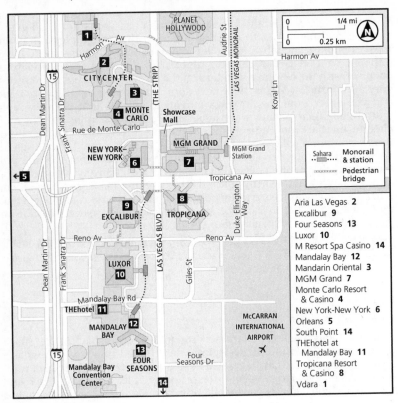

Map legend (right side):

Aria Las Vegas **2**
Excalibur **9**
Four Seasons **13**
Luxor **10**
M Resort Spa Casino **14**
Mandalay Bay **12**
Mandarin Oriental **3**
MGM Grand **7**
Monte Carlo Resort
  & Casino **4**
New York-New York **6**
Orleans **5**
South Point **14**
THEhotel at
  Mandalay Bay **11**
Tropicana Resort
  & Casino **8**
Vdara **1**

Caesars Palace
$$$$$ Center Strip

This is the archetypal sprawling Vegas hotel, where high class meets high kitsch. When in Rome, after all. Over the last decade or so, Caesars has thrown billions of dollars into the place, expanding and remodeling, and then remodeling some more. It's more Vegas than ever — at least, in the modern sense of Vegas, which has redefined *elegant* since the days of kitsch glory. But have no fear: The campy Roman theme lives on, with marble columns, copies of famous statues, and toga-wearing employees. True glamour has replaced most of the tacky stuff (kind of sad for those of us who love all things kitschy), but the hotel still has that great Vegas feel. Our only problem with Caesars is that it's one of the most confusingly laid-out hotels in the entire city. Despite that one negative, we've nearly been reduced to tears when it's been time to leave.

Center Strip Accommodations

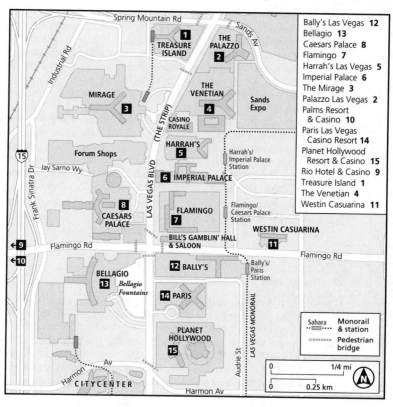

Bally's Las Vegas **12**
Bellagio **13**
Caesars Palace **8**
Flamingo **7**
Harrah's Las Vegas **5**
Imperial Palace **6**
The Mirage **3**
Palazzo Las Vegas **2**
Palms Resort
  & Casino **10**
Paris Las Vegas
  Casino Resort **14**
Planet Hollywood
  Resort & Casino **15**
Rio Hotel & Casino **9**
Treasure Island **1**
The Venetian **4**
Westin Casuarina **11**

The newer rooms in the towers are generic-beautiful and huge — some with his and hers baths. And even the older rooms have character; some have sunken tubs in the sleeping areas. For every fabulous new touch — a stunning swimming-pool area and health club/spa, each with a classical Roman theme — there remains some of the Vegas cheese we love so well, such as the talking, stiffly moving statues in the shopping area. That shopping area is also a Vegas wonder: a reproduction of an Italian street, down to the sky overhead, full of famous-name stores — plus a replica of the Colosseum in Rome, a state-of-the-art showroom currently hosting Cher, with Celine Dion returning in March 2011. Add to this quite a few terrific restaurants (including **Spago** and the **Palm**) and one of the best casinos in town, and Caesars remains the place to go for all facets of Vegas life.

See maps p. 96 and above. 3570 Las Vegas Blvd. S. (just north of Flamingo Road). ☎ **877-427-7243** *or 702-731-7110. Fax: 702-697-5706.* www.caesarspalace.com. *Rack rates: $129 and up double. AE, DC, DISC, MC, V.*

Circus Circus
$ **North Strip**

If you have the kids in tow, consider staying at this massive 3,700-room hotel, unless you're "clownphobic." (Don't laugh — many people are.) It's the original (and now pretty much the only) hotel that specifically caters to children. The theme is, well, circus, complete with a chaotic carnival and arcade games on the midway. Don't miss the circus acts (trapeze, high wire, jugglers, and so on) that run most of the day and are visible from the midway and much of the casino. The kiddies will be properly entertained by the myriad amusements: an aerial tramway, an arcade, the **Adventuredome** indoor theme park, several swimming pools, and even an attached RV park, run by KOA. Circus Circus does come off a bit worn at the edges, but it's almost always a great deal for travelers on a budget — and don't underestimate the value of its family-friendly attitude. Try to avoid the Manor rooms, which are in glorified motel buildings that have seen better days.

See maps p. 96 and p. 102. 2880 Las Vegas Blvd. S. (between Sahara Avenue and Convention Center Drive). ☎ **877-434-9175** *or 702-734-0410. Fax: 702-734-5897.* www. circuscircus.com. *Rack rates: $59 and up double. AE, DC, DISC, MC, V.*

El Cortez
$ **Downtown**

The El, as it's colloquially known, was built in 1941 and was owned at one point by Bugsy Siegel, before all that unpleasantness with his "bosses" of course. In recent years, it was an also-ran in the downtown market, which, in turn, is an also-ran to the more popular Strip, but the El has gotten a rebirth recently that has made it a much more attractive possibility for all budget-conscious tourists. The casino and other public spaces were given a makeover, with lovely stone, wood, and copper accents turning a smoky dive into a slightly less-smoky and a lot more eye-pleasing affair. Rooms are still pretty basic but well kept and usually dirt cheap, which is the primary lure of this hotel. Of note are the Cabana Suites, a separate building that used to be the rattrap Ogden House but is now a funky-chic boutique hotel with retro '60s furnishings and concierge-level service.

See maps p. 96 and p. 104. 600 Fremont St. (between Sixth and Seventh streets). ☎ **800-634-6703** *or 702-385-5200. Fax: 702-474-3626.* www.elcortezhotel casino.com. *Rack rates: $35 and up double. AE, DC, DISC, MC, V.*

Encore Las Vegas
$$$$$ **North Strip**

Although built as a figurative encore (see what they did there?) to the hugely successful Wynn Las Vegas, Encore stands on its own elegant feet as a destination worthy of being the main act. Smaller in square footage and more intimate in vibe than Wynn, the Encore is done in springtime reds and florals with lots of natural light spilling into the casino and public spaces, a relative rarity in Las Vegas. There are several terrific restaurants, including Sinatra and Switch, two pool areas, a shopping arcade linking it to Wynn Las Vegas, and a showroom featuring one of the best entertainment offerings in town, with Garth Brooks. The casino itself is tiny by comparison, made to feel even more so by the columns and drapes that turn it into a series of gambling parlors instead of one big hall. Rooms are bigger than at the Wynn and even more luxurious; most are minisuites with a cozy sitting area separated from the bedroom by a partial wall and a giant TV (one of three in the room). Everything that is supposed to be plush (towels, bedding, robes, chairs) is to a tee, and everything that is supposed to be solid (the marble in the bathroom, the sturdy furnishings) practically screams quality. What price quality? High, just about everywhere you go. This is one of the most expensive hotels in Las Vegas, but here you really feel like you're getting your money's worth.

See maps p. 96 and p. 102. 3121 Las Vegas Blvd. S. (just north of Spring Mountain Road). ☎ **888-320-7125** *or 702-770-7171. Fax: 702-770-1571.* www.encorelas vegas.com. *Rack rates: $159 and up double. AE, DC, DISC, MC, V.*

Excalibur
$$ South Strip

This gigantic medieval castle comes complete with (faux) moat and draw-bridge — don't you just love a theme run wild? This used to be a good and reasonably priced choice for families, but it's not nearly as kid-friendly as it used to be (witness the male strip show in one of the theaters). Worse, step-by-step, the theme is getting toned down. Kids will still be pleased with the attractive swimming pools with waterfalls and waterslides, and love the sheer enormity and spectacle of it all. Adults often quickly tire of the place for the same reasons. Budget travelers also love its well-priced rooms, some of which got a redo and look quite spiffy (ask for the Widescreen rooms to get the nicer ones) — good deals happen here more often than at most other hotels.

The vast size of the hotel — more than 4,000 rooms, five restaurants, and a food court, a casino, and medieval-themed video and shopping arcades — means that it's mostly hectic and noisy (Camelot was a "shining spot" not a "quiet spot"). Still, it's perfectly located at the bustling south end of the Strip. A handy monorail connects Excalibur to its southern neighbors, Luxor and Mandalay Bay.

See maps p. 96 and p. 98. 3850 Las Vegas Blvd. S. (at Tropicana Avenue). ☎ **800-937-7777** *or 702-597-7700. Fax: 702-597-7163.* www.excalibur.com. *Rack rates: $59 and up double. AE, DC, DISC, MC, V.*

Fitzgeralds Casino & Hotel
$$ Downtown

Here's a solid, middle-of-the-road choice for affordable downtown accommodations. Once it was an understated ode to the luck o' the Irish, but the current owner (the first African-American casino owner in Vegas) has eliminated virtually all such references. Along the way, the place got a subtle but solid makeover to brighten up the public areas and add a pool, a rare thing for downtown Vegas. Rooms are pretty standard, but

North Strip Accommodations

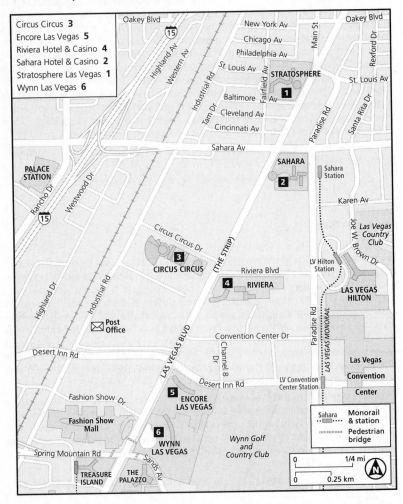

Circus Circus **3**
Encore Las Vegas **5**
Riviera Hotel & Casino **4**
Sahara Hotel & Casino **2**
Stratosphere Las Vegas **1**
Wynn Las Vegas **6**

comfortable; slightly larger Jacuzzi units are available for a few bucks more. The tall tower offers great views of the mountains or the Strip. Fitzgeralds still has a couple decent restaurants as well. Be sure to stop by the outdoor balcony off the casino to get a cool view of the **Fremont Street Experience** (see Chapter 12).

See maps p. 96 and p. 104. 301 E. Fremont St. (at Third Street). ☎ **800-274-5825** *or 702-388-2400. Fax: 702-388-2181.* www.fitzgeralds.com. *Rack rates: $59 and up double. AE, DC, DISC, MC, V.*

Flamingo
$$$ Center Strip

Infamous gangster Bugsy Siegel would no longer recognize his baby, which he opened in 1946 on what would eventually become the Strip. After more than 60 years and several renovations, nothing is left from Bugsy's day but a rumor of escape tunnels under the grounds. Flamingo currently sports a vaguely Art Deco/tropical theme (no wonder Jimmy Buffett put one of his Margaritaville cafe/nightclubs here) and is every bit as neon as you'd like. Many of the rooms have gotten a makeover to turn them ring-a-ding fabulous — we're suckers for judicious use of hot pink. The rest are nice but bland in comparison. The gorgeous, lush pool and spa area (the former with a couple excellent water slides) is a major draw. It also has a bustling casino, excellent tennis facilities, a wedding chapel, a showroom featuring Donny & Marie, and some indifferent bars and restaurants. It's all too far removed from its past self for nostalgia, but the Central Strip location and those new rooms make Flamingo viable.

See maps p. 96 and p. 99. 3555 Las Vegas Blvd. S. (just north of Flamingo Road). ☎ **800-732-2111** *or 702-733-3111. Fax: 702-733-3353.* www.flamingolv.com. *Rack rates: $85 and up double. AE, DC, DISC, MC, V.*

Four Queens
$$ Downtown

This is another downtown property that once felt dated but has been spruced up to make it feel, well, not exactly current but certainly closer than it used to be. The casino is still crowded and a bit smoky, but the overall ambience is brighter and cleaner than before. The same can be said of the rooms — simple but clean and comfortable. You get a handful of restaurants on-site but no pool. Nostalgia buffs and budget travelers will be very pleased.

See maps p. 96 and p. 104. 202 Fremont St. (at Casino Center Boulevard). ☎ **800-634-6045** *or 702-385-4011. Fax: 702-387-5122.* www.fourqueens.com. *Rack rates: $49 and up double. AE, DC, DISC, MC, V.*

Four Seasons
$$$$$ South Strip

If you have money to burn, you can't go wrong by joining the other fat cats at Vegas's version of a true luxury resort. Not only does the Four Seasons have a degree in pampering, but with just 400 rooms, it can give far more personal attention than any other high-profile hotel. Its unusual location within Mandalay Bay was a bit of an experiment for Vegas. The Four Seasons is accessible through its own entrance on the other side of the Mandalay Bay building and has its own lobby, high-speed elevators, pool, and health club/spa. You don't, however, have to miss any Vegas fun. On the Four Seasons side, all is calm and serene. But open a door and — presto! — you're back in the hustle and bustle of Vegas, heading right into

Downtown Accommodations

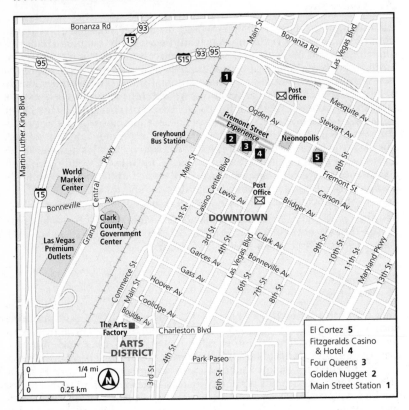

El Cortez **5**
Fitzgeralds Casino
& Hotel **4**
Four Queens **3**
Golden Nugget **2**
Main Street Station **1**

Mandalay Bay's casino. It's the best of both worlds. Still, after you've experienced the Four Seasons kind of serenity, you may find it hard to return to the typical adrenaline rush.

At first glance, rooms don't appear all that special — but when you notice the many comforts (down comforters, fancy amenities, DVD players, bathrobes), you don't mind. The staff members are brilliant at fulfilling and even anticipating needs, and they love to pamper your children even more than they pamper you. Health-club privileges are included here; other hotels often charge extra for these delights. As a result, the high rack rates aren't all that out of line with other high-end, but less accommodating choices — and you can get good deals here nearly all the time. The Four Seasons also boasts the excellent (but pricey) **Charlie Palmer Steak** restaurant.

See maps p. 96 and p. 98. 3960 Las Vegas Blvd. S. ☎ **877-632-5000** *or 702-632-5000. Fax: 702-632-5195.* www.fourseasons.com. *Rack rates: $199 and up double. AE, DC, DISC, MC, V.*

Golden Nugget
$$$ Downtown

Indisputably the nicest downtown hotel, the Golden Nugget is all the better thanks to a recent makeover that has given it a much fresher feeling. The larger-than-average, updated rooms are comfortable and pretty, size-wise on a par with those found at the Mirage, especially those in the new (as of 2009) Rush Tower. The large, multilevel pool (rare for downtown) features an incredibly cool glass tunnel that passes through a shark tank and an adults-only (meaning no kids, not topless) infinity pool. Other highlights include a particularly good health club and spa and several different restaurants. Like any place downtown, it can be a little cramped, but at least you won't feel as if you're stuck in a time warp. Despite its superior status, the Nugget can be a surprisingly good deal; if you catch the prices even close to the lower end, it's hard to justify spending the big bucks at a mega-resort on the Strip.

See maps p. 96 and p. 104. 129 E. Fremont St. (at Casino Center Boulevard). ☎ **800-846-5336** *or 702-385-7111. Fax: 702-386-8362.* www.goldennugget.com. *Rack rates: $69 and up double. AE, DC, DISC, MC, V.*

Green Valley Ranch Resort
$$$ Henderson

We won't kid you — it's a drive from here to the Strip. But we picked this fabulous resort because it combines all the things we like best in a hotel — the grown-up style and comfort of places like the Ritz and the playful kickiness of the W or the Palms. The latter is particularly evident in the pool area, with its geometric beach pool and mattresses tossed here and there for supreme and slightly suggestive lounging comfort. The workout room is small, but the spa is hip. The nicely old-school casino and a number of affordable restaurants are located in a complex a longish stroll away (through indoor corridors) that includes a multiscreen movie theater. This resort is a good choice for families (especially because Green Valley Ranch is away from all the obvious sinning of Vegas), as well as for couples seeking a little romantic privacy.

See map p. 96. 2300 Paseo Verde Pkwy. (at I-215). ☎ **866-782-9487** *or 702-617-7777. Fax 702-617-7778.* www.greenvalleyranchresort.com. *Rack rates: $129 and up double. AE, DC, DISC, MC, V.*

The Hard Rock Hotel & Casino
$$$$ Paradise Road

Gen Xers and baby boomers should run to the Hard Rock: Your people await! Rock music blares in the wildly and playfully decorated casino, the center of the circular public area, with rock 'n' roll memorabilia everywhere you turn. This hotel is not for someone looking for a quiet getaway (it's loud, loud, loud), but it's definitely the epicenter of happening Las Vegas. And sometimes, we can't help but think that if we were Lady Gaga or Britney, or just looked like Lady Gaga or Britney, we'd get better treatment.

And now the place rocks even harder, or at least larger, with the completion of a nearly $1-billion expansion. Two new hotel towers serve up sleek, high-tech rooms (check out the wall-unit MP3 docks that connect to the hotel's "jukebox"), all with different pros and cons. The original rooms have French doors that open to small balconies but are smaller and less chic; the Paradise Tower rooms are swank black-and-gray wonders but don't have tubs; and the HRH suites are big white wonders but are the most expensive, naturally. The Beach Club has more than doubled in size, with multiple pools, swim-up blackjack, indoor/outdoor bars (including a branch of the famed L.A. hot spot SkyBar), and plenty of hard bodies to intimidate the rest of us. The casino was expanded, a new Joint concert venue was built, restaurants were added, a new spa and workout facility is available, and there are more exclusive nightclubs than ever before. It's all thrilling and/or exhausting — depending on your point of view or energy level.

See maps p. 96 and p. 108. 4455 Paradise Rd. (at Harmon Avenue). ☎ **800-473-7625** *or 702-693-5000. Fax: 702-693-5588.* www.hardrockhotel.com. *Rack rates: $109 and up double. AE, DC, MC, V.*

Harrah's Las Vegas
$$$ Center Strip

Harrah's is one of the friendliest places in town, with its price and location (smack in the center of the Strip) making it a solid pick. Still, it does look dated and as if it's trying too hard — and not in the good, over-the-top theme way — next to the splashier places right around it. Don't come here thinking you're getting more than just a good deal on a hotel room. The carnival atmosphere is not overwhelming, and the rooms are large and comfortably furnished. The carnival-themed casino is certainly festive, and you can spend some quality time relaxing in the pool, dining at one of the several restaurants, browsing the shopping and live entertainment plaza (where our favorite lounge singer, Cook E. Jarr, has a recurring gig), and hopping the monorail out back to a more interesting destination.

See maps p. 96 and p. 99. 3475 Las Vegas Blvd. S. (between Spring Mountain and Flamingo roads). ☎ **800-427-7247** *or 702-369-5000. Fax: 702-369-5283.* www.harrahslasvegas.com. *Rack rates: $79 and up double. AE, DC, DISC, MC, V.*

Imperial Palace
$$ Center Strip

You gotta love the IP. Despite years of rumors that it was going to be torn down to make way for something nicer, it soldiers on with a few improvements but mostly the same old inexpensive and cheap (two very different things) hotel that it always has been. The rooms are as bargain-basement as you can find in a major hotel on the Strip in terms of the amenities and furnishings. You get a bed, a phone, a small TV, an air conditioner, a postage-stamp-size bathroom, and that's about it. The casino, showroom, attractions, bars, and most of the restaurants are equally, uh, "budget conscious" — although many of the offerings are solidly satisfying and, in the case of Hash House A Go Go, absolutely fantastic. The good news is that the low-rent feeling extends to the bill you get at the end of your stay. If you pay more than $100 a night here you're doing something really wrong.

See maps p. 96 and p. 99. 3535 Las Vegas Blvd. S. (between Flamingo and Spring Mountain roads). ☎ *800-351-7400 or 702-731-3311. Fax: 702-735-8328.* www.imperial palace.com. *Rack rates: $59 and up double. AE, DC, DISC, MC, V.*

Las Vegas Hilton
$$$$ Paradise Road

Elvis spent the bulk (sorry) of his Fat Years performing at this hotel, but it caters primarily to business travelers because it's adjacent to the **Las Vegas Convention Center.** The rooms here are large and comfortable, if not all that striking. Recently upgraded here and there, this hotel has a little bit of everything people look for in Vegas. The casino is smaller than most and not in the way — it's handy, but you don't have to pass through it every time you leave your room. The atmosphere is more elegant and expensive than not. The Las Vegas Hilton has an extensive selection of restaurants, a superior recreation deck with a swimming pool and tennis courts, and a terrific health club/spa where you really feel pampered.

See maps p. 96 and p. 108. 3000 Paradise Rd. (at Riviera Boulevard). ☎ **888-732-7117** *or 702-732-5111. Fax: 702-732-5805.* www.lvhilton.com. *Rack rates: $49 and up double. AE, DC, DISC, MC, V.*

Luxor
$$$ South Strip

It's hard to miss the Luxor — it's the 30-story pyramid with the Sphinx in front. And no, the Great Pyramid of Giza is not similarly covered in glass, nor does it have a 315,000-watt light beam shooting from the top. The Luxor used to be the epitome of a tacky theme park, but a huge renovation has stripped it of all the ridiculous silliness, to the point that the generic interior no longer matches the thematic promise of its exterior. It's a darn shame. Although some of the Egyptian detail remains in the otherwise bland rooms, at least the ones in the pyramid still have cool sloped walls (the baths in those rooms have showers only). And let's not forget those "inclinators" (the elevators that go at an angle) — they're the best free rides in town! The hotel houses five big pools, a large and airy casino, some hot nightclubs and bars, interesting shows, and an attractions level featuring artifacts from the *Titanic* and the gruesomely fascinating pre-served bodies science exhibit called, appropriately enough, Bodies: The Exhibit. A mini-monorail connects you with **Mandalay Bay** and **Excalibur.**

See maps p. 96 and p. 98. 3900 Las Vegas Blvd. S. (between Reno and Hacienda avenues). ☎ **888-777-0188** *or 702-262-4000. Fax: 702-262-4478.* www.luxor.com. *Rack rates: $59 and up double. AE, DC, DISC, MC, V.*

Paradise Road Accommodations

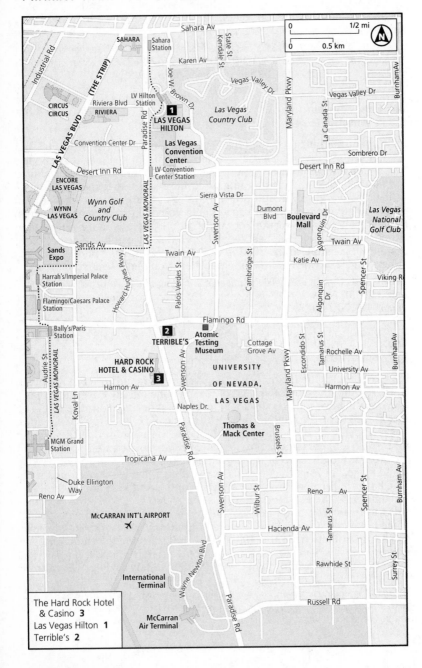

The Hard Rock Hotel
& Casino **3**
Las Vegas Hilton **1**
Terrible's **2**

Main Street Station
$$ Downtown

This surprisingly sweet hotel — hard to believe in Vegas, but true — is one of the nicest downtown choices and a really great bargain, to boot. It does a good job of evoking turn-of-the-century San Francisco with charming décor that includes gas lanterns, stained-glass windows, and lazy ceiling fans in the casino, plus plantation shutters and comfy furniture in the average-size rooms. Although it isn't located right on **Fremont Street,** like most other downtown hotels, it's less than a 5-minute walk away. And the in-house dining and entertainment options are better than those at many of the other downtown hotels, including the best buffet found downtown (and maybe in all of Vegas), a particularly handsome steakhouse, a microbrewery that's great for snacking, and bar-type nighttime hangouts. The only drawbacks are potential freeway noise and the lack of a health club and pool, although you can use the one at the California across the street.

See maps p. 96 and p. 104. 200 N. Main St. (between Fremont Street and I-95). ☎ *800-465-0711 or 702-387-1896. Fax: 702-386-4466. www.mainstreetcasino. com. Rack rates: $59 and up double. AE, DC, DISC, MC, V.*

Mandalay Bay
$$$$ South Strip

In case you were wondering, it's named after a Kipling poem. (Who says Vegas can't be educational?) A Kipling-themed hotel? No such luck. There aren't any mini-Mowglis or Baloos running around singing about the bare necessities. Perhaps that's just as well. Immediate access to the guest elevators off the aquarium and bird-studded lobby avoids the usual tiring slog through casino mayhem such as that found at so many of its peers, and the superb unimpeded views of the entire Strip includes the planes landing at the airport. The hotel has particularly large, handsome rooms (king rooms come off better than doubles) with large bathrooms (some of the biggest and nicest around — you may never get out of that sunken tub). The pool area is, hands down, the best in Vegas — with a wave pool, a lazy "river," an open-air casino, and some basic pools, there is something here for every water taste. And the giant aquarium — oops, we mean **Shark Reef Aquarium** — is a blood-pressure-lowering pleasure (if a tad expensive).

You'll find a branch of the **House of Blues** here, plus more than a dozen restaurants, many of which are quite good. Although the emphasis is on adult pleasures, Mandalay Bay isn't a bad option for parents traveling with offspring, and not just because of a version of the Broadway hit *The Lion King* playing in the main theater. It offers variety, and you don't have to negotiate through R-rated territory to get Junior to his fun.

See maps p. 96 and p. 98. 3950 Las Vegas Blvd. S. (at Hacienda Avenue). ☎ *877-632-7800 or 702-632-7108. Fax: 702-632-7228. www.mandalaybay.com. Rack rates: $99 and up standard double. AE, DC, DISC, MC, V.*

Mandarin Oriental
$$$$$ South Strip

Aiming to fill the void left by the closure of the Ritz-Carlton, the Mandarin Oriental doesn't pull any punches when it comes to the level of luxurious service and amenities it offers. Staying here is more than just checking in and sleeping — it's an "experience." Arriving guests are whisked to the 23rd-floor Sky Lobby with its floor-to-ceiling windows showing off unparalleled views of the Strip — be sure to stop in after dark to get the full impact. Rooms are standard in terms of size — no massive multiroom suites here unless you upgrade — but everything in them is of a higher caliber, with rich woods, silky fabrics, cushy furnishings, gleaming marble, high-end bath products, and plenty of technology gizmos to make you feel either really smart or really stupid depending on how well you can figure out stuff like that. A pool and spa on the seventh and eighth floors provide more great views and pampering, but although the hotel has a couple on-site restaurants, it has no casino, showroom, or roller coaster to offer distractions from how well you're being treated by the superb staff. If you want all that, it's merely steps away at the other CityCenter properties, so you get the best of both worlds here. The price for the experience can be crazy-expensive but, wow, is it ever worth it.

See maps p. 96 and p. 98. 3752 Las Vegas Blvd. S. (at Harmon Avenue). ☎ **888-881-9578** *or 702-590-8881. Fax: 702-590-8880.* www.mandarinoriental.com. *Rack rates: $299 and up double. AE, DC, DISC, MC, V.*

MGM Grand
$$$$ South Strip

This is not the biggest hotel in the world. It's only the second-biggest hotel in the world. Rhode Island could comfortably fit inside its casino, which is the biggest in Las Vegas. Clearly, this is not a cozy, intimate locale. The theme, such as it is, is classic MGM movies; some of the rooms, in addition to having stand-out minimalist 1930s glamour-evoking furniture, also feature black-and-white movie-star photos. Other rooms are a bit more hotel pedestrian, while still others — in the so-called West Wing — are tiny but stylish, with the kind of sleek W-style appointments that are all the rage these days. The staff somehow manages to be attentive despite the overwhelming hugeness of the place.

The pool area is fabulous, with big bodies of water, a lazy river, and many acres to play and splash around in, but note that during the off season (most non-summer months), much of it can be closed. The Asian-Zen spa is luxurious and grown-up. The MGM Grand has a fine lineup of restaurants: **Joël Robuchon at the Mansion** and Robuchon's **L'Atelier,** Emeril Lagasse's **New Orleans Fish House,** the **Rainforest Cafe,** and Tom Colicchio's **Craftsteak,** to name just a few. The whole thing is overseen outside by a four-story-tall gleaming gold lion. He's photo-op ready, but you may want to save your film for the **Lion Habitat,** which allows you to visit and even have your photo taken with real-life Simbas.

See maps p. 96 and p. 98. 3799 Las Vegas Blvd. S. (at Tropicana Avenue). ☎ *800-929-1111 or 702-891-7777. Fax: 702-891-1030.* www.mgmgrand.com. *Rack rates: $99 and up double. AE, DC, DISC, MC, V.*

The Mirage
$$$$ Center Strip

We just dig this hotel. Others may be doing it somewhat better, but they're merely building on what the Mirage began.

Marvel at the rejiggered "lava"-spewing volcano out front; sniff the interior's vanilla-scented air; soothe jangled nerves by staring at the 200,000-gallon aquarium behind the reception desk; stroll through the indoor rain forest; loll by the tropical pool with much foliage, waterfalls, and water slides; go play with some dolphins; have a fab meal (the buffet is a particularly good); rejuvenate at the luxe spa and health club; or gamble in the jolly casino. And when your clock winds down, you can sleep it off in one of the nicest rooms in town for the price, all sleekly modern glory (see if you can get one that overlooks the volcano's action). We've done it all here, and we'll do it again. What don't we like? Navigating the twisting paths through the casino to go just about anywhere, paying extra for that spa and the Dolphin Habitat, the dinky bathrooms that pale in comparison to the lush ones at newer hotels, and the long lines for food. When you're ready to try something new, you can take a free tram over to **Treasure Island** (it runs daily 7 a.m.–2 a.m.).

See maps p. 96 and p. 99. 3400 Las Vegas Blvd. S. (between Flamingo Road and Sands Avenue). ☎ *800-627-6667 or 702-791-7111. Fax: 702-791-7446.* www.mirage.com. *Rack rates: $109 and up double. AE, DC, DISC, MC, V.*

Monte Carlo Resort & Casino
$$$ South Strip

Overshadowed both literally and figuratively by it's wackier (New York–New York) and more modern (CityCenter) neighbors, Monte Carlo still reaches for grandeur on the outside by reproducing the opulence of its namesake with colonnades, arches, fountains, and enormous statues that are nearly in good taste. Inside, it's a much more sedate affair, all muted earth tones — in the casino and most of the rooms — that can be a bit yawn-inducing. The lone exception is the top floor Hotel 32 rooms and suites, done in bold red and offering concierge-level service (including free limo rides to and from the airport). Of course, you find the usual array of restaurants and bars, plus a showroom. The hotel's pool area has pleased many a guest, but it's kind of tame compared to Mandalay Bay. (Kids generally like this area a lot, but they'll probably be bored by the rest.) Grown-ups love the fabulous spa, which offers all the equipment and treatments you could want.

See maps p. 96 and p. 98. 3770 Las Vegas Blvd. S. (between Flamingo Road and Tropicana Avenue). ☎ *800-311-8999 or 702-730-7777.* www.montecarlo.com. *Rack rates: $59 and up double. AE, DC, DISC, MC, V.*

M Resort Spa Casino
$$$ Henderson

Just because it's located far from the places you'll want to go in Las Vegas (and just about everything else) doesn't mean you should bypass the M Resort. Designed primarily as a destination for locals, it offers a great value in a really attractive package. Public spaces are flooded with light and the entire resort is done in a delightfully warm mix of stone, wood, glass, crystal, and mother-of-pearl accents, making it not only comfortable but nice to look at as well. Rooms are modern wonders, all sleek lines, plush furnishings, and high-tech touches such as an auto-save function that turns out all the lights when you leave and restores them when you come back. The bathrooms are big and marbled, although they tend to echo and carry more sound into adjoining rooms than we like. It has a large casino with more lower-limit gambling than you'll find on the Strip, plus several restaurants, a buffet, lounges, a very nice pool area, and a full-service health club and spa. If this hotel were located on the Strip it would probably cost two or three times more, but the money you'll save by staying here could make the 10-mile drive to the heart of Sin City totally worth it.

See maps p. 96 and p. 98. 12300 Las Vegas Blvd. S. (at St. Rose Parkway). ☎ **877-673-7678** *or 702-797-1000. Fax: 702-797-3010.* www.themresort.com. *Rack rates: $129 and up double. AE, DC, DISC, MC, V.*

New York–New York
$$$$ South Strip

Now this is more like it. None of that namby-pamby "luxury resort" good-taste crap. No, this is Vegas at its finest, following the honored tradition of taking a theme and beating it into the ground. And good golly, is it fun. It's almost impossible to do this place justice in just a few sentences, but here goes. The exterior is an actual reproduction of the New York skyline, with one-third-scale replicas of the Empire State Building, the Chrysler Building, the Statue of Liberty, and the Brooklyn Bridge. Inside, you stroll through versions of Greenwich Village and Times Square, and although the casino has gotten some of the Gotham taken out of it by a remodeling, there's still more than enough left to giggle over. The arcade is tricked up like Coney Island, there are cobblestone streets in the Village, and there's even (not naughty) graffiti. Hey, and just for flavor, a roller coaster runs through the whole thing.

Thankfully, the theme doesn't carry over into the rooms, which can be smallish (just like New York!) and sedate enough to induce yawns — but isn't that what you want where you're going to be sleeping? Note that it can be a very long, confusing, tortuous walk to just about anywhere in the hotel, even from the elevator to your room. Guests with disabilities should make this clear when reserving, or perhaps skip this hotel altogether. The spa and pool aren't as great as those at other hotels. The hotel is nearly always crowded, and there's definitely a sensory-overload factor, especially in the casino. But boy, is it a hoot! If you don't stay here, you have to at least stop by to see it.

See maps p. 96 and p. 98. 3790 Las Vegas Blvd. S. (at Tropicana Avenue). ☎ *800-693-6763 or 702-740-6969. Fax: 702-740-6920. www.nynyhotelcasino.com. Rack rates: $79 and up double. AE, DC, DISC, MC, V.*

Orleans
$$ West of the Strip

This is one terrific value. As the name implies, this is the Las Vegas interpretation of New Orleans, complete with French Quarter influences, Mardi Gras beads given away just for stopping in, and Cajun and zydeco music playing in the casino. It's located about a mile west of the Strip. We recommend this place primarily for the rooms — they're roomier than most, with comfortable Victorian-parlor-style furnishings (although, as in a true Victorian parlor, the clutter can make matters cramped). You often can get terrific prices here — so what's a little distance? This is a medium-size hotel with the usual array of bars and restaurants (including a moderately priced buffet and a very good Mexican restaurant that makes its own tortillas), plus two medium-size swimming pools, movie theaters, a large child-care center, a 70-lane bowling alley open nearly round-the-clock, a sports arena, and much more.

See maps p. 96 and p. 98. 4500 W. Tropicana Ave. (west of I-15). ☎ *800-675-3267 or 702-365-7111. Fax: 702-365-7505. www.orleanscasino.com. Rack rates: $59 and up standard double. AE, DC, DISC, MC, V.*

Palazzo Las Vegas
$$$$ Center Strip

This relatively staid sequel to the Venetian suffers a bit in comparison to its more ostentatious sibling. It's not that Palazzo isn't nice — it is nice, and then some. The rooms are similar to those at the original with a huge, showy bathroom (people want them for their own homes), a sleeping area, and a separate sunken living room, all done in a much more modern and elegant scheme. The casino is big and airy. There are several restaurants, a spa, a pool, a showroom featuring *Jersey Boys,* nightclubs, a shopping mall, and all the other things you've come to expect in a major Las Vegas casino hotel. But it's all a bit bland. Where the Venetian is all themed glory (complete with canals!), Palazzo is significantly more subtle in its design approach, which is a polite way of saying "yawn." There are no "wow" moments at Palazzo, which may appeal to some travelers, but it really doesn't do it for us. Of course, when we see the bill for staying a few nights here, that definitely wakes us up.

See maps p. 96 and p. 99. 3325 Las Vegas Blvd. S. (at Spring Mountain Road). ☎ *877-883-6423 or 702-414-4100. Fax: 702-414-4805. www.palazzolasvegas.com. Rack rates: $199 and up double. AE, DC, DISC, MC, V.*

Palms Resort & Casino
$$$ **West of the Strip**

Staying at the Palms (across from the Rio, a few blocks off the Strip) is pretty much a toss-up, and your decision to stay here should be based on your priorities. Want one of the hottest hotels in town, one that tries to straddle the line between posh and friendly? Want a place that actively caters to the hip and the happening, with trendy nightclubs **(Rain, Moon)** and bars **(ghostbar, the Playboy Club)**? Want some of the most comfortable beds in town? Want movie theaters and a really good, inexpensive buffet? Want to stay where Britney spent her first ill-fated honeymoon night? Then stay here. Want something with thematic punch? Want to be right on the Strip? Want not to pay near-Strip prices for an off-Strip room, even a nice room with big TVs and bathrooms? Want to avoid having to deal with a lot of zero-percent-body-fat riffraff? Then go elsewhere. We love the beds, the collection of better-than-average chain restaurants in the food court, and the restaurant Alizé — but man, do we hate the crowds at night. But maybe that's because we can't fit into size-2 jeans.

See maps p. 96 and p. 99. 4321 W. Flamingo Rd. (at I-15). ☎ 866-942-7777 or 702-942-7777. Fax: 702-942-6859. www.palms.com. Rack rates: $99 and up double occupancy. AE, DC, DISC, MC, V.

Paris Las Vegas Casino Resort
$$$$ **Center Strip**

Ooh la la. If the French get snippy over foreigners mangling their language, what on earth must they think of this place: a hotel, fashioned by vulgar Americans, no less, that re-creates all their most cherished monuments (the Eiffel Tower, looming nearly as large as the original, the Louvre, and the Arc de Triomphe)? You find signs in somewhat dubious French ("Le Car Rental") and employees who sprinkle all transactions with various phrases *("Bonjour et merci, Madame!")*. Who cares? We do. That's the kind of smile-inducing devotion to theme we can really get behind. Most rooms here are perfectly nice and perfectly forgettable — although the newer Red Rooms, with their bordello colors and couches, are kicky fun. The health club has pretensions of posh, and the pool area is cold and sterile. A number of restaurants will appeal, in varying degrees, to the Francophile; we particularly like **Mon Ami Gabi.** You can ride up to the near-top of the half-size Eiffel Tower and kiss your amour. Put it that way, and *pourquoi pas* (why not)?

See maps p. 96 and p. 99. 3655 Las Vegas Blvd. S. ☎ 888-266-5687 or 702-946-7000. Fax: 702-946-4405. www.parislv.com. Rack rates: $119 and up standard double. AE, DC, DISC, MC, V.

Planet Hollywood Resort & Casino
$$$$ **Center Strip**

As sentimentalists, we were sorry to see the old Aladdin go — it's where Elvis married 'Scilla, don't you know. As chroniclers of modern Vegas, we shake our heads with wonder over the transformation of the new Aladdin into the even newer Planet Hollywood. It's not that the new Aladdin was that spectacular, but its brief existence dramatically demonstrates how fast Vegas changes these days. So, Planet Hollywood it is now (owned by Harrah's as of 2010), and that means another wacky theme bites the dust. In its place are admittedly striking acres of gleaming wood and dazzling glass, plus an eye-catching shiny new exterior. We really do like the rooms, each of which contains a central piece of memorabilia — from Judy Garland's dress from *The Good Old Summer Time* or the sword from the Wesley Snipes movie *Blade* — with more souvenirs contained in a glass-topped table. It's a good gimmick in a town that is strangely moving away from gimmicks, and it does give the quite comfortable rooms some zingy personality. The newer PH Tower rooms are bigger and swankier with prices to match. Note that self-parking here means leaving your car at the other side of the adjoining shopping mall, the Miracle Mile, which you then have to schlep bags through to reach the registration desk. Guests with mobility issues must be sure to use the casino valet parking, which is located right outside check-in.

See maps p. 96 and p. 99. 3667 Las Vegas Blvd. S. ☎ **877-333-9474** *or 702-785-5555. Fax: 702-785-5558.* www.planethollywoodresort.com. *Rack rates: $99 and up double. AE, DC, DISC, MC, V.*

Red Rock Resort
$$$$ West Las Vegas

This billion-dollar resort was created by the same people behind the splendid Green Valley, so it would already be something even before you take in the setting, perched overlooking the incredible formations that make up the Red Rock National Conservancy area. If what you're looking for is a true luxury resort retreat getaway, this place has it all: lush, colorful rooms (42-inch plasma TVs!); a fancy swimming area; excellent restaurants; and even a terrific-looking casino. It's a resort of choice for tabloid favorites looking for a lower-profile vacation, and no wonder. For the rest of us mortals, we hope that the habit of sneaking in extra charges (A "resort fee"? Are they kidding?), to say nothing of a high ticket price (remember, this is still 11 miles from the Strip, and this is a *Vegas* vacation), all gets ironed out, because we really, really want to stay here.

See map p. 96. 11011 W. Charleston Rd. ☎ **866-767-7773** *or 702-797-7625. Fax: 702-797-7053.* www.redrockstation.com. *Rack rates: $119 and up for up to 4 people per room. AE, DC, DISC, MC, V.*

Rio Hotel & Casino
$$$$ West of the Strip

Although it's not at the top of our list, lots of people love this hotel for its carnival ambience, tropical theme, and oversized rooms. The rooms are big, all right, featuring sectional sofas, small refrigerators, and very nifty floor-to-ceiling windows with fab views; but they're not quite the "suites" the hotel touts. Downsides here include location (a solid 20-minute walk from the Strip) and a sometimes unfriendly staff. If you're easily over-whelmed, you may not enjoy the hectic, party-all-the-time atmosphere; plus, it's not a good choice for families with kids.

The hotel includes a 41-story tower and a European-style "village" of shops and restaurants that's worth strolling through. A live-action show with a carnival theme (sort of a mock Mardi Gras parade that moves about on tracks overhead), called *Show in the Sky,* runs hourly during the eve-nings on weekends. The Rio is justly proud of its array of restaurants and bars, which includes a popular buffet, a wine bar where you can indulge in tastings, and the **Voodoo Lounge.** The swimming pools are a bit of a bust compared with some others in town, and the older parts of the casino can be too confining; head to the section housed in the newer expansion. Finally, the **Penn & Teller** show, surely the smartest show in Vegas, is in residency here.

See maps p. 96 and p. 99. 3700 W. Flamingo Rd. (just east of I-15). ☎ 888-752-9746 or 702-777-7777. Fax: 702-777-7611. www.playrio.com. *Rack rates: $99 and up double. AE, DC, MC, V.*

Riviera Hotel & Casino
$$ North Strip

This 50-something-year-old Vegas institution is showing its age, sadly; we include it here as an option only if you can get a good deal and you simply must stay on the Strip. Its once-elegant décor now seems more than a touch seedy, an impression that's reinforced by the topless revues that are heavily featured (and even enshrined — the Riviera displays a bronze statue commemorating the remarkable derrières featured in its show *Crazy Girls* in full view of the street). The **Riviera** is definitely *not* a good choice for families; but the rooms are adequate, and you can choose from tons of shows and snacking places. Amenities here include a vast casino, an Olympic-size pool and sun deck, a large video arcade, a health club, and a wedding chapel.

See maps p. 96 and p. 102. 2901 Las Vegas Blvd. S. (at Riviera Boulevard). ☎ 800-634-6753 or 702-734-5110. Fax: 702-794-9451. www.rivierahotel.com. *Rack rates: $59 and up double. AE, DC, MC, V.*

Sahara Hotel & Casino
$$ North Strip

This Vegas institution, a major player since 1952, is now a bit of an also-ran. New owners promised changes that haven't come, and in 2009 many of the hotel rooms were temporarily mothballed due to lack of demand. Whether things are back on track by the time you read this is really up to the gods of tourism. Meanwhile, she's an old hotel with spots of wear. Chandeliers and marble vie with the onion domes and mosaic tile they've thrown in for the *Arabian Nights* theme. We're not really sure how the roller coaster fits in. These public areas aren't bad at all, but the guest rooms are on the smallish side and despite cosmetic upgrades, they can never compare to the grander palaces down the street. Still, the rates can be cheap. The hotel is located in an out-of-the-way spot on the North Strip, which is a plus or a minus, depending on how you look at it. A very attractive Olympic-size pool has Moroccan tiles and a sun deck, plus there are several restaurants and bars and a large casino.

See maps p. 96 and p. 102. 2535 Las Vegas Blvd. S. (at Sahara Avenue). ☎ **888-696-2121** *or 702-737-2654. Fax: 702-791-2027.* www.saharavegas.com. *Rack rates: $45 and up double. AE, DC, DISC, MC, V.*

South Point
$$$ South Strip

Given how vast the distance can be from one major hotel to another on the Strip (blocks and blocks, sometimes), you don't need to actually stay on it, especially if you take our advice and rent a car. Much of the time, you're going to be driving or cabbing it from one location to another anyway. Given that, do your wallet a favor and stay here. Just 6 miles down Las Vegas Boulevard South from Mandalay Bay, this "locals hotel" offers genuinely attractive rooms (500 sq. ft., flatscreen TVs, handsome linens) for a fraction of the price of, say, a Wynn or a Bellagio. Add to that a number of affordable dining options, movie theaters, a bowling alley, an equestrian center, and more, and those staying farther north begin to look like real suckers. Meanwhile, you take the money you've saved each night, hop in your rental car, and go spend it on a good show or a fancy meal. Now who's the Dummy?

See maps p. 96 and p. 98. 9777 Las Vegas Blvd. S. ☎ **866-796-7111** *or 702-796-7111. Fax: 702-365-7505.* www.southcoastcasino.com. *$79 and up double. AE, DC, DISC, MC, V.*

Stratosphere Las Vegas
$$$ North Strip

A 108-story observation tower makes this the tallest building west of the Mississippi. Aside from really stunning views (the lights, the desert, the mountains — day or night, Vegas looks mighty fine from way above ground), the tower has the world's highest thrill rides, including a free-fall contraption, a whirligig-style device that spins you around in midair, a giant teeter-totter-style thing that sends you flying off the side of the building, and opportunity to literally jump off the top of the building. (Why you'd want to do all this is beyond us.) A wedding chapel completes the aforementioned views. Cool! And the staff is incredibly nice. But it does have drawbacks: It's quite a trek to anything else on the Strip, and this end of the Strip isn't very attractive. The rooms aren't in the tower itself, so don't expect those tremendous views from your own windows; plus, they really can't be described more generously than "really nice for a motel." Other extras include a casino, a huge pool, and a shopping arcade with a World's Fair theme.

See maps p. 96 and p. 102. 2000 Las Vegas Blvd. S. (between St. Louis Street and Baltimore Avenue). ☎ **800-998-6937** *or 702-380-7777. Fax: 702-383-5334.* www.stratospherehotel.com. *Rack rates: $49 and up double. AE, DC, DISC, MC, V.*

Terrible's Casino and Hotel
$ Paradise Road

Now, you've got to be thinking, "Hey, there's no way I'm going to stay in a place called Terrible's!" Would we steer you wrong? No fear: It's named after the owner (his nickname; let's not ask). And it's anything but. It's actually a complete renovation of a former dumpy old hotel (plus a newish tower), now all smarted up in a Tuscany-esque style, with decent, well-stocked rooms (some of which are considerably larger than others, so if personal space is an issue, make that clear when making reservations), a sweet pool, a really good coffee shop, and a casino with penny slots. All that, and would you look at those prices?

See maps p. 96 and p. 108. 4100 Paradise Rd. (at Flamingo Road). ☎ **800-640-9777** *or 702-733-7000. Fax: 702-765-5109.* www.terriblescasinos.com. *Rack rates: $39 and up double. AE, DC, DISC, MC, V.*

THEhotel at Mandalay Bay
$$$$ South Strip

If we had to pick *one* place to stay on the Strip, and assuming price were not a major issue, we would not hesitate in choosing THEhotel. Heck, even if price *were* an issue, we would still pick it, we're so in love with it right now. For all intents and purposes an entire separate hotel entity within Mandalay Bay, this is as sophisticated and mature as any happening hotel in Manhattan, swanky and stylish enough so that one seasoned traveler we know declared it perhaps the nicest she'd ever experienced. Because it has an entirely different entrance, you're in a different world than Mandalay Bay, one that makes that oh-so-Vegas hotel suddenly seem rather crass. A sleek and modern black-and-tan palette follows you from the lobby to the rooms, each of which is a genuine one-bedroom suite, complete with extra half-bath, wet bar, three plasma TVs, and the most heavenly bathroom in Vegas. The soaking tub is so deep that the water came to our chin. And the beds! Divine! Sure, it's another of these wannabe boutique hotels that are blown up so large that they can't possibly deliver the service of a real such place. At the same time, the design concept and resulting comfort are so successful, it's hard to care much. Best of all, all the frolicking noisy fun of Mandalay Bay is but a stroll down a hallway. Guests have access to the famous Mandalay Bay pool; their own pool area; a couple handsome if ordinary cafes and bars; and one grand, gorgeous, and overpriced spa/gym complex.

See maps p. 96 and p. 98. 3950 Las Vegas Blvd. S. ☎ **877-632-7800** *or 702-632-7777. Fax: 702-632-9215.* www.thehotelatmandalaybay.com. *$160 and up. AE, DC, DISC, MC, V.*

Treasure Island
$$$$ Center Strip

Once upon a time, this was a silly, pirate-themed hotel, one that epitomized the "family-friendly" Vegas vacation experiment. That it has since been stripped of nearly all pirate references demonstrates how much, and we cannot stress this enough, *Vegas is not for families anymore.*

And although the goal to turn the resort into a hipster or posh adult hang-out wasn't reached, it's still a fine place to stay. The rooms are not as stylish as those at its former sister, the Mirage, but expect a decent amount of space, particularly nice bathrooms, and good beds, done in a brown palette. Not a single doubloon in sight. The pirates are still present in one form: in the free, Strip-side *Sirens of TI* pirate battle, where they now, sadly, battle sexy scantily clad showgirls in one of the worst pieces of trash ever to hit Vegas — and that's saying a lot. Poor pirates. The pool is minimally interesting, but the spa and health club are quite good. There are a few restaurants and bars, including a branch of the yeehaw favorite **Gilley's**, and the few kids who still come here, if they're more sophisti-cated than much of the short-attention-span generation, will enjoy **Cirque du Soleil's** *Mystère,* which is housed in a wonderful theater.

See maps p. 96 and p. 99. 3300 Las Vegas Blvd. S. (at Spring Mountain Road). ☎ *800-944-7444 or 702-894-7111.* www.treasureisland.com. *Rack rates: $89 and up double. AE, DC, DISC, MC, V.*

Tropicana Resort & Casino
$$$ **South Strip**

You remember the Tropicana, don't you? The dingy and faded affair that was once known as the Tiffany of the Strip had been rightfully overshad-owed by its newer and better neighbors. Tell the truth: You forgot it even existed. Well, take another look. New owners have thrown a couple hun-dred million dollars at the place, almost literally changing everything. The new look is tropical South Beach Miami, all white and gold with bold splashes of orange and red everywhere you look. The exterior, the casino, the rooms, the restaurants, the showroom, the pool, the convention center — it has all gotten a major makeover, and it's not only nicer than it has been in decades but now totally competitive with those fancy neigh-bors. Rooms are all sandy earth tones with rattan and bamboo furnish-ings, crisp white linens, and extensively remodeled bathrooms turning what had been almost depressing floral nightmares into light and bright accommodations in which you may actually want to spend some time. Of course, prices have gone up — they have to pay for all this "new" some-how — but it's still a relative bargain. Welcome back, Tropicana! We missed you. Note: Construction on all this was supposed to be done by the end of 2010, but there may be some lingering affects, including the pool area, which is getting a Miami beach makeover and is set to debut in the spring of 2011.

See maps p. 96 and p. 98. 3801 Las Vegas Blvd. S. (at Tropicana Avenue). ☎ **888-826-8767** *or 702-739-2222. Fax: 702-739-2469.* www.tropicanalv.com. *Rack rates: $79 and up double. AE, DC, DISC, MC, V.*

Vdara
$$$$ South Strip

The least interesting of the CityCenter hotels is still a nice option, especially for families. Designed as a condominium hotel, rooms here range from studios to multibedroom apartments, and each has a kitchen, which could come in handy if you want to save a little bit of dough on meals. The design and décor of the entire building is gray and brown, making it muted in comparison to the rest of CityCenter (and all of Vegas for that matter) and certainly more grown-up (which is good), quiet (which can be good depending on what you're after), and a little boring (not so good). A pool and spa and one on-site restaurant is it in terms of amenities. If you want to gamble or see a show or check out a buffet, you'll have to go to one of the other nearby hotels, but the good news is that Vdara is connected by a long hallway to Bellagio and by a monorail to the rest of CityCenter, so getting to the good stuff is easy.

See maps p. 96 and p. 98. 2600 W. Harmon Ave. (just west of the Strip). ☎ **866-745-7767** *or 702-590-2767. Fax: 702-669-6233.* www.vdara.com. *Rack rates: $159 and up double. AE, DC, DISC, MC, V.*

The Venetian
$$$$$ Center Strip

Normally, we get all smug and patronizing about Vegas re-creations of famous locales and feel the need to gently remind you, "now, this isn't *really* like seeing the actual place, you know." But when we walk around the outside of the Venetian, through some re-creations of famous portions of Venice, Italy, noting the meticulous attention to detail, we think, "Well, actually, this *is* a great deal like the original." Your jaw will drop upon seeing the grand, sweeping, heavily marbled galleria, its ceiling covered in handmade re-creations of noted Venetian paintings, and the ambitious and amazing shopping area, where Venetian buildings line an actual canal, complete with singing gondoliers. You can take a ride with them while listening to costumed strolling minstrels burst into Italian arias, or you can flirt with Casanova and other famous Venetians in a small-scale clone of St. Mark's Square.

And then there are the rooms, each a junior suite measuring 700 square feet (the largest and probably most handsome in Vegas), with grand bathrooms and steps leading down to a sunken living room. Don't expect rooms like these in the real Venice. A 2004 addition, the **Venezia,** offers the same rooms, only even frillier, plus separate check-in and public areas entirely apart from the main hotel's. This option is perfect for adults wanting to have their Vegas cake and eat it, too. And the restaurants rival those at Bellagio for high-quality food (and prices to match) made by celebrity chefs, including the superlative bistro **Bouchon,** by famed chef Thomas Keller. The swimming-pool area is a disappointment, lacking the lush greenery and style of similar hotels. The spa area is provided courtesy of the highly touted **Canyon Ranch Spa;** there is nothing else like it (alas, including the cost) in Vegas.

See maps p. 96 and p. 99. 3355 Las Vegas Blvd. S. ☎ **877-283-6423** *or 702-414-1000. Fax: 702-414-4805.* www.venetian.com. *Rack rates: $169 and up double. AE, DC, DISC, MC, V.*

Westin Casuarina Las Vegas Hotel & Spa
$$$$ Center Strip

We were excited when the old seedy Maxim was stripped to its iron girder bones in order to get entirely made over as a Westin. Vegas needs a true boutique hotel, and although this isn't the hippest choice, it's still a good brand name. The results, however, are mixed: The casino may be new, but it sure looks old, even more so when stacked next to the streamlined new lobby, all business-class posh. Rooms are in good taste and comfortable (though the much-touted, admittedly cloudlike Heavenly Beds use too much polyester for our persnickety selves), but even our love of sage green is not enough for us to ignore the fact that compared to the dazzling wonders at, say, THEhotel, this hotel is rather plain. What it comes down to is this: Who wants business traveler good taste in Vegas? Still, the gym is decent; there is a pool and a cafe; and the entire place (with the exception of the small casino) is a nonsmoking zone, which is nice for those who are sensitive to smoke. Overall, the size is so refreshingly manageable that it may be just what you need, if what you need is a smart and sharp hotel with no Vegas personality at all, and just enough removed from Vegas distractions so that you can get some work done, but close enough so that you can get distracted when your work *is* done.

See maps p. 96 and p. 99. 160 E. Flamingo Rd. ☎ **866-837-4215** *or 702-836-5900. Fax: 702-836-5996.* www.westin.com. *$139 and up double. AE, DC, DISC, MC, V.*

Wynn Las Vegas
$$$$$ North Strip

Steve Wynn's $3-billion homage to excess is gorgeous, for sure; the rooms are large and snazzy with Warhol silk screens, flatscreen TVs, deep soaking tubs, and oomphy beds. The collection of restaurants is terrific. But the hotel is structured old-school style; you have to wiggle through the mazelike casino to get anywhere. The check-in area is too cramped for a facility this large. The fabled 150-foot manmade mountain can be glimpsed only in bits from inside the hotel, and the high-tech free show displayed there is only visible from a viewing platform that fits about a dozen people or from an expensive restaurant or bar. And everything seems to cost a lot. Finally, at no time do you think, "Wow, this is something else, again!" There is no particular theme apart from "posh resort." We want glitz, but we want it silly, too. And if we go to a resort, we want a certain level of personal service that's hard to pull off on a nearly 4,000-room scale. Don't get us wrong — we'd stay here in an instant. But in the end, it's still just another big fancy Vegas hotel, with a big fancy nightly price to match.

See maps p. 96 and p. 102. 3131 Las Vegas Blvd. S. (at Flamingo Road). ☎ **888-320-9966** *or 702-770-7100. Fax: 702-770-1571.* www.wynnlasvegas.com. *Rack rates: $199 and up double. AE, DC, MC, V.*

Coming soon

For the last several decades, Vegas has been in an almost constant state of construction — so much so that residents jokingly call the construction crane their state bird. New hotels and casinos fueled much of the tourism boom during the '90s and '00s, justifying the more than two dozen massive mega-resorts that opened around town in the past 20 years.

But the economic meltdown of 2008 has driven a stake into the chest of the casino industry, leaving it on life support.

As of this writing only one major hotel-casino is scheduled to open in Las Vegas, which is pretty remarkable considering the development boom of the last two decades.

That hotel is The Cosmopolitan of Las Vegas. Located between CityCenter and Bellagio, the modern glass and chrome structure will have more than 3,000 rooms all with private terraces and kitchenettes, a 150,000 square-foot casino, three pools, over a dozen restaurants and bars, and more. Although not branded a Marriott, it will be available for bookings through that chain's Web site.

The next one to emerge will likely be Fontainebleau, the 3,000-plus room resort that was under construction just north of The Riviera. It fell into bankruptcy and construction halted, leaving the project mothballed until billionaire Carl Icahn bought the place with plans to complete it. When? Good question. Probably not before 2012.

Other major projects for the Strip that are all on hold or dead include Echelon, the 5,000 room replacement for the Stardust that was supposed to open in 2011; The Plaza, a recreation of the New York landmark hotel where The Frontier used to be; the partnership between MGM Resorts and South African casino magnate Sol Kerzner that was going to result in a big hotel across from The Sahara; and the CityCenter like project slated for the land just north of Circus Circus.

At this point if any of these projects get the green light to move forward again, it'll be the second half of the decade before they open. Hope you like what's already there!

No Room at the Inn?

Not able to find a room in any of our main choices (listed in the preceding section)? It happens all too often, frankly, which never ceases to amaze us. The good news is that there are more than 140,000 rooms in Las Vegas, so the odds are good that you'll find some place to rest in between gambling sessions.

Here are some other reliable choices to call with your pleas and tales of woe:

✔ **Best Western Mardi Gras Inn ($$).** 3500 Paradise Rd. (between Sands Avenue and Desert Inn Road). ☎ **800-634-6501** or 702-731-2020.

- ✔ **Courtyard by Marriott ($$$).** 3275 Paradise Rd. (between Convention Center Drive and Desert Inn Road). ☎ **800-321-2211** or 702-791-3600.

- ✔ **Fairfield Inn by Marriott ($$$).** 3850 Paradise Rd. (between Twain Avenue and Flamingo Road). ☎ **800-228-2800** or 702-791-0899.

- ✔ **La Quinta Inn ($$$).** 3970 Paradise Rd. (between Twain Avenue and Flamingo Road). ☎ **800-531-5900** or 702-796-9000.

- ✔ **Marriott Suites ($$$$).** 325 Convention Center Dr. ☎ **800-228-9290** or 702-650-2000.

- ✔ **Palace Station ($$).** 2411 W. Sahara Ave. (just west of I-15). ☎ **800-634-3101** or 702-367-2411.

- ✔ **Residence Inn by Marriott ($$$$).** 3225 Paradise Rd. (between Desert Inn Road and Convention Center Drive). ☎ **800-331-3131** or 702-796-9300.

- ✔ **Sam's Town Hotel & Gambling Hall ($$$).** 5111 Boulder Hwy. (at Flamingo Road). ☎ **800-634-6371** or 702-456-7777.

- ✔ **Tuscany ($$$).** 255 E. Flamingo Rd. ☎ **877-887-2261** or 702-893-8933.

Index of Accommodations by Neighborhood

Center Strip
Bally's Las Vegas ($$$)
Bellagio ($$$$$)
Caesars Palace ($$$$$)
Flamingo ($$$)
Harrah's Las Vegas ($$$)
Imperial Palace ($$)
The Mirage ($$$$)
Palazzo Las Vegas ($$$$$)
Paris Las Vegas Casino Resort ($$$$)
Planet Hollywood Resort & Casino ($$$$)
Treasure Island ($$$$)
The Venetian ($$$$$)
Westin Casuarina Las Vegas Hotel & Spa ($$$$)

Downtown
El Cortez ($)
Fitzgeralds Casino & Hotel ($$)
Four Queens ($$)
Golden Nugget ($$$)
Main Street Station ($$)

Henderson
Green Valley Ranch Resort ($$$)
M Resort Spa Casino ($$$)

North Strip
Circus Circus ($)
Encore Las Vegas ($$$$$)
Riviera Hotel & Casino ($$)
Sahara Hotel & Casino ($$)
Stratosphere Las Vegas ($$$)
Wynn Las Vegas ($$$$$)

Paradise Road
The Hard Rock Hotel & Casino ($$$$)
Las Vegas Hilton ($$$$)
Terrible's Casino and Hotel ($)

South Strip
Aria Las Vegas ($$$$)
Excalibur ($$)
Four Seasons ($$$$$)
Luxor ($$$)
Mandalay Bay ($$$$)

Mandarin Oriental ($$$$$)
MGM Grand ($$$$)
Monte Carlo Resort & Casino ($$$)
New York–New York ($$$$)
South Point ($$$)
THEhotel at Mandalay Bay ($$$$)
Tropicana Resort & Casino ($$$)
Vdara ($$$$)

West of the Strip
Orleans ($$)
Palms Resort & Casino ($$$)
Rio Hotel & Casino ($$$$)

West Las Vegas
Red Rock Resort ($$$$)

Index of Accommodations by Price

$$$$$
Bellagio (Center Strip)
Caesars Palace (Center Strip)
Encore Las Vegas (North Strip)
Four Seasons (South Strip)
Mandarin Oriental (South Strip)
Palazzo Las Vegas (Center Strip)
The Venetian (Center Strip)
Wynn Las Vegas (North Strip)

$$$$
Aria Las Vegas (South Strip)
The Hard Rock Hotel & Casino
(Paradise Road)
Las Vegas Hilton (Paradise Road)
Mandalay Bay (South Strip)
MGM Grand (South Strip)
The Mirage (Center Strip)
New York–New York (South Strip)
Paris Las Vegas Casino Resort (Center
Strip)
Planet Hollywood Resort & Casino
(Center Strip)
Red Rock Resort (West Las Vegas)
Rio Hotel & Casino (West of the Strip)
THEhotel at Mandalay Bay (South Strip)
Treasure Island (Center Strip)
Vdara (South Strip)
Westin Casuarina Las Vegas Hotel &
Spa (Center Strip)

$$$
Bally's Las Vegas (Center Strip)
Flamingo (Center Strip)

Golden Nugget (Downtown)
Green Valley Ranch Resort
(Henderson)
Harrah's Las Vegas (Center Strip)
Luxor (South Strip)
Monte Carlo Resort & Casino (South
Strip)
M Resort Spa Casino (Henderson)
Palms Resort & Casino (West of the
Strip)
South Point (South Strip)
Stratosphere Las Vegas (North Strip)
Tropicana Resort & Casino (South Strip)

$$
Excalibur (South Strip)
Fitzgeralds Casino & Hotel (Downtown)
Four Queens (Downtown)
Imperial Palace (Center Strip)
Main Street Station (Downtown)
Orleans (West of the Strip)
Riviera Hotel & Casino (North Strip)
Sahara Hotel & Casino (North Strip)

$
Circus Circus (North Strip)
El Cortez (Downtown)
Terrible's Casino and Hotel (Paradise
Road)

Chapter 10

Dining, Las Vegas Style

. . . .

In This Chapter

▶ Exploring the Las Vegas dining scene
▶ Figuring out dress codes
▶ Cutting food costs
▶ Snacking on the go
▶ Making reservations

. . . .

*L*as Vegas is not only about gambling and having fun. Although you may be tempted to spend all your time in front of a slot machine, you've gotta keep that blood sugar up, you know. Las Vegas has a real dining scene; in fact, in some of the larger hotels, you can hang out for a week and never eat in the same place twice. But there's more to Las Vegas dining than what you find adjacent to a casino.

Getting the Dish on the Local Scene

It used to be that food snobs, foodies, chowhounds, gourmands, or simply anyone with well-developed taste buds never put the words *good, food,* and *Vegas* in the same sentence. But in the last few years, that has changed dramatically. All kinds of celebrity chefs — you know, the ones who have very famous (and usually expensive) restaurants that are often written about in glossy magazines, or their own line of frozen foods, or their own show on the Food Network — have opened restaurants in Vegas. You can thank the owners of those fancy luxury resort hotels. Apparently, they figured that budget travelers will eat anything put before them, but if they wanted the well-heeled to come to Vegas, they had to feed them in the manner to which they were accustomed. It's rather snobby, but no matter — we're mighty glad. You should be, too.

Meals for high rollers

If you really want to eat well in Vegas, and you don't have a trust fund, hit that jackpot and feel free to start in at the top. Alas, that's probably the only way to afford it all. If it's some consolation, you wouldn't have time to eat at all the amazing places now open.

Ease your wallet's strain a little by having just one or two blowout meals — that is, if you can narrow your decision down to just one or two. We certainly can't. Just look at this partial (and mouth-watering) list: Aside from Wolfgang Puck's half-dozen or so places, and those of Emeril Lagasse, Vegas has branches of such New York City favorites as **Mesa Grill** and **Aureole;** branches of such Los Angeles favorites as **Pinot, Nobu,** and **Border Grill;** a branch of the San Francisco favorite **Michael Mina** (aka Aqua); and restaurants by famed chefs such as Thomas Keller, Mario Batali, Julian Serrano, Paul Bartolotta, Daniel Boulud, Jean-Georges, Alex Stratta, and Todd English, not to mention now local, by way of New Orleans, chef Michael Jordan. Most significantly, multi-Michelin-starred chef **Joël Robuchon** opened up two eponymous restaurants in the MGM Grand, to universal shouts of hosanna (not to mention cries of "$350 a person — are you out of your mind?"). Whew! By the time you get through all that, you may well be a foodie yourself. You certainly will have been exposed to some dining that is every bit as significant and special as that found in more traditional culinary capitals.

Not all the good news is strictly at the top end of the scale, just a lot of it. "But I thought Vegas was supposed to have such cheap food!" Well, it does, but it's often not much more than fuel. The good news is the recent trend toward more moderately priced restaurants, many of which are featured in this chapter.

Belly up to the buffet

Buffets used to be *the* way to eat in Vegas. They've been an institution in Vegas since the 1940s, when **El Rancho Hotel** offered an all-you-can-eat spread for a buck! Unlimited prime rib and shrimp — $1! Wahoo! Heck, nothing says "vacation" like that.

But along with everything else in Vegas, buffets have gone upscale. You still find them everywhere — every major hotel and most minor ones have one. Unfortunately, they aren't really such bargains anymore, particularly the good ones where it's hard to eat $20 (or more) of food in one sitting (though, heaven knows, you feel compelled to try). You can find a few relatively inexpensive ones in town, but the quality of those . . . well, sometimes it just doesn't bear thinking about. Still, a Las Vegas vacation isn't really complete without at least one visit to a buffet. We review some of the best bets in this chapter.

Dressing to dine, Las Vegas style

For the most part, Las Vegas is a very informal town. You see people in jeans at even the best restaurants. A few places require jackets and forbid all-American denim, so bring at least one nice outfit. A general rule: If you have to call to make a reservation, ask about a dress code while you're on the phone. If you don't have to make reservations, don't worry about what you're wearing.

Smoking etiquette: Lighting up

Smokers still can enjoy cigarettes in Vegas in the way they can't in many major American cities. It's legal to smoke in casinos, which, of course, counts for a large area of indoor public places. But it's illegal to smoke in enclosed areas in restaurants (and bars that serve food), stores, malls, or in any restaurant that adjoins said casino areas. Confused? Figure you can light up freely in the casino and your basic bars, but not anywhere else.

Reserving a table: The only sure bet in Vegas

If you plan on going to any of the high-profile fancy-schmancy places, make your reservations as far in advance as possible. Unless you're a high roller, it's unlikely that you'll get a table at the best hotel restaurants without making a reservation beforehand. If you didn't reserve ahead, try to go on off-hours — 6 p.m. or 10 p.m. — when the restaurant is less likely to be full.

Trimming the Fat from Your Budget

You easily can feed a family of four for under $40 (though not in a nutritionally sound way) in Las Vegas; on the other hand, you can quickly blow $200 on dinner for two. We discuss the latter earlier in this chapter; the former can be achieved through careful application of those famous Vegas meal specials, as well as by seeking out your favorite chain restaurants.

If you want to try all the mouth-watering, foodie-heaven, critically acclaimed restaurants but your budget doesn't allow for it, note which ones are open for lunch. You often find similar menu offerings at much more affordable prices.

Also keep in mind that the farther away from tourist areas you are, the better the food bargains. You aren't going to find those famous cheap Vegas food specials at many of the name-brand hotels, but check the hotels downtown, on the northern end of the Strip, and just off the Strip Just follow the locals.

Where the locals meet to eat

If you don't have a trust fund, your best bet is to dine with the locals. Many a local has sworn to us that they don't bother cooking because eating out in Vegas is so cheap. With all the great meal deals offered by the hotels, it can be more affordable to eat out. Obviously, this doesn't hold true at those celebrity-chef, name-brand places — though you will find locals there, to be sure, on special occasions.

Keep in mind that when it comes to dining bargains, *great* refers to price, not quality. Oh, don't worry — that $1.99 shrimp cocktail is safe enough. People chow down on these bargain meals all the time, happy to save a few bucks that may have been spent at the blackjack table, and they all seem to live to tell about it. Actually, we know someone who loves the meal deals simply because they're often offered in the middle of the night; when he can't sleep, he just tromps downstairs and munches on a steak.

Listing specifics is almost impossible, because they change weekly, but here are a few places that offer bargain-basement food prices. Please remember that these are just a random recent sampling. These more than likely will not be available when you're in town, as these sorts of deals can change weekly. Don't worry, though — something else will have taken their place:

- **The Burger Joint** at the Flamingo, 3555 Las Vegas Blvd. S. (☎ 702-733-3111): This place is bringing the meal deal back to the Strip with $2 burger and fries and $5.99 steak and egg specials from midnight to 6 a.m. on weekends.

- **Market Street Café** at California Hotel & Casino, 12 E. Ogden Ave. (☎ 702-385-1222): What would Vegas be without the prime-rib special? Here it's $7.95 and includes soup or salad, potato, vegetable, and dessert from 4 p.m. until 11 p.m. nightly.

- **Ellis Island,** 4178 Koval Lane, near the Flamingo (☎ 702-733-8901): Legendary for its meal-deal specials, Ellis Island offers a 10-ounce steak, potato, bread, green beans, and a beer for $6.99.

- **Bill's Victorian Room,** 3595 Las Vegas Blvd. S. (☎ 702-737-7111): Got $15? It buys you your choice of prime rib or steak, soup or salad, and multiple potato options.

- **Gold Coast Sports Book,** 4000 W. Flamingo Rd., just west of the Strip (☎ 702-367-7111): What goes better with the big game than a hot dog, served from an authentic vendor's cart for just $1.25!

- **Bougainvillea Café,** at Terrible's Hotel Casino, 4100 Paradise Rd. (☎ 702-733-7000): The 24-hour cafe has several daily specials that aren't listed on the menu, including a $6.99 New York steak or $9.99 for a T-bone steak or prime rib. Just ask the server for the hidden deals.

The best way to find other bargains is to read the signs in front of the various casinos and check for coupons inside the many free magazines that are available inside Vegas hotel rooms and on the Strip. They always advertise current meal deals.

Chow down on the chain gang

You also can find a slew of national chain restaurants in Las Vegas — **Denny's, Tony Roma's, Olive Garden,** and so on — but they aren't the great bargains that they are in other cities. Obviously, the amount of money you spend on food depends on whether you can be satisfied with eating on the chain gang or the hotel's spiritual equivalent. If you avoid the celeb joints, food generally sets you back around $30 to $50 per person, per day. You can do it for less if you want to pinch pennies: Fill up at one buffet — even cram your pockets and purse with transportable leftovers, though you didn't hear that from us — and the rest of the day can be handled with light snacking.

Las Vegas's Best Restaurants

For help picking a place that suits your particular tastes, consult the indexes at the end of this chapter. Restaurants are indexed by price, so you can budget yourself; by location, so you can find a good place to eat in the area that's most convenient for you; and by cuisine, so you can satisfy your cravings.

But first are our picks for the most noteworthy restaurants in town. Each restaurant is followed by its price range, the part of town where it's located, and the type of cuisine you find there. You may notice that the picks are a bit heavy on the expensive food; that's because there just aren't as many recommendable places at more reasonable prices. The good news is that you often can enjoy a more affordable meal at expensive restaurants, and we let you know if this is an option. (All you have to do is eat there at lunch, when the menu is cheaper.) You should, however, let your hotel know that it needs to work on better budget options. After all, if you don't complain, who will?

The price categories used in this chapter are based on the average cost of a dinner entree (a la carte). Table 10-1 gives you the rundown.

Table 10-1	Key to Restaurant Dollar Signs	
Dollar Signs	**Category**	**Price Range**
$	A mind-blowing deal	Most main courses less than $9
$$	Inexpensive	Most main courses $10–$19
$$$	Moderate	Most main courses $20–$29
$$$$	Expensive	Most main courses $30–$34
$$$$$	Very expensive	Main courses more than $35

The dollar signs give you a general idea of how much a place costs. Don't rely solely on the price symbols, as some restaurants offer *prix-fixe* (set-price) meals or other deals that will affect the price rankings.

To help you figure out what to expect for your money, here's the low-down on the restaurants in a given price category:

- ✔ **$ (Dirt Cheap):** These are the popular places that have been around for a while. You can expect plain food in simple surroundings.

- ✔ **$$ (Inexpensive):** Some buffets and decent, if not stellar, restaurants fall into this category. They're cheaper than you may expect, because they're located a little out of the way or the food emphasizes quantity over quality.

- ✔ **$$$ (Moderate):** Think theme restaurants and smaller hotel joints. These are good bets for a decent dinner that won't blow your budget out of the water. Expect a unique décor, good service, and better-than-average food.

- ✔ **$$$$ (Expensive):** These are among the top Vegas restaurants: tops for food, chefs, service, décor, and ambience. You usually get what you pay for in this life, so be prepared to fork over a bundle.

- ✔ **$$$$$ (Very Expensive):** We're talking foodie nirvana here. These restaurants deserve respect. Here's where the well-heeled come for dinner. The food is above reproach, and the décor may include priceless artwork. One thing's for certain: People come here because the restaurant is well known, usually for its chef, atmosphere, or high-rolling clientele.

Las Vegas Restaurants from A to Z

Alizé
$$$$$ Center Strip   FRENCH

Love this place, oh yes, we do. Another restaurant from the capable and commendable hands of André Rochat (formerly of the much-lauded André's downtown restaurant), and though another chef is in the kitchen, that just means another clever soul is thrilling our palate — along with our eyes. This is one of the prettiest dining spaces in all of Vegas, thanks to a room (at the top of the Palms) bordered on three sides by windows, with panoramic views of all of Vegas. (*Note:* The right-hand side of the restaurant now looks at the newish Palms tower, so it's probably the least desirable spot to sit.) We've had any number of courses at this restaurant and have not been disappointed by one, though we do tend to prefer meat courses over fish. The menu changes often, but you could be trying a marinated jumbo lump crabmeat and avocado salad with heirloom tomato consommé, or a fabulous New York steak with summer truffle jus and potato herb pancakes, or meltingly tender lamb chops with shredded lamb shank wrapped in a crispy fried crepe. Desserts are often quite silly

Las Vegas Dining Overview

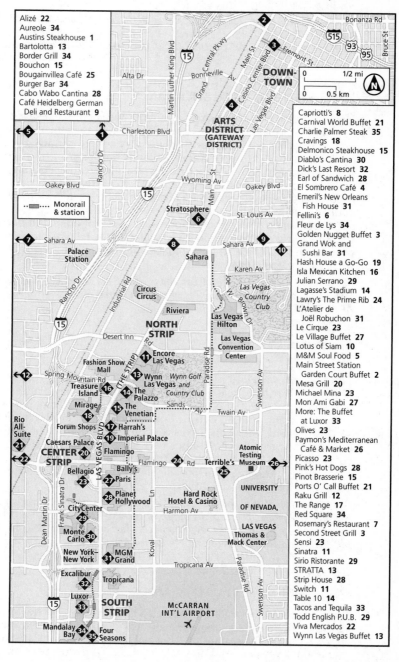

Alizé **22**
Aureole **34**
Austins Steakhouse **1**
Bartolotta **13**
Border Grill **34**
Bouchon **15**
Bougainvillea Café **25**
Burger Bar **34**
Cabo Wabo Cantina **28**
Café Heidelberg German
  Deli and Restaurant **9**

Capriotti's **8**
Carnival World Buffet **21**
Charlie Palmer Steak **35**
Cravings **18**
Delmonico Steakhouse **15**
Diablo's Cantina **30**
Dick's Last Resort **32**
Earl of Sandwich **28**
El Sombrero Café **4**
Emeril's New Orleans
  Fish House **31**
Fellini's **6**
Fleur de Lys **34**
Golden Nugget Buffet **3**
Grand Wok and
  Sushi Bar **31**
Hash House a Go-Go **19**
Isla Mexican Kitchen **16**
Julian Serrano **29**
Lagasse's Stadium **14**
Lawry's The Prime Rib **24**
L'Atelier de
  Joël Robuchon **31**
Le Cirque **23**
Le Village Buffet **27**
Lotus of Siam **10**
M&M Soul Food **5**
Main Street Station
  Garden Court Buffet **2**
Mesa Grill **20**
Michael Mina **23**
Mon Ami Gabi **27**
More: The Buffet
  at Luxor **33**
Olives **23**
Paymon's Mediterranean
  Café & Market **26**
Picasso **23**
Pink's Hot Dogs **28**
Pinot Brasserie **15**
Ports O' Call Buffet **21**
Raku Grill **12**
The Range **17**
Red Square **34**
Rosemary's Restaurant **7**
Second Street Grill **3**
Sensi **23**
Sinatra **11**
Sirio Ristorante **29**
STRATTA **13**
Strip House **28**
Switch **11**
Table 10 **14**
Tacos and Tequila **33**
Todd English P.U.B. **29**
Viva Mercados **22**
Wynn Las Vegas Buffet **13**

(either in theme or construction), which is appropriate given how much we giggle with delight through meals here.

See maps p. 131 and p. 138. 4321 W. Flamingo Rd. (in the Palms Hotel). ☎ **702-951-7000.** *Fax: 702-951-7002.* www.alizelv.com. *Reservations strongly recommended. Main courses: $34–$67. AE, DC, DISC MC, V. Open: Daily 5:30–10:30 p.m.*

Aureole
$$$$$ South Strip   NEW AMERICAN

Many people recognize this restaurant because of its namesake establishment in New York City, home to famed chef Charlie Palmer. Or they think of it only because of its signature, four-story wine tower, where cat-suited lovelies are hauled up by wires to fetch bottles from the uppermost heights. Lost in this is some of the best, most interesting cooking in Vegas. Aureole does beautiful things with the prix-fixe three-course menu (though it does tend to coddle favored guests by sending out curious little extra courses) that may include tender roasted lamb, or a rack of venison accompanied by sweet potato puree and chestnut crisp. But don't forget the wine tower, made even more playful with the help of a handheld computer wine list, which will even make suggestions for pairings based on what you ordered that evening.

See maps p. 131 and p. 133. 3950 Las Vegas Blvd. S. (in Mandalay Bay). ☎ **877-632-1766.** www.aureolelv.com. *Reservations required. Fixed-price dinner: $55–$95. AE, DISC, MC, V. Open: Daily 5:30–10:30 p.m.*

Austins Steakhouse
$$$ Off the Beaten Path   STEAKHOUSE

You find lots and lots of places to eat steak in Vegas, that's for sure. Although we're busy recommending some really pricey places, we ought to recommend one that is a bit less so. Not that it's cheap, but as we say again and again, split an entree. Your heart and stomach (room for dessert!) will thank you. This Texas Station restaurant is a favorite among locals, who swear by the 24-ounce rib-eye and the filets so tender you can cut them with a fork. Not only are the steaks fantastic, but they're significantly more affordable than most similar cuts of beef at restaurants on the Strip. Definitely worth the drive.

See map p. 131. 2101 Texas Star Lane, North Las Vegas (in Texas Station Gambling Hall and Hotel, 6 miles north of the Strip). ☎ **702-631-1000.** www.texasstation.com/dining. *Reservations recommended. Main courses: $15–$50. AE, DC, DISC, MC, V. Open: Sun–Thurs 5–10 p.m., Fri–Sat 5–11 p.m.*

Bartolotta
$$$$$ North Strip   ITALIAN/SEAFOOD

Steve Wynn went to a lot of trouble to make his hotel the swellest ever, and while debates rage about the success of some of his efforts, none is directed toward the restaurants. Not only did Wynn want top-name chefs,

South Strip Dining

PLANET HOLLYWOOD

Harmon Av

Aria Crystals

CITYCENTER

(THE STRIP)

LAS VEGAS MONORAIL

Audrie St

Koval Ln

Harmon Av

0   1/4 mi
0   0.25 km

MONTE CARLO

Showcase Mall

Rue de Monte Carlo

NEW YORK–NEW YORK

MGM GRAND

MGM Grand Station

Sahara Monorail & station
Pedestrian bridge

Tropicana Av

EXCALIBUR

TROPICANA

Duke Ellington Way

Reno Av

Reno Av

Dean Martin Dr

Frank Sinatra Dr

LUXOR

LAS VEGAS BLVD

Giles St

Mandalay Bay Rd

THEhotel

MANDALAY BAY

McCARRAN INTERNATIONAL AIRPORT

Dean Martin Dr

Frank Sinatra Dr

Mandalay Bay Convention Center

FOUR SEASONS

Four Seasons Dr

Aureole **7**
Border Grill **7**
Burger Bar **7**
Charlie Palmer Steak **8**
Diablo's Cantina **3**
Dick's Last Resort **5**
Emeril's New Orleans Fish House **4**
Fleur de Lys **7**
Grand Wok and Sushi Bar **4**
Julian Serrano **1**
L'Atelier de Joël Robuchon **4**
More: The Buffet at Luxor **6**
Red Square **7**
Sirio Ristorante **1**
Tacos and Tequila **6**
Todd English P.U.B. **2**

but he wanted those chefs to be physically in their kitchens. This is the dirty little secret about all those celebrity-chef outposts in town: Many, if not most chefs, not only don't do their own cooking but are physically elsewhere. Not only is James Beard Foundation Award–winning Paul Bartolotta in his kitchen, but so is his fish — that is, the fish he insists must be flown fresh from the Mediterranean every day. Everything is deceptively simple (easy little sauces over charbroiled fish, for example), but it all depends on the right ingredients — the best olive oil, the ripest tomatoes, the most perfect pasta, and the best fish. The result: nominated for Best New Restaurant for the 2006 Beard Awards and one of our favorite places to eat in Vegas.

See maps p. 131 and p. 143. 3131 Las Vegas Blvd. S. (in Wynn Las Vegas). ☎ **888-352-3463** *or 702-248-3463.* www.wynnlasvegas.com. *Reservations recommended. Main courses: $20–$58. AE, DC, DISC, MC, V. Open: Daily 5:30–10:30 p.m.*

Border Grill
$$$ South Strip   MEXICAN

You may think that you love Mexican food, but unless you've been to Mexico, you've probably never eaten real Mexican food. You've only eaten American interpretations. You don't find cheesy combo platters in Mexico, except at places catering to tourists. Not that there's anything wrong with a cheesy combo platter, but you owe it to yourself to try the real thing. The chef/owners of this Los Angeles–based restaurant (once on the Food Network as "The Two Hot Tamales") went to Mexico and learned to cook at street markets and in homes. Consequently, Border Grill features the real home cooking of Mexico, and it bursts with flavor (all the chicken and pork dishes are especially delicious).

Note that this visually delightful restaurant (interior colors are drawn from a slightly subdued Easter palate) has a separate *cantina,* where the reasonable lunch prices stay in play even at dinner.

Hey, and if you want to try to cook your own Mexican cuisine, check out *Mexican Cooking For Dummies* (published by Wiley), which happens to have been written by the Two Hot Tamales themselves, Mary Sue Milliken and Susan Feniger!

See maps p. 131 and p. 133. 3950 Las Vegas Blvd. S. (in Mandalay Bay). ☎ *702-632-7403.* www.bordergrill.com. *Reservations recommended. Main courses: Lunch $15–$24, dinner $21–$34 ($15–$24 in cantina). AE, DC, DISC, MC, V. Open: Mon–Fri 11 a.m.–10 p.m., Sat–Sun 11 a.m.–11 p.m.*

Bouchon
$$$$ Center Strip   BISTRO

Given that there are those (and we don't argue with them) who think Thomas Keller is the best chef in America, we were mighty happy when he opened up a Vegas outlet. We were less so when we heard it was going to be a branch of his Napa Valley bistro, Bouchon, because Bouchon has never impressed us as we had hoped (unlike Keller's French Laundry, which is everything and more). So we were back to mighty happy when we ate our way through the Vegas Bouchon menu and had not a single misstep. Don't be deceived by the simplicity of what's on offer; even humble "peasant" food is lifted into glory when thoughtfully prepared with fine ingredients. The sweet oysters, the impossibly rich, days-in-the-preparing pâté (which could probably serve four); the bacon and poached egg frisée salad; the garlic-intensive lamb; the perfect beef bourguignon — oh, so good, we're growing a bit faint writing about it.

See maps p. 131 and p. 138. 3355 S. Las Vegas Blvd. S. (in the Venetian). ☎ *702-414-6200.* www.bouchonbistro.com. *Reservations strongly recommended. Main courses: Breakfast $10–$20, dinner $22–$45, Sat/Sun brunch $21–$25. AE, DC, DISC, MC, V. Open: Mon–Fri 7–10:30 a.m. and 5–10 p.m., Sat–Sun 8 a.m.–2 p.m. and 5–10 p.m.; oyster bar daily 3–10 p.m.*

Bougainvillea Café
$ Paradise Road COFFEE SHOP

The Vegas hotel coffee shop is a dying institution. For shame. But this curiously named hotel (the owner's nickname, for some reason) has provided a stalwart version of a vintage coffee shop, with all-day breakfasts, late-night specials (steak and eggs: $5!), and a variety of other options, from prime rib to Chinese to a soup-and-half-sandwich lunch special. It's open all the time. The food is hearty and a serious value. Race you there!

See maps p. 131 and p. 147. 4100 Paradise Rd. (in Terrible's Hotel Casino). ☎ *702-733-7000.* www.terriblescasinos.com. *Main courses: $5–$13. AE, MC, V. Open: Daily 24 hours.*

Burger Bar
$$ South Strip DINER

Sheesh, Vegas and its need for gimmicks. You can't just have a burger place — you have to have one where you "build" your own burger. They don't just mean "add cheese, bacon, and avocado," either; the menu has to have such pricey (and absurd, really) options as anchovies and lobster. Add foie gras, and watch your budget meal suddenly cost $60 per person. But still, start with Ridgefield Farm or Black Angus beef, add a few extras, not to mention some excellent fries and shakes, and its tempting — and fun! — to get a bit creative. Just keep an eye on your tab while you do so. Note the later weekend evening hours.

See maps p. 131 and p. 133. 3930 Las Vegas Blvd. S. (in the Mandalay Place shopping center). ☎ *702-632-9364.* www.mandalayabay.com. *Main courses: $8–$24 (burgers start at $8, depending on kind of beef; toppings start at 65¢ and go way up). AE, DISC, MC, V. Open: Sun–Thurs 11 a.m.–11 p.m., Fri–Sat 10 a.m.–1 a.m.*

Cabo Wabo Cantina
$$ Center Strip MEXICAN

Rocker Sammy Hagar's Cabo San Lucas den of spring-break iniquity attempts a similar vibe on the Las Vegas Strip, and although it may not reach those staggering heights of drunken mayhem, it certainly has more of a party atmosphere than most other restaurants/bars of its ilk. Where else can the wait staff drop everything to do a performance of the Cha Cha slide? Whether or not that's a good thing is up to you, but we can absolutely vouch for the simple Mexican dishes served mostly as a way to soak up the excessive tequila intake. The Cadillac Nachos, where every chip is loaded individually, are a billion times better than the soggy, lightly dressed ones you usually get at Mexican restaurants, and the fajitas are a sizzling wonder, especially the steak variety, which features specially seasoned meat that delivers lots of spicy punch. Or you could simply say to heck with all that and concentrate on Hagar's Cabo Wabo–brand tequila. Nothing wrong with that.

See maps p. 131 and p. 138. 3663 Las Vegas Blvd. S. (in Planet Hollywood). ☎ *702-385-2226.* www.cabowabocantinalv.com. *Main courses: $10–$24. AE, DISC, MC, V. Open: Daily 11 a.m.–2 a.m.*

Café Heidelberg German Deli and Restaurant
$$ Off the Beaten Path   DELI/GERMAN

It's true that Germany is no France when it comes to food, but the hearty menu options here may be a good choice if truffles are simply smelly fungus to you. You can either battle the locals for one of the six booths or order food to go from the deli. Come for the very reasonably priced lunch, and plan on sharing the huge portions . . . or live to regret it. Try some schnitzel or liebchen, or learn the difference between bratwurst and knockwurst, courtesy of their sausage sampler. Wash it all down with German beer.

See maps p. 131 and p. 143. 604 E. Sahara Ave. ☎ *702-731-5310. Reservations highly recommended Fri–Sat nights. Main courses: Lunch mostly under $13, dinner $20–$26. DISC, MC, V. Open: Mon–Tues 11 a.m.–3 p.m., Wed–Sun 11 a.m.–8 p.m.; deli opens daily at 10 a.m.*

Capriotti's
$ Off the Beaten Path   SANDWICHES/AMERICAN

Actually, this place is barely a block off the north part of the Strip, so it's an easy swing — one you owe to yourself to make. Some of the best sandwiches we've ever had came from Capriotti's. Possibly it's because they roast their own beef and turkey on the premises, and certainly because they then stuff those contents (or Italian cold cuts, meatballs, sausages, and even some entirely veggie options) into monster-size submarine sandwiches. Even the "small" is too big — two people can share it, which makes this place easier on the wallet. The most popular is the Bobby; with turkey, stuffing, and cranberry sauce combined on a French roll, it's a complete Thanksgiving dinner in handy packaging, any time of year. We prefer the Slaw B. Joe: roast beef, provolone, coleslaw, and Russian dressing. Grab a couple sandwiches if you want to pack a lunch for a day's sightseeing out of the city, or do like we do and pick up a few for your trip out of town.

See maps p. 131 and p. 143. 324 W. Sahara Ave. (at Las Vegas Boulevard South). ☎ *702-474-0229.* www.cappriotis.com. *Most sandwiches under $10. AE, MC, V. Open: Mon–Sat 10 a.m.–8 p.m., Sun 11 a.m.–7 p.m.*

Carnival World Buffet
$$ Center Strip   BUFFET

This is an excellent buffet with cheerfully decorative food booths set up like stations in an upscale food court. And it serves up an incredible selection, including cooked-to-order "South American" stir-fries, a Brazilian mixed grill, barbecue and ribs, Mexican, Chinese, sushi and teppanyaki, Italian, and diner food (burgers and hot dogs). The desserts are especially indulgent. Everything is fresh and well prepared. There's a good reason it's the most popular in town, but that means longer lines than just about any other buffet.

See maps p. 131 and p. 138. 3700 W. Flamingo Rd. (in the Rio Hotel & Casino). ☎ *702-252-7777.* www.riolasvegas.com. *Reservations not accepted. Buffet prices: Breakfast $15, lunch $17, dinner $24, Sat–Sun champagne brunch $24. AE, DC, MC, V. Open: Daily 8 a.m.–11 p.m.*

Charlie Palmer Steak
$$$$$ South Strip   STEAKHOUSE

We mentioned Charlie Palmer a few pages earlier; this is his version of that Vegas staple, the steakhouse. Every hotel has one. Some of them are cheaper than others. Some are better than others. This one isn't cheap, but it does head the list of "better than." But don't fret too much about the price. The portions (22–44 oz. each, no kidding) are so large, not only *can* you share, you really, really should. We prefer the tender rib-eye to the more authoritatively flavored Kansas City. If you also share some (generously portioned) sides like truffled potato puree and citrus-braised asparagus, you'll still have room for a stylish dessert.

See maps p. 131 and p. 133. 3960 Las Vegas Blvd. S. (in the Four Seasons Hotel). ☎ **702-632-5120.** www.charliepalmersteaklv.com. *Reservations suggested. Main courses: $30–$42. AE, DC, DISC, MC, V. Open: Daily 5–10:30 p.m.*

Cravings
$$$ Center Strip   BUFFET

Our favorite midrange buffet choice, this place features a lavish, diverse spread of much better quality than that found at cheaper spots. The enormous salad bar, with more than 25 types of salads, and the dessert table, laden with sweet temptations (it sounds silly, but can we say that the chocolate pudding is particularly good?), are especially notable. You can probably skip the hot entrees in favor of Asian or Mexican choices. Sunday brunch adds free champagne, smoked salmon, and fruit-filled crepes for starters.

See maps p. 131 and p. 138. 3400 Las Vegas Blvd. S. (in the Mirage). ☎ **702-791-7111.** www.mirage.com. *Reservations not accepted. Buffet prices: Breakfast $14, lunch $18, dinner $25, Sun brunch $23; kids 5–10 eat for reduced prices, kids 4 and under eat free. AE, DC, DISC, MC, V. Open: Daily 7 a.m.–10 p.m.*

Delmonico Steakhouse
$$$$$ Center Strip   STEAKHOUSE

You watch his Food Network shows (or you've at least heard about them), and even though you didn't watch his CBS sitcom (who did?), you want to sample his food. But you don't like fish, so you aren't going to Emeril's Seafood over in the MGM Grand. Thoughtfully, Emeril (Bam!) Lagasse opened a steak restaurant in Vegas just for you, where you can try some

Center Strip Dining

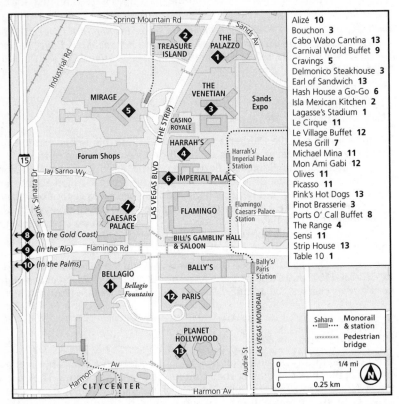

Alizé	**10**
Bouchon	**3**
Cabo Wabo Cantina	**13**
Carnival World Buffet	**9**
Cravings	**5**
Delmonico Steakhouse	**3**
Earl of Sandwich	**13**
Hash House a Go-Go	**6**
Isla Mexican Kitchen	**2**
Lagasse's Stadium	**1**
Le Cirque	**11**
Le Village Buffet	**12**
Mesa Grill	**7**
Michael Mina	**11**
Mon Ami Gabi	**12**
Olives	**11**
Picasso	**11**
Pink's Hot Dogs	**13**
Pinot Brasserie	**3**
Ports O' Call Buffet	**8**
The Range	**4**
Sensi	**11**
Strip House	**13**
Table 10	**1**

of his special dishes (smoked mushrooms and tasso ham over pasta), his twists on classic New Orleans Creole cuisine, and wonderful cuts of red meat. Portions are generous, so think about sharing.

See maps p. 131 and above. 3355 Las Vegas Blvd. S. (in the Venetian). ☎ *702-414-3737.* www.emerils.com. *Reservations strongly recommended for dinner. Main courses: $40–$50. AE, DC, DISC, MC, V. Open: Sun–Thurs 11:30 a.m.–2 p.m. and 5–10 p.m., Fri–Sat 11:30 a.m.–2 p.m. and 5–10:30 p.m.*

Diablo's Cantina
$$$ South Strip   MEXICAN

It used to be difficult to find a good, moderately priced Mexican meal on the Strip, but these days joints that specialize in just that very thing are popping up everywhere. What sets Diablo's apart from the pack is the quality of the food, which rivals restaurants twice its price for freshness and flavor. The stuffed quesadillas are a meal unto themselves, with our favorite being the Club variety with steak, pulled pork, guacamole, and sour cream. The Mexican pizzas on crispy tortillas are topped with so much cheese and meat (mmm, chorizo!) that you'll never want a "regular" pizza again. Empanadas, burritos, fajitas, and the like give you lots of traditional choices while hamburgers, wraps, ribs, and even filet mignon provide options for those with more sensitive taste buds. With its Strip-facing wall of windows and airy second-floor patio, you get great people-watching opportunities to go with your dinner.

See maps p. 131 and p. 133. 3663 Las Vegas Blvd. S. (in the Monte Carlo). ☎ *702-385-2226. www.montecarlo.com. Main courses: $12–$30. AE, DISC, MC, V. Open: Daily 11 a.m. to midnight.*

Dick's Last Resort
$$ South Strip   DINER

You think all we care about is truffles and foie gras and chichi food and servile wait staff. Good heavens, no. We like that stuff a lot, don't get us wrong. But we also like a good, rowdy spot with hearty food that needs lots of napkins. Maybe the gimmick at this place — where the waiters are good-naturedly surly and abusive — is a bit much. But so are the portions, and we mean that in a good way. Buckets (literally!) of fried goodies, such as ribs or honey-glazed chicken, overly generous portions of chicken-fried steak, and one heck of a massive burger — it's definitely the food you get while watching the Big Game or when you want to fill up one of those bottomless-pit teenagers (though the atmosphere is a little bit closer to R than PG-13). And what's wrong with that? Nothing, we say.

See maps p. 131 and p. 133. 3850 Las Vegas Blvd. S. (in Excalibur). ☎ *702-597-7991. www.dickslastresort.com. Main courses: $13–$24. AE, MC, V. Mon–Thurs 1 p.m. to "late," Fri–Sun 11 a.m. to "late."*

Earl of Sandwich
$ Center Strip   SANDWICHES

Don't you wish your ancestor invented the sandwich? (Well, someone had to.) The 11th Earl of Sandwich, descendent of that culinary hero, has given his heraldic stamp of approval to this venture, where they serve — oh, you know. (You may be a Dummy, but you aren't stupid!) Actually, they have more than just sandwiches — including wraps (a sandwich by any other name), salads, and smoothies — but with options like three-cheese grilled cheese with bacon, and roast beef with horseradish cream and cheddar cheese, it may be hard to get to that part of the menu. The sandwiches aren't the monsters you find at Capriotti's, but at these prices, you can always get two. And with these hours, you've got later-night munchies covered as well.

See maps p. 131 and p. 138. 3667 Las Vegas Blvd. S. (in Planet Hollywood). ☎ *702-463-0259. www.earlofsandwichusa.com. Main courses: Everything under $6. AE, MC, V. Open: Sun–Thurs 6 a.m. to midnight, Fri–Sat 6 a.m.–2 a.m.*

El Sombrero Café
$ Downtown MEXICAN

We want you to go here simply because it's the kind of mom-and-pop joint that's fast disappearing in Vegas. What's more, it's been around since 1950, which, for Vegas, makes it practically prehistoric. You want to go here if you like real Mexican food (well, what Americans perceive as real Mexican food). It's not in the nicest part of town, but you find the inside to be quite a bit friendlier than its neighborhood. Portions (such as the large enchilada and taco combo) are generous, reliably good, and nicely spicy, and they won't mind if you ask for the beef burrito to be made with chicken.

See map p. 131. 807 S. Main St. ☎ **702-382-9234.** *Main courses: Everything under $15. AE, MC, V. Open: Mon–Thurs 11 a.m.–4 p.m., Fri–Sat 11 a.m.–8:30 p.m.*

Emeril's New Orleans Fish House
$$$$$ South Strip AMERICAN/SEAFOOD/CAJUN

New Orleans–based celebrity chef Emeril Lagasse may be spreading himself a bit thin, between all his restaurants and all his shows on the Food Network. At least, it seemed that way to us after we ate here not many days after eating at his original (and still terrific) New Orleans restaurant, an experience that only highlighted the somewhat more pallid meal here. Again, this may be the fish-house-in-Vegas syndrome. How else to explain why the spiced rib-eye here was better than the foie-gras-topped ahi tuna? You may be best off trying some appetizers, because you haven't lived until you've tried Lagasse's savory lobster cheesecake, or the barbecue shrimp, drenched in a garlicky Worcestershire-butter sauce and served with a rosemary biscuit. The banana cream pie is the star of a sinful dessert menu.

See maps p. 131 and p. 133. 3799 Las Vegas Blvd. S. (in the MGM Grand). ☎ **702-891-7374.** *www.emerils.com. Reservations required. Main courses: $17–$30 lunch, $28–$45 dinner. AE, DC, DISC, MC, V. Open: Daily 11:30 a.m.–2:30 p.m. and 5–10:30 p.m.*

Fellini's
$$ North Strip ITALIAN

Okay, so we love Bartolotta's authentic — and expensive — Italian food. *Love it.* But seriously? Italian red sauce is the comfort food of our childhood. And when it's done well, there is nothing we love more. Fellini's has it all — the garlicky cheesy bread, the *Amatriciana* with generous helpings of pancetta, basic pizza, even tenderloin tips in a Gorgonzola and shallot cream sauce. Pretty much everyone in your party will find something they secretly love here, unless they're deeply picky eaters or even deeper snobs. A Vegas institution, Fellini's is just the antidote to all the pricier event dining going on elsewhere on the Strip.

See maps p. 131 and p. 143. 2000 Las Vegas Blvd. S. (in the Stratosphere). ☎ **702-383-4859.** *Main courses: $9–$24. AE, DISC, MC, V. Open: Mon–Thurs 5–11 p.m., Fri–Sat 11:30 a.m.–1 a.m.*

Fleur de Lys
$$$$$ South Strip FRENCH

Of the many sophisticated restaurants to choose from in Vegas these days, we single this one out for its combination of mature sexy food and atmosphere. The chef made his name at his highly regarded San Francisco establishment, and his reputation continues unsullied here. The two-story room, half-hidden by billowing drapes, reminds you to dress up to dine while playing footsie with your dining companion. The three- to five-course tasting menus don't come cheap (though they're practically bargains compared to similar high-end restaurants in town), but they're so playful and clever that it feels like a treat, not a mugging. Options are seasonal, but always beautifully composed; plus, a thoughtful vegetarian menu is available. So *ooh la la.*

See maps p. 131 and p. 133. 3950 Las Vegas Blvd. S. (in Mandalay Place). ☎ *702-632-7200.* www.mandalaybay.com. *Reservations recommended. Main courses: 3-course menu $79, 4-course menu $89, 5-course menus $99. AE, DC, DISC, MC, V. Open: Daily 5:30–10:30 p.m.*

Golden Nugget Buffet
$$ Downtown BUFFET

This is the fanciest of the downtown buffets by far, and one of the only two downtown where we can guarantee quality. The salad bar is loaded with extra goodies, former owner Steve Wynn's mom's bread pudding is still featured among the desserts, there's fresh seafood every night, and the Sunday brunches are what that meal should be — even more decadent and indulgent. It's all set in a very plush space with big windows overlooking the pool.

See map p. 131. 129 E. Fremont St. (in the Golden Nugget). ☎ *702-385-7111. Reservations not accepted. Buffet prices: Breakfast $7, lunch $8, dinner $13–$17, Sun brunch $14. AE, DC, DISC, MC, V. Open: Mon–Sat 7 a.m.–10 p.m., Sun 8 a.m.–10 p.m.*

Grand Wok and Sushi Bar
$$$ South Strip PAN-ASIAN

Does your family love Asian food but can't choose between Chinese, Japanese, Vietnamese, or Korean? (Hey, our family has that problem, why wouldn't yours?) Well, here you don't have to, because they serve it all. Surprisingly, it's all done quite well, including the fine sushi. Note that the soups come in huge portions and easily can feed four for a bargain price.

See maps p. 131 and p. 133. 3799 Las Vegas Blvd. S. (in the MGM Grand). ☎ *702-891-7777.* www.mgmgrand.com. *Reservations not accepted. Main courses: $15–$38, sushi $7–$30. AE, DC, DISC, MC, V. Open: Restaurant Sun–Thurs 11 a.m.–10 p.m., Fri–Sat 11 a.m.–1 a.m.; sushi bar Mon–Thurs 5–10 p.m., Fri–Sat 11 a.m.–1 a.m., Sun 11 a.m.–10 p.m.*

Hash House A Go Go
$$$ Center Strip   AMERICAN

So there you are at a breakfast buffet, faced with warming trays full of runny scrambled eggs and limp bacon and you think to yourself, "Wouldn't it be nice if there were a place where I could get a pancake the size of a pizza instead?" Your prayers are answered at Hash House, one of the most deliriously enjoyable restaurants in town. Its "twisted farm food" is all served in portions that are meant to be shared, but everything is so good you may want to hoard it for yourself. We're not joking about those mammoth pancakes (the brown-sugar banana version is perfection, but the Snickers variety is worth consideration), and the super-sizing continues with the waffles (checkerboard size with bacon baked right into it — genius!), fried chicken with bacon mashed potatoes, pork tenderloins topped with scrambled eggs, and its signature hashes, which cover the gamut from corned beef to meatloaf with spinach. Partied too much the night before? How about the "O'Hare of the Dog That Bit You" — a 24-ounce Budweiser served in a paper bag with a side of bacon. How can you not love a place that has something like that on the menu? Prices seem high until you remember the portions and take a bite. It has a full lunch and dinner menu as well (burgers, pastas, and more). The Imperial Palace branch is the most convenient for most visitors, but keep in mind there is another location at 6800 W. Sahara Ave., if you find yourself out exploring and get really hungry.

See maps p. 131 and p. 138. 3535 Las Vegas Blvd. S. (in the Imperial Palace). ☎ *702-731-3311.* www.hashhouseagogo.com. *Main courses: $9–$14 breakfast, $6–$14 lunch, $7–$24 dinner. AE, DISC, MC, V. Open: Sun–Thurs 7 a.m.–11 p.m., Fri–Sat 7 a.m.–2 a.m.*

Isla Mexican Kitchen
$$ Center Strip   MEXICAN

Isla is a good choice for a party, given how the "modern Mexican cuisine" menu — not to mention largest collection of tequila in Vegas — lends itself to sharing and silliness. Consider guacamole made on demand (including variations made with lobster and passion fruit) and sharable starters, such as empanadas with dried cherries and a chipotle tomato sauce, not to mention roast pork with a pumpkin-seed sauce, along with typical tacos and burritos for those who would rather stick with the familiar. Caramel cupcakes come with a chocolate cactus stuck into them, a kind of playfulness we're total suckers for. Somewhat late nights make this a good place for a drop in during a night of fun.

See maps p. 131 and p. 138. 3300 Las Vegas Blvd. S. (in Treasure Island). ☎ *866-286-3809 or 702-894-7223.* www.treasureisland.com. *Main courses: $10–$30. AE, DC, DISC, MC, V. Open: Daily 4–10 p.m.*

Julian Serrano
$$$$ South Strip   SPANISH

The big-time chef behind the big-ticket restaurant Picasso at Bellagio has turned his attention to things of a smaller nature here at his eponymously named restaurant. Tapas is the main feature of the menu, with the

North Strip Dining

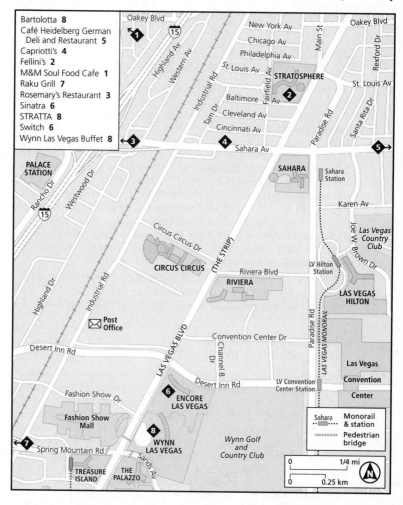

Bartolotta **8**
Café Heidelberg German
  Deli and Restaurant **5**
Capriotti's **4**
Fellini's **2**
M&M Soul Food Cafe **1**
Raku Grill **7**
Rosemary's Restaurant **3**
Sinatra **6**
STRATTA **8**
Switch **6**
Wynn Las Vegas Buffet **8**

selections both delicate (lobster with molecular pineapple) and hearty (eggs, fried potatoes, and chorizo) all served on appetizer-style sticks. Spanish flair is everywhere, but there is surprisingly little in the way of set-your-mouth-on fire spiciness, a welcome change from most Latin restaurants, which seem to want to set your mouth on fire the second you sit down. If you don't want to do the small-plate samba, it has several big-people-sized main courses, including several wonderful paellas with saffron rice and your choice of vegetables, meats, and/or seafood. The version with chorizo, chicken, and rabbit is so good you'll forget that you're eating rabbit. It's easy to ring up a big bill here — tapas prices seem cheap until you realize you have to order at least three per person to make a full meal.

See maps p. 131 and p. 133. 3730 Las Vegas Blvd. S. (in Aria Las Vegas). ☎ **877-230-2742.** www.arialasvegas.com. *Reservations recommended. Tapas: $8–$25. Main courses: $18–$35. AE, DC, DISC, MC, V. Open: Daily 11 a.m.–11 p.m.*

Lagasse's Stadium
$$$ Center Strip   AMERICAN

The mission of Emeril's latest Vegas venture seems mostly to be to serve sports fanatics. With more than 100 television screens showing virtually every sport imaginable and the ability to bet on just about any of them, the Stadium (so named because of the area with tiers of couches facing some really big screens) is probably most satisfying for those who just want to watch the big game. But it also serves food — some of Emeril's signature dishes, such as his crab cakes, are offered, but it's mostly fancy pub grub, from burgers and sandwiches to pastas and steaks, with lots and lots of Buffalo-wing-style munchies available for the more casual diner. Although nothing is particularly "Bam!" worthy, it's all good and portioned to satisfy the appetites of the most unruly of sports fans — and plenty of them show up, so don't expect a quiet meal. Prices are surprisingly affordable until you get to the part where most tables have a $25- to $50-per-person minimum, so no crab-cakes-and-a-beer meals for you, sorry.

See maps p. 131 and p. 138. 3325 Las Vegas Blvd. S. (in Palazzo Las Vegas). ☎ **702-607-2665.** www.emerils.com. *Main courses: $12–$29. AE, DC, DISC, MC, V. Open: Mon–Fri 11 a.m.–10 p.m., Sat 7:30 a.m.–10 p.m., Sun 8 a.m.–10 p.m.*

L'Atelier de Joël Robuchon
$$$$$ South Strip   FRENCH

People who care about such things know that Chef Robuchon has won all sorts of fancy culinary awards, from coveted Michelin stars for his earlier establishments in Europe to the James Beard award for Best New Restaurant 2007 for this very spot. They get all giddy over that sort of thing. So do food critics, who have given his other restaurant, Joël Robuchon at the Mansion, their highest accolades. We were hard-pressed to choose between the two but decided that the counter-seating setup here, where you can interact with wait staff and chefs alike, makes for a more fun foodie experience. Also, as expensive as this is, it's not heart-stoppingly expensive like the Mansion. Portions come in both small-plate-tasting and main-course sizes, and the menu changes seasonally. Look for playful — yes, fun — dishes such as La Pied de Cochon (pâté made of pig's feet topped with shaved truffle and parmesan on toast) or quail with foie gras stuffed under the skin, with curious desserts such as sheep's milk yogurt panna cotta with Bergamot tea infusion. Under the circumstances, the tasting menu is the way to go, even if it doesn't allow you the freedom of random grazing.

See maps p. 131 and p. 133. 3799 Las Vegas Blvd. S. (in MGM Grand). ☎ **702-891-7358.** www.mgmgrand.com. *Reservations strongly recommended. 8-course discovery menu: $135. Small plates: $16–$32. Main courses: $38–$70. AE, DC, DISC, MC, V. Open: Sun–Thurs 5:30–10:30 p.m., Fri–Sat 5–10:30 p.m.*

Lawry's The Prime Rib
$$$$$ Paradise Road   STEAKHOUSE

Sure, you can get prime rib anywhere in town for under $6. But it's not going to taste like this. Lawry's didn't invent prime rib, but it may as well have. Dare we say that no one does it better? Sure, we dare. The elaborate meal presentation includes 50 years' worth of traditional touches, such as the spinning salad bowl (a production you have to see to appreciate) and the metal carving carts piled high with meat for you to select from. You can find other things on the menu these days (fresh fish, for example), but why bother? Come here for a seriously satisfying carnivorous experience.

See maps p. 131 and p. 147. 4043 Howard Hughes Pkwy. (just west of Paradise Road). ☎ *702-893-2223.* www.lawrysonline.com. *Reservations recommended. Main courses: $32–$49. AE, DC, DISC, MC, V. Open: Mon–Thurs 11:30 a.m.–2:30 p.m. and 5–10 p.m., Fri 11:30 a.m.–2:30 p.m. and 5–11 p.m., Sat 5–11 p.m., and Sun 5–10 p.m.*

Le Cirque
$$$$$ Center Strip   NOUVELLE FRENCH

Le Cirque originated in New York and was practically legendary there. This branch varies between user-friendly and just a touch frightening. We've had excellent meals here, and ones that made us wonder what all the fuss was about. The menu changes regularly but some things we loved: anything with truffles (especially the sweet and tender lobster salad topped with truffle dressing); foie gras pâté, also topped with the truffle dressing; and the roasted honey-glazed duck with figs. All the desserts are playful, pretty creations that are almost too good-looking to eat. Almost.

See maps p. 131 and p. 138. 3600 Las Vegas Blvd. S. (in Bellagio). ☎ **702-693-7223.** www.bellagio.com. *Reservations required. Jacket required for gentleman; no jeans, T-shirts, shorts, or sneakers. Prix fixe dinner: $98 and up. AE, DC, DISC, MC, V. Open: Tues–Sun 5:30–10 p.m.*

Le Village Buffet
$$$ Center Strip   BUFFET

You may wonder why we would suggest coming to such a comparatively expensive buffet when there are much cheaper options. Mainly it's because the more expensive restaurants that we're so cheerfully telling you to eat at are *still* more costly than the most expensive buffets. And do they give you the same amount of food? No, they do not. Not only is this buffet rather pretty, but the food stations also represent the different regions of France, offering choices indigenous to the region (Alsace, Provence, Burgundy) in question. You enjoy a more imaginative (to say nothing of larger) meal than those found at the usual buffet suspects.

See maps p. 131 and p. 138. 3665 Las Vegas Blvd. S. (in Paris Las Vegas). ☎ **888-266-5687.** www.parislasvegas.com. *Buffet prices: Breakfast $15, lunch $18, dinner $25, brunch $25. AE, DC, DISC, MC, V. Open: Daily 7 a.m.–10 p.m.*

Lotus of Siam
$ **Off the Beaten Path** THAI

Yeah, it's out in the middle of nowhere in one god-awful ugly strip mall, but this nothing of a place has been called no less than the best Thai restaurant in North America. That claim now exhausts us — how can we prove it? At least you know it's not going to stink, no matter what. It makes all your usual Thai favorites very well, but be sure to ask for the special north Thailand menu, because that's where it shines and where it's made its reputation. Skip the lunch buffet, even though it's a bargain price, and try some sour pork Issan sausage or *nam kao tod* (sour pork Issan sausage ground up with lime, green onion, fresh chili, and ginger served with crispy rice). We love *sua rong hai* (literally "weeping tiger" — soft marinated, grilled beef). Have some sticky rice, just like it is off a cart in Bangkok, for dessert. And then congratulate yourself for eating perhaps the most authentic food in all of Vegas.

See maps p. 131 and 147. 953 E. Sahara Ave., no. A-5. ☎ **702-735-3033.** *www. saipinchutima.com. Reservations strongly suggested for dinner. Main courses: Lunch buffet $9, other dishes $9–$20. AE, MC, V. Open: Mon–Fri 11:30 a.m.–2 p.m. and 5:30–9:30 p.m., Sat–Sun 5:30–10 p.m.*

Main Street Station Garden Court Buffet
$$ **Downtown** BUFFET

This is the best buffet in downtown, and possibly the city. It has succeeded in rising above the rest, with a pretty dining room (high ceilings and actual windows provide real sunlight — a rarity in Vegas) and food that is decidedly a cut above what you get in the other buffets around town. Selections are prepared at stations that dish out barbecue and soul food, Chinese and Hawaiian specialties, and wood-fired brick-oven pizzas. On Friday nights, you can dine on a seafood buffet that features lobster and other fresh fish.

See map p. 131. 200 N. Main St. (in the Main Street Station). ☎ **702-387-1896.** *www. mainstreetcasino.com. Reservations not accepted. Buffet prices: Breakfast $7, lunch $8, dinner $11–$16, Sat–Sun champagne brunch $11. AE, DC, DISC, MC, V. Open: Daily 7–10:30 a.m., 11 a.m.–3 p.m., and 4–10 p.m.*

M&M Soul Food Cafe
$$ **Off the Beaten Path** AMERICAN/SOUTHERN

Would you like gravy with that? If the answer is yes, then M&M Soul Food is just your kind of place. Authentic deep-South home cooking is the specialty here with barbecue, chitterlings, collard greens, corn bread, okra, and black-eyed peas just the tip of the finger-lickin'-good iceberg. Get the fried chicken — a little spicy and more moist than it has any right to be — and then get it "smothered" (yes, covered in gravy), and you'll never want to talk to the Colonel again. Portions are enormous, and all the main courses come with a choice of three sides, which makes the high-at-first-glance prices much more palatable. It's worth noting that this is a no-frills

Paradise Road Dining

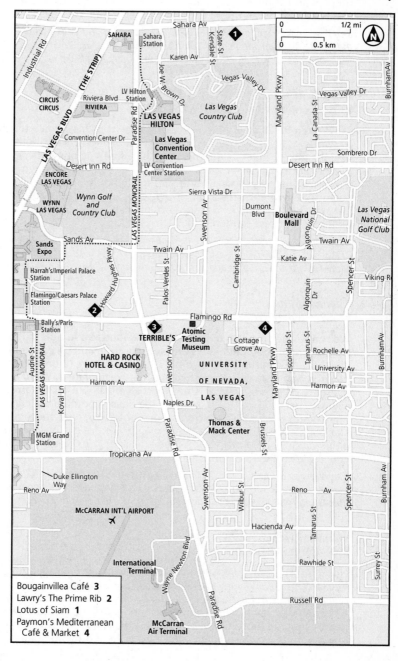

Bougainvillea Café **3**
Lawry's The Prime Rib **2**
Lotus of Siam **1**
Paymon's Mediterranean
Café & Market **4**

restaurant in a no-frills neighborhood that could be a little intimidating to those who rarely venture out of suburbia or away from the Strip, but you're probably safer here than you are crossing Las Vegas Boulevard.

See maps p. 131 and p. 143. 3923 W. Charleston Blvd. (at Valley View Boulevard in the Westgate Shopping Center). ☎ *702-453-7685.* www.mmsoulfoodcafe.com. *Main courses: $6–$17. AE, DISC, MC, V. Open: Daily 7 a.m.–8 p.m.*

Mesa Grill
$$$$ Center Strip   SOUTHWESTERN

Celebrity chef Bobby Flay is well known from his shows on the Food Network, so if you've been wondering what his food is all about, here's an opportunity to find out. (Remember that Bobby is busy with restaurants in New York and the aforementioned TV career, so although he created the menu, you likely won't find him in the kitchen here.) Like so many celebrity-chef joints, it's a bit overpriced; so come here for lunch to try such over-the-top dishes as blue corn pancakes with BBQ duck and ancho-chili honey-glazed salmon.

See maps p. 131 and p. 138. 3570 Las Vegas Blvd. S. (in Caesars Palace). ☎ *702-731-7731.* www.bobbyflay.com. *Main courses: $23–$45. AE, DC, DISC, MC, V. Open: Mon–Fri 11 a.m.–2:30 p.m. and 5–11 p.m., Sat–Sun 10:30 a.m.–3 p.m. and 5–11 p.m.*

Michael Mina
$$$$$ Center Strip   SEAFOOD

We're always somewhat dubious about seafood restaurants in the desert — yes, we know about jet planes and refrigeration and other modern conveniences — and although our initial experience here (a branch of a terrific place in San Francisco) soothed our concerns, more recent visits have made us skeptical again. It's not the fish itself, but all the preparations seemed just a bit blah. Miso-glazed sea bass, a noted dish, came out like really fancy sukiyaki (a traditional one-pot soup), and the signature lobster pot pie was too soupy and overpriced. Service can be kind but absent-minded. Get silly with the homemade root-beer float, complete with chocolate straws and homemade cookies.

See maps p. 131 and p. 138. 3600 Las Vegas Blvd. S. (in Bellagio). ☎ *702-693-7223.* www.michaelmina.net. *Reservations recommended. Main courses: $36–$72 (lobster and whole foie gras higher). AE, DISC, MC, V. Open: Thurs–Tues 5:30–10 p.m.*

Mon Ami Gabi
$$$ Center Strip   BISTRO

Ooh la la! This cute-as-a-button place is one of our favorite dining spots in Vegas. You get all your classic bistro fare, from hearty onion soup to *croque-monsieur* (grilled ham and cheese) to steak and *pomme frites.* Although you can run up a hefty tab here, note that just eating that same hearty soup or those clever sandwiches will keep the prices down while filling you up most satisfactorily. And although it's absolutely a Vegas version of a bistro, even cynics have to admit that it got the décor just right. Seat your amour on the patio right on the Strip and gaze into each other's eyes, but don't get so swept up in each other that you forget to order desserts — they're huge here.

See maps p. 131 and p. 138. 3655 Las Vegas Blvd. S. (in the Paris Las Vegas). ☎ *702-944-4224.* www.monamigabi.com. *Reservations recommended. Main courses: $18–$40. AE, DC, DISC, MC, V. Open: Sun–Fri 7 a.m.–11 p.m., Sat 7 a.m. to midnight.*

More: The Buffet at Luxor
$$ South Strip BUFFET

This buffet offers great value and better-than-average food. Set inside an amusing "archaeological dig," it has all the buffet standards (salads, fresh fruit, a carving station with turkey and ham), plus some interesting twists, such as Mexican, Chinese stir-fry, and Italian pastas. You may feel like lying down in King Tut's tomb after negotiating the long lines at peak dining times; try to come during off-hours after the rush has died down.

See maps p. 131 and p. 133. 3900 Las Vegas Blvd. S. (in the Luxor). ☎ *702-262-4000. Reservations not accepted. Buffet prices: Breakfast $12, lunch $14, dinner $20. AE, DC, DISC, MC, V. Open: Daily 7 a.m.–10 p.m.*

Olives
$$$$ Center Strip ITALIAN/MEDITERRANEAN

Todd English, the man behind this restaurant, is considered to be a major American chef, so you know you're in for something good. Although the prices here can be budget busting, you actually can eat here for *moderate* cost. First of all, come when the cheaper lunch menu is in play (11 a.m.–3 p.m.), and stick to pastas and the flatbread pizzas. The latter are a cracker-thin-crust creation topped with such unusual items as Moroccan lamb and feta cheese, and prosciutto and figs. They're really quite good — we wish this place were in our neighborhood so that we could eat these regularly. One pizza can feed two people, though you may want to add a fresh, pretty salad, a large sandwich (note the pressed Cuban), or a bowl of pasta, such as the spaghetini with roasted garlic and tomatoes (wonderful, with just the right amount of richness).

See maps p. 131 and p. 138. 3600 Las Vegas Blvd. S. (in Bellagio). ☎ *702-693-7223.* www.toddenglish.com. *Reservations recommended for parties of 6 or more. Main courses: Lunch $15–$25, dinner $24–$52. AE, DC, DISC, MC, V. Open: Daily 11 a.m.–2:45 p.m. and 5–10:30 p.m.*

Paymon's Mediterranean Café & Lounge
$$ Paradise Road GREEK/MIDDLE EASTERN

This authentic, family-owned Middle Eastern restaurant offers solid food with no glitz or neon in sight. In fact, the semi-outdoors courtyard area is one of the few nonhotel dining choices that succeeds at a non-mini-mall identity. The *gyros* (lamb and beef in a pita) are probably your best choice.

The menu also features other favorites, such as phyllo pie served with a side of hummus, and chicken and vegetable kabobs. Eat here and then get some at the adjoining market to take home. There's also a "hookah lounge" attached to the restaurant, where you have a few drinks, get a bite to eat, and, yes, smoke a hookah pipe.

See maps p. 131 and p. 147. 4147 S. Maryland Pkwy. (at Flamingo Road). ☎ *702-731-6030.* www.paymons.com. *Reservations not accepted. Main courses: $10–$19; most sandwiches $8 or less. AE, MC, DISC, V. Open: Daily 11 a.m.–1 a.m.*

Picasso
$$$$$ **Center Strip**   **NOUVELLE FRENCH**

Former Bellagio owner Steve Wynn spent nearly a year wooing superstar chef Julian Serrano — a man who works a kitchen the way Springsteen works a concert — away from his highly praised San Francisco restaurant. Wynn succeeded, and it's your gain. Yep, the prices are what you may expect from a place with more than $30 million worth of genuine Picassos hanging on the wall, but Serrano's cooking produces really good food the way Picasso's painting produced really good art. The menu changes nightly (though lately it seems to rotate among a number of regular dishes), giving you a choice of two multicourse tasting menus (portions are small so that you can finish everything without feeling as if you're going to explode). We fell hard for the corn flan (like eating solid sunshine) with chunks of lobster, and the perfectly tender lamb crusted with black truffles. For dessert, we got silly over the molten chocolate soufflé cake with homemade chocolate ice cream — then dreamed about it all night long.

See maps p. 131 and p. 138. 3600 Las Vegas Blvd. S. (in the Bellagio). ☎ *702-693-7223. Reservations recommended. Main courses: 4-course prix fixe $113, 5-course degustation $123. AE, DC, DISC, MC, V. Open: Wed–Mon 6–9:30 p.m.*

Pink's Hot Dogs
$ **Center Strip**   **AMERICAN**

Over on La Brea Avenue in Los Angeles is a tiny little shack of a joint serving up hot dogs, and at most times of the day and night, there's a line down the block to get one. As soon as word gets out that these hot dogs have made their way to Vegas, you may see the same kind of lines down the Strip. Pink's has been in business since 1939 and its all-beef dogs, cooked with a "snap" to them, are good on their own, but the wild-and-wooly toppings are what make people sit up and take notice. Its chili is legendary — meaty and not too spicy — but that's kid's play. How about bacon or guacamole or pastrami? Maybe some nacho cheese and jalapeños? Sauerkraut and sour cream? The possibilities are almost endless. Each dog comes piled high almost to the point of being impossible to eat, but we're sure you'll find a way. Pink's also serves burgers and burritos, plus some non-beef hot dogs, but we sort of feel like eating any of that would be sacrilegious. The dogs are so good that the fact that they're so cheap is almost like a bonus.

See maps p. 131 and p. 138. 3663 Las Vegas Blvd. S. (in Planet Hollywood). ☎ *702-785-5555.* www.pinkslv.com. *Main courses: $5–$9. AE, MC, V. Sun–Thurs 10:30 a.m. to midnight, Fri–Sat 10:30 a.m.–3 a.m.*

Pinot Brasserie
$$$$ Center Strip   BISTRO

Here's a perfect choice if you want a really nice meal but don't want food that's too — how shall we say? — froufrou. Here's a secret about French food: An actual French person's favorite thing to eat is a small steak, a handful of french fries, and some wine. *Voilá!* Sound scary? Of course not. And so although this charming bistro (we love the clubby, intimate interior here) serves "French" fare, it's going to be things that you can easily recognize and immediately love. Favorites include the roast chicken accompanied by a heap of garlic fries, a lovely onion soup, even more lovely and crunchy salads (sometimes with toasted slices of bread topped with such things as herbed goat cheese), and a sublime homemade chocolate ice cream. Simple. Delicious. Perfect. It also offers some more complicated — but not outrageously so — items, if you feel inclined. Consider coming at lunch, when prices fall into the *moderate* category.

See maps p. 131 and p. 138. 3355 Las Vegas Blvd. S. (in the Venetian). ☎ *702-414-8888.* www.patinagroup.com. *Reservations suggested for dinner. Main course: Lunch $16–$31, dinner $32–$46. AE, DISC, MC, V. Open: Sun–hurs 11:30 a.m.–3 p.m. and 5:30–10 p.m.; Fri–Sat 11:30 a.m.–3 p.m. and 5:30–10:30 p.m.*

Ports O' Call Buffet
$ East of Strip   BUFFET

Bummed that the glory days of Vegas buffets — and by that we don't mean quality-of-food-wise, we mean ratio-of-quantity-to-cost-wise — seem to be behind it? Us, too. That's why we're sending you off the Strip and over here. Cheaper than anything on the Strip, but not that far away, Ports O' Call has as much of a range as any buffet ought, keeps the warm food warm, and has an all you-can-eat-steak night. Ah, nostalgia.

See maps p. 131 and p. 138. 4400 W. Flamingo Rd. (in the Gold Coast). ☎ *702-367-7111.* www.goldcoastcasino.com. *Buffet prices: Breakfast $7, lunch $9, dinner $13–$17 (for specialty nights), brunch $13. Open: Mon–Sat 7 a.m.–10:30 a.m., 11 a.m.–3 p.m., and 4–9 p.m.; Sun 8 a.m.–3 p.m. and 4–9 p.m.*

Raku Grill
$$$ Off the Beaten Path   JAPANESE

When many of the chefs in town get off work, they come here to eat — that should tell you just about everything you need to know. This tiny hidden gem specializes in small plates from its Robata grill, most served on skewers, ranging from the offbeat (pork ear, pork cheek, Kobe beef liver) to the mainstream (chicken breast, Kobe with wasabi, lamb, seared foie gras, grilled duck, asparagus or tomato wrapped in bacon, ground chicken, and much more). Daily specials include seafood flown in from Japan and there is also an Oden (broth pot) and rice, noodle, and soup dishes, but the Robata grill should dominate your choices. The smoky charcoal grill brings everything to life but allows each dish to have its own distinct flavors. Although most of the selections are only a few bucks (most under $5), it's easy to ring up a sizable check at the end — the food is so good here it's like that famous potato chip saying: "You can't eat just one." Nor should you.

See maps p. 131 and p. 143. 5030 W. Spring Mountain Rd. #2 (at Decatur Boulevard). ☎ *702-367-3511.* www.raku-grill.com. *Reservations required. Main courses: Robata grill items $2@nd$14; other items $3.50–$16. AE, MC, V. Open: Daily 6 p.m.–3 a.m.*

The Range
$$$$$ Center Strip   STEAKHOUSE

This very fine steakhouse has a warm copper-and-mahogany interior that's classy and plush without being intimidating. Panoramic windows offer incredible views of the Strip below. The kitchen does chicken, sea-food, salads, and, of course, wonderful tender steaks best, so the menu naturally features these items. As an added touch, side dishes are served family style. Try not to miss the five-onion soup appetizer (baked in a large onion with cheese) or the chicken quesadillas.

See maps p. 131 and p. 138. 3475 Las Vegas Blvd. S. (in Harrah's Las Vegas). ☎ *702-369-5084. Reservations highly recommended. AE, DC, DISC, MC, V. Main courses: $20–$59. Open: Daily 5:30–10:30 p.m.*

Red Square
$$$$ South Strip   CONTINENTAL

No one parties like the Red Party, and this restaurant sets out to prove it. No, no, no — no Communist propaganda here; quite the opposite, as sym-bols and artifacts from the days of the Iron Curtain are defaced or otherwise turned into capitalist décor. Heck, when folks protested the giant statue of Lenin (like the one found in the real Red Square), the restaurant promptly decapitated it and covered it with fake pigeon poop. Enjoy the toppling of sacred cows as you dine on real cow — the Chef's Special is a terrific filet mignon topped with Roquefort — or caviar (pricey ounces allow you to taste several varieties), or other Russia-meets-the-rest-of-the-world fare. Be sure to have a drink at the bar, which is partially constructed out of a block of ice, the better to keep that vodka glass nicely chilled.

See maps p. 131 and p. 133. 3950 Las Vegas Blvd. S. (in Mandalay Bay). ☎ *702-632-7407.* www.mandalaybay.com. *Reservations recommended. Main courses: $26–$40. AE, DC, MC, V. Open: Sun–Thurs 5–10:30 p.m., Fri–Sat 5–11 p.m.*

Rosemary's Restaurant
$$$$ Off the Beaten Path   AMERICAN/SOUTHERN

Now we like those fancy Strip restaurants such as Picasso and Fleur de Lys — we like 'em a lot. But when asked, "What's the best restaurant in Vegas?", we may just have to answer "Rosemary's." Then we'd go on to explain that it's about a 20-minute drive from the Strip — one reason why we tell people to rent cars when they come here — and the chef-owners used to cook in New Orleans. (They opened Emeril's Seafood here, and in fact, this is the most reliable place in town to eat fish.) And now they've got their own place where they create twists on classic Southern fare. (Try that bleu cheese slaw! Or the jalapeño hush puppies!) We'd go on to explain that we've tried both the humble (crispy bass) and the fancy (foie gras with peach coulis or a pan-seared honey-glazed salmon), and both were wonderful. Plus, in addition to wine-pairing suggestions, Rosemary's offers you pairings for beer (which we've never seen before). But enough explaining, already: We're losing valuable time that's better spent eating here.

See maps p. 131 and p. 143. 8125 W. Sahara Ave. ☎ *702-869-2251.* www.rose marysrestaurant.com. *Reservations strongly suggested. Main courses: Lunch $14–$17, dinner $27–$42. AE, MC, V. Open: Mon–Fri 11:30 a.m.–2:15 p.m. and 5:30–10:30 p.m., Sat–Sun 5:30–10:30 p.m.*

Second Street Grill
$$$$ Downtown   INTERNATIONAL

Downtown really isn't keeping up with the big changes on the Strip, in terms of either lodging or culinary options. Sure, you still have the classic Vegas cheap meal deals here, but for swankier occasions, options are still either old-fashioned chophouses (nothing wrong with that, by the way) or well-intentioned muddles like this place. Which is still likable, and certainly more affordable than comparable places uptown. Stick to the grill dishes and have some fun with Hunan pork and beef lettuce-wrap appetizers. Steamed fish in a bamboo pot is reliable (and lower fat!) as well, although portions remain generous — a relief in these days of wee servings.

See map p. 131. 200 E. Fremont St. (in the Fremont Hotel). ☎ *702-385-3232.* www. fremontcasino.com. *Main courses: $17–$30. Reservations recommended. AE, DC, DISC, MC, V. Open: Sun, Mon, and Thurs 5–10 p.m.; Fri–Sat 5–11 p.m.*

Sensi
$$$$ Center Strip   INTERNATIONAL

Sort of a higher-priced version of those jack-of-all-trades restaurants (like Jillian's and Triple George) you find downtown — pan-Asian is the most prominent cuisine influence here, but how else to explain the pizza al prosciutto, not to mention the burgers? Still, it's much healthier than those other places — especially when you try the bento box at lunch, which usually features such heart-happy options as miso-glazed sea bass and sashimi, all cleverly displayed in a traditional Japanese lunch box. Probably too costly to consider for dinner, but worth a lunchtime visit.

See maps p. 131 and p. 138. 3600 Las Vegas Blvd. S. (in Bellagio). ☎ *702-693-8800.* www. bellagio.com. *Reservations recommended. Main courses: Lunch $14–$22, dinner $22–$44. AE, DC, DISC, MC, V. Open: Mon–Thurs 5–9:45 p.m., Fri–Sat 5–10:15 p.m.*

Sinatra
$$$$$ **North Strip** **ITALIAN**

The music and life of Old Blue Eyes is the theme here, but thankfully it's much more subtle than what you might expect from a Las Vegas restaurant. There are a few pictures, some of his awards (Oscar, Grammy, and so on), and a soundtrack of Frank's music, but this is no overdone memorabilia extravaganza. That's great because it allows you to concentrate on the sublime Italian/Mediterranean dishes prepared under the watchful eyes of Italian-born chef Theo Schoenegger. Everything that comes across the table is bursting with freshness and flavor, tasting as though it was in the ground, in the sea, or in a field moments before it was served to you. Everything on the antipasti plate is bursting with such flavor that it's practically dizzying, including a prosciutto that's probably the best you'll ever taste. Handmade pastas are king here with a stunning three-meat lasagna (pork, beef, and veal) and seasonal selections to die for: pray it has the ravioli stuffed with ricotta cheese and topped in a buttery asparagus sauce — it'll change your life or at least your relationship with asparagus. And if you want to go the full Frank route, the menu offers a few of his favorite dishes, such as Oso Bucco Milanese and Clams Possilipo. You'll be singing "I Did It My Way" all the way home.

See maps p. 131 and p. 143. 3121 Las Vegas Blvd. S. (in Encore Las Vegas). ☎ 702-248-3463. www.encorelasvegas.com. Reservations required. Main courses: $22–$49. AE, DISC, MC, V. Open: Daily 5:30–10 p.m.

Sirio Ristorante
$$$$ **South Strip** **ITALIAN**

Although our hearts still long for a really good Americanized Italian restaurant (think red-checkered tablecloths and spaghetti and meatballs), we can't deny that the Tuscany-based fine cuisine at Sirio is "Mamma Mia!" delicious. Done by the same family that runs the famous Le Cirque and Circo restaurants up the street at Bellagio, Sirio specializes in upscale Italian dishes, all handmade using the freshest of natural ingredients. The meatball appetizer trio (duck, lamb, and veal) is a genius stroke that will make you get into arguments with your table mates over which one is the best — we're leaning toward the sweet veal in the spicy tomato/onion compote. Pasta selections include an eggy handmade spaghetti in a robust three-meat ragu that qualifies as the best example of this particular noodle we've tasted pretty much anywhere. Hey, wait! We did get spaghetti and meatballs after all! Designer pizzas and a wide selection of seafood and meat entrees (loved the tenderloin, and not just because of the garlic and gorgonzola) fill out the menu, but be sure to save room for dessert. Its sampler trio of tiramisu — traditional, chocolate-caramel, and strawberry — will inspire those "which–is–best" arguments all over again . . . provided you're willing to share it in the first place, of course.

See maps p. 131 and p. 133. 3730 Las Vegas Blvd. S. (in Aria Las Vegas). ☎ 877-230-2742. www.arialasvegas.com. Reservations recommended. Main courses: $18–$45. AE, DC, DISC, MC, V. Open: Daily 5–10:30 p.m.

STRATTA
$$$ North Strip   ITALIAN

Alessandro Stratta is the James Beard Award–winning chef behind Wynn Las Vegas's Alex restaurant, which regularly garners the type of breathless praise usually reserved for dining experiences most people can't afford. STRATTA is sort of like the test kitchen for Alex, offering the same type of cuisine (Southern Italian) as Alex but at much more reasonable prices. The gnocchi, only served when they can get the exact right crop of potatoes, is a delicate wonder as it practically melts in your mouth while you're savoring the creamy tomato sauce and kicky mozzarella. Gourmet-style pizzas and pastas make up a big chunk of the menu (the baked lasagna is a cheesy, meaty temptation), but don't ignore the meat and seafood entrees. Traditional *osso bucco,* veal marsala, and beef short ribs in a red-wine sauce are examples of the types of dishes you can expect, although you really should hope that it's offering the stuffed pork chop when you visit — it's stuffed with cheese and prosciutto, and if there's anything better than that, we're having a hard time thinking of what it might be. Meals are still pricey here, but not as pricey as Alex, and they're just as good.

See maps p. 131 and p. 143. 3121 Las Vegas Blvd. S. (in Encore Las Vegas). ☎ **702-248-3463.** *www.encorelasvegas.com. Main courses: $10–$35. AE, DC, DISC, MC, V. Open: Daily 5:30–11 p.m.*

Strip House
$$$$ Center Strip   STEAKHOUSE

Vegas is home to roughly nine billion steakhouses. Okay, that's an exaggeration, but there are a lot of them and they're pretty much all the same. So, a steakhouse like Strip House is a breath of fresh air, serving up interestingly prepared cuts of meat in a fun atmosphere. The Strip in its name refers not to the street on which it's located but rather the act of shedding one's clothing. The room is done with a bordello theme — flocked red wallpaper and lots of peek-a-boo photos of scantily clad ladies from the '20s, '30s, '40s, and '50s. They were probably scandalous back in the day, but now, at the most, it's a PG-13 experience. The food served under these lovely ladies' watchful eyes is almost as cheeky, with the steaks done in a bold pepper rub that may be a little too much for some taste buds but certainly makes them distinctive. And how can you not love the idea of a garlic bread/gorgonzola fondue appetizer?

See maps p. 131 and p. 138. 3663 Las Vegas Blvd. S. (in Planet Hollywood). ☎ **702-737-5200.** *www.planethollywoodresort.com. Reservations recommended. Main courses: $25–$60. AE, DISC, MC, V. Open: Sun–Thurs 5–11 p.m., Fri–Sat 5 p.m. to midnight.*

Switch
$$$$ North Strip   FRENCH/STEAKHOUSE

Most restaurants with a gimmick use that to cover up the fact that the food they serve is not that great. Not so, here. The French-inspired steakhouse from Chef Marc Poidevin offers just enough of a Gallic twist to the proceedings that it's accessible to less-refined palates but adventurous enough to satisfy those looking for something more than just meat and potatoes. Cornish game hen and rabbit fricassee are for the latter crowd, while steaks of all varieties and lots of accompanying sauces and sides can titillate the taste buds of the former. Try the fantastic blue cheese as a topping for your meat, and consider the grilled onions and jalapeños to really kick things up a notch. And while you're dining, enjoy that gimmick we mentioned, wherein every 20 minutes or so the room "switches" to a new theme, with the walls rolling up and down and the music and lighting changing to match. It's cute and certainly a good diversion if conversation at the table is lagging.

See maps p. 131 and p. 143. 3121 Las Vegas Blvd. S. (in Encore Las Vegas). ☎ *702-248-3463.* www.encorelasvegas.com. *Reservations recommended. Main courses: $22–$61. AE, DC, DISC, MC, V. Open: Daily 5:30–10:30 p.m.*

Table 10
$$$$ Center Strip   AMERICAN

There does seem to be an awful lot of Emeril in town, and you have to wonder if there's a need for any more. Table 10 puts those doubts to rest. Possibly the most successful of his local establishments, it's also a relative bargain compared to other high-end dining in town. (It's even more affordable at lunch.) Figure on the menu changing regularly; also figure on dishes that do justice to Emeril's contemporary Creole cooking, such as oyster fritters with a Rockefeller dipping sauce and pasta jambalaya, as well as offerings imbued with a hearty dose of fun, such as lamb sliders made with roasted leg of lamb. Top it all off with malasadas, deep-fried dough balls filled with white chocolate.

See maps p. 131 and p. 138. 3328 Las Vegas Blvd. S. (in the Palazzo). ☎ *702-607-6363.* www.palazzolasvegas.com. *Reservations recommended. Main courses: Lunch $11–$29, dinner $25–$38. AE, MC, V. Open: Sun–Thurs 11 a.m.–10 p.m., Fri–Sat 11 a.m.–11 p.m.*

Tacos and Tequila
$$$ South Strip   MEXICAN

We'd like to be able to say the primary reason you should come here is because of the food. Don't get us wrong: The Mexican specialties it serves are good — certainly fresh and satisfying — especially its epic list of tacos, including chicken, beef, carne asada, beer-battered Tilapia, pulled pork, Kobe beef, Maine lobster, and many more. Oh, and its fajitas are divine — juicy steak and soft, moist, flavorful flour tortillas and all the fixings. But let's be honest: The primary reason you should come here are for the margaritas, which are, in our humble estimation, the best in Las Vegas. All are made with fresh-squeezed lime and organic agave nectar, and you can choose from more than 100 different types of tequila. Have a couple of these bad boys and you won't care whether the food is any good. We're not wild about the dining room, which is a little too open and loud for our tastes, and the prices are on the high side for Mexican food, but did we mention the margaritas?

See maps p. 131 and p. 133. 3900 Las Vegas Blvd. S. (in Luxor Las Vegas). ☎ **702-262-5225.** *www.luxor.com. Main courses: $12–$25. AE, DC, DISC, MC, V. Open: Daily 11 a.m.–11 p.m.*

Todd English P.U.B.
$$$ South Strip AMERICAN

Of the more than two dozen new restaurants at CityCenter, this one is by far our favorite and one of our favorites in the entire city. Why? First, we're fans of Chef English anyway; his Olives restaurant at Bellagio is simply terrific. Second, our wallets are grateful that English chose to do a moderately priced eatery instead of yet another insanely priced affair, something this city needs absolutely no more of. And third, and most important, our stomachs are grateful for the flat-out fantastic food. It's basically pub grub — burgers, sandwiches, fish and chips, bangers and mash, pot pies, and the like — but it's all done with such hearty goodness that it far exceeds bar-food expectations. Our recommended menu: Start with the prime-rib beef chili, not too spicy and filled with tender chunks of meat; sample from the Carvery, where you get to choose from a big list of meats (roasted chicken, brisket, sirloin, duck, turkey, and so on), breads, and accompaniments; and finish off with the giant platter of cookies and cream, with everything from a giant chocolate-covered Oreo to a red velvet cupcake and a side of ice cream. The fact that you can do all that for around $30 is amazing — and you'll have some dough left over to sample one of the dozens of on-tap beers from all over the globe.

See maps p. 131 and p. 133. 3720 Las Vegas Blvd. S. (in Crystals at CityCenter). ☎ **702-489-8080.** *www.toddenglishpub.com. Reservations recommended. Main courses: $12–$26. AE, DISC, MC, V. Open: Sun–Thurs 11 a.m.–11 p.m., Fri–Sat 11 a.m. to midnight.*

Viva Mercados
$$ Off the Beaten Path MEXICAN

Locals consider this the best Mexican restaurant in town, and surprisingly enough, the fare is healthy. Everything is cooked in canola oil, and you can choose from lots of vegetarian and seafood selections. You find 11 varieties of salsa, from extremely mild to call-the-fire-department hot. The food is fresh, the staff is friendly, and the price is right. It's definitely worth the ten-minute drive from the Strip.

See map p. 131. 6182 W. Flamingo Rd. (about 3 miles west of the Strip on your right). ☎ **702-871-8826.** *www.vivamercados.com. Reservations not accepted. Main courses: $10–$20. AE, DISC, MC, V. Open: Sun–Thurs 11 a.m.–9:30 p.m., Fri–Sat 11 a.m.–10 p.m.*

Wynn Las Vegas Buffet
$$$$ **North Strip   BUFFET**

Here's your proof the $5.99 dinner buffet is gone. Don't think of this place as a traditional Vegas buffet — you know, a place where you can fill up for hardly anything at all. Think of it as an alternative to some of those fancy-pants places where a three-course meal will set you back at least twice what all-you-can-eat will cost you here. Notice the honey-glazed pork, the tandoori chicken, the honest-to-goodness pastry chef working the dessert section. . . . Sample sushi and wood-fired pizza — though probably not at the exact same moment. Go back for seconds, maybe thirds. Have a cookie while contemplating which dessert(s) to try. Think about those diners who are paying a premium for tiny little portions. Notice how it's all really quite good, and how much of it you can have. Meetcha there.

See maps p. 131 and p. 143. 3131 Las Vegas Blvd. S. (in Wynn Las Vegas). ☎ *702-770-3340.* www.wynnlasvegas.com. *Buffet prices: Breakfast $20, lunch $23, dinner $35–$39, Sat–Sun brunch $26–$32. AE, DC, DISC, MC, V. Open: Sun–Thurs 8 a.m.–10 p.m., Fri–Sat 8 a.m.–10:30 p.m.*

On the Lighter Side: Munchies and Meals to Go

If you're not in the mood for a major meal or you're just looking for something to nibble on before you head off to a show, you have a number of options to choose from. Many of the big hotels have food courts that are similar to what you find in your local mall, although prices are slightly higher than what you're used to paying for similar fare at home. And there are also some alternatives to the brand-name generic sameness these places mostly offer.

Food courts

The best of the hotel food courts is **Cypress Street Marketplace,** in **Caesars Palace,** 3570 Las Vegas Blvd. S. (☎ 702-731-7110), with a selection of vendors (pulled-pork sandwiches at the barbecue stand, pot stickers and bowls of noodles at the Asian stand, wrap sandwiches, very fine pizza slices, large salads, even hamburgers — there's enough here to please every palate in even the most diet-divided family). Prices are low, but the choices and quality are such that you may get a bit carried away. Hours may vary at each place, but, collectively, the food court is open from 11 a.m. to 11 p.m. daily. It's opposite the entrance to the **Forum Shops** at the northern end of the casino.

On the South Strip, the **Monte Carlo Resort & Casino,** 3770 Las Vegas Blvd. S. (☎ 702-730-7777), has a food court featuring **Häagen-Dazs, McDonald's, Nathan's Hot Dogs,** and **Sbarro.** It's open (varying from stand to stand) from 6 a.m. to 3 a.m. Look for it between the lobby (which is at the back of the hotel's first floor) and casino (at the front).

New York–New York, 3790 Las Vegas Blvd. S. (☎ 702-740-6969), has the nicest food court, thanks to its Greenwich Village–style setting. There, and up near Coney Island, are New York–themed eateries — **Schrafft's Ice Cream** (yippee!), a good pizza place, and a good hamburger joint, plus **Jodi Maroni's Sausage Kingdom,** which serves up some of the best dogs this side of the Hudson River.

For the sweet tooth

Let's see . . . home to the world's largest chocolate fountain and a World Pastry Champion. Oh, you need more reason to come to **Jean-Philippe Patisserie** in **Bellagio,** 3600 Las Vegas Blvd. S. (☎ 702-369-5000)? How about perfect gourmet chocolates, brioche stuffed with dulce de leche, pastries that are works of art, and thick ice cream? Decadence run amok. Race you there!

Harrah's, 3475 Las Vegas Blvd. S. (☎ 702-892-8447), has a **Ghirardelli Chocolate Shop and Soda Fountain** in the outdoor Carnival Court. You can't watch the chocolate being mixed in vats (darn!) as you can at its flagship store in San Francisco, but this is where we like to spend time on a hot Vegas day.

Speaking of chocolate, how about the frozen hot kind served at the Las Vegas branch of the famed **Serendipity 3** at **Caesars Palace,** 3570 Las Vegas Blvd. S. (☎ 877-346-4642)? Basically a big chocolate shake but with a hot-chocolate flavor, it's worth its reputation as a sinfully delicious dessert. You can find some heavenly baked goods served up by **Freed's Bakery,** 4780 S. Eastern Ave. (☎ 702-456-7762; www.freeds bakery.com), where it smells just like grandma's kitchen.

We used to try to send you to Henderson for the best cupcakes in Vegas, but now a branch of the **Cupcakery** has opened at the **Monte Carlo,** 3770 Las Vegas Blvd. S. (☎ 702-207-2253; www.thecupcakery.com)! Little morsels of cake and frosting wonder, sometimes filled with even more sweetness, such as the Boston cream pie packed with custard cream.

When the heat is on in Vegas, we think ice cream — or variations on that theme — is as much a necessity as water. We head right to **Luv-It Frozen Custard,** 505 E. Oakey, at the Strip (☎ 702-384-6452), open Monday through Thursday 11 a.m. to 10 p.m., Friday 11 a.m. to 11 p.m., Saturday noon to 11 p.m., and Sunday 1 to 10 p.m. It varies slightly in taste — and caloric content (yay!) — from regular ice cream, and the batches here are made fresh every few hours.

Man cannot live by cake alone (we've tried), so vary your diet with bagels from either **Einstein Bros. Bagels,** 4624 S. Maryland Pkwy. (☎ 702-795-7800; www.einsteinbros.com), or **Bagelmania,** 855 Twain Ave. (☎ 702-369-3322), both of which provide good alternatives to expensive hotel breakfasts.

What's your theme?

It shouldn't be too surprising to learn that a town devoted to gimmicks has just about every gimmick restaurant there is. Almost all have prominent celebrity co-owners and tons of "memorabilia" on the walls, which can be fun or cheesy depending on your viewpoint. Most offer good (but not great) food for higher-than-average prices. So, why go? Who doesn't want to have a burger next to a margarita-spewing volcano, a Lady Gaga costume, or a signed jersey from (insert the name of your favorite athlete here)?

You can hear "Yeehaw" all over Vegas now that **Gilley's** has returned, this time at **Treasure Island,** 3300 Las Vegas Blvd. S. (☎ **702-894-7111;** www.gilleyslasvegas. com). The mechanical bull is there, of course, along with line-dancing instructions, but the restaurant part is worth knowing about. Expect huge portions of down-home country cooking, including everything from burgers to barbecue, and its pork green chili deserves all the awards it's won.

New to the theme party is **BB King's Blues Club** in the **Mirage,** 3400 Las Vegas Blvd. S. (☎ **702-242-5464;** www.bbkingclubs.com), a casual, moderately priced concert venue, bar, and restaurant from Blues singer/guitarist/legend BB King. Breakfast, lunch, and dinner is all of the deep South variety, heavy on the kind of calories-be-darned flavors and portions that you'd expect. Stick around after dinner to enjoy the nightly performances from blues bands that are worthy of playing a joint with BB King's name on it.

The House of Blues, in **Mandalay Bay,** 3950 Las Vegas Blvd. S. (☎ **702-632-7607;** www. hob.com), for our money, food- and theme-wise, is the best of the theme restaurants. The food is really pretty good (if a little more costly than it ought to be in a theme restaurant), and the mock Delta/New Orleans look works well, even if it is unavoidably commercial. Dining, drinking, concerts, and a weekend gospel brunch make this a well-rounded theme party.

People rave about the warm Tollhouse-cookie pie at the **Harley-Davidson Cafe,** 3725 Las Vegas Blvd. S., at Harmon Avenue (☎ **702-740-4555;** www.harley-davidson cafe.com). But before you get to dessert, a full menu of southern staples (barbecue being chief among them) awaits.

The Hard Rock Cafe, 4475 Paradise Rd., at Harmon Avenue (☎ **702-733-8400;** www. hardrockcafe.com), has decent burgers, and the serious hipster quotient at the adjacent hotel means that the people-watching opportunities are best here. Note a second Hard Rock Cafe is now open on the Strip at 3771 Las Vegas Blvd. S. (☎ **702-733-7625),** a 42,000-square-foot, three-level behemoth with all sorts of high-tech gadgetry like interactive tables, a gigantic gift shop, a 1,000-seat concert venue, and more. Bigger, yes. Better? You decide.

Parrot Heads like to party it up at **Margaritaville,** singer Jimmy Buffett's tropical-themed cafe/bar/club, at the Flamingo ("Parrot Heads" is how his fans refer to themselves). The menu runs a range from Mexican to something sort of Caribbean-themed to basic American, and it's not all that bad, considering. Partaking in lots of fruity tropical drinks doesn't hurt, either. It's in the **Flamingo,** 3555 Las Vegas Blvd. S. (☎ **702-733-3302;** www.margaritavillelasvegas.com).

We may have spent too much time on the Jungle Cruise ride at Disneyland during our impressionable youth, and that's probably why we rather enjoy the **Rainforest Cafe,** in the MGM Grand, 3799 Las Vegas Blvd. S. (☎ **702-891-8580;** www.rainforest cafe.com). The fake foliage, animatronic animals, and real fish give everyone, especially kids, plenty to look at while dining on some needlessly busy but better-than-average (for a theme restaurant) food. In theory, your child (or you) can also learn about environmental issues, which to our way of thinking is a better use of everyone's time than gawking at used football jerseys.

Index of Restaurants by Neighborhood

Center Strip

Alizé (French, $$$$$)
Bouchon (Bistro, $$$$)
Cabo Wabo Cantina (Mexican, $$)
Carnival World Buffet (Buffet, $$)
Cravings (Buffet, $$$)
Delmonico Steakhouse (Steakhouse, $$$$$)
Earl of Sandwich (Sandwiches, $)
Hash House A Go Go (American, $$$)
Isla Mexican Kitchen (Mexican, $$)
Lagasse's Stadium (American, $$$)
Le Cirque (Nouvelle French, $$$$$)
Le Village Buffet (Buffet, $$$)
Mesa Grill (Southwestern, $$$$)
Michael Mina (Seafood, $$$$$)
Mon Ami Gabi (Bistro, $$$)
Olives (Italian/Mediterranean, $$$$)
Picasso (Nouvelle French, $$$$$)
Pink's Hot Dogs (American, $)
Pinot Brasserie (Bistro, $$$$)
The Range (Steakhouse, $$$$$)
Sensi (International, $$$$)
Strip House (Steakhouse, $$$$)
Table 10 (American, $$$$)

Downtown

El Sombrero Café (Mexican, $)
Golden Nugget Buffet (Buffet, $$)
Main Street Station Garden Court Buffet (Buffet, $$)
Second Street Grill (International, $$$$)

East of the Strip

Buffet (Buffet, $)

North Strip

Bartolotta (Italian/Seafood, $$$$$)
Fellini's (Italian, $$)
Sinatra (Italian, $$$$$)
STRATTA (Italian, $$$)
Switch (French/Steakhouse, $$$$)
Wynn Las Vegas Buffet (Buffet, $$$$)

Off the Beaten Path

Austins Steakhouse (Steakhouse, $$$)
Café Heidelberg German Deli and Restaurant (Deli/German, $$)
Capriotti's (Sandwiches/American, $)
Lotus of Siam (Thai, $)
M&M Soul Food Cafe (American/Southern, $$)
Raku Grill (Japanese, $$$)
Rosemary's Restaurant (American/Southern, $$$$)
Viva Mercados (Mexican, $$)

Paradise Road

Bougainvillea Café (Coffee Shop, $)
Lawry's The Prime Rib (Steakhouse, $$$$$)
Paymon's Mediterranean Café & Lounge (Greek/Middle Eastern, $$)

South Strip

Aureole (New American, $$$$$)
Border Grill (Mexican, $$$)
Burger Bar (Diner, $$)
Charlie Palmer Steak (Steakhouse, $$$$$)

Diablo's Cantina (Mexican, $$$)
Dick's Last Resort (Diner, $$)
Emeril's New Orleans Fish House
(American/Seafood/Cajun, $$$$$)
Fleur de Lys (French, $$$$$)
Grand Wok and Sushi Bar
(Pan-Asian, $$$)
Julian Serrano (Spanish, $$$$)

L'Atelier de Joël Robuchon
(French, $$$$$)
More: The Buffet at Luxor (Buffet, $$)
Red Square (Continental, $$$$)
Sirio Ristorante (Italian, $$$$)
Tacos and Tequila (Mexican, $$$)
Todd English P.U.B. (American, $$$)

Index of Restaurants by Cuisine

American

Capriotti's (Off the Beaten Path, $)
Emeril's New Orleans Fish House
(South Strip, $$$$$)
Hash House A Go Go (Center Strip, $$$)
Lagasse's Stadium (Center Strip, $$$)
M&M Soul Food Cafe (Off the Beaten
Path, $$)
Pink's Hot Dogs (Center Strip, $)
Rosemary's Restaurant (Off the Beaten
Path, $$$$)
Table 10 (Center Strip, $$$$)
Todd English P.U.B. (South Strip, $$$)

Bistro

Bouchon (Center Strip, $$$$)
Mon Ami Gabi (Center Strip, $$$)
Pinot Brassiere (Center Strip, $$$$)

Buffets

Carnival World Buffet (Center Strip, $$)
Cravings (Center Strip, $$$)
Golden Nugget Buffet (Downtown, $$)
Le Village Buffet (Center Strip, $$$)
Main Street Station Garden Court
Buffet (Downtown, $$)
More: The Buffet at Luxor (South Strip,
$$)
Ports O' Call Buffet (East of the Strip, $)
Wynn Las Vegas Buffet (North Strip,
$$$$)

Cajun

Emeril's New Orleans Fish House
(South Strip, $$$$$)

Coffee Shop

Bougainvillea Café (Paradise Road, $)

Continental

Red Square (South Strip, $$$$)

Deli/Sandwiches

Café Heidelberg German Deli and
Restaurant (Off the Beaten Path, $$)
Capriotti's (Off the Beaten Path, $)
Earl of Sandwich (Center Strip, $)

Diner

Burger Bar (South Strip, $$)
Dick's Last Resort (South Strip, $$)

French

Alizé (Center Strip, $$$$$)
Fleur de Lys (South Strip, $$$$$)
L'Atelier de Joël Robuchon (South
Strip, $$$$$)
Switch (North Strip, $$$$)

German

Café Heidelberg German Deli and
Restaurant (Off the Beaten Path, $$)

Greek/Middle Eastern

Paymon's Mediterranean Café &
Lounge (Paradise Road, $$)

International

Second Street Grill (Downtown, $$$$)
Sensi (Center Strip, $$$$)

Italian/Mediterranean
Bartolotta (North Strip, $$$$$)
Fellini's (North Strip, $$)
Olives (Center Strip, $$$$)
Sinatra (North Strip, $$$$$)
Sirio Ristorante (South Strip, $$$$)
STRATTA (North Strip, $$$)

Japanese
Raku Grill (Off the Beaten Path, $$$)

Mexican
Border Grill (South Strip, $$$)
Cabo Wabo Cantina (Center Strip, $$)
Diablo's Cantina (South Strip, $$$)
El Sombrero Café (Downtown, $)
Isla Mexican Kitchen (Center Strip, $$)
Tacos and Tequila (South Strip, $$$)
Viva Mercados (Off the Beaten Path, $$)

New American
Aureole (South Strip, $$$$$)

Nouvelle French
Le Cirque (Center Strip, $$$$$)
Picasso (Center Strip, $$$$$)

Pan-Asian
Grand Wok and Sushi Bar
(South Strip, $$$)

Seafood
Bartolotta (North Strip, $$$$$)
Emeril's New Orleans Fish House
(South Strip, $$$$$)
Michael Mina (Center Strip, $$$$$)

Southern
M&M Soul Food Cafe (Off the Beaten
Path, $$)
Rosemary's Restaurant (Off the Beaten
Path, $$$$)

Southwestern
Mesa Grill (Center Strip, $$$$)

Spanish
Julian Serrano (South Strip, $$$$)

Steakhouse
Austins Steakhouse (Off the Beaten
Path, $$$)
Charlie Palmer Steak (South Strip,
$$$$$)
Delmonico Steakhouse (Center Strip,
$$$$$)
Lawry's The Prime Rib (Paradise Road,
$$$$$)
The Range (Center Strip, $$$$$)
Strip House (Center Strip, $$$$)
Switch (North Strip, $$$$)

Thai
Lotus of Siam (Off the Beaten Path, $)

Index of Restaurants by Price

$$$$$
Alizé (French, Center Strip)
Aureole (New American, South Strip)
Bartolotta (Italian/Seafood, North Strip)
Charlie Palmer Steak (Steakhouse,
South Strip)

Delmonico Steakhouse (Steakhouse,
Center Strip)
Emeril's New Orleans Fish House
(American/Seafood/Cajun, South Strip)
Fleur de Lys (French, South Strip)
L'Atelier de Joël Robuchon (French,
South Strip)

Lawry's The Prime Rib (Steakhouse, Paradise Road)

Le Cirque (Nouvelle French, Center Strip)

Michael Mina (Seafood, Center Strip)

Picasso (Nouvelle French, Center Strip)

The Range (Steakhouse, Center Strip)

Sinatra (Italian, North Strip)

$$$$

Bouchon (Bistro, Center Strip)

Julian Serrano (Spanish, South Strip)

Mesa Grill (Southwestern, Center Strip)

Olives (Italian/Mediterranean, Center Strip)

Pinot Brasserie (Bistro, Center Strip)

Red Square (Continental, South Strip)

Rosemary's Restaurant (American/ Southern, Off the Beaten Path)

Second Street Grill (International, Downtown)

Sensi (International, Center Strip)

Sirio Ristorante (Italian, South Strip)

Strip House (Steakhouse, Center Strip)

Switch (French/Steakhouse, North Strip)

Table 10 (American, Center Strip)

Wynn Las Vegas Buffet (Buffet, North Strip)

$$$

Austins Steakhouse (Steakhouse, Off the Beaten Path)

Border Grill (Mexican, South Strip)

Cravings (Buffet, Center Strip)

Diablo's Cantina (Mexican, South Strip)

Grand Wok and Sushi Bar (Pan-Asian, South Strip)

Hash House A Go Go (American, Center Strip)

Lagasse's Stadium (American, Center Strip)

Le Village Buffet (Buffet, Center Strip)

Mon Ami Gabi (Bistro, Center Strip)

Raku Grill (Japanese, Off the Beaten Path)

STRATTA (Italian, North Strip)

Tacos and Tequila (Mexican, South Strip)

Todd English P.U.B. (American, South Strip)

$$

Burger Bar (Diner, South Strip)

Cabo Wabo Cantina (Mexican, Center Strip)

Café Heidelberg German Deli and Restaurant (Deli/German, Off the Beaten Path)

Carnival World Buffet (Buffet, Center Strip)

Dick's Last Resort (Diner, South Strip)

Fellini's (Italian, North Strip)

Golden Nugget Buffet (Buffet, Downtown)

Isla Mexican Kitchen (Mexican, Center Strip)

Main Street Station Garden Court Buffet (Buffet, Downtown)

M&M Soul Food Cafe (American/ Southern, Off the Beaten Path)

More: The Buffet at Luxor (Buffet, South Strip)

Paymon's Mediterranean Café & Lounge (Greek/Middle Eastern, Paradise Road)

Viva Mercados (Mexican, Off the Beaten Path)

$

Bougainvillea Café (Coffee Shop, Paradise Road)

Capriotti's (Sandwiches/American, Off the Beaten Path)

Earl of Sandwich (Sandwich, Center Strip)

El Sombrero Café (Mexican, Downtown)

Lotus of Siam (Thai, Off the Beaten Path)

Pink's Hot Dogs (American, Center Strip)

Ports O' Call Buffet (Buffet, East of the Strip)

Part IV
Exploring Las Vegas

"Would you mind not sitting at
that machine? It throws off the
feng shui in this row."

In this part . . .

Yes, it's true: You can do more in Las Vegas than drop dollar bills into a slot machine. Ultimately, this city is one big amusement park, with a healthy dose of resort pampering thrown in for good measure. Where else can you ride a roller coaster, play a few hands of blackjack, watch Elvis return to the stage, go bowling, take an 800-foot plunge from the top of a tower, play with a dolphin, practice your golf swing, get a massage, and get hitched? In this part, we give you tips on how to gamble, see the top attractions, shop 'til you drop, and get in as much fun as is humanly possible.

Chapter 11

Luck Be a Lady: Gambling Tips and Tricks

*H*ey, did you know that they have gambling in Vegas?

Well, of course, you did. If you knew only one thing about Vegas before you picked up this book, we'd bet dollars to donuts it was that. See how quickly the gambling begins? In fact, what you may not realize, and may not fully comprehend until you actually get here, is how much gambling there is in Vegas. It starts at the airport, follows you to the gas station, and then hits hyperdrive when you finally get to your hotel.

Clearly, it's time to get serious.

Ante Up: Gambling Basics

If you want to try the gambling scene, but you've never done it before and don't know all the rules, don't worry. We can get you started. Gambling isn't as fun if you aren't savvy enough to know when to "double down," and the last thing you want to do in Vegas is lose your shirt. So, in this section, we give you the basics (although we can't guarantee a win — you have to rely on Lady Luck for that one!).

Entire books have been written about the nuances of casino gambling, so if you're looking for an in-depth analysis, we suggest that you go grab an additional reference. *Casino Gambling For Dummies,* by Kevin Blackwood and Max Rubin (published by Wiley) seems like a good place to start — symmetry, you know.

Before you even walk into a casino, you need to keep some basic rules in mind.

✔ **You have to be at least 21 years old to even enter a casino area, much less play the games.** If you bring your kids to Vegas and plan on spending significant time inside the casino, check into finding a baby sitter or child-care center at your hotel (see the Quick Concierge for baby-sitting resources). If you happen to look younger than 21, be sure to carry a valid driver's license (or other piece of ID) with you. Casino officials and cashiers can and do card patrons.

If you're under 21 and somehow manage to make it to a table or slot machine, don't think that you're home free: A while back, a big slot winner had his jackpot taken away when the casino found out he was only 17.

✔ **Join the casino club to save money.** Most hotels offer free enrollment in their slot and gaming clubs. After you fill out a form, you get a card (it looks kind of like a credit card) that you insert into a special reader on slot machines or turn in at gaming tables. Each time you place a bet or pull the handle on a slot machine, you rack up points on your account. (Just remember to take your card with you when you leave!) Later, you can trade in these points for discounts on meals, shopping, and accommodations. If you gamble enough, you may even get a free room.

Getting a club card is one of the best deals in Vegas. Even if you think that you aren't going to gamble enough to make it worthwhile, sign up for as many of these as you can. After all, you never know — vows to drop only small amounts of cash on the tables often have the longevity of New Year's resolutions, so you may as well get something out of all this if you can. Signing up for the club also puts you on the hotel's mailing list, which can be a plus, because hotels often offer special deals on room rates and packages to their club members. Every casino has a casino club desk — just ask any employee where it is to get started.

✔ **You can drink.** In fact, almost all the casinos offer free drinks (alcoholic and nonalcoholic) if you're gambling. All you need to do is flag down one of the many cocktail servers who roam the casino floor. (The servers often pop up mere moments after you've seated yourself.) It may be a while, however, before your drink arrives. Servers blame the delay on the long trek they have to make to get from the kitchens to the casino, but the suspicious among us suspect that they just want you to keep pumping quarters into that slot machine while you wait. And suddenly, that free beer costs you $20.

✔ **You can light up.** Smokers, who must often take to the streets to light up in other U.S. cities, will be happy to know that the huff-'n'-puff crowd rules in Las Vegas's casinos. Some casinos even offer free packs of cigarettes to gamblers. A few casinos have no-smoking sections, but you still share the same air with the rest of the casino.

Nonsmokers should take solace in the Vegas legend that says that casinos constantly pump in fresh oxygen to keep players from getting tired.

✔ **Cheaters really don't prosper.** Don't even think about cheating. If you don't believe us, just look up at the ceiling when you walk into any casino. Those innocuous little black domes or opaque glass panels are actually cameras poised to watch your every move. They're extremely high-tech and can cover every square inch of the casino. And somebody is always watching. Floor staff and undercover operators also roam the floors just trying to catch you doing anything out of the ordinary. They've seen every trick in the book, and many not in the books. They know more than you do, and they *will* catch you. And although there may no longer be goons named Guido ready to rearrange your face for your transgressions, legal punishment is pretty humiliating. Save the cheating for your Monday-night bridge club.

✔ **You must be prepared to lose.** One thing you must understand before you set out to play: Losers outnumber winners in any casino. They don't build these super-casinos on winners. After all, they have to have some way to pay for those big chandeliers, mammoth volcanoes, and Celine Dion's salary — and they do, and then some. In 2009, Las Vegas–area casinos raked in just under $9 billion — and that was considered a down year for the city. Chew on that for a minute.

Don't budget any more gambling money than you can afford to lose. After you set aside your bankroll for the casinos, consider it gone. If you leave the city with some jingle left in your pocket, consider yourself very lucky.

✔ **Never forget that it's just a game.** You won't find the key to successful gambling in any strategy book or streak of good luck. It's a state of mind. Success means having fun without losing the farm. And so, although it must be very nice (not that we would know) to bet $10,000 and win $30,000, remember that it must really hurt all the other times when that $10,000 goes bye-bye. If you remember that this is just a game, for your entertainment, you can have plenty of fun playing nickel slots. Sure, you won't get rich, but you won't send your children to the poorhouse, either. If you're looking for an investment opportunity, consider the stock market (although lately, that's not a sure bet either).

The Slot Machines: Bells and Sirens

Old-timers will tell you that slots were invented to give wives something to do while their husbands gambled. Slots used to be stuck on the peripheries of the casinos and could be counted on one hand, maybe two. But now they *are* the casino: The casinos make more from slots than from craps, blackjack, and roulette combined. In fact, you can find nearly 200,000 slot machines in the state of Nevada.

A slot machine (shown in Figure 11-1) is actually a computer with a highly specialized program that randomly decides how much and how often you'll win on any given play. Most of the time, the computer decides that you lose, but occasionally it decides that you win, and then you hear the coins raining down into the little bin below. The good news is that Las Vegas slot machines are the *loosest* (the house keeps less money) in the country. The bad news is that the house still holds a 3 percent to 25 percent advantage on the slot machines. (There's a reason they're nicknamed "one-armed bandits.")

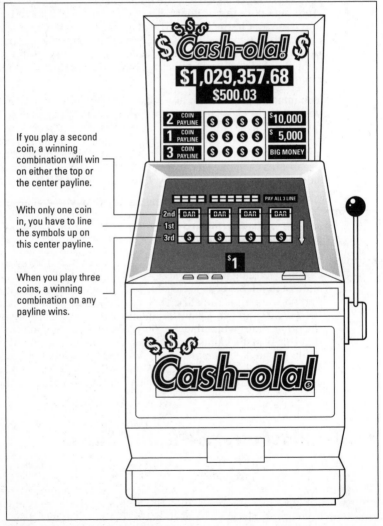

If you play a second coin, a winning combination will win on either the top or the center payline.

With only one coin in, you have to line the symbols up on this center payline.

When you play three coins, a winning combination on any payline wins.

Figure 11-1: A basic slot machine.

How they work

You put bills in the slot and pull the handle. What, you thought that there was a trick to this? Well, maybe there is a bit more to tell. In order to keep up with increasing competition, the plain old machine, where reels just spin, has become nearly obsolete. Now, they are all computerized, have fun graphics, and have added buttons to push so that you can avoid developing carpal tunnel syndrome yanking the handle all night. (The handles are still there on some of them so that you can feel more involved in the play.) The idea is still simple: Get three (sometimes four) cherries (Elvi, sevens, dinosaurs, whatever) in a row and you win something.

Increasingly popular are the video-based machines, which complicate matters even further by offering multiple pay lines (that barely qualify as a line, they're so convoluted) and multiple ways to play.

Each machine has its own combination, so be sure to check the chart (included on the front of every machine or in the help section on video-based slots) that tells you all the winning combinations. Some pay you something with just one symbol showing; on most, the more combinations there are, the more opportunities for loot. Some even pay a little if you get three blanks.

Different slots for different pots

Slot machines take paper currency ($1–$100) inserted into a slot to get started and then pay you with a paper ticket that can be either inserted into other machines or cashed in. Even though most don't accept actual coins, they still refer to them with their old monikers: Nickel machines are usually the lowest limit (although penny slots are making a big comeback), followed by dimes (fairly rare), quarters, half-dollars, dollars, and $5. The high-limit machines, usually cordoned off in their own area, can cost you anywhere from $10 to $500 or even more for a single pull of the handle. Each machine shows you how much you have left to gamble on a credit meter.

After you decide how much you want to blow (er, bet), you have to decide between *progressive* and so-called *flat-top* machines. Here's the lowdown on each of these machines:

- ✓ **Flat-top machines** have a fixed high-end limit of how much you can win. For example, hit three gold bars and you win 1,000 coins — but never any more or less.

- ✓ **Progressive machines** offer unlimited high-end winnings as the jackpot grows, and the pot grows each time you put a coin in. If you play on a progressive machine, those three gold bars can win you different amounts, depending on how much money has accumulated in the jackpot. Most progressive slots are located in *carousels* (groups of machines that contribute to one central jackpot). The first person to hit the big one wins the big jackpot. Carousels are easy to find: Just look for the large electronic signs above them displaying the jackpot amount. Some machines offer their own individual progressive jackpot. Play these, and you won't have to worry about the guy sitting next to you winning the big prize.

Most machines take two *credits* (the denomination of the machine — penny, quarter, dollar, and so on), three credits, or up to 45 credits at a time. Many even have more than one set of reels (meaning, you can win on more than one "line" horizontally, vertically, or diagonally). Some include bonus wheels that spin and award you extra dough. Don't worry, though — it's not all that complicated. If you study a machine carefully for just a few moments before you play it (or watch someone else who's playing a similar machine), you get a good handle on all the rules and your possible winnings.

What to do if you hit the jackpot

If you're half asleep and mindlessly pumping credits into a machine, don't worry that you won't recognize if you hit the big one. Bells and sirens often blare, just in case you weren't paying attention (and just in case others in the casino need a little help deciding to play!). If this happens, but the credit meter doesn't show your winnings, relax. Most machines have *payout limits;* any jackpot that exceeds the limit is paid in cash by an attendant (who will no doubt double-time it to your frantic side).

Be aware that the casino automatically reports any jackpot of $1,200 or more to the IRS. Yes, that big win is considered income and is taxable — Uncle Sam takes 25 percent of your winnings. (You also can deduct losses, but only if you have winnings and you've kept a record of your play.) So, maybe instead of trying for that one big jackpot, you should go after a bunch of smaller ones. And be sure to check with your accountant if you're unsure how to report your winnings or losses.

Tips and tricks

There is no such thing as a slots expert (just someone who's played them a whole lot), but we still have a few hints for you to take to the slot machines. These hints are not guaranteed to make you a penny, but if you stick to them, you may do pretty well.

- ✔ **Be prepared to walk away.** If you sit down at a slot machine, and it doesn't pay out anything within the first ten or so pulls, move your butt to the next one. Odds are that it isn't going to get any better.

- ✔ **For bigger pots, play bigger money.** The lower the denomination required to play a slot machine, the less likely you are to hit the jackpot. In general, nickel machines pay off less frequently than quarter machines, which pay off less frequently than dollars, and so on.

✔ **Play the max.** This one is a tough call. If you play the maximum number of credits, and you win, you win much more. Of course, if you lose, you go through your money that much faster. Most machines, progressive or not, offer higher payout odds on maximum bets. Bet 25¢, get three cherries, and you get 50¢ back, for example. The payout is 2:1. However, bet 75¢, hit those same three cherries, and you get $2.25 as a payoff. This makes the payout 3:1. In addition, if you want to win the big jackpot, you must put in the maximum number of credits. It's a hook to make you spend more money, but it's a hook that's hard to argue with. True slot junkies always play the maximum.

When you're ready to leave, just press the Cash Out button on the machine. But don't expect to hear that lovely *chingchingchingch-ingCHANG* sound any more. Well, you will hear it, but it's a recording, and no actual coins will come cascading out when you press the button. As we mention earlier, casinos have switched most of the gaming machines to credit slips only. All payouts now are done this way. It allegedly makes matters more convenient and less costly for the casino, and although our hearts may yearn for the "good old days," even we have to admit that it's a lot easier for the gambler, too.

✔ **Look for busy carousels.** When you look for a machine to park yourself in front of, take note of whether the machine is in a carousel that's empty or teeming with players. There's a method to this madness — empty carousels likely have machines that aren't paying well. Take your time to find a carousel where lots of people have lots of money listed on their credit readouts. Again, we're not going to guarantee that you'll do better here, but you may have more luck.

✔ **Investigate progressive payouts.** If you're thinking about playing at a bank of progressive slots, ask an attendant what the jackpot starts at and when it usually hits. Most of the time, she'll be happy to give you this "insider" information. Here's a good general rule: If you discover that a progressive slot carousel jackpot starts at $10,000, usually hits before it reaches $15,000, and is currently at $14,500, sit down and start playing! If it's only at $10,500 (meaning that somebody recently won), it probably won't hit again anytime soon.

✔ **Ask the experts.** Feel free to ask the floor attendants if they know of a certain area that's doing well. It sure beats wandering around from machine to machine looking for that special vibe. Technically, the attendants aren't supposed to tell you this, but many do — especially those in the change areas above slot carousels.

The ins and outs of slot etiquette

You won't need to consult your Emily Post etiquette guide before tackling the slots in Vegas, but you would be wise to keep a few unwritten rules in mind:

✔ **Don't assume that a slot machine isn't in use because nobody is sitting at it.** Slot fanatics often play two or three machines at a time and can be extraordinarily territorial. If people are playing machines adjacent to the one you're thinking of using, ask before you sit down.

✔ **If the chair is tilted toward the machine so no one else can sit down, it's a safe bet that it's in use.** Technically, if you're alone, and you get up and walk away from a machine — even if it's to go to the bathroom — you've relinquished all rights to it, even if you tilt the chair. In reality, unless the casino is mobbed, in which case all bets are off, etiquette holds that you don't touch a machine that is being "held." However, players can't hold slot machines indefinitely. If the "owner" doesn't show up after 10 to 15 minutes, sit down and start playing.

Video Poker: Virtual-Reality Card Games

Video poker works the same way as regular poker, except that you play on a machine. This is one of the few games in Vegas where, if you play perfectly and on the right machine, you actually can break even or, perhaps — gasp! — ahead of the house. It would take a lot more space than we have in this book to expound on perfect video-poker strategy and the proper machines to play on, but in this section we give you the game's basics.

How they work

To play a round of video poker, put in your money, press the Deal button, and five virtual-reality cards pop up (out of a 52-card virtual deck that the machines use for each deal). Select the cards you want to keep with the Hold buttons located under each card, and press Deal again to get replacement cards for the ones you didn't hold. You have only one chance to draw for a winning poker hand. The machine doesn't have a hand of its own, so you aren't competing *against* it. You're just trying to get a hand that's high enough to win something.

This game is a bit more challenging and more active than slots because you have some control (or at least illusion of control) over your fate, and it's easier than playing actual poker with a table full of folks who probably take it very seriously. Even better, some video-poker machines — admittedly, they're very hard to find — actually offer favorable odds if you play perfectly.

Pick your poison

When push comes to shove, your choice of video-poker machine is affected by three factors: denomination, payout schedules, and availability. Unfortunately, you're going to have to do some footwork if you want a machine that meets your expectations for all three, because the poker machines in Vegas are in a constant state of flux.

Just like slot machines, you can play video poker in many different denominations, although quarter and dollar machines are the most played (and most available). Progressive video poker is popping up everywhere, but most are still flat, offering a fixed payout. You also can find a huge range of add-ons that may include a wild card, a double-down feature (where you double your money on a winning hand), or special bonuses for certain hands.

 If you're a beginner, stick to the basic games that offer payouts starting with jacks or better until you get used to the concept. Try to get a machine that pays more than just a return of your money for two pairs. If you can find it, the best machine to play on is called a **9/6 machine,** because, for a single credit bet, it pays out 9 credits for a full house and 6 coins for a flush. Most machines in Vegas are **8/5 machines,** which pay out less money. So, before you play, check the pay schedule on a video-poker machine to determine what its payout percentage is.

A winning hand

Many video-poker machines have a minimum of **jacks or better** to win. This means that out of five cards, you must have at least two jacks of any suit (the ace is always the highest card value, and the two is the lowest) to win. Two matching cards that are higher than jacks is also a winner. If you've never played poker, consult Figure 11-2 to find out more about poker hands.

Just like slots, video-poker machines have gone to a cashless, ticket-in/ticket-out technology, so don't expect to hear the jingle-jangle of coins in the metal tray if you hit it big.

Here's how various poker hands stack up against one another, moving from lowest to highest:

- ✔ **One pair:** Out of your five cards, you have two that have the same face value. Most video-poker games require a pair of jacks as the minimum before they pay.

- ✔ **Two pair:** Two pairs have matching card values — for example, two 5s and two 8s.

- ✔ **Three of a kind:** Three cards out of your five have matching values (for example, three kings).

- ✔ **Straight:** All five of your cards are in sequential order. It doesn't matter what suit they are — they don't have to match. The lowest possible straight is 2-3-4-5-6, and the highest is 10-J-Q-K-A.

✔ **Flush:** Five cards of the same suit, regardless of value (for example, five diamonds).

✔ **Full house:** A combination of one pair and three of a kind (two aces and three 7s, for example).

✔ **Four of a kind:** Not hard to figure out, but also not easy to get. Four of the five cards have the same face value (4-4-4-4-9, for example).

✔ **Straight flush:** Five cards in sequential order, all in the same suit, such as the 5-6-7-8-9 of spades.

✔ **Royal flush:** This is the ultimate poker hand and the highest possible straight flush. If you wind up with the 10-J-Q-K-A of all spades, clubs, diamonds, or hearts, you win big time.

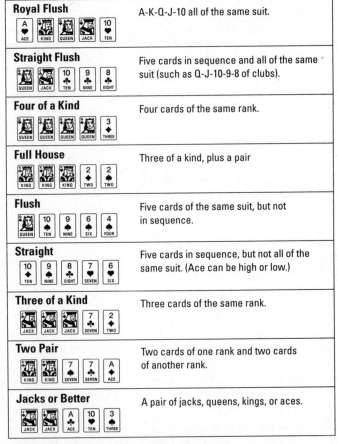

Royal Flush	A-K-Q-J-10 all of the same suit.
Straight Flush	Five cards in sequence and all of the same suit (such as Q-J-10-9-8 of clubs).
Four of a Kind	Four cards of the same rank.
Full House	Three of a kind, plus a pair
Flush	Five cards of the same suit, but not in sequence.
Straight	Five cards in sequence, but not all of the same suit. (Ace can be high or low.)
Three of a Kind	Three cards of the same rank.
Two Pair	Two cards of one rank and two cards of another rank.
Jacks or Better	A pair of jacks, queens, kings, or aces.

Figure 11-2: The hierarchy of video poker hands.

John Caldwell's poker-room picks

Poker in Las Vegas has changed a lot over the past five years, with dozens of new rooms opening and the "old" classics getting a facelift to try to compete. If you're staying in a casino hotel, chances are, your casino has a poker room, and if you just want to play, that may be your best choice. The ten rooms we review here either are clearly top-shelf rooms or have something that makes them special. Wherever you play, have fun and make the most out of the experience.

Bellagio (☎ 702-693-7291; www.bellagio.com**):** Although not as far ahead as it once was, the Bellagio is still the epicenter of the Las Vegas poker scene. At least four major poker events are held here each year. The skill level varies greatly at the lower levels, but at the top levels, this is as tough a room as there is out there. Bring your A game if you're coming to the Bellagio to play. Although the legendary "big game" (the biggest game in town where the elite of the elite get together to exchange hundreds of thousands of dollars over the course of a night) rarely comes together these days, fans of television poker can sit in the adjacent bar and see the top names in the game shuffle in and out of the most notable poker room in town.

Binion's (☎ 702-366-7397; www.binions.com**):** Most of the great moments in tournament poker history have occurred within these walls, as Binion's was the host casino of the World Series of Poker for the first 34 years of the event. Pictures of each world champion from 1970 to 2005 are prominently placed. If these walls could talk, poker fans would never stop listening. The current poker room hosts many daily tournaments, and always has no limit games in play. Go and play poker here, just so you can say you did.

Caesars Palace (☎ 702-785-6566; www.caesars.com**):** One of the biggest rooms in town, the Caesars Palace poker room could host 1,000 players if it needed to. The atmosphere in the room isn't great — it basically converted an old convention room into the new poker room. The room is off the casino floor, which some players like, as there are very few external distractions. For fans of low-limit buy-in tournaments, Caesars has some of the best blind structures of any casino in town. Daily tournaments often last in excess of eight hours, giving the better players time to outmaneuver the competition.

MGM Grand (☎ 702-891-7434; www.mgmgrand.com**):** The MGM poker room is very upscale and hosts daily tournaments that, in our opinion, have some of the weakest fields out there. Many tourists and recreational players play here, and the vibe is decidedly relaxed and friendly. Few know about the private room upstairs, where most of the monitors in the sports book can be watched while you play, and the games are . . . less friendly.

The Mirage (☎ 702-791-7291; www.mirage.com**):** Once the center of the poker world, the Mirage is still a great place to play. Recent additions and upgrades to the surrounding casino (such as the Beatles Cirque Du Soleil show) make the Mirage feel a lot "nicer" than it had in recent years. Big action can be found here, and the daily tournaments are still something of a draw.

The Palms (☎ 702-942-6961; www.palms.com**):** If your TV poker event was not shot at Bellagio, it may have been shot at the Palms. Everything from *Celebrity Poker Showdown* to the "U.S. versus the World" poker TV programs were shot here. The room

(continued)

(continued)

is small, but the "baby" buy-in no-limit games are some of the most action filled of any in town. Bring your money, and your heart — chances are, you'll have to put your money in play frequently at the Palms to have a profitable trip.

Red Rock (☎ 702-797-7766; www.redrocklasvegas.com): The Red Rock poker room has become very popular with locals. One of the more high-tech rooms in town, each dealer has a screen that shows the names of everyone who is playing at the table; it's a little odd at first to have the dealer call you by name, but it's a nice touch. Also, the room has card-tracker and seat-tracker technology so that an unfilled seat doesn't stay unfilled for long, assuming there's a live body to take its place. The room offers food service at the table, but only from 7 a.m. to 7 p.m.

The Rio (☎ 702-777-7650; www.worldseriesofpoker.com): The Rio is notable in that it hosts poker's finest in the World Series of Poker (WSOP) each year. The poker room has gotten a recent facelift and hosts daily tournaments that are quite popular. Check the schedule, and if you want to play against poker's best in the WSOP, the Rio is the place to do it.

Venetian (☎ 702-414-7657; www.venetian.com): The Venetian offers a special parking area for players, has an aggressive comp program, and has, in the past, hosted the legendary "big game." The room has an experienced poker staff, mostly culled from other poker rooms. The Venetian offers table-side food service, which is becoming rarer at top rooms. The Venetian "Deep Stack" Series, held several times a year, is one of the most popular mid-buy-in poker tournament series around.

Wynn Las Vegas (☎ 702-770-3090; www.wynnlasvegas.com): Opened to much fanfare, the Wynn poker room is very upscale and a nice place to play. Most of the action seems to be at the lower levels, but you occasionally find some of the bigger players in town plying their craft here. If you're staying in the hotel, you can put yourself on a waiting list for a game while you relax in your room — and monitor your position on the list from your room instead of sitting in the poker room chomping to get into the game. The room hosts tournaments most days at noon, and the prize pools can get fairly juicy at times ($300 or $500 buy-in).

A note about games: At any given time, you probably will find at least one active low-limit Hold'em game running at any given poker room. However, if you want to play Stud, Omaha, or any other game, call ahead and see if your game of choice is being offered. Also, keep in mind that if you and four or five friends want to play Draw just like you do at home, ask! It's possible the room may provide you a dealer (as long as you pay the time charge).

When you approach the poker room, you'll see a podium or desk staffed by an attendant who will put you right into the game of your choice or on the waiting list. (Know which game[s] you want to be put on the list for in advance — many rooms have a board on the wall describing the games in action at that time.)

Very soon, you'll find yourself with a stack of chips at a poker table with six to nine other people. Here are some do's and don'ts for first-timers:

✔ **Do tip the dealer if you win the hand.** Observe how others have tipped, and follow suit. If you don't know, it's okay to ask! Tip the waitresses, too.

✔ **Don't hold up the game by taking more than 15 to 20 seconds to decide what to do.** If you need a *little* extra time, say "time" so everyone knows you're thinking and not sleeping. Veteran players get very testy with people who take three minutes to decide whether to call an $8 bet.

✔ **Don't act out of turn.** Acting prematurely can give away the strength of your hand. When you're just starting out, take an extra beat to make sure it's your turn to act.

✔ **Do place the chips far enough out in front of you so the dealer can easily reach them when you're going to make or call a bet.** Don't throw the chips at the pot — this is called "splashing the pot" and will not only anger the other players but identify you as the newbie.

✔ **Do protect your hand.** Place a chip or something on your cards to protect them from being accidentally grabbed by the dealer (you'd be surprised how often this happens). Also, carefully cover your cards with your hands when checking them. You can't believe how good a player the guy next to you is when he knows what you have.

✔ **Do say the word *raise* when you want to raise.** If you put a larger chip in and don't say raise (or anything at all), it will be considered a call.

✔ **Do feel free to engage in a bit of table talk.** A little light chat is fine, but if you notice you're the only one talking, either pipe down or find a friendlier game. Games vary a lot in this way, and you have to feel out the table's "temperature" for yourself.

✔ **Don't talk about a hand when it is still going on.** It could influence the play.

✔ **When you win, do wait until the chips are pushed to you before you give your cards back to the dealer.**

John "Schecky" Caldwell is the editor-in-chief of PokerNews.com, the Web's largest poker news site. John lives in Carlsbad, California, where he stays on top of the news and generally thinks way too much about poker.

Tips and tricks

Not enough information for you? Here are a couple other handy tips to remember when you play video poker:

> ✔ **Keep the rules in mind.** A pair of 3s, for example, isn't going to win you anything on a jacks-or-better machine. Drawing three cards to try to get another 3 (for a winning three of a kind) means that you have only two chances to get it right (there are only two more 3s in the deck). If you have an ace and a jack with those two 3s, however, you can keep the high cards and draw for a possible jacks-or-better pair. By doing so, you increase your odds of winning. (You now have six chances of getting a winning hand — three more aces and three more jacks.)

✔ **Don't risk a sure thing.** Unless you're bent on hitting all or nothing, consider keeping a winning hand, regardless of the potential of hitting the mother lode. Say you're dealt the A-K-10 of spades, and the jacks of hearts and diamonds. You may be tempted to go for the royal flush by keeping the A-K-10, but the odds of you getting it are around 1 in 40,000. Keep your sure-thing pair of jacks, and try to build on that.

Blackjack: Hit Me!

Most casino gaming tables are devoted to the game of blackjack. It's very popular, probably because it's very simple to learn the basics and develop a strategy. You should, however, be aware of a few quirks of playing this game in a casino.

In short, you compete *against the dealer* — not the other players — to get as close to 21 points per hand without going over (known as *busting*). Numbered cards are worth their face value, face cards (J-Q-K) are worth 10, and the ace is worth either 1 or 11 points (your choice).

The primary differences among blackjack games are the number of decks used and the minimum bets allowed. Games range anywhere from one to six decks per game, and table minimums range from $1 to $500 per hand, although $5 to $10 per hand is the most common. (It's usually at least $10 on the Strip.) Most tables also have a maximum bet, so make sure that you find out what the betting range is for a given table before you sit down to play.

How to play the game

The first thing you need to do is place your bet on the table. After you place your bet, the dealer gives you two cards, usually face up, and then deals himself two cards: one face up and one face down. If your two cards equal 21 (a 10 or face card plus an ace), the dealer calls blackjack and you win automatically.

If the dealer has a 10 or an ace showing, he'll check his hidden card. If he has a blackjack, everyone sitting at the table loses.

If you don't have 21, you're allowed as many additional cards as you want to try to reach 21. You lose (or bust) if you go over.

If you didn't bust, and you've gone as high as you can (or want to), the dealer reveals his hidden card and attempts to beat your score. If he does, you lose; if he doesn't, you win. If you tie, it's called a *push,* and neither of you wins or loses.

Know the finer points

Blackjack really isn't all that complicated, but you should know a few things before you sit down to play a hand. After you read the following tips, watch a few hands when you enter the casino, and then sit down and press your luck. And if you still have questions, ask the dealer.

- ✔ **You need chips to play.** Casino blackjack is played with chips, not cash. You can buy chips in different denominations at the main cashier or at the table itself. And after you've placed a bet on the table and the dealer starts dealing, don't touch your bet. If you do, you're likely to get a verbal slap on the wrist (often accompanied by a stern look) from the dealer.

- ✔ **Pay attention to the dealer minimum.** Most casino blackjack games require the dealer to draw to at least 17. In other words, the dealer can't quit drawing cards until her hand totals 17 or higher. Keep this in mind when devising your own strategy.

- ✔ **Know the difference between multideck and single-deck games.** Most Vegas blackjack games use six decks of cards all mixed together in a *shoe,* which is a special card dispenser. The cards are dealt face up in front of you. *Don't touch them!* The dealer is the only one allowed to handle the cards in these multideck games. (You're scolded if you touch them.) Occasionally, you can find a single-deck game in which the dealer deals the cards by hand, face down in front of you. In this case, you're allowed to touch the cards — they're face down, so you have to pick them up to look at them. It's worth noting that most single-deck games now pay only 6:5 on a natural blackjack instead of the 3:2 at multideck tables.

  No matter which type of blackjack game you play, you need to know the hand signals for *hitting* (asking for another card) or *standing* (telling the dealer that you don't want another card). It's kind of like the secret handshake of blackjack players. (Luckily, no decoder rings are involved.) You signal for an additional card by making a light scratching motion toward yourself on the table with your hand (or with your cards, if you're holding them). This is sort of a nonverbal way of saying, "Gimme another one." If you don't want to draw, wave your hand once above your cards to signal "no more" (or if you're holding your cards, tuck them face down on the table gently under your bet).

What's your strategy?

You better your chances of winning at the blackjack table if you have a basic strategy going into the game.

If your two cards total 17 or above, don't draw. Your chances of getting a higher hand are slim (and the dealer has a decent chance of busting while trying to beat your hand). If you have a two-card total of 11 or less, draw a card — it's impossible to go over 21 with one additional card.

When you have 12 to 16 points, regardless of how many cards you have, things start to get a bit tricky. This is when you should take a long, hard look at the dealer's single upturned card. If you fall into that 12- to 16-point range, and the dealer has a 7 or higher showing, you should probably draw a card. Chances are, the dealer has a 10-point card hidden, and you lose if you don't draw a card. If the dealer has a 6 or lower card showing, she'll probably have to draw (to reach at least 17), and there's a good chance of her going over 21 and losing. Consider staying, even with a hand as low as 12.

Insurance

When the dealer has an ace upturned, she asks if you want to take out **insurance.** When taking out insurance, you're allowed to place an additional bet of up to half your original wager — for example, if you bet $10, you can wager up to $5 on an insurance bet. If the dealer has 21, you lose your original bet but are paid 2:1 on your insurance bet. By doing so, you come out even if your insurance bet was half your original bet. (You lose your $10 bet but gain an additional $5 on the insurance bet — are you following us on this?) If the dealer doesn't have 21, you lose your insurance bet, and the game proceeds as usual. Many gambling aficionados, including our humble selves, consider this a sucker bet, because the odds are that the dealer won't have 21. We suggest that you don't bother with insurance.

Doubling down

If you want to do even more fancy stuff at the blackjack tables, you can **double down.** You place this bet after you're dealt your first two cards but before any additional cards are dealt. You must double the amount you bet by placing additional chips on the table — for example, if you originally bet $10, you put out another $10 in chips. By doing this, you're hoping that your next card will give you a high enough hand to win — but you get only one additional card. The odds are that your one additional card will be worth 10 points (a 10 or a face card), so you should go with this option when your first two cards total 10 or 11, and the dealer has a low card showing. If you're lucky, you wind up with 20 or 21 and will probably win the hand and double your entire bet. If you get a low card, however, you don't get another card to boost your point total, and you're likely to lose it all. Hey, that's why they call it gambling!

Splitting

Splitting is another option you can try if you're feeling adventurous. Here's the deal: You're allowed to split when the first two cards you're dealt are of the same value (for example, two 7s). If you tell the dealer that you want to split this hand, the two cards on the table will be separated; then you lay down additional chips equal to your original bet. The dealer then treats each card as a separate hand, and you can draw as many cards as you like to get as close to 21 as possible *for each hand.* Whichever hand beats the dealer wins double that bet (and you may even win with both hands). If either (or both) of your hands doesn't beat the dealer, you lose the bet.

When deciding whether to split your hand, consider this: Most people agree that two aces or two 8s should always be split into separate hands. This is generally a good bet because the odds are in your favor that you wind up with two better hands than the one you would've had otherwise.

Tips and tricks

Blackjack is an easy game to play and can be a lot of fun under the right conditions:

- ✔ **Find a fun dealer.** Before you choose your table, watch the dealer to see if she's one of the stone-faced, boring ones, or if she has some kick. A fun dealer often chats, offers advice, and generally makes the entire experience more enjoyable. On the other hand, if you're in a somber mood, you may want a no-nonsense dealer. Your choice.

- ✔ **Look for fun tablemates.** Same concept as in the preceding bullet, only this one has to do with the other gamblers at the table. If everyone is sitting around looking sour and concentrating mightily on his cards, you may want to bypass the table. Scope out a table where your tablemates are whooping it up, and you may have a better time.

- ✔ **Keep a stash.** Any financial planner will tell you that you should always save, and it's no different when gambling. Keep two piles of chips — one for betting and one for saving. Every time you win a hand, set aside part of your winnings (maybe half?) into the "don't touch" pile, and then, well, don't touch it. If your luck takes a bad turn, and you go through your betting pile, walk away. At least you still have money left.

- ✔ **Practice with video blackjack.** Most of the better casinos have nifty computerized video-blackjack games that cost a quarter a try. Because most blackjack tables on the Strip start at $10, this is an economical way to at least get a feel for the game before you start laying down real money. It's not precisely the same as working with a real dealer, and the odds aren't the same, but the rules are, and that's what matters if you're a beginner.

- ✔ **Gamble downtown.** Serious gamblers — and by that we mean those who play to win, pure and simple — particularly blackjack players, always gamble downtown. They don't care about glitz and flash and themes. They want single-deck play, because they believe that the odds are better, and because they stand a better chance of card counting (not that they do that, nosirree — that's their story and they're stickin' to it!). You may want to join them for these same reasons, and also because the minimum stakes are lower — as low as $5 a hand as opposed to $10 on the Strip.

While playing blackjack, be sure to ask the dealer or the *pit boss* (the employee overseeing a group of tables) about restaurants, shows, and attractions in that particular hotel. If you've been betting a decent amount of money per hand (think $25 per hand for a few hours in the big hotels) and have been playing a while, you may get a *comp* (complimentary) meal, show ticket, or other discount. You have to ask for these, however, because they're rarely offered.

Roulette: Take a Spin

Lots of people have seen roulette wheels, but few ever sit down to play. The game is actually quite easy to learn and can be a lot of fun to play. It does, however, have a huge house advantage, so keep that in mind.

Here are the basics of playing roulette: A ball is spun on a wheel with 38 numbers (0, 00, and 1 through 36). The 0 and 00 spaces are green, and the other numbers are either red or black (divided evenly between the two colors). You place your bets on the *field,* which is a grid layout on the table showing all the numbers and a variety of different combinations (see Figure 11-3). *Inside bets* are those placed on the 0 through 36 number part of the field. *Outside bets* are placed in the boxes surrounding the numbers and include red, black, even, odd, 1 through 18, 19 through 36, 1st 12, 2nd 12, 3rd 12, and the columns bets. The object is for the ball to settle on one of the numbers (or other options) that you've placed bets on.

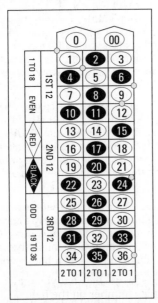

Figure 11-3: A standard roulette table.

Note that you can win on more than one bet on a single spin, depending on the outcome. For example, if you place a bet on 8, even, and 1st 12, you can potentially win all three bets if the ball lands on 8. Pretty cool, huh?

How to bet on roulette

After you choose your table, you can exchange some cash or chips for special roulette chips. Each player at the table has a different color of chips, so it's easy to keep track of yours. Then you can start placing your bets on the field (refer to Figure 11-3). You're allowed to bet even after the ball begins spinning, but once the ball starts to fall toward the numbers, bets are cut off.

Inside bets are complicated, so we're going to stick to the outside bets, with one exception: single-number bets (see the upcoming description). Outside bets don't pay out as much, but beginners should probably stick with them at first.

- ✓ **Odd-Even:** If you place a bet in the Odd field and an odd number comes up on the wheel, you win double your bet placed on that field. If it comes up as an even number, you lose that bet. It follows, then, that if an even number comes up, you win for bets placed in the Even field. If either 0 or 00 comes up, you lose bets placed in either field.

- ✓ **Red-Black:** This one is really simple. Place your chips on a color, and you win if a number comes up in the color you bet. If you bet red, and the ball lands on a red number, you double your bet (but you lose if black comes up). If 0 or 00 comes up — you guessed it! — you lose.

- ✓ **1–18, 19–36:** If you place chips in either of these boxes, and the winning number falls within the range listed, you double your money for that bet. Suppose that you bet on 1–18, and the number 15 comes up on the wheel; you win. If the number 32 comes up, you lose. If 0 or 00 comes up on the wheel, you lose these bets.

- ✓ **1st 12, 2nd 12, 3rd 12:** This is similar to the 1–18 and 19–36 bets, only a little more specific. Bet on the 1st 12, and if any number between 1 and 12 hits, you win triple your bet. If any other number hits, you lose your bet. The same concept applies with bets on the 2nd 12 (numbers 13–24) and the 3rd 12 (numbers 25–36).

- ✓ **Column bets:** At the end of the Inside fields are three boxes that are marked *2 to 1* (refer to Figure 11-3). If you place chips here, you're betting that the winning number on the wheel is going to be one of the numbers in the column above that box. If it is, you triple your bet. If it isn't, you lose it all.

- ✓ **Single-number bets:** This is the one inside bet that you may want to try. Place your chips on any single number on the field (17 or 34, for example), and if that number comes up, you win 35 times your bet. This is fun to play, and the winnings can be big, but the odds are way against you.

Tips and tricks

Here's some common-sense advice for first-timers:

- ✔ **Look for single-zero roulette.** As we mention earlier, most tables and wheels have both 0 and 00. A few have only the 0. If you can find one of these single-zero tables, play it, because your odds are slightly better with fewer possible numbers (only 37 instead of 38) on the wheel.

- ✔ **Stick with the outside bets.** Placing all your money on your one single lucky number is tempting. Doing so can be exciting, but the problem is that you're much more likely to lose. The outside bets may not seem as glamorous, and they certainly don't pay out as much, but your money goes farther, and the odds of winning are a lot better.

Keno: The Lotto of the Casinos

The ancient Chinese played a game that was very similar to your local lotto, and keno is based on the same concept. It may not be as adrenaline-filled as craps, but it's a good diversion while you're sitting in a hotel restaurant or lounge.

In the game of keno, a computer randomly draws 20 numbers from a field of 1 through 80. You place various bets on which numbers will come up, and if enough of your numbers do come up, you win.

Large keno boards (with the 80 numbers displayed) are scattered throughout casinos — often in the coffee shops and lounges. You can get a keno ticket from the restaurant tables or at the bar. The ticket shows the 80 numbers (called *spots*) and has boxes for the amount of your bet and the number of sequential games you want to play (see Figure 11-4). You place a bet by filling out the ticket and giving it to the *runner,* who then takes it to the keno lounge. You can find keno runners walking around the casino floor and inside the hotel's restaurants and bars. Their uniforms usually identify them as keno runners, but they also announce their presence as they drift around.

Casinos vary wildly regarding the possible bets you can make and the payout odds for bets, but the most common bets are 6-, 7-, 8-, 9-, and 10-spot bets. If you play a 6-spot game, for example, you mark six numbers on the ticket and hand it in. Just as with the lotto, if your six numbers come up, you win. If five of your six numbers are selected, you also win, but substantially less than you would have with all six numbers. Four matching numbers will likely pay even money, and three or fewer matching numbers loses.

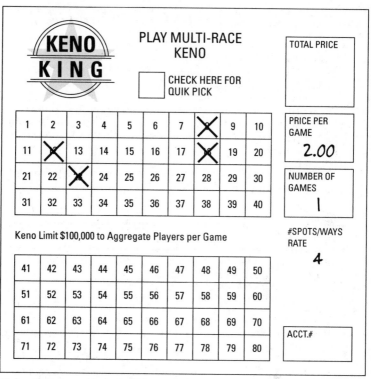

Figure 11-4: A sample keno ticket.

 Keep in mind that you have to cash in winning tickets *before the start of the next game,* or you lose it all. If you can't find a keno runner, take your ticket to the keno cashier right away to get paid. Also, before you go dreaming about hitting the big jackpot, know this: The house advantage on keno is greater than in any other game in the casino.

In true Vegas style, you can change your betting strategy so that this fundamentally simple game takes a complex turn. For example, you can make bets involving groupings and splits. However, this is much more than you need to know if you're just looking for something to do while waiting for your drink. Just pick your lucky numbers and go. The best advice we can offer is that betting on fewer spots means better odds of winning. It's a lot easier to get six out of six than it is to get 10 out of 10. Plus, if you get five numbers on a six-spot ticket, you win something, whereas five numbers on a 10-spot will probably get you zippo. You won't win as much on a lower-spot ticket, but you're likely to win more often.

Craps: Roll the Dice and Play the Odds

If you've ever heard that craps is really complicated, you've heard right. Oh, we struggled with it. We read books. We had people explain. Our eyes always glazed over. We considered and wondered if a quick course in quantum physics. . . .

Now, we think we've finally gotten it. Despite our initial handicap, many people figure it out rather quickly (or else are faking it by randomly hurling money at the table — that works, too). Playing craps can be a little intimidating, but it's possible to play a simple game. Basically, bets are placed on what number will come up on a pair of dice thrown. You can place bets even if you're not the one throwing the dice. Table 11-1 shows how the 36 combinations stack up.

Table 11-1   Craps Combinations and Odds

Number Rolled	How Many Ways to Roll That Number	True Odds	Winning Combinations
Two	1	35 to 1	
Three	2	17 to 1	
Four	3	11 to 1	
Five	4	8 to 1	
Six	5	6.2 to 1	
Seven	6	5 to 1	
Eight	5	6.2 to 1	
Nine	4	8 to 1	
Ten	3	11 to 1	
Eleven	2	17 to 1	
Twelve	1	35 to 1	

The person who is rolling the dice is called the *shooter*. When the shooter makes her first roll, it's called *coming out*. The object is for the shooter to get a 7 or 11 in any combination (2 and 5, 5 and 6, and so on) on the first roll. That's an automatic winner for anyone playing the *pass line* (see upcoming section, "The pass-line bet"). If the shooter rolls a 2, 3, or 12, she *craps out,* and it's an automatic loser for anyone playing the pass line. If any other number comes up on the come-out roll (4, 5, 6, 8, 9, or 10), this number becomes the *point,* and the object of the game switches a little. After a point number has been established, the goal is for the shooter to roll the point number again before rolling a 7. If a 7 comes up before the point, then the shooter has crapped out, and you lose your pass-line bet. Any time the shooter craps out, the dice are passed to the next shooter, and the game starts over.

The following sections describe how you place bets on various parts of the gaming table (see also Figure 11-5).

There's a lot more to this game than what we describe in this section. For example, you can *play the odds* (make side bets that are placed on the point number), *buy bets,* and *lay bets.* If you're a beginner, we suggest that you stick with the pass line and come bets (see the upcoming section, "The come bet") at first. These are the easiest to play, and they offer the best odds. If you're interested in knowing more about the intricacies of craps, check out the upcoming section, "More Information on Gambling."

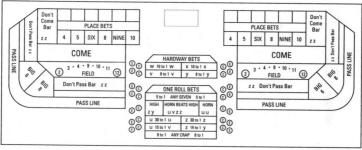

Figure 11-5: A standard craps table.

The pass-line bet

You should stick with the pass-line bet if you're a beginner. When playing this type of bet, you place your initial bet on the pass line, which means that you're betting that the player won't crap out. A roll of 7 or 11, or establishing a point number and rolling it before a 7, wins double your bet. Here's an example to help you out: Say that you place your bet on the pass line. After you place it on the pass line, you can't touch it until you win or lose. The shooter rolls a 4. This is now the point. The next roll is a 5 and then a 10. Finally, on the fourth throw, the shooter rolls a 4 and you win. If that fourth throw had turned up a 7, you would've lost.

The don't pass bar bet

The *don't pass bar bet,* placed on the don't pass bar, is exactly the opposite of the pass bet. You're betting that the shooter will crap out before winning. If the shooter rolls a 7 or 11, or establishes and then makes a point number, you lose a don't pass bet. If the shooter rolls a 2, 3, or 12, or craps out before making his point, then you win double.

The come bet

You place a *come bet* after the shooter establishes a point number. For example, say the shooter throws a 6 on his first throw. That is the point number, and placing a bet in the come field is now just like a pass-line bet. You're wagering that the next throw of the dice will be 7 or 11. If it is, you win double. If the next throw is a 2, 3, or 12, you lose. If it's any other number, the bet is moved into the corresponding box (4, 5, 6, 8, 9, or 10), where it remains until the shooter either rolls the number again (you win) or rolls a 7 (you lose).

The don't come bet

The *don't come bet,* placed on the don't come bar, is the pessimists' version of the come bet: You win double if the throw is 2, 3, or 12, and lose if it's a 7 or 11. If any other number appears (4, 5, 6, 8, 9, or 10), you win if a 7 is thrown before that number is repeated, but lose if it's not.

The place bet

To make a *place bet,* put your chips in the place bets field above any number. You're betting that the number will be rolled before a 7 is rolled. You can increase, decrease, or remove your bet entirely at any time during play.

The Hard Way, Big 6/8, Field, and Proposition bets

The Hard Way, Big 6, Big 8, Field, and Proposition bets make up the remainder of the gaming table. If you win on one of these bets, you can win big; but these bets are, according to most people, not worth the effort, because the odds are against you in every single case.

- The **Hard Way bets** wager that 4, 6, 8, or 10 will be rolled, with one catch: The numbers must come up on the dice as double numbers (two 2s, 3s, 4s, or 5s, depending on which box you choose), and the combination has to appear before the number is thrown in any other combination or before a 7 appears.

- The **Big 6 and Big 8 bets** say that the shooter will throw a 6 or 8 before a 7 appears — the same as a place bet but with lower payback odds.

- A **Field bet** wagers that the next throw of the dice will be a 2, 3, 4, 9, 10, 11, or 12, which are the seven least likely numbers to appear.

This bet is based on one single roll of the dice; avoid it if you're a beginner.

✔ **Proposition bets** say that the next roll will be a 2, 3, 7, 11, or 12 (there's a box for each), or any craps (2, 3, or 12). This bet is also based on one single roll of the dice and, again, should be avoided if you're a beginner.

Tips and tricks

Okay, so we're not seasoned craps players. But we do listen, and we've managed to pick up some tips that we're happy to pass on to you.

✔ **If you can find a table with any room, just stand and watch for a while.** Even if you think that you still don't understand the game, it'll become a lot clearer when you see it in action. Maybe.

✔ **It's definitely exciting to be the shooter, but it's a lot easier to bet and watch your money if you let someone else roll the dice.** Feel free to pass when your turn as shooter comes around if you're not comfortable trying to roll and manage your bets. Alternatively, just don't bet when you're shooting.

✔ **Avoid the Hard Way and one-roll bets like the plague.** You almost always lose.

The Other Games in Town

The games that we mention earlier in this chapter are the most popular games, but they certainly are not the only ones in town. In addition, you can find the following games:

✔ **Standard poker:** This game is pretty much the same as video poker, only with real players and real cards. You don't play against the house (although the house does take a percentage of the pot), so you have a better shot at winning here than in any other game.

✔ **Three-card poker:** Once a rarity, this game has gotten so popular that you usually can find several tables in most of the major casinos. It's actually much more difficult to explain than it is to play — basically, you're dealt three cards with no draw and you have to make the best poker hand out of those three cards. We recommend that you watch a table for a bit before giving it a try.

✔ **Baccarat:** This is a complex card game that is similar to blackjack. Actually, the main thing you need to know is that you bet on either the bank or the player — the dealer does all the rest of the work.

✔ **Mini-baccarat:** This is pretty much the same as baccarat, only a little simpler.

✔ **Pai-gow poker:** This is a Chinese take on seven-card stud poker.

✔ **Let-it-ride and Caribbean stud:** These are two more poker-based card games.

✔ **Sports betting:** Yep, you can bet on just about any game in the world by stopping in at your hotel's *sports book* (the area of a casino where sports betting occurs) and placing a wager.

More Information on Gambling

The information we provide throughout this chapter gives you a good, basic overview on the most popular games in the casinos. If you want to know even more, check out the following valuable resources:

✔ **Hotel gaming lessons:** If you want some nitty-gritty details on the table game of your choice, ask if your hotel offers gaming lessons. Many do. These lessons are very helpful, and they're usually taught in an easy-to-understand manner, right at the table, so that you can see what's going on. Plus, they're often free.

✔ **Computer games:** You can find tons of computer games for sale at retail stores. These games simulate live play and enable you to learn the rules of casino gambling. Search online for "casino games" and you'll likely find a bunch of shareware programs that you can download for free.

Where to Play

Trust us: In Las Vegas, you won't lack for opportunities to gamble. If you're in a gambling frame of mind, you can start with the slot machines at the airport baggage carousel and keep going at restaurants, coffee shops, bars, and so on. We won't take up your time by listing every single casino in town; suffice it to say that every hotel on the Strip has a gigantic casino with all the games you could ever want to play.

In many ways, a casino is a casino is a casino. They all have machines and tables and chances for joy or heartbreak. Some people may want a casino with a theme because it's fun and gambling is fun, while others may find the themes distracting because gambling is serious business. Let's face it: Ultimately, your favorite casino is one you've won at. Here are some casinos that we like (and some that we don't — only because we've lost there).

Casinos for the serious gambler

The **Mirage,** 3400 Las Vegas Blvd. S. (☎ **702-791-7111**), is one of our favorite place to gamble — and not even because we've won all that much there. Quite the opposite, in fact. This casino is large and surprisingly quiet, allowing for minimal distractions from your desire to win. If you want to play serious poker on the Strip, this is the place to go.

But if you really want to gamble in high-class style, you should go to **Mandalay Bay**, 3950 Las Vegas Blvd. S. (☎ 702-632-7777), the **Monte Carlo**, 3770 Las Vegas Blvd. S. (☎ 702-730-7777), or the **Venetian**, 3355 Las Vegas Blvd. S. (☎ 702-414-1000). All these casinos are variations on a theme: classy, European-style casinos, full of towering ceilings, marble, and glitzy lights. Tacky touches are kept at bay. Although these casinos are attractive places, we think that the results are pretty interchangeable — when you've seen one of them, you've seen them all. On the other hand, they tend to be less noisy and chaotic than some of the others.

Outstripping even these casinos in the hoity-toity department is **Bellagio**, 3600 Las Vegas Blvd. S. (☎ 888-987-6667). Bellagio was built with high rollers and lovers of class in mind, as were the casinos mentioned earlier, but Bellagio takes it up a notch or two on the grand meter. Oh, does it feel serious. We've heard that the slot machines have been constructed to make less of a crash-clang than usual, but this may be a nuance too subtle for us to really notice. If you love the look of Bellagio, you should also try **Wynn Las Vegas**, 3131 Las Vegas Blvd. S. (☎ 702-770-7700), given that a common first impression is "It looks like Bellagio!"

For a little architectural eye candy with your gaming, try **Encore**, 3121 Las Vegas Blvd. S. (☎ 800-320-7125), with its red walls, white plantation shutters, and plenty of natural light, or **Aria**, 3730 Las Vegas Blvd. S. (☎ 702-590-7111), which is a veritable riot (but in a good way) of dramatic design using everything from luxurious woods to shaped glass to rich fabrics to give it a modern air.

Casinos for the not-so-serious gambler

Harrah's Las Vegas, 3475 Las Vegas Blvd. S. (☎ 702-369-5000), has a festive European carnival theme. This place may have the friendliest dealers in town.

The casino at the **Hard Rock Hotel & Casino**, 4455 Paradise Rd. (☎ 702-693-5000), is a masterpiece of Vegas silliness. The craps tables are shaped like grand pianos, some slot machines have guitar necks for handles, and the gaming chips have faces of famous rock stars on them. The decibel level is high — be prepared for blaring rock music — but it makes for a much looser vibe. Try to bet to the beat. And if you're staying there, don't forget to visit the pool's swim-up blackjack table. And yes, we asked — they give you little waterproof pouches for holding your money.

Caesars Palace, 3570 Las Vegas Blvd. S. (☎ 702-731-7110), offers serious luxury for serious gamblers, but lovers of the absurd will have a great time here, too. After all, the cocktail waitresses are wearing togas, and faux marble Roman statues keep an eye on the proceedings. And that's not even counting regular appearances by Roman gladiators and soldiers, and Caesar and Cleopatra.

Hey, and speaking of silly, don't overlook the fabulous **New York–New York,** 3790 Las Vegas Blvd. S. (☎ 702-740-6969). Although some of the Gotham madness has been stripped away, there's still enough of the Big Apple — Times Square, Greenwich Village, and so on — left to giggle about.

In summer, **Tropicana Resort & Casino,** 3801 Las Vegas Blvd. S. (☎ 702-739-2222), offers swim-up blackjack in its beautiful tropical pool area (which is getting a major redo for 2011). And then there's **Circus Circus,** 2880 Las Vegas Blvd. S. (☎ 702-734-0410), which hits new heights in distractions — literally — with frequent live circus aerial acts over its casino. Is that trapeze artist going to miss and land on your winning blackjack hand? And if he does, does that count as a push?

And speaking of overhead distractions, the **Rio,** 3700 W. Flamingo Rd. (☎ 702-252-7777), interrupts play (or it would, if you find that you can't pull a slot handle while looking up at the ceiling) several times on week-end nights with its "Show in the Sky" Mardi Gras performance. This show takes place in the much more appealing part of the Rio's casino, an extension that has a very high ceiling (the better to accommodate said show).

Casinos for the budget gambler

If you're gambling on a budget (and you don't want to break the bank), head downtown to make your money last the longest. Or just rejoice that just about every casino, even on the Strip, has added at least one bank of penny slots. C'mon, even the tightest tightwad in Miserville can afford to play those babies.

Binion's, 128 E. Fremont St. (☎ 702-382-1600), is a great example of Old Las Vegas. Because of its reputation, those people claiming to be *real* gamblers won't play anywhere but Binion's.

A few blocks down the street from Binion's is **El Cortez Hotel & Casino,** 600 E. Fremont St. (☎ 702-385-5200), offering roulette with minimum bets as low as $1, and $3 craps.

A casino for those who think bigger is better

The **MGM Grand,** 3799 Las Vegas Blvd. S. (☎ 702-891-7777), has one of the largest casinos in the world. And it is, needless to say, really, really big. Four football fields would fit in here, with room left over for several basketball courts. You can decide if that's a good thing or a bad thing. Slot lore has it that the Majestic Lions slot machines here are always a sure thing.

A cozy casino for your gambling pleasure

Or go in the completely opposite direction and head to one of our favor-ites, the **Main Street Station,** 200 N. Main St. (☎ 702-387-1896). This is actually a sweet little place (pretty, even), with its turn-of-the-century San Francisco style. We love it.

 Many of the casinos in the downtown area are small and not affiliated with any hotel. You often see employees standing out front trying to lure you inside with the promise of free stuff. Avoid these places, because, almost without exception, your free gift isn't worth it.

Chapter 12

Discovering Las Vegas's Best Attractions

. . . .

In This Chapter

▶ Prioritizing your activities
▶ Discovering the best things to see and do in Las Vegas
▶ Entertaining your kids and teens
▶ Getting hitched in Vegas
▶ Scoping out museums and cultural activities
▶ Finding a place to work out
▶ Taking an organized tour

. . . .

*W*hat truly separates Sin City from other destinations is, of course, gambling — were you expecting cathedrals or something? But you can't sit at a slot machine forever. (Or maybe you can.) If there is one sure bet in Las Vegas, it's that you won't lack for things to do, regardless of your personal tastes or budget. However, Vegas being Vegas, the attractions here are not quite the same as what you find in other destinations. The city's most notable must-sees are those mammoth theme hotels.

But glitzy, over-the-top hotels are not all there is to Vegas — although, by the time you're through investigating all the jaw-dropping architecture on the Strip, you may be too exhausted to learn otherwise. Sure, Vegas has lavish shows and Elvis impersonators, but it also has off-the-wall museums and free street-side extravaganzas. Rest assured that you can find plenty of action-packed fun to fill your time in between poker hands. Having said that, please note that there are fewer and fewer family-appropriate activities, even for the locals. And as Vegas continues to build and dazzle, newer resorts seem less likely to put up an amusement park or a shark exhibit, and more inclined to build saucy burlesque nightclubs or another posh spa. In other words, a growing emphasis is being placed on relaxation or nighttime partying — neither of which is a bad thing on its own, of course!

Las Vegas Attractions Overview

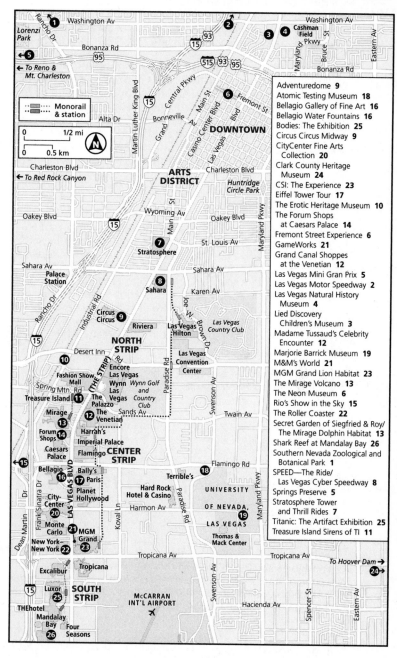

Adventuredome **9**
Atomic Testing Museum **18**
Bellagio Gallery of Fine Art **16**
Bellagio Water Fountains **16**
Bodies: The Exhibition **25**
Circus Circus Midway **9**
CityCenter Fine Arts
  Collection **20**
Clark County Heritage
  Museum **24**
CSI: The Experience **23**
Eiffel Tower Tour **17**
The Erotic Heritage Museum **10**
The Forum Shops
  at Caesars Palace **14**
Fremont Street Experience **6**
GameWorks **21**
Grand Canal Shoppes
  at the Venetian **12**
Las Vegas Mini Gran Prix **5**
Las Vegas Motor Speedway **2**
Las Vegas Natural History
  Museum **4**
Lied Discovery
  Children's Museum **3**
Madame Tussaud's Celebrity
  Encounter **12**
Marjorie Barrick Museum **19**
M&M's World **21**
MGM Grand Lion Habitat **23**
The Mirage Volcano **13**
The Neon Museum **6**
Rio's Show in the Sky **15**
The Roller Coaster **22**
Secret Garden of Siegfried & Roy/
  The Mirage Dolphin Habitat **13**
Shark Reef at Mandalay Bay **26**
Southern Nevada Zoological and
  Botanical Park **1**
SPEED—The Ride/
  Las Vegas Cyber Speedway **8**
Springs Preserve **5**
Stratosphere Tower
  and Thrill Rides **7**
Titanic: The Artifact Exhibition **25**
Treasure Island Sirens of TI **11**

If you're spending a lot of time (or money) gambling in one casino, check with the dealer or casino attendant to find out if you can get a discounted (or free) admission to the hotel's attractions. A simple "How much is it to get into (fill in the blank)?" may get you a free pass if you're dumping money into their coffers via the casino.

On a strict budget? Lost all your money in the slots? No problem. You can find lots of inexpensive diversions in town to keep you amused (and away from the casinos). Many of the free publications in town, such as *LVM*, include coupons for discount admissions to attractions. In addition, some hotels have people at the front door passing out coupons for discounted admission to the hotel's attractions. And don't forget that you can check out the free hotel shows, such as **Bellagio**'s exquisite water fountains or the **Mirage** volcano.

What's Your Priority?

Although we include only Vegas's most entertaining or unusual sights in the following listings, unless you're planning on being here for a while, you're going to need to prioritize. For consistency's sake, we're sticking with the South Strip, North Strip, and Central Strip neighborhoods, which parallel those set up in the hotel and restaurant chapters. Remember that a Paradise Road designation means that an attraction is located somewhere *near* Paradise Road and not necessarily *on* it. As in other chapters, we use the Off the Beaten Path designation for places that are located outside the defined neighborhoods but are worth the extra time and mileage.

If your time in Las Vegas is limited, try to plan the attractions you want to see by neighborhood, instead of running all over town. If you stick to one area at a time, you maximize your sightseeing opportunities.

Unless we note otherwise, all the following attractions offer free valet or do-it-yourself parking.

Las Vegas's Top Sites from A to Z

Adventuredome
North Strip

Though showing its age, this miniature amusement park under a giant pink dome may be a good place to head on a hot day. It has a double-loop roller coaster, a water flume, laser tag, and a few other rides — plus a separate video/carnival game arcade, food stands, and a couple of non-stomach-churning rides for the smaller kids. Kids and adults alike will have their fill of this place after a couple hours.

See maps p. 197 and p. 205. 2880 Las Vegas Blvd. S. (in Circus Circus). ☎ **702-794-3939.** *www.adventuredome.com. Admission: All-day ride pass $25 for everyone*

South Strip Attractions

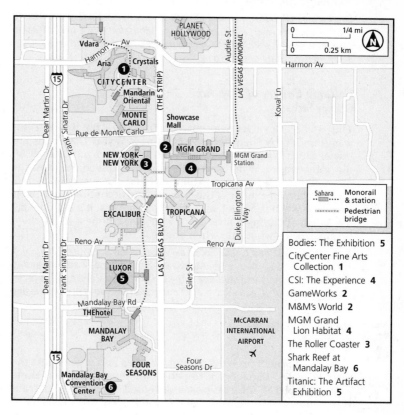

48 in. or taller, $15 for everyone 33–47 in. tall. Per-ride prices: $4–$7. Open: Park hours vary season to season, but generally Mon–Thurs 11 a.m.–6 p.m., Fri–Sat 10 a.m. to midnight, Sun 10 a.m.–9 p.m.

Atomic Testing Museum
Off the Beaten Path

A 1950s-era souvenir from Binion's hotel and casino memorializes a "dreaded atomic bomb blast" with pictures of a mushroom cloud blooming over the Nevada desert just outside of Las Vegas. The Nevada Test Site was home to many such tests for the better part of four decades, and the fact that it turned into a bit of a tourist attraction is just one of the aspects covered at the Atomic Testing Museum, a fascinating facility devoted to the history of the atomic age both in the area and around the world. Far from a dry examination of science, this interactive interpretative center boasts exhibits, video, memorabilia, and more designed to help visitors understand the good and the bad that came from setting off radioactive bombs 60 miles away from a major tourist destination.

See map p. 197. 755 E. Flamingo Rd. (just east of Paradise Road). ☎ *702-794-5151. www.atomictestingmuseum.org. Admission: $12 adults; $9 seniors, military, students with ID, and Nevada residents; free for kids 6 and under. Open: Mon–Sat 9 a.m.–5 p.m., Sun noon to 5 p.m.*

Bellagio Gallery of Fine Art
Center Strip

This isn't black velvet paintings or motel art — but it is hotel art, in that it was founded by then **Bellagio** (and now **Wynn Las Vegas** and **Encore**) owner Steve Wynn, a most respected art collector. When MGM took over his hotel empire, Wynn's art collection was moved out. Now the gallery is home to notable traveling exhibitions and other events, including a critically acclaimed exhibit of the collection of actor Steve Martin, plus shows featuring Warhol, Monet, and Picasso ceramics. It's not cheap, but surely it's worth spending a little money for some honest-to-goodness cultcha. Be sure to see what's up when you're in town.

See maps p. 197 and p. 201. 3600 Las Vegas Blvd. S. (in the Bellagio). ☎ *702-693-7871. www.bellagio.com. Admission: $15 adults; $12 seniors and Nevada residents; $10 teachers and students with I.D. Open: Sun–Tues and Thurs 10 a.m.–6 p.m., Wed and Fri–Sat 10 a.m.–7 p.m. Last admission half-hour prior to closing.*

Bodies: The Exhibition
South Strip

This exhibition of preserved human bodies and organs puts the "eewww" back in "cool." Cadavers, stripped to the muscle and sometimes beyond, are displayed in athletic poses designed to vividly illustrate just how those muscles work, while other body parts are dissected for similar demonstrative purposes (cross sections of lungs showing the damage inflicted by smoking, for example). It's completely scientific rather than exploitative, but we won't kid you — if you think too much about the source of the contents of the informative displays, it is a little icky. Some people may find it too intense, but many others will be so intrigued and fascinated that they'll want to make a return visit. There certainly is nothing else like it in Vegas.

See maps p. 197 and p. 199. 3900 Las Vegas Blvd. S. (in the Luxor). ☎ *702-262-4400. www.bodiestheexhibition.com. Admission: $31 adults, $29 seniors 65 and over, $28 Nevada residents, $23 kids 4–12, free for kids 3 and under. Open: Daily 10 a.m.–10 p.m.*

The Erotic Heritage Museum
Off the Beaten Path

What better place than Las Vegas to put a museum all about sex? You'd think it might be nothing more than a paean to cheap thrills, but

Center Strip Attractions

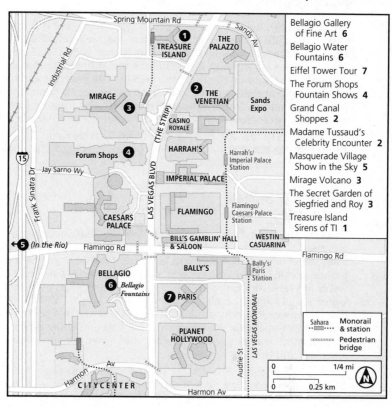

it somehow manages to find a sweet spot somewhere between tawdry, titillating, and thought-provoking. Paintings and sculpture co-mingle with video screens showing everything from documentaries to hard-core porn, and in between you'll find exhibits about free speech, Larry Flynt, the history of peep shows, AIDS, and more. Shepherded by the Institute for Advanced Study of Human Sexuality, the facility covers the full spectrum of the topic, meaning that it isn't for the squeamish, the prudish, or children — but for everyone else it offers a fascinating display of the range of human possibility and is the best museum of any type in Las Vegas.

See map p. 197. 3275 Industrial Rd. (at Fashion Show Drive). ☎ *702-369-6442.* www.eroticheritagemuseum.org. *Admission: $15; discounts for college students. Not appropriate for children. Open: Wed–Thurs 6–10 p.m., Fri 3 p.m. to midnight, Sat–Sun noon to midnight.*

The Forum Shops at Caesars Palace Fountain Shows
Center Strip

Toga, toga! No, it's not a tribute to *Animal House,* nor is it John Belushi springing to life in the center of two giant marble fountains in this snazzy shopping arcade. It's really Bacchus, the Roman god of wine and debauchery (and thus, if we may mix religious metaphors, the patron saint of Vegas). Every hour on the hour, the faux-marble Bacchus and his buddies creakily (and creepily) move and speak to the accompaniment of lasers, water, and smoke. In the **Roman Great Hall,** the Atlantis fountain uses hydraulics, projection-screen TVs, and fire effects to entertain the crowd.

See maps p. 197 and p. 201. 3500 Las Vegas Blvd. S. (at the Forum Shops at Caesars Palace). ☎ *702-893-4800. Admission: Free. Open: Shows hourly Sun–Thurs 10 a.m.– 11 p.m., Fri–Sat 10 a.m. to midnight.*

Fountains of Bellagio
Center Strip

Okay, so you've probably seen water fountains that shoot geysers into the air, cued to some musical number. Ho-hum. But if you trust us on anything, trust us on this: This is far, far better than what you've experienced before, and it is easily the coolest, classiest free show in Vegas. Yeah, it's water geysers shooting into the air, keyed to musical numbers, but this water shoots into the air to an impossible height, and then flirts and dances, moves like Baryshnikov, and is as witty as it is pretty. The music ranges from opera to Sinatra, with some pop and show tunes thrown in. Make a point of seeing at least one number — we bet you stick around for a second and third.

See maps p. 197 and p. 201. 3600 Las Vegas Blvd. S. (at Flamingo Road outside the Bellagio). Admission: Free. Performances take place every 30 min. Mon–Fri 3–8 p.m. and Sat–Sun noon to 8 p.m., every 15 min. nightly 8 p.m. to midnight.

Fremont Street Experience
Downtown

This high-tech light-and-laser show is Lazerium, Vegas-style. The **Fremont Street Experience** is a 5-block open-air pedestrian mall, a landscaped strip of outdoor cafes, vendor carts, and colorful kiosks purveying food and merchandise. Overhead is a 90-foot-high steel-mesh "celestial vault"; at night, it's the *Viva Vision,* a high-tech light-and-laser show enhanced by a concert-hall-quality sound system, which takes place several times nightly. It got a major overhaul in 2005, which turned the display from a basic animated LED thing to something more high-tech and clear, like the full video display hotel marquees on the Strip. With a soundtrack of everything from Ol' Blue Eyes to the Rolling Stones, it's just slightly cheesy, but it's still good gawking fun. Shows rotate throughout the night and seasonally (the Christmas show is a lot of fun). Aerialists and live bands perform between shows on some nights. The crowd it attracts is more upscale than in years past, and of course, downtown is a lot less crowded than the hectic Strip.

Fitzgeralds hotel has an upstairs balcony and a downstairs McDonald's, both of which offer good views of the show.

See map p. 197. On Fremont Street, between Main Street and Las Vegas Boulevard. ☎ *702-678-5777.* www.vegasexperience.com. *Admission: Free. Open: Nightly, with shows every hour, on the hour, from dusk to midnight.*

Grand Canal Shoppes at the Venetian
Center Strip

If you haven't made it to Venice this year, you might try strolling through the grand shopping arcade at the **Venetian.** Oh, it's not *really* like being in Venice, but between the nifty Venetian facades, the re-creation of St. Mark's Square and other Venetian landmarks, the actual canal complete with singing gondoliers (who will give you a ride if you give them money), the flower girls who sing arias, and the attentions of a flirty Casanova, it's not an unacceptable substitute. Costumed characters roam the area, bursting into song or interacting with visitors, while glass blowers and other vendors inhabit the square. As if this weren't enjoyable enough, there are over 70 brand-name stores where you can drop all your gambling winnings.

See maps p. 197 and p. 201. 3355 Las Vegas Blvd. S. (in the Venetian). ☎ *702-414-1000.* www.venetian.com. *Open: Sun–Thurs 10 a.m.–11 p.m., Fri–Sat 10 a.m. to midnight.*

Lied Discovery Children's Museum
Off the Beaten Path

A hands-on science museum designed for curious kids, the bright, airy, two-story **Lied** makes an ideal outing for toddlers and young children. Clever, thoughtful exhibits are everywhere, allowing children to experience life from all angles. Play a steel drum. Mine soft-sculpture "boulders." See how much sunscreen the giant stuffed mascot needs to keep from burning. Drop-in art classes are offered on weekend afternoons. Teenagers may find it to be a big yawn, but it's a terrific diversion for younger kids, as long as you don't tell them it's educational; adults enjoy it, too.

See map p. 197. 833 Las Vegas Blvd. N. (about 1½ miles north of Fremont Street). ☎ *702-382-5437.* www.ldcm.org. *Admission: $8.50 adults; $7.50 seniors, military, and kids 1–17. Open: Tues–Fri 9 a.m.–4 p.m., Sat 10 a.m.–5 p.m., Sun noon to 5 p.m.*

Madame Tussauds Celebrity Encounter
Center Strip

Forget any of the cheesy wax museums you may have previously visited — they're all amateurs compared with the genuine (though still a wee bit hokey) art created by the legendary Madame Tussauds. (The original is still the most popular tourist attraction in London.) Waxing nostalgic? Every figure here represents a noted person in the entertainment or sports world, and you're free to get up close to take pictures with them. You also find a section where you can see the incredible, painstaking effort that goes into perfectly replicating a celebrity in wax. Although their "Scream" section is good ghoulish fun it's not as scary as "Chamber of Horrors," and we're a little sad about that. Frankly, we think the whole thing is way too much money to look at big lifelike dolls, but what the heck — if nothing else, consider how nicely air-conditioned this exhibit has to be!

See maps p. 197 and p. 201. 3355 Las Vegas Blvd. S. (in the Venetian). ☎ *702-862-7805.* www.mtvegas.com. *Admission: $25 adults, $18 seniors and students, $15 kids 7–12, free for kids 6 and under. Open: Sun–Thurs 10 a.m.–9 p.m., Fri–Sat 10 a.m.–10 p.m., but hours vary seasonally, and museum may close early for private events.*

The Mirage Volcano
Center Strip

After dark, this active "volcano" erupts every hour on the hour, spewing fire 100 feet above the lagoons below. Originally such a hit that it literally stopped traffic on the Strip, an extremely expensive overhaul has made it even more lava-rific, with actual fireballs shot out in rhythm to a percussion soundtrack by Grateful Dead drummer Mickey Hart. Get there at least ten minutes before the spewing starts for the best vantage point near the main driveway entrance.

See maps p. 197 and p. 201. 3400 Las Vegas Blvd. S. (in front of the Mirage). ☎ *702-791-7111. Admission: Free. Open: Dusk to midnight. Eruptions take place every hour on the hour.*

Rio's Show in the Sky
Center Strip

Spend enough time in a casino, and you may swear you see Mardi Gras parades floating in the sky. Oh, wait, it's the Rio's free carnival-themed extravaganza! Giant floats filled with "performers" travel on tracks in the ceiling two stories above the floor. ***Parental warning:*** This is meant to invoke blissful visions of the naughty Brazil Mardi Gras, so there are some moments (including a sequence that takes place on a bed) that are probably closer to PG-13 than you may feel comfortable. It's meant to be risqué, is what we're saying, and if it's more silly than anything else, well, you still may not want to have to explain it to Junior. Luckily, the shows are in the evening now, a more adult timeline.

See map p. 197. 3700 W. Flamingo Rd. (in the Rio Hotel & Casino, just west of I-15). ☎ *702-777-7777.* www.riolasvegas.com. *Admission: Free to view, $13 to ride in a float. Open: Shows hourly Thurs–Sun 6 p.m. to midnight.*

North Strip Attractions

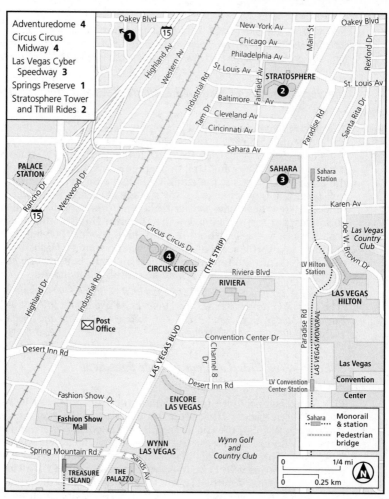

Adventuredome **4**
Circus Circus
  Midway **4**
Las Vegas Cyber
  Speedway **3**
Springs Preserve **1**
Stratosphere Tower
  and Thrill Rides **2**

The Roller Coaster
South Strip

Apparently, the designers of **New York–New York** didn't think that their little Big Apple looked busy enough, so they threw in a roller coaster. It's designed to look like a New York City cab, and it plummets, loops, and rolls in and around the hotel's re-created New York skyline. A unique feature of the ride is the barrel-roll drop, which turns you upside down and then drops you straight toward the ground. (And you thought nothing was as scary as a New York City cab ride.) Enter through the second-level arcade and be prepared for a long line. You need to be at least 54 inches tall to ride.

See maps p. 197 and p. 199. 3790 Las Vegas Blvd. S. (in New York–New York). ☎ 702-740-6969. www.nynyhotelcasino.com. *Admission: $14; multiride, all-day, and group packages also available. Open: Daily 10:30 a.m. to midnight.*

The Secret Garden of Siegfried & Roy/The Mirage Dolphin Habitat
Center Strip

The **Secret Garden** is a small zoo where rare lions, tigers, leopards, and the like from Siegfried & Roy's show are exhibited while they aren't at home with S & R (yes, they really do live with the boys). Guests get ear-phones so that they can listen to prerecorded facts and fun tidbits about the animals. Obviously, the exhibit has had a bit of an unintentional sub-text for some time, thanks to Roy's stage accident. But don't forget: He himself loves these cats and critters, and this exhibit has always been about respect for the animals. The **Dolphin Habitat** allows you to play "catch" with and learn about our flippered friends. Playing ball with the dolphins is a thrill; see if singing the theme song to *Flipper* makes them toss it to you more often. Allow at least an hour, but you can stay as long as you like. If you're like us, it may be quite a while indeed.

See maps p. 197 and p. 201. 3400 Las Vegas Blvd. S. (behind the Mirage). ☎ 702-791-7111. www.miragehabitat.com. *Admission: $15 adults, $10 kids 4–10, free for kids 3 and under. Open: Mon–Fri 11 a.m.–5:30 p.m., Sat–Sun and holidays 10 a.m.–5:30 p.m. Hours may vary seasonally.*

SPEED — The Ride/Las Vegas Cyber Speedway
North Strip

This wild, eight-minute motion-simulator ride puts you in replicas of NASCAR-style racers (three-fourths the size of the real cars) and lets you careen through the Las Vegas Motor Speedway or around (and even inside — whoops, there went the Forum Shops) the hotels on the Strip and downtown. The realistic details — down to the wind in your hair and the required pit stops if you crash — are impressive. **SPEED — The Ride** is a wild roller coaster that blasts you through loops and dips, and even the marquee of the hotel, before you go up a tower and then do the whole thing backward.

See map p. 197. 2535 Las Vegas Blvd. S. (in the Sahara Hotel & Casino). ☎ 702-737-2111. www.saharavegas.com/NASCAR. *Admission: Cyber Speedway (simula-tor) $10, $6 per re-ride; SPEED — The Ride (roller coaster) $10 for single ride; combination ticket $18 for 1 ride on each; $23 for all-day pass to both rides. Hours: Cyber Speedway daily noon to 10 p.m.; SPEED — The Ride Mon–Thurs noon to 8 p.m., Fri–Sun noon to 10 p.m. Hours may vary. Minimum height requirement for Cyber Speedway is 45 inches and for SPEED — The Ride is 54 inches.*

Stratosphere Tower and Thrill Rides
North Strip

If you think that confronting your fears is the best way of dealing with them, come test your vertigo here. You can get a spectacular view of Vegas and the surrounding landscape from the indoor and outdoor observation decks of this 110-story tower. Adrenaline junkies (or the certifiably insane) can try the **Big Shot,** an open car that rockets up 160 feet to the tip of the tower before dropping back down in a bungee effect. Or, if that thrill isn't quite thrilling enough, you have the **X-Scream,** a giant teeter-totter-style device that shoots you off the edge of the tower in a floorless, sideless car at about 30 mph. Yikes! Still not scared? Try the aptly named **Insanity: The Ride,** a whirligig-style spinner that sends you in circles as you look almost straight down. Need more crazy? Then we recommend **SkyJump,** which lets you literally jump off the top of the building in a 40-mph, "controlled" descent of more than 800 feet. Now that's insanity! *Note:* The rides are shut down on windy days. Thank goodness.

See maps p. 197 and p. 205. 2000 Las Vegas Blvd. S. (in Stratosphere Las Vegas). ☎ 702-380-7777. www.stratospherehotel.com/thrills. Admission: $13 for Big Shot, $12 for X-Scream and Insanity, plus fee to ascend Tower ($16 adults; $12 locals, seniors, hotel guests; $10 kids 4–12; free for kids 3 and under); $99 for SkyJump (tower admission waved). Multiride and all-day packages also available for varying costs. Hours: Sun–Thurs 10 a.m.–1 a.m., Fri–Sat 10 a.m.–2 a.m. Hours vary seasonally. Minimum height requirement for Big Shot is 48 inches and for X-Scream and Insanity is 52 inches. SkyJump has weight restrictions.

Titanic: The Artifact Exhibition
South Strip

The *Titanic* may be gone, but it's hardly forgotten. Actually, given the number of salvage operations that journey down to the wreck, it's not even all that gone. This exhibition neatly and cleverly educates visitors on the significance of the movie-inspiring 1912 disaster via informative displays, re-creations of sample cabins from first through third class, and relics taken from the wreck. A disaster that claimed the lives of over 1,500 is not precisely the kind of cheery subject with which one looks to occupy one's mind while visiting a happy-go-lucky town, but then again it has been enshrined in the cultural imagination as a blockbuster romance.

See maps p. 197 and p. 199. 3900 Las Vegas Blvd. S. (in the Luxor). ☎ 702-262-4400. www.luxor.com. Admission: $27 adults, $24 locals (with valid ID), $25 seniors 65 and over, $20 kids 4–12, free for kids 3 and under. Open: Daily 10 a.m.–10 p.m. (last admission 9 p.m.).

Treasure Island Sirens of TI
Center Strip

Another victim of the "Vegas is for adults, and we mean it, dammit" wave was the popular pirate stunt show. Oh, there are still pirates, and they still do stunts, but now, instead of the British, they "battle" a bunch of scantily clad damsels who try to — oh, why are we acting like "plot" is a vital component of this attraction? It's all about the lingerie, and that tells you everything you need to know. It's junky and awful, but there are bosoms on those bosoms, so there you go. And indeed, there you *may* go, but don't take the kids with you.

See maps p. 197 and p. 201. 3300 Las Vegas Blvd. S. (in front of Treasure Island). ☎ *702-894-7111.* www.treasureisand.com. *Admission: Free. Hours: Shows nightly at 5:30 p.m. (winter only), 7 p.m., 8:30 p.m., 10 p.m., and 11:30 p.m. (summer only).*

Finding Fun for the Younger Set

For a New York minute, Vegas tried to position itself as a suitable family destination — this despite being a town built around gambling, drinking, and sex. Although these pursuits are all fine if you're over the magical age of 21, for the underage crowd, the Strip is something of a drag. The great "Vegas Is Really for Families" marketing campaign failed precisely because gambling, drinking, and sex are more profitable than thrill-park rides and kiddie shows. Nevertheless, the city recognizes that you may have occasion to bring children to town, so we include some entertainment options for the little rug rats, in addition to those marked with a Kid Friendly icon elsewhere in this chapter.

Vegas for kids

Circus Circus Midway
North Strip

A solid, time-tested bet. Back in the pre–"Vegas Is for Families" days, this was about the only option for kids. Your kids will enjoy carnival games (complete with prizes) and arcade games. While they're having fun, they can catch circus acts — trapeze artists, stunt cyclists, jugglers, magicians, and acrobats — that perform continuously under the big top Sunday through Thursday from 11 a.m. to 11 p.m. and Friday and Saturday from 11 a.m. to midnight.

See maps p. 197 and p. 205. 2880 Las Vegas Blvd. S. (in Circus Circus). ☎ *702-734-0410. Admission: Free; game prices vary. Open: Daily 24 hours.*

Ethel M Chocolates Las Vegas Factory Tour
Off the Beaten Path

The fastest way to get to Henderson for the **Ethel M Chocolates Las Vegas Factory Tour** is to take the Strip south to Sunset Road, about a mile past the last of the big hotels. Turn left, and it's a straight shot across to Mountain Vista. There you find the chocolate factory, which offers free tours and has a surprisingly attractive 2½-acre **Botanical Cactus Garden** featuring rare and exotic succulents, providing a serene escape from the clang of slots.

2 Cactus Garden Dr. (just off Mountain Vista and Sunset Way in the Green Valley Business Park). ☎ *702-433-2500 for recorded information or 702-458-8864.* www. ethelschocolate.com. *Admission: Free. Open: Daily 8:30 a.m.–4:30 p.m. Closed Dec 25.*

Las Vegas Mini Gran Prix
Off the Beaten Path

Even though we insist that Vegas really isn't for families, citing a lack of affordable G-rated activities, we have to admit that this place is sure to make kids happy. It's got everything they need to work off all that nervous energy, from go-kart tracks requiring different skill levels to a mini roller coaster to a well-stocked arcade with decent prizes. The staff is friendly, and the cafe serves pizzas bigger and cheaper than any in your hotel. The one drawback: It's far away from main Strip action — here's where you need that rental car, for sure. *Note:* Kids have to be at least 36 inches tall to ride any of the attractions.

See map p. 197. 1401 N. Rainbow Rd. (just off US 95 N.). ☎ **702-259-7000.** www. lvmgp.com. *Admission: Free. Ride tickets $6.50 each, $6 for 5 or more; tickets good on all rides and at any time. Unlimited ride wristbands $18 per hour. Open: Sun–Thurs 11 a.m.–10 p.m., Fri–Sat 10 a.m.–11 p.m. Closed Dec 25.*

M&M's World
South Strip

M&M's World is a shrine devoted to the four basic food groups: milk chocolate, dark chocolate, white chocolate, and chocolate truffles. This four-story retail and exhibit space, brought to you by the company that makes M&M's, Milky Way, and Snickers, is more gift shop than museum; but it's still fun to wander around — plus, they give free samples! All those people holding their stomachs as they exit? That's a *good* sign. (Actually, the samples are usually small. Meanies.) Check out the little film/show that runs every half-hour; it's quite cute and clever.

See maps p. 197 and p. 199. 3875 Las Vegas Blvd. S. (just north of the MGM Grand Hotel, in the Showcase Mall). ☎ **702-736-7611.** *Admission: Free. Open: Sun–Thurs 9 a.m.–11 p.m., Fri–Sat 9 a.m. to midnight.*

MGM Grand Lion Habitat
South Strip

Oooh, pretty lions. Lions lying there. Lions occasionally getting up and stretching. That's about all you see at this free exhibit, but hey, if you want to see lions stalking an elk, then go on a safari. Having said that, it is free and the cats are undeniably beautiful, so if you have an extra ten minutes with nothing to do, wander on over. After those ten minutes are up, you'll probably be just as bored as the lions appear to be, but the wee ones can spend hours gaping. Note that despite the lack of elk hunting, crowds around the glass enclosure can be thick, so go early or late for the best viewing opportunities.

See maps p. 197 and p. 199. 3799 Las Vegas Blvd. S. (in MGM Grand). ☎ **702-891-7777.** www.mgmgrand.com. *Admission: Free. Open: Daily 11 a.m.–10 p.m.*

Video arcades to keep the kids busy

Also of note are the video-game arcades in the **New York–New York** and **Excalibur** hotels. All are large and feature lots of high-tech (and low-tech) diversions for the kids. New York–New York's arcade, in particular, is nicely done, modeled more or less on Coney Island, with plenty of non-video arcade games.

Many of the video- and carnival-game arcades offer tickets to winners of certain games. These tickets can be redeemed for merchandise. Now this may just be a ploy to get the little tykes introduced to the idea of gambling at an early age, but one would hope that your kids will learn pretty quickly that spending $10 on Skee-Ball just to win a stuffed animal worth a buck doesn't make much sense. (On the other hand, those stuffed animals can be pretty cute.)

Shark Reef at Mandalay Bay
South Strip

Kids love fish. Kids love this big giant aquarium. We think it's too small, but it is prettily designed and educational, and sharks swim overhead in glass tunnels. It's so much better than letting kids watch TV.

See maps p. 197 and p. 199. 3950 Las Vegas Blvd. S. (in Mandalay Bay). ☎ *702-632-7000. Admission: $17 adults, $13 kids 5–12, free for kids 4 and under. Open: Sun–Thurs 10 a.m.–8 p.m., Fri–Sat 10 a.m.–10 p.m. Last admission 1 hour before closing.*

Southern Nevada Zoological and Botanical Park
Off the Beaten Path

Although this zoo is on the smallish side, it boasts more than 150 species from around the world, plus a petting zoo for younger kids. Do remember that it can get quite hot in the desert; if the animals are sleeping in the shade when you come by, that's just because they're smart and don't go out in the noonday sun. Try to time a visit for early-morning or late-afternoon hours (when it's cooler) to see the most activity.

See map p. 197. 1775 N. Rancho Dr. ☎ *702-647-4685.* www.lasvegaszoo.org. *To get there, take Charleston west from the Strip to Rancho Drive and turn right. It's up about 2½ miles on your left. Admission: $9 adults, $7 seniors and kids 2–12. Open: Daily 9 a.m.–5 p.m.*

Vegas for teens

If Vegas is frustrating for kids, it's even more frustrating for teens, who can see the promised land in the form of slot machines glistening in the distance (or, more accurately, at their elbow), tantalizing them, but remaining untouchable for a few more years. If they even slow down (as they pass through the casino to the outside world) to gawk when someone hits a jackpot, security guards show up to hustle them along. Plus,

Vegas has a **curfew law:** Local ordinances forbid anyone under 18 from being on the Strip without a parent after 9 p.m. — for many teens (at least the ones we know), a chilling prospect.

What to do? Well, outside the curfew hours, you can send them off on the thrill rides listed earlier in this chapter, to the video arcades listed above, or to your hotel pool. And there's always shopping (see Chapter 13). Following are a couple things that teens may not find totally boring.

CSI: The Experience
South Strip

Someone has been murdered and it's your job to figure out whodunit, using all the tricks of the Crime Scene Investigation trade. Based on the popular TV series, and featuring video of the stars of the show in character guiding you along the way, the facility features three different crime scenes that allow you to look for clues, run analysis of the evidence, and identify a culprit (if you're paying attention, of course). Just like the show, it's a bit gory (blood spatter! autopsies!), so teens may love it.

See maps p. 197 and p. 199. 3799 Las Vegas Blvd. S. (in MGM Grand). ☎ **877-660-0660.** www.csiexhibit.com. *Admission: $30 for the first crime scene, $26 for additional crime scenes. Open: Daily 10 a.m.–10 p.m.*

GameWorks
South Strip

This 47,000-square-foot facility boasts the latest interactive video games (some of them designed by Steven Spielberg's DreamWorks company), motion-simulator rides, plus a giant rock-climbing wall, and such mundane games as air hockey and pool. This is more adult arcade fun, often too sophisticated for those under 10 — or at least, without parents to hover over and help, which takes precious time away from all the big fun said parents could be having themselves. It's also the perfect place for your teens to get their ya-yas out.

See maps p. 197 and p. 199. 3785 Las Vegas Blvd. S. (in the Showcase Mall just north of the MGM Grand). ☎ **702-432-4263.** www.gameworks.com. *Open: Sun–Thurs 10 a.m. to midnight, Fri–Sat 10 a.m.–1 a.m. Hours may vary.*

Going to the Chapel: Vegas Weddings

Birds do it, bees do it, and as we know, Britney and What's-His-Name-the-First-Husband sure did it — got married in Vegas, that is. (Okay, birds and bees don't bother with ceremonies, but it worked as a line, all right?) And you can, too, with tremendous ease, as the unfortunate Spears/What's-His-Name union demonstrated. We profoundly hope that you put more thought into this step than they did, but regardless, this is a most accommodating town for impulsive lovers. All you need is a license, a couple of minutes, and someone to recite vows with you. More

Las Vegas Wedding Chapels

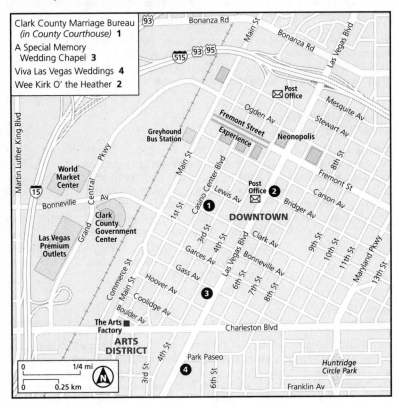

Clark County Marriage Bureau
  (in County Courthouse) **1**
A Special Memory
  Wedding Chapel **3**
Viva Las Vegas Weddings **4**
Wee Kirk O' the Heather **2**

than 100,000 weddings are performed in Las Vegas annually. The two busiest days are **Valentine's Day** (some chapels perform more than 80 services in one day) and **New Year's Eve.**

Many of the major hotels have wedding chapels and services, but the bulk of the independent places are located between the Strip and downtown on Las Vegas Boulevard. In this section, we describe a few of our favorite wedding venues, but remember that you have many to choose from. Just cruise the chapels and pick the one that appeals to you the most. Note that fees vary depending on what kind of ceremony you opt for, so call the chapel ahead of time for prices. Even if you're not getting married, you may be able to watch other couples tie the knot. Just ask. You can decide for yourself whether a $100, 15-minute wedding is as likely to last as that $50,000 ceremony with badly dressed bridesmaids.

If you want to find out more about getting hitched in Vegas, make a call to **Las Vegas Weddings** (☎ 800-498-6285; www.lasvegasweddings.com).

Clark County Marriage License Bureau
Downtown

Your first stop on your way to marital bliss has to be at the courthouse to visit the Clark County Marriage License Bureau. All that's required is for both of you to be there and for one of you to have $60. That's it — not even a blood test.

See map p. 212. 201 Clark Ave. ☎ *702-761-0600. Open: Daily 8 a.m. to midnight.*

A Special Memory Wedding Chapel
Off the Beaten Path

Here you find a more traditional style, with somewhat less of a Vegas approach to weddings. It's a clean, modern, new building, complete with a churchlike steeple and a demi-shopping arcade for flowers, tuxes, and the like. If you're in a hurry, you can even use its drive-up window! (So much for it not being too Vegas.)

See map p. 212. 800 S. Fourth St. (at Gass Avenue). ☎ *800-962-7798.* www.a specialmemory.com. *Fees: $25 for drive-up service. Open: Sun–Thurs 8 a.m.– 10 p.m., Fri–Sat 8 a.m. to midnight.*

Viva Las Vegas Weddings
Downtown

Feel the need to get hitched by Elvis after riding into the chapel in the back of a pink Cadillac? Want to walk down the aisle amidst dry ice fog while Dracula performs your ceremony? This is the place to do it. The epicenter of the themed Vegas wedding has multiple chapels, tux and costume rentals, florists, theme rooms for receptions, and a staff of former stage performers who love to put on a show. *This* is what a Vegas wedding should be like.

See map p. 212. 1205 Las Vegas Blvd. S. ☎ *800-574-4450.* www.vivalasvegas weddings.com. *Open: Sun–Thurs 9 a.m.–9 p.m., Fri–Sat 8 a.m.–10 p.m.*

Wee Kirk O' the Heather
Downtown

Originally built in 1925 as the house for a local minister, marriage bureau officials kept sending couples there to get married. In 1940, the owners just gave up and turned it into a chapel, making it the oldest in Vegas. It's not really that special from a looks point of view, but if there's a competition for friendliest chapel in town, this one would win hands-down.

See map p. 212. 231 Las Vegas Blvd. S. (between Bridger and Carson avenues).
☎ *800-843-2566 or 702-382-9830.* www.weekirk.com. *Open: Daily 10 a.m.–8 p.m.*

If You're Sick of Neon

Just about everything in Las Vegas has some neon on it — even the 7-Eleven and the airport parking garages. If it all gets to be a little much for you, there are places you can go that don't involve bright lights, marble, and concrete.

CityCenter Fine Art Collection
South Strip

Maya Lin, Nancy Rubins, and Henry Moore are just a few of the artists who have contributed works to the massive CityCenter complex. Spread across the acreage both indoors and outdoors are more than a dozen major pieces and several smaller ones, turning the development into one big art gallery. Although you most likely need to be an appreciator of fine art to really get the full impact of most of the works, some of it is pop-art enough to amuse even the most casual of viewers. In the latter category is the 266-foot-long LED display by street artist Jenny Holzer, located on the lower level of the north entrance of Aria. Visit the concierge at that hotel for a map and explanatory brochure.

See map p. 197. 3730 Las Vegas Blvd. S. (at Harmon Avenue). ☎ *702-590-7111.* www. citycenter.com. *Admission: Free. Open: Most artworks are outdoors or in 24-hour public spaces.*

Clark County Heritage Museum
Off the Beaten Path

Here you can go through 12,000 years of local history, including exhibits on Native American tribes, pioneer settlements, the gold-rush era, and the dawn of gambling (with old slot machines and a life-size statue of Bugsy Siegel). The 25-acre facility also has an authentic ghost town and several houses from the early to mid-1900s that have been fully restored with period furnishings.

See map p. 197. 1830 S. Boulder Hwy. Take Tropicana Avenue east to Boulder Highway and turn right. It's down about 8 miles on your left. ☎ *702-455-7955. Admission: $1.50 adults, $1 seniors and kids 3–15. Open: Daily 9 a.m.–4:30 p.m.*

Las Vegas Natural History Museum
Off the Beaten Path

This museum has exhibits of (stuffed) bears, elk, and the like, plus a few roaring dinosaurs. There's also a hands-on activity room that's great for kids, and a gift shop for you. In truth, the exhibits are a bit moldy and creaky, but there's not a speck of neon anywhere in sight.

See map p. 197. 900 Las Vegas Blvd. N. It's a couple of miles north of downtown. ☎ *702-384-3466.* www.lvnhm.org. *Admission: $8 adults; $7 seniors, students, and military personnel; $4 kids 3–11. Open: Daily 9 a.m.–4 p.m.*

Lorenzi Park
Off the Beaten Path

If you want to ditch the glitz and enjoy a lake, playgrounds, jogging paths, and acres of grassy lawns and lush gardens, Lorenzi Park is the place for you. This, the largest park in Las Vegas, is located just west of Rancho Drive, northwest of the Strip.

Washington Street. Take Charleston Boulevard west from the Strip, turn right on Rancho Drive, and then travel about 2 miles to Washington Street and turn left. You see the park on your left in a few short blocks.

Marjorie Barrick Museum
Paradise Road

This attractive, if simplistic, display of Native American craftwork and Las Vegas history is conveniently located on the grounds of the University of Nevada Las Vegas (UNLV). It's more of a small-town museum than a big-city museum, but it's free. It has snakes in glass cages and air-conditioning.

See map p. 197. At UNLV, located between Paradise Road and Maryland Parkway, just east of the Strip and just north of Tropicana Avenue. ☎ **702-895-3381**. www. barrickmuseum.unlv.edu. *Admission: Free. Open: Mon–Fri 8 a.m.–4:45 p.m., Sat 10 a.m.–2 p.m.*

Springs Preserve
Off the Beaten Path

This is an absolute jewel of a facility, designed to educate visitors about the environmental impact of Sin City (in summation: huge). Sure, you come to Vegas for fantasy, not for a lecture on grim reality, but the attitude here is anything but scolding. Plus, they put their money where their mouth is. With the exception of the interpretative center, all the buildings were constructed with the least amount of environmental impact possible, using green techniques. Exhibits range from a simulation of a flash flood to kid-geared instruction on the fun of recycling, including a compost tunnel you can crawl through. The gardens demonstrate environmentally friendly gardening, with an emphasis on the possibilities for the elderly and physically disabled. All this is set amid nature and hiking trails. Even the playground is made of recycled materials. Plenty to do and even more to learn — maybe it'll make you think twice before asking for a daily sheet change in your hotel room.

See map p. 197. 3333 S. Valley View Blvd. ☎ **702-822-8344**. www.springs preserve.com. *Admission: $19 adults, $17 seniors and students with I.D., $11 kids 5–17. Admission to trails is free. Open: Daily 10 a.m.–6 p.m.*

If You Just Can't Get Enough Neon

Face it. No matter how hard you try, it's hard to avoid neon in Las Vegas. The stuff is so much a part of the city that it shouldn't come as a surprise that Vegas authorities have preserved some of the city's neon treasures.

The Neon Museum
Downtown

This terrific museum is helping to preserve a piece of Vegas history by rescuing classic neon signs, restoring them, and putting them on public display. Given how fast bits of Las Vegas get tossed into the wastebasket of memory, this project is a most worthy one. After all, these signs are what originally gave Vegas its unique look. They deserve better, and it's nice to know that some are getting it. At the end of the **Fremont Street Experience** (described earlier in this chapter), you find the **horse and rider** from the Hacienda Hotel, the **genie's lamp** from the Aladdin Hotel, the **Anderson Dairy milkman,** and the **Chief Hotel Court** sign, among others prominently displayed. Construction is underway on a visitor center and park nearby, which should be open in 2011.

See map p. 197. Located at Fremont Street and Las Vegas Boulevard. ☎ **702-229-4872.** www.neonmuseum.org. *Admission: Free.*

If You Want to See Neon from a Great Vantage Point

Eiffel Tower Tour
Center Strip

We love Paris in the springtime, but we can't always make it there, so it's nice — or really hokey — that Paris Las Vegas has provided us with a half-scale replica of the City of Lights' famous Eiffel Tower. The "tour" consists of a few factoids about this tower and its more famous Parisian sister given in the 90 seconds or so it takes for the elevator to zoom to the observation platform. You can get a nice view from up there, though.

See maps p. 197 and p. 201. 3655 Las Vegas Blvd. S. (at Paris Las Vegas). ☎ **702-946-7000.** www.parislasvegas.com. *Admission: 9:30 a.m.–7:15 p.m. $10 adults, $7 kids; 7:30 p.m. to close $15 adults. (Children not allowed after 7:30 p.m.). Open: Daily 9:30 a.m.–12:30 a.m., weather permitting.*

Vegas for the Sports-Minded

For many years, recreation in Las Vegas meant lying by the pool, and exercise came in the form of pulling handles on slot machines. But when the **Mirage** opened in the late 1980s, it signaled a change in attitude that would revolutionize the way visitors spent their time. This major resort was the first in town to offer such an unprecedented array of sporting and exercise alternatives. Sure, other hotels in town had golf courses and health clubs, but nobody did it quite the way the Mirage did.

Virtually every major hotel built since then has tried to imitate the Mirage's success. Odds are, your own hotel will have a huge array of options and probably even a full-fledged spa.

Biking

Whether you're a biking fanatic or you just want to take a gentle cruise through the city or outlying areas, Vegas has plenty to offer. Just be careful of the traffic; many Vegas drivers are tourists who may be less familiar with the roadways.

Las Vegas Cyclery

This rental company offers a variety of street and mountain bikes for your riding pleasure. It even drops off your bike for you at any downtown or Strip hotel or picks you up to take you on a guided tour.

Consider taking a trip out to Red Rock Canyon using Charleston Boulevard. A nice wide bike lane starts at Rainbow Lane (in the western part of town) and runs all the way to the canyon's visitor center, about 11 challenging but not impossible miles in total. If you're in really good shape, you may consider a bike tour of the canyon. Contact the **Red Rock Canyon Visitors Center** (☎ **702-363-1921**), or ask the bike rental agent for other options.

8221 W. Charleston Blvd. ☎ *702-596-2953.* www.lasvegascyclery.com. *Rates vary, starting at $30 for the first day, $25 for a half-day or the following whole consecutive days, and $110 for a week (major credit card required).*

Bowling

Bowlers can find a few good spots to knock down some pins, if the mood, um, strikes. Here's a favorite recommendation.

Orleans
Off the Beaten Path

Orleans has a great 70-lane facility. It's on the second floor of the hotel, which you see on your right as you travel west from the Strip on Tropicana Avenue.

4500 W. Tropicana Ave. ☎ *702-365-7411. Fees: Starting at $2.90 per game ($1 from midnight to 8 a.m. Mon–Fri); $2.75 shoe rental. Open: Daily 24 hours.*

Golfing

Las Vegas is a favorite destination for the PGA's annual tour, so it makes sense that the city has dozens of great golf courses for you to try.

If you're an avid golfer and you intend to play the links in Las Vegas, consider bringing your own clubs. We know of more than one golfer who didn't want to haul his equipment halfway across the country but was horrified at the outrageous rental fees at the local courses.

Angel Park Golf Club
Off the Beaten Path

One notable course is the Angel Park Golf Club, which has a 36-hole, par-70/71 public course that was designed by Arnold Palmer. Pretty spiffy, in our humble opinion.

100 S. Rampart Blvd. To get there, take the Strip to Charleston Boulevard and travel west about 10 miles; then turn right on Rampart Boulevard. ☎ **888-446-5358.** *www. angelpark.com. Greens fees: $49–$99. Open: Hours vary; call for times.*

Las Vegas National Golf Club
Paradise Road

Another exceptional course is located at the Las Vegas National Golf Club, which was formerly part of the Las Vegas Hilton Country Club (and before that affiliated with the Stardust way back in the day). You can find its 18-hole, par-71 public course just past Paradise Road on your left.

1911 Desert Inn Rd. ☎ **702-794-1796.** *www.lasvegasnational.com. Greens fees: $89–$119. Open: Hours vary; call for times.*

Health clubs

Just about every hotel in town has a health club/spa, so you can probably find a place to work out without a problem. We especially like the outstanding facilities at **Encore Las Vegas,** the **Mirage, Bellagio,** the **Golden Nugget,** and **Caesars Palace,** which features a rock-climbing wall and Zen meditation garden. Most hotel facilities are open only to hotel guests, but there is one facility of note that welcomes all.

Canyon Ranch Spa
Center Strip

This is an outpost of what is generally considered the finest spa in the United States. But it's so costly that we have trouble even typing in the numbers. For sheer physical beauty (and we're not even talking about the clientele) and the vast number of exotic services offered (such as Subtle Energy Therapies that use Reiki healing methods), this place has no equal in town. However, the prices are virtually prohibitive. A day pass (which just covers use of the fitness center, steam room, whirlpool, sauna, and locker rooms) will set you back $40, and a 50-minute facial will run you $175.

See map p. 201, Venetian. 3355 Las Vegas Blvd. S. (in the Venetian). ☎ **877-220-2688** *(toll-free) or 702-414-3600. www.venetian.com. Admission: Spa packages available. Hours: Daily 6 a.m.–8 p.m.*

Tennis

You can find places to play at only a couple hotels.

Bally's Las Vegas
Center Strip

The hotel has eight lighted hard courts that are available to both guests and nonguests. The pro shop can help if you leave any equipment at home.

3645 Las Vegas Blvd. S. ☎ 702-739-4111. www.ballyslasvegas.com. Fees: $20 guests of all Bally's hotels, $25 nonguests. Hours vary; call ahead. Reservations highly recommended.

Flamingo
Center Strip

The hotel has four outdoor hard courts (all are lit for night play) available to the public. Lessons are available.

3555 Las Vegas Blvd. S. ☎ 702-733-3444. www.flamingo-las-vegas.com. Fees: $15 guests, $20 nonguests. Hours vary; call ahead. Reservations required.

Vegas for the Sports Spectator

Las Vegas has no major-league sporting teams, so most of the local action comes from **UNLV**. The main campus is located just off Paradise Road between Tropicana Avenue and Flamingo Road. If you just have to get a football or basketball fix, there may be a game playing at the **Thomas and Mack Center (☎ 702-895-3900)** on campus. This 18,500-seat facility hosts the college teams and a variety of boxing tournaments, NBA exhibition games, and rodeos.

The **MGM Grand's Garden Arena (☎ 800-929-1111)** and **Mandalay Bay's Events Center (☎ 877-632-7800)** host major sporting events year-round, including gymnastics, figure skating, and boxing. Remember the bite that Mike Tyson took out of Evander Holyfield's ear in 1997? That happened at the MGM — how proud they must be.

Las Vegas Motor Speedway
Off the Beaten Path

The Las Vegas Motor Speedway is a 176,000-seat, $200-million, state-of-the-art, motor-sports entertainment complex. Its 1½-mile oval hosts Indy and NASCAR events, a road course, a drag strip, and a motocross course.

7000 Las Vegas Blvd. N. ☎ 702-644-4443. www.lvms.com. Admission: Ticket prices vary wildly, so call ahead to find out what's happening and how much it costs. Open: Hours vary. If you're driving, take I-15 north to the Speedway exit (exit 54) and follow the signs.

National Finals Rodeo

Every December, Las Vegas hosts the National Finals Rodeo, considered to be the "Super Bowl of rodeos." Nearly 200,000 people attend the two-week event, which is held at the **Thomas and Mack Center** on the UNLV campus.

Tropicana Avenue and Swenson Street (located in the Thomas and Mack Center on the UNLV campus). ☎ **702-895-3900.** *www.nfrexperience.com. Everything sells out quickly, so call as far in advance as possible.*

Vegas by Sightseeing Tour

You won't find many organized sightseeing tours in Vegas, but the ones that are offered are very reasonably priced. Also, a good tour guide can fill you in on entertaining and historical tidbits that you won't get wandering around by yourself.

Hotels as attractions

Although this chapter focuses on the formal attractions — the ones with ticket prices and/or operating hours — keep in mind that in Vegas, the hotels are attractions in and of themselves. Wandering around and appreciating the extravagant, over-the-top, historic — and in some cases awe-inspiring — architecture is a great way to spend some time outside of the casinos.

Luxor, New York-New York, Paris Las Vegas, and The Venetian are the pinnacles of the theme madness design aesthetic that gripped much of the 1990s building boom. Although Luxor and New York-New York have had their themes de-emphasized inside, the exteriors of the buildings are still giggle-inducing wonders. Inside at Paris and Venetian, the romance of France and Italy are alive and well and worth a gander.

If you're looking for history, you can find some of it on The Strip at places like Caesars Palace (see that tower in the center? It's been there since the joint opened in 1966) but the most classic of Vegas hotels are located downtown. The Golden Nugget's south entrance has been there, in some form or another, since the mid-1940s, and the El Cortez dates back to 1941.

But as Vegas marches forward, so do the design themes, which now are much more modern. Take a few minutes to appreciate the sinuous curves of the glass and steel CityCenter or the graceful bronze arc that is Wynn Las Vegas. They may not be as wacky as a pyramid or the Empire State Building in the middle of the desert, but they are beautiful hotels.

Char Cruze's Creative Adventures

For something really special, get a personalized tour from **Char Cruze** and her **Creative Adventures** tour company. Char is a fourth-generation Las Vegas native (yeah, people really do raise families here), and if there's a story she hasn't heard, it's not worth repeating. She also does marvelous tours of **Red Rock Canyon, Hoover Dam,** and other non-city sights. She charges a flat fee that's more than the others listed, but her tour is quite a bit more personal; she can tailor any tour to your specifications and interests. And the more people you have in your group, the more cost-effective it is. It's terrific for families and highly recommended in general.

☎ **702-893-2051.** *www.creativeadventuretours.net. Admission: Prices vary according to size of group and method of transportation. Tours start at $150 per day, per family.*

Gray Line Tours

The most reputable company around offers a variety of interesting tours, including a 5½-hour journey around town that includes the **Strip, Fremont Street,** and a visit to the **Clark County Heritage Museum.**

795 E. Tropicana Ave. ☎ **702-735-4947.** *www.grayline.com. Admission: Tours start at $55 per day and go way up.*

Index of Attractions by Neighborhood

Center Strip
Bellagio Gallery of Fine Art
Eiffel Tower Tour
The Forum Shops at Caesars Palace
Fountain Shows
Fountains of Bellagio
Grand Canal Shoppes at the Venetian
Madame Tussauds Celebrity Encounter
The Mirage Volcano
Rio's Show in the Sky
The Secret Garden of Siegfried & Roy/
The Mirage Dolphin Habitat
Treasure Island Sirens of TI

Downtown
Fremont Street Experience
The Neon Museum

North Strip
Adventuredome
Circus Circus Midway

Speed — The Ride/Las Vegas Cyber Speedway
Stratosphere Tower and Thrill Rides

Paradise Road
Marjorie Barrick Museum

Off the Beaten Path
Atomic Testing Museum
Clark County Heritage Museum
The Erotic Heritage Museum
Ethel M Chocolates Las Vegas Factory Tour
Las Vegas Mini Gran Prix
Las Vegas Natural History Museum
Lied Discovery Children's Museum
Lorenzi Park
Southern Nevada Zoological and Botanical Park
Springs Preserve

South Strip

Bodies: The Exhibition
CityCenter Fine Art Collection
CSI: The Experience
GameWorks

M&M's World
MGM Grand Lion Habitat
The Roller Coaster
Shark Reef at Mandalay Bay
Titanic: The Artifact Exhibition

Index of Attractions by Type

Amusement Parks/Arcades/ Thrill Rides

Adventuredome (North Strip)
Circus Circus Midway (North Strip)
CSI: The Experience (South Strip)
GameWorks (South Strip)
Las Vegas Mini Gran Prix (Off the Beaten Path)
The Roller Coaster (South Strip)
Speed — The Ride/Las Vegas Cyber Speedway (North Strip)
Stratosphere Tower and Thrill Rides (North Strip)

Museums/Memorabilia Exhibits

Atomic Testing Museum (Off the Beaten Path)
Bellagio Gallery of Fine Art (Center Strip)
Bodies: The Exhibition (South Strip)
CityCenter Fine Art Collection (South Strip)
Clark County Heritage Museum (Off the Beaten Path)
Eiffel Tower Tour (Center Strip)
The Erotic Heritage Museum (Off the Beaten Path)
Ethel M Chocolates Las Vegas Factory Tour (Off the Beaten Path)
Las Vegas Natural History Museum (Off the Beaten Path)
Lied Discovery Children's Museum (Off the Beaten Path)

Lorenzi Park (Off the Beaten Path)
Madame Tussauds Celebrity Encounter (Center Strip)
Marjorie Barrick Museum (Paradise Road)
MGM Grand Lion Habitat (South Strip)
The Neon Museum (Downtown)
The Secret Garden of Siegfried & Roy/ The Mirage Dolphin Habitat (Center Strip)
Shark Reef at Mandalay Bay (South Strip)
Southern Nevada Zoological and Botanical Park (Off the Beaten Path)
Springs Preserve (Off the Beaten Path)
Titanic: The Artifact Exhibition (South Strip)

Shows/Entertainment/Shopping

The Forum Shops at Caesars Palace Fountain Shows (Center Strip)
Fountains of Bellagio (Center Strip)
Fremont Street Experience (Downtown)
Grand Canal Shoppes at the Venetian (Center Strip)
M&M's World (South Strip)
The Mirage Volcano (Center Strip)
Rio's Show in the Sky (Center Strip)
Treasure Island Sirens of TI (Center Strip)

Chapter 13

Shopping the Local Stores

. . . .

In This Chapter

▶ Checking out the malls
▶ Hitting the hotel shops
▶ Shopping for necessities
▶ Searching for antiques
▶ Seeking out hip and happening clothes
▶ Buying gambling gadgets for the home

. . . .

*W*ay back in the good ol' days, when hotel boutiques carried merchandise that could charitably be described as taste-free, Vegas was no shopping mecca. If you're a penny pincher, it still isn't. But as the luxury hotels have risen (and gotten better at extracting your cash at every opportunity), the shopping has escalated — in both price and quality — to the level of that found in Beverly Hills and Manhattan. Which isn't to say that you won't find plenty of dubious items still available for purchase — you will, in spades. From campy souvenir shops to ritzy designer boutiques, die-hard shoppers can find plenty of places to empty their wallets. This chapter takes a look at the basics, the bargains, and the bizarre shopping options.

Shopping, Vegas Style

Naturally, this being Las Vegas and all, the show must go on — ordinary malls aren't enough to lure jaded shoppers. Theme malls proliferate — you can window-shop on the Appian Way or sail past stores along the Grand Canal — and many of these malls include shows and rides designed to amuse people as they spend any cash the casinos may have missed. You can find some smaller places where you can drop a few (or considerably more) dollars, but for the most part, like the hotels here, the megajoints rule.

Dedicated fashionistas will want to note that the best of the new season's offerings are found mid-September and mid-March, while the best sales occur from mid-July to the end of August and mid-December to the end of February. We're talking 50 percent to 70 percent off the most luscious of designer goods! Happy hunting!

Las Vegas Shopping

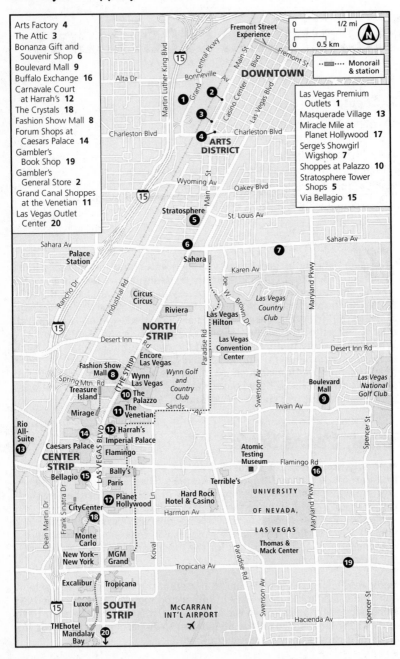

Arts Factory **4**
The Attic **3**
Bonanza Gift and
  Souvenir Shop **6**
Boulevard Mall **9**
Buffalo Exchange **16**
Carnavale Court
  at Harrah's **12**
The Crystals **18**
Fashion Show Mall **8**
Forum Shops at
  Caesars Palace **14**
Gambler's
  Book Shop **19**
Gambler's
  General Store **2**
Grand Canal Shoppes
  at the Venetian **11**
Las Vegas Outlet
  Center **20**

Las Vegas Premium
  Outlets **1**
Masquerade Village **13**
Miracle Mile at
  Planet Hollywood **17**
Serge's Showgirl
  Wigshop **7**
Shoppes at Palazzo **10**
Stratosphere Tower
  Shops **5**
Via Bellagio **15**

0   1/2 mi
0   0.5 km

······ Monorail
        & station

Fremont Street
Experience

DOWNTOWN

Martin Luther King Blvd
Grand Central Pkwy
Bonneville Av
Main St
Fremont St
Blvd
Las Vegas Blvd
Casino Center

Alta Dr

Charleston Blvd   Charleston Blvd

ARTS
DISTRICT

Wyoming Av

Main St

Oakey Blvd

Stratosphere

St. Louis Av

Sahara Av   Sahara Av

Palace
Station

Sahara

Karen Av

Rancho Dr
Industrial Rd

Circus
Circus

Riviera

NORTH
STRIP

Desert Inn
Rd

Las Vegas
Hilton

Las Vegas
Country
Club

Joe W. Brown Dr
Paradise Rd
Maryland Pkwy

Las Vegas
Convention
Center

Desert Inn Rd

Encore
Las Vegas

Fashion Show
Mall

Spring Mtn. Rd
Treasure
Island

Wynn
Las Vegas

Wynn Golf
and
Country
Club

Boulevard
Mall

Las Vegas
National
Golf Club

The
Palazzo

(THE STRIP)

Mirage

The
Venetian

Sands
Av

Twain Av

Swenson Av
Spencer St

Rio
All-
Suite

Harrah's
Imperial Palace

Caesars Palace

CENTER
STRIP

Flamingo

Atomic
Testing
Museum

Flamingo Rd

Bellagio

LAS VEGAS BLVD

Bally's

Paris

Terrible's

UNIVERSITY

Dean Martin Dr
Frank Sinatra Dr

CityCenter

Planet
Hollywood

Hard Rock
Hotel & Casino

Harmon Av

OF NEVADA,

Koval

LAS VEGAS

Monte
Carlo

New York–
New York

MGM
Grand

Tropicana Av

Paradise Rd

Thomas &
Mack Center

Swenson Av

Spencer St

Excalibur

Tropicana

Luxor

SOUTH
STRIP

McCARRAN
INT'L AIRPORT ✈

THEhotel
Mandalay
Bay

Hacienda Av

If you do decide to splurge here, don't forget to factor in an 8.1 percent sales tax to the price of whatever you buy.

Do keep in mind that, just like pricing for hotels and restaurants, shopping is more expensive on the Strip. If you're more intent on serious bargain hunting than fun browsing, head elsewhere.

The Malls: Tried and True

Just across the street from Treasure Island is the **Fashion Show Mall,** 3200 Las Vegas Blvd. S. (☎ **702-784-7000;** www.thefashionshow.com), which tries to impersonate an "attraction." (How else to explain those giant LED video screens and that enormous flying-saucer-shaped thingy on the roof?) The Fashion Show Mall boasts more than 250 shops, restaurants, and services, including **Abercrombie & Fitch, Apple, Bloomingdale's Home, Macy's, Neiman Marcus, Nordstrom,** and **Saks Fifth Avenue,** plus your usual mall denizens, such as **Bath & Body Works, Gap,** and **Victoria's Secret.** If your Caddy is looking a little dull, you can even arrange to have your car washed while you shop. Free self-parking and valet parking are available, and the mall is open Monday through Saturday from 10 a.m. to 9 p.m. and Sunday from 11 a.m. to 7 p.m.

For a more traditional shopping experience, head over to the **Boulevard Mall,** 3528 S. Maryland Pkwy. (☎ **702-735-8268;** www.boulevardmall.com). It has 140-plus stores geared to the average traveler. Anchors here include **JCPenney, Marshalls,** and **Sears.** Its wide variety of shops offers moderately priced shoes and clothing for the entire family, books, gifts, jewelry, and home furnishings, plus more than a dozen fast-food eateries. To get there, take any of the major east–west streets (**Flamingo, Tropicana,** or **Sahara**) to **Maryland Parkway,** which is about 2 miles east of the Strip. The mall is located just south of **Desert Inn Road** and north of **Flamingo.** Hours are Monday through Saturday from 10 a.m. to 9 p.m. and Sunday from 11 a.m. to 6 p.m.

Outlet Malls: Bargain City

Americans' love for factory-outlet malls has not gone unrequited in Las Vegas. At many of these stores, you can get slightly (sometimes imperceptibly) flawed or overstocked merchandise for up to 75 percent off retail prices. Of course, by the time it gets to the outlet, the stuff is often no longer first-run — but at these prices, who cares?

Before you buy something in a regular mall in Las Vegas, ask the sales staff if the store has a local outlet. You can save big bucks by exploring this alternative.

Las Vegas Premium Outlets, 875 Grand Central Pkwy. (☎ **702-474-7500;** www.premiumoutlets.com), can be disappointing. It looks sharp enough, but it's a structure that's entirely outdoors. We don't know about you, but when it's 110°F out, we're simply not interested in buying leather — or anything other than water and ice cream. The shops are an adequate range, but too many had too much merchandise at essentially full price. Call to see who's there currently, but when we last went in, **Armani, Calvin Klein, Dolce & Gabbana, Kenneth Cole, Lacoste, Nike,** and **Perry Ellis** all had stores here. It's open Monday through Saturday from 10 a.m. to 9 p.m. and Sunday from 10 a.m. to 8 p.m.

Having said that, the indoor **Las Vegas Outlet Center,** 7400 Las Vegas Blvd. S. (☎ **702-896-5599;** www.premiumoutlets.com), is a bargain hunter's dream. Housed in a friendly and spacious mall-like setting are 130 outlets, including **Burlington, Converse, Corningware/Corelle, Levi's, Nike, Reebok,** and **Tommy Hilfiger.** You can even find entertainment for kids (or bored spouses) in the form of a giant indoor carousel. It's open Monday through Saturday from 10 a.m. to 9 p.m. and Sunday from 10 a.m. to 8 p.m.

You can get to this mall by heading south on the Strip. It's located a few miles past the southernmost major hotel, Mandalay Bay.

The Hotel Shops: From Trinkets to Toys

Just about all the big hotels offer some shopping opportunities, ranging from fancy clothing emporiums to gift shops. Avoid these latter places like the plague if at all possible; the prices are astronomically higher than in the outside world. The hotels get away with this kind of price gouging because they assume that hotel guests or fervent gamblers don't want to leave the property to pick up a bottle of shampoo or a pack of gum.

Most of the hotels have small gift shops (also known as **logo shops**) that offer a variety of trinkets for you to bring home to friends and family. Such souvenirs are usually overpriced junk, but some of what's offered in the better hotels is of good quality — but still overpriced. In other words, expect to pay through the nose no matter what you buy at a hotel shop. You can try an independent souvenir shop, which will still charge too much, but it may be slightly less outrageous.

The big guns

No matter what your budget, a few shopping spots inside the major hotels are attractions in their own right; put them at the top of your to-do list.

Mix equal amounts of Rodeo Drive and the Ancient Roman Empire, and then add a dash of Disney, and you may get something close to the **Forum Shops at Caesars Palace,** 3570 Las Vegas Blvd. S. (☎ **702-731-7110**). It's designed to look like a Roman street scene, complete with columns, marble, and animatronic statues under a "sky" that somehow transforms from day to night as time passes. You find mostly high-rent joints, such as **Armani, Christian Dior, Louis Vuitton,** and **Versace,** alongside fancy restaurants such as **Spago.** (Even if you don't like shopping, it's worth the stroll just to giggle.) Need more? Okay, they also have a large aquarium in the center of a fiery-fountain show and one of only two circular escalators in the world. So maybe not as exciting as a roller coaster, but you get to shop in between floors so that must be worth something! For a truly Vegas (and somewhat bizarre) experience, take in one of the every-hour-on-the-hour light-and-laser shows at the **Festival Fountain** or the **Atlantis Fountain.** Store hours may vary but the bulk of them are open Sunday through Thursday from 10 a.m. to 11 p.m. and Friday and Saturday from 10 a.m. to midnight.

Just up the street from the eye-popping Forum Shops is gotta-see-to-believe stop number two — the **Grand Canal Shoppes at the Venetian,** 3355 Las Vegas Blvd. S. (☎ **702-414-1000**). If the **Forum Shops** are a street out of Rome, this is a street out of Renaissance Venice, with a cloud-studded sky overhead and a canal running down the middle of it, complete with singing gondoliers. (A ride costs $15. It's not inexpensive, but it's still a heck of lot cheaper than the real thing in Venice.) The "canal" ends at a reproduction of St. Mark's Square, a stalled market where glass blowers and flower sellers ply their trades. You can even find strolling musicians. You find more than 70 retail shops — **Davidoff, Kenneth Cole,** and **Sephora,** to name a few — to choose from. The Grand Canal Shoppes (accessible from the outside world via its own, casino-bypassing entrance) is open Sunday through Thursday from 10 a.m. to 11 p.m. and Friday and Saturday from 10 a.m. to midnight.

Right next door (and accessible from the interior) in the Venetian's sister hotel are the **Shoppes at Palazzo.** They lack thematic splendor but more than make up for it with fashion fabulousness. They're anchored by the superb department store **Barneys of New York,** which is as aesthetically pleasing as it is crammed with lust-inducing labels. The Shoppes have many another drool-worthy stores, such as **Bottega Veneta, Chloe, Christian Louboutin, Diane von Furstenberg,** and **Fendi.** Open Sunday through Thursday 10 a.m. to 11 p.m. and Friday and Saturday 10 a.m. to midnight.

Speaking of aesthetics, we no longer adore the visuals at **Miracle Mile at Planet Hollywood,** 3667 Las Vegas Blvd. S. (☎ **702-866-0710**), since its transformation from the Middle Eastern–themed Desert Passage. Trying for a sort of "Madison Avenue" glitz and glam it's really now just a very large, sprawling, bland (if sparkly), fancy-pants mall. That's not a theme, dang it. But although perhaps lacking the high-end heaven of the previously mentioned hotel shopping, it does have more accessible venues. It has **bebe, Betsey Johnson, Frederick's of Hollywood, Gap,** cheap-chic nirvana **H&M, Sephora,** and much more. With something for just about every taste or need, it's our shopping mall of choice for practical reasons, if nothing else. Open Sunday through Thursday 10 a.m. to 11 p.m., Friday and Saturday 10 a.m. to midnight.

If you want a more Rodeo Drive experience, head straight for the **Via Bellagio** shops in the **Bellagio**, 3600 Las Vegas Blvd. S. (☎ 702-693-7111; hours for stores vary). Not one place in this mall offers prices that we can afford (we can't even afford the oxygen — we make guidebook-writer wages, you know), but we sure like to browse and fantasize. **Armani, Gucci, Prada, Tiffany** — they're all here. And the setup, topped in its entirety by an overhead skylight that actually allows for — gasp! — natural lighting, is most attractive. Speaking of this sort of experience, the slightly smaller, but essentially same idea **Esplanade at Wynn Las Vegas**, 3131 Las Vegas Blvd. S. (☎ 702-770-7100; hours for stores vary), has the same kind of fantasy stores — **Cartier, Chanel, Jean Paul Gaultier, Manolo Blahnik** — but seems maybe just a touch less intimidating. Just a touch, mind you.

Presuming you haven't reached your credit limit yet, the hotel shopping tour wouldn't be complete without a visit to the newest addition to the city, or rather CityCenter, at the **Crystals**, 3720 Las Vegas Blvd. S. (☎ 702-590-9299; www.crystalsatcitycenter.com). It's architectural drama on the outside — all angular shapes, glass, and steel. Inside, it's a really expensive mall and not much else, featuring **Louis Vuitton, Porsche Design, Prada, Tiffany & Co.,** and **Tom Ford** among others, at which normal people can't afford to shop. On-site restaurants include offerings from Todd English, Wolfgang Puck, and *Desperate Housewives* star Eva Longoria Parker. The mall is open daily from 10 a.m. to midnight.

The rest of the pack

Two levels of shopping and dining surround a casino at **Masquerade Village**, 3700 W. Flamingo Rd. (☎ 702-777-7777), a 60,000-square-foot addition to the Rio Hotel & Casino. It's done up as a European village, and it sports mostly clothing boutiques and small curio or jewelry shops. Be sure to stop by the '**Nawlins** store, which sells voodoo items, Mardi Gras masks, and the like.

Shopping is definitely no afterthought at the **Stratosphere Las Vegas,** 2000 Las Vegas Blvd. S. (☎ 702-380-7777); you have to pass through its Tower Shops promenade in order to get to the tower itself. More than 40 stores are set along different international streetscapes that attempt to evoke Paris, Hong Kong, and New York City.

Harrah's Las Vegas, 3475 Las Vegas Blvd. S. (☎ 702-369-5000) is unusual in that it has an outdoor shopping promenade: the **Carnavale Court.** Assuming that it's not deathly hot, this is a small but sweet place to wander, stocked with open-air carts featuring floaty dresses, naughty underwear, purses, and more. Among the store highlights is a branch of San Francisco's famous **Ghirardelli Chocolate** shop.

Most of the hotel shopping arcades are adjacent to or in the middle of casinos. Perhaps they hope that you use your shopping money on a slot machine instead? Avoid these machines if at all possible — they're rumored to offer lower winnings than machines in other areas of the casinos.

Can't go home without a tacky souvenir?

The **Bonanza Gift and Souvenir Shop**, 2460 Las Vegas Blvd. S. (☎ 702-385-7359), located at the northwest corner of Sahara, bills itself as the "largest souvenir shop in the world." We have no way of verifying this, but it does have an enormous selection of souvenirs. Your best bet in the tacky department is earrings made out of poker chips or bracelets made out of dice.

Or head over to the **Arts Factory**, 101–107 E. Charleston Blvd. (☎ 702-383-3133), which offers, in addition to several art galleries (where you can pick up a really expensive souvenir, such as an original painting), a very fine gift shop that caters to all camp sensibilities. Pink flamingos, fuzzy dice, and truly marvelous retro-Vegas items — they're all here, along with so much more.

Where to Find the Bare Necessities

Forgot to pack your shampoo and don't want to waste your kid's college tuition by buying it in the hotel gift shop? Consider driving down **Maryland Parkway,** which runs parallel to the Strip on the east and has one of everything: **Target, Toys "R" Us,** several major department stores, major drugstores, some alternative-culture stores (tattoo parlors and hip clothing stores), and so forth. It goes on for blocks.

If you need to fill a medical prescription, you can do it at **Walgreens,** in between the Venetian and the Palazzo, 3339 Las Vegas Blvd S. (☎ 702-369-8166), or at **Sav-On** at 1360 E. Flamingo Rd. (☎ 702-737-0595). Another, more retro option is **White Cross Drugs,** just north of the Stratosphere Tower, 1700 Las Vegas Blvd. S. (☎ 702-382-1733).

Road-trippers whose cars need an emergency tune-up can try **Pep Boys,** 637 E. Sahara Ave., just east of Paradise (☎ 702-796-0600), which is part of a major auto parts and service chain.

Angling for Antiques

If you're an antiques hound, you may want to poke around **East Charleston Road,** where more than 20 small, good-quality antiques stores are located within a few blocks of each other. We know an interior designer who got most of her best pieces here. Go north on the Strip to Charleston Road and turn right — the stores begin at about the 1600 block.

Shopping for Cool Clothes and Accessories

If you want hip and cool outfits, take a drive over to the **Buffalo Exchange,** 4110 S. Maryland Pkwy. (☎ 702-791-3960). It's one of a chain of used-clothing stores filled with vintage and current discards. Comb the racks and find something that will instantly upgrade your trendy image. It's in a small shopping strip at the southeast corner of Maryland Parkway and Flamingo Road. The **Attic,** 1018 S. Main St. (☎ **702-388-4088;** www.atticvintage.com), is another vintage/used-clothing store, with a generally excellent selection. It was featured for several years in an eye-catching, too-cool-for-words Visa ad. It also makes its own poodle skirts!

If you crave showgirl hair (and why not?), stop in at **Serge's Showgirl Wigshop,** 953 E. Sahara Ave., No. A-2 (☎ **702-732-1015;** www.showgirl wigs.com), located in the Sahara Commercial Center just east of Paradise. This place has been supplying the Strip for more than 20 years, and it has some 2,000 wigs ranging from $130 to $1,500. It has wigs by Dolly Parton and Revlon, and men's and women's hairpieces. You can customize your own special creation.

 If the prices at Serge's main shop are too steep for you, check out **Serge's Wig Outlet,** just across the shopping center at 953 E. Sahara Ave. (☎ **702-732-3844**). The store offers discontinued wigs that run around $60 to $70.

Buying Gambling Gear

If you're not content blowing your money at the blackjack table, you can blow it on gambling-related stuff downtown at the **Gambler's General Store,** 800 S. Main St. (☎ **800-322-2447;** www.gamblersgeneralstore.com), located 8 blocks south of Fremont. Another "World's Largest" (who decides these things?), the store has actual gaming equipment (dice, craps tables, old slot machines, and more), plus a selection of gambling books.

If you want to read up on strategy, try the **Gambler's Book Shop,** 1550 E. Tropicana Ave. (☎ **800-522-1777;** www.gamblersbook.com), located just east of Maryland Parkway. The store's motto is "Knowledge Is Protection." You can browse more than 4,000 gambling-related titles here, all designed to help you beat the odds. Don't forget to check out *Casino Gambling For Dummies,* by Kevin Blackwood and Max Rubin (published by Wiley), for clear, concise tips on gambling strategies.

 The store's knowledgeable clerks are happy to provide on-the-spot expert advice on handicapping the ponies and other aspects of sports betting.

Chapter 14

Doubling Your Odds: A Pair of Itineraries

Arguably, there are really only two ways to spend your time in Las Vegas — gambling and looking at hotels.

Okay, that's not exactly true. But if that's all you do, unlike in most cities, you haven't missed much. These two activities, after all, are exactly what Las Vegas is all about.

But you can organize your time in Vegas to get the most out of what the city has to offer.

Seeing Las Vegas in Four Days

As we said, you can just plunk yourself down at a poker table, heave yourself back off the chair four days later, and consider your time well spent. But if you want to check out the sights beyond that cute dealer, here are some suggestions.

Day one

Ignore those slot machines — come on, you can do it, and you can get back to them eventually, we promise — and head right out to the **Strip.** This is one of the great wonders of the artificial world; it's as important a sight, for entirely different reasons, as the Grand Canyon. And you must take it all in, because you don't know what will be gone by your next visit. If you haven't been to Vegas in more than six years — heck, if it's been more than six *weeks* — the town may be nearly unrecognizable to you. This is a city that sheds its skin about every ten years. Things change that fast, so go ogle it all. A lot of people spent many hours and a whole lot of money erecting these behemoths; you may as well admire their work, because, after all, you're paying for it!

We give you a suggested itinerary for viewing the Strip's hotels in the upcoming section, "Seeing the World-Famous Las Vegas Strip," but here's the gist: Be sure to see the **Venetian** (including the **Grand Canal Shoppes**), **Wynn Las Vegas, Bellagio,** the **Mirage** (including the white tigers), **Paris, Caesars Palace** (including the **Forum Shops** and the talking statues), **CityCenter** (primarily its centerpiece **Aria Las Vegas**), **New York–New York,** the **MGM Grand,** and the exteriors of the **Luxor,** and the **Excalibur.** Then, at night, take a drive (if you can) down the Strip. When the street is lit up, it's even more extraordinary than it is during the day.

Turn to Chapter 9 for more on all the Strip's hotels. Be sure to note the free evening entertainment: **Bellagio's** water fountains, which "perform" to various musical genres; the pirate battle at **Treasure Island** (even though it kinda stinks, thanks to a reworking to turn the focus to less-than-nautical nekked ladies); and the volcano explosion next door at the **Mirage** (see Chapter 12 for more on these attractions). Have at least one meal at the quintessential Vegas dining experience, the **buffet** (details in Chapter 10), and have a drink at the top of the **Stratosphere,** the tallest building west of the Mississippi and, not surprisingly, the best view in town (see Chapter 17).

Oh, all right, maybe you should go gamble a little now (see Chapter 11 for gambling tips).

This is your budget day — the buffet (depending on where you go) probably doesn't cost much, and with unlimited portions, you should eat your fill! Hotel gazing is free — but we're not responsible for what you spend gambling.

Day two

Unless you were really energetic (and the temperatures weren't extremely hot!), you probably didn't cover the whole Strip on day one, so pick up where you left off. Then go see some smaller sights, such as the **Atomic Testing Museum,** the **Erotic Heritage Museum,** or the significantly less bejeweled or naughty **Dolphin Habitat** (see Chapter 12 for more on these and other attractions). Because day one was your budget day, tonight it's time to kick out the jams, budget-wise. First, you must take in a show. We think **Cirque du Soleil's** *O* and *KÀ* and **Garth Brooks** are the finest shows in Vegas, but see Chapter 16 for many other choices that may have greater ticket availability (not to mention cheaper prices, if you refuse to let us spend your money for you). Having done the buffet thing, take advantage of the celebrity-chef invasion and have at least one haute cuisine meal — it's as over the top as the buffets, but in a different way; and face it, mass-prepared buffet food is, shall we say, not of the same quality. **Alize, Bartolotta's, Bouchon, L'Atelier, Picasso, Rosemary's,** and **Sinatra** are our top choices, but you can't go wrong with **Alex, Aureole,** or **Fleur de Lis.** You'll also enjoy any of the following: the **Border Grill, Isla, Olives, Sensi, Strip House,** or **Todd English P.U.B.** All are reviewed in Chapter 10.

Day three

Loving this decadent thing, are you? Went into the casino "just to play for a few minutes," only to find that two days have passed without your noticing?

It's time to get out into the fresh air. Get off that slot-machine stool and drive out to **Red Rock Canyon.** The panoramic 13-mile **Scenic Loop Drive** is best seen early in the morning when traffic is light. If you have the time and energy, get out of your car and take a hike. You can even give your gambling budget a break by spending the whole day out. If so, have a bite to eat at nearby **Bonnie Springs Ranch,** and afterward take a guided trail ride into the desert wilderness or enjoy the silliness at **Old Nevada.** You can find out more about these side trips later in Chapter 15. Be sure to take along a submarine sandwich from **Capriotti's** (see Chapter 10) for your lunch — they're cheap, large, and delicious.

Tonight, continue to enjoy that fresh air — of a sort — and head downtown. This neighborhood is often neglected because it simply can't stand up to the over-the-top excess of the Strip, but it's far more user-friendly. About a dozen hotels and casinos lie within a five-minute walk of one another, all grouped around a pedestrian mall, which, at night, lights up overhead with the colorful and musical **Fremont Street Experience** light show (see Chapter 12). Stick your head out of the casino to look at it and think, "Look, I'm outside! I am!"

Day four

This is Culture and History Day! Go see the marvel of modern engineering that is the **Hoover Dam.** Leave early in the morning, returning to Las Vegas after lunch via **Valley of Fire State Park,** while stopping at the **Lost City Museum** in Overton en route (see Chapter 15 for more information on all these attractions). Or spend time with some incredible works of art courtesy of the **Bellagio Gallery of Art** or the **CityCenter Fine Art Collection** (see Chapter 12). Nothing like real art to remind you of the artificial reality that is Las Vegas. Plus, think how smug you can feel after enjoying some honest-to-gosh culture.

Too exhausted to do that, are you? And it's kinda hot, is it? Oh, all right. Another option is to recharge your batteries by spending the day by the hotel pool or going to the hotel spa for some detoxing and pampering.

All rested up? Then get out again and enjoy the city that never sleeps. Hit the casinos some more — you can take them down; we know you can! Catch another show — if you went with our **Cirque** suggestion, that means you haven't seen a classic Vegas topless revue, so get thee over to *Jubilee!* (at **Bally's**) pronto. Or you can enjoy some retro fun with **Barry Manilow** (at the **Paris**) or **Donny and Marie** (at the **Flamingo**), up your intelligence quotient with the smartest show in town, **Penn & Teller** (at the **Rio**), or laugh yourself silly with comedienne **Rita Rudner** (at **Harrah's**); see Chapter 16 for reviews of all these shows. Get back into the decadent swing of things with another buffet orgy, or worship at the shrine of a second celebrity chef.

After all, you're on vacation.

Seeing the World-Famous Las Vegas Strip

One of the main activities in town is wandering around and gawking at the gigantic, splashy, gimmick-filled hotels. This should be your first order of business, and getting through them all (especially if you stop for a hand or two of blackjack at each) can take most of your trip. We describe the hotels in detail in Chapter 9, but for sheer spectacle, here's the best way to see our favorites.

Start south on the Strip at **Mandalay Bay** to get a gander at its South Seas theme. As far as themes goes, this one is pretty subtle, but it's still worth taking a look.

Walk through the Mandalay Place shops to get to the **Luxor,** where you can experience the Vegas version of Ancient Egypt. The Sphinx (don't worry, the real one is still in Egypt) stands guard in front of a 30-story pyramid that's big enough to house nine jumbo jets. Be sure to visit the dizzying interior of the pyramid. It's been de-Egypt-ified for mystifying reasons, but it's still neck-craning interesting.

Now hop on the moving sidewalk — and exit at Camelot. Oh, not really, but it is a giant medieval castle — or at least, a cartoon version of one. It's the **Excalibur,** one of the largest hotels in the world.

Take the pedestrian bridge across the Strip to the **Tropicana** to get a look at the rebirth of a legend. Its 2010 makeover has turned it into a South Beach paradise worth visiting again. Then take another overhead pedestrian walkway across Tropicana Avenue so that you can get up close and personal with the highly impersonal **MGM Grand.** It's the second-largest hotel in the world, and at night, it's very, very green. If you're looking for photo-ops, that molten-gold, four-stories-high lion out front is just begging for your camera to snap away. Here, kitty, kitty, kitty! Then turn around and grab a few shots of New York City across the street — that's where you're headed next.

Mosey right across the Strip (a pedestrian overhead walkway can get you there) to **New York–New York.** Don't worry, you'll find it — it's that little place (ha!), on the corner of Trop and the Strip, that looks like the New York City skyline, complete with the Empire State Building and the Statue of Liberty. Take time to really appreciate all the silly touches, such as the graffiti-covered mailboxes and the manhole covers.

Head north along the Strip and wander through **Monte Carlo,** mainly to get to the monorail that will take you to **CityCenter**, a $9 billion complex of hotels, shopping, entertainment, gambling, and art; its modern, glass-and-steel skyline looks completely out of place on the Strip yet somehow still works.

At this point, you can go back across the street via a pedestrian bridge to **Planet Hollywood** and wander through its **Miracle Mile** shopping mall. Its Madison Avenue theme is not quite as interesting as the former Middle East extravaganza that was the Desert Passage back when the whole mess was called Aladdin, but it's still worth a look if you're not too pooped and not ready to call it a day. It's also one of our favorite places to shop.

Head north along the Strip for a stop at **Paris Las Vegas** to appreciate the replica of the Eiffel Tower and Arc de Triomphe, and then turn west to catch the **Fountains of Bellagio** show across the street (shows every 15 or 30 minutes daily). You can use the pedestrian bridge in front of **Bally's** to go to **Bellagio** and appreciate its **Conservatory,** a riot of color thanks to fresh flowers and plants that are re-landscaped every few weeks to reflect the changing seasons.

If you still have energy and ambition (or you skipped the Planet Hollywood step), your next stop is **Caesars Palace,** where you can gawk at the silly wonder that is a re-creation (well, kinda) of ancient Rome, and the oldest theme hotel in Vegas. The **Forum Shops** (see Chapter 13) are tied with the **Venetian Grand Canal Shoppes** for thematic silliness, but over here they have talking statues. Head next to the **Mirage,** where, after dusk, the **volcano** out front explodes every hour (see Chapter 12). Inside, you find a simulated (well, partially, anyhow) rain forest.

Proceed right next door to **Treasure Island,** if you want to see the sorta-naughty free pirate stunt show we endlessly mock elsewhere in this book (particularly in Chapter 12). Otherwise, cross the Strip via the overhead pedestrian walkway to the **Venetian** and sister **Palazzo.** Unlike the appealing but off-limits exteriors of the other theme hotels, you actually can wander through the outside of this replica of Venice, that most charming of Italian cities. And with its (nonsmelly) canal, tall street-lights, and promenades, it's supremely charming — for Vegas, at least. Dash inside for a cup of gelato (stopping to admire the heavily marbled and art-covered grand entrance galleria), and bring it outside for a snack. Or head upstairs to the **Grand Canal Shoppes** (see Chapter 13), and pay a gondolier to row you about.

Finally, take yet another pedestrian walkway to **Wynn Las Vegas** and its sequel **Encore Las Vegas** to see the luxurious empire that casino impresario Steve Wynn runs. Then grab a cab, hoof it, or ride the Las Vegas Monorail (the nearest station is at the **Venetian**) home.

Chapter 15

Going Beyond Las Vegas: Day Trips

....

In This Chapter

▶ Heading to Hoover Dam, Lake Mead, and the Valley of Fire

▶ Winging off to Red Rock Canyon and Bonnie Springs

....

*L*as Vegas can be a bit overwhelming, so if you've already blown your bankroll or you need to take a breather from the blackjack table, a day trip may be just the thing to recharge your batteries.

Day Trip No. 1: Hoover Dam, Lake Mead, and Valley of Fire State Park

A couple thousand people visit Hoover Dam daily to pay homage to the engineering marvel, without which, frankly, there would be no Las Vegas. A visit to the dam doesn't fill an entire day, but two other magnificent spots nearby — **Lake Mead** and **Valley of Fire State Park** — also deserve your attention.

Getting there

To get to **Lake Mead,** go east on Flamingo or Tropicana to U.S. 515 south, which automatically turns into 93 south and takes you right to the dam. This involves a rather dramatic drive, as you go through **Boulder City,** come over a rise, and suddenly behold Lake Mead spread out before you. It's a beautiful sight. At about this point in the drive, the road narrows to two lanes, and traffic can slow considerably. On busy tourist days, the drive can take an hour or more.

To continue on to **Hoover Dam,** go past the turnoff to **Lake Mead.** As you near the dam, you see a five-story parking structure tucked into the canyon wall on your left. Park here ($7 charge) and take the elevators or stairs to the walkway leading to the visitor center.

To get to the spooky, otherworldly landscape of the **Valley of Fire** from Las Vegas, take I-15 north to exit 75 (Valley of Fire turnoff). For a more scenic route, take I-15 north, travel Lake Mead Boulevard east to North Shore Road (Nev. 167), and proceed north to the Valley of Fire exit. The first route takes about an hour; the second, 1½ hours. From the Lake Mead area, take Nev. 166 (Lakeshore Scenic Drive) north, make a right turn on Nev. 167 (North Shore Scenic Drive), turn left on Nev. 169 (Moapa Valley Boulevard) west — a spectacularly scenic drive — and follow the signs. Valley of Fire is about 65 miles from **Hoover Dam.**

Taking a tour

If you didn't rent a car, or if you'd rather go on an organized tour, contact **Gray Line** (☎ **800-634-6579** or 702-384-1234; www.grayline.com). The company offers several packages inside and outside Las Vegas. The 4½-hour **Mini Hoover Dam Tour** ($60) departs daily at 8:30 a.m. There's also a **Neon Lights Tour** ($55) of Las Vegas that includes a narrative tour past the mega-resorts and a visit to the **Fremont Street Experience.** You can inquire at your hotel tour desk about other bus tours.

Numerous sightseeing tours also go to **Valley of Fire.** Inquire at your hotel tour desk. Char Cruze of **Creative Adventures** (☎ **702-893-2051;** www.creativeadventuresltd.net) also does a fantastic tour.

 When you're in Las Vegas, look in the numerous free publications available at hotels for discount coupons that offer significant savings on tours to Hoover Dam and Valley of Fire State Park.

Seeing the sights

Start your day with Hoover Dam itself or, rather, the **Hoover Dam Visitor Center** (☎ **702-494-2517**). There, you can check out exhibits on the dam and buy tickets for tours. The visitor center is open daily from 9 a.m. to 6 p.m., except Thanksgiving and Christmas. You can purchase tickets until 5:15 p.m. Admission for the Powerplant Tour is $11 for adults, $9 for seniors and kids 4 to 16, while the more extensive Hoover Dam Tour is $30 (no kids under 7 allowed). There is a $7 parking fee. *Note:* Due to heightened security, visitors are not allowed on top of the dam after dark.

It takes about two hours, either on the tour or on your own, to see all that Hoover Dam has to offer. Although it's not compulsory, it's not a bad idea to call in advance for the tour (☎ **866-730-9097**). Kids may be bored by the dam, unless they are budding engineers or just love big things — but your parents probably took you to things you didn't want to see for your own good when you were a kid, so why should your kids get off the hook?

Hoover Dam fun facts

Surely this is one of the few examples of primo government efficiency. Construction on Hoover Dam began in 1931. Some 5,200 workers labored around the clock to complete the dam in 1936, two years ahead of schedule and $15 million under budget. The dam stopped the annual floods and conserved water for irrigation, as well as industrial and domestic use. Equally important, it became one of the world's major electrical generating plants, providing low-cost, pollution-free hydroelectric power to scores of surrounding communities. The dam itself is a massive curved wall, measuring 660 feet thick at the bottom and tapering to 45 feet where the road crosses it at the top. It towers 726 feet above bedrock (about the height of a 60-story skyscraper) and acts as a plug between the canyon walls to hold back up to 9.2 trillion gallons of water in Lake Mead — the reservoir created by its construction.

After touring the dam, you can have lunch in **Boulder City** (see the upcoming section, "Dining locally"), or you can go to the **Lake Mead National Recreation Area.** Start at the **Alan Bible Visitor Center,** 4 miles northeast of Boulder City on U.S. 93 at Lakeshore Scenic Drive (☎ **702-293-8990**), which provides information on all area activities and services. You can pick up trail maps and brochures here, view informative films, and find out about scenic drives, accommodations, ranger-guided hikes, naturalist programs and lectures, bird-watching, canoeing, camping, lakeside RV parks, and picnic facilities. The center also sells books and videotapes about the area. It's open daily from 8:30 a.m. to 4:30 p.m., except Thanksgiving and Christmas. For information on accommodations, boat rentals, and fishing, call the **Las Vegas Boat Harbor** (☎ **702-293-1191**).

If you don't want to spend your post-dam time on outdoor activities, you always can drive back to Vegas via the **Valley of Fire State Park,** or you can spend a day just on the park alone. This is an awesome, foreboding desert tundra, full of flaming red rocks. It looks like the setting of any number of sci-fi movies — not surprisingly, considering that a number of them have been filmed here.

Plan on spending a minimum of an hour in the park, though you can spend a great deal more time here. It can get very hot — there's nothing to offer relief from the sun beating down and reflecting off all that red. No water is available, so be sure to bring a liter, if not two, with you in the summer. Without a guide, you must stay on paved roads, but don't worry if they end — you can always turn around and come back to the main road. You can soak up a lot of the park from the car, but try one of the hiking trails if you feel up to it.

Pick up information on **Valley of Fire** at the **visitor center** on Nev. 169, 6 miles west of North Shore Road (☎ **702-397-2088**). Open daily from 8:30 a.m. to 4:30 p.m., it's worth a quick stop for information and a bit of history before entering the park.

At the southern edge of **Overton** (15 miles northwest on Nev. 169). is the **Lost City Museum,** 721 S. Moapa Valley Blvd. (☎ **702-397-2193**), a sweet little museum commemorating an ancient Anasazi village that was discovered in the region in 1924. Admission is $3 for adults, $2 for seniors, and free for kids 17 and under. The museum is open daily from 8:30 a.m. to 4:30 p.m. and is closed New Year's Day, Thanksgiving, and Christmas.

Dining locally

After touring **Hoover Dam,** have lunch in **Boulder City,** 7 miles northwest of the dam on U.S. 93. You may want to check out some of the antiques and curio shops while you're there. For lunch, you have your choice of a number of family-style restaurants and burger and Mexican joints, including **Totos,** 806 Buchanan Blvd. (☎ **702-293-1744**), a reasonably priced Mexican restaurant in the Vons shopping center. There are no food concessions or gas stations in **Valley of Fire State Park;** however, you can grab meals or gas on Nev. 167 or in Overton. We recommend eating at **Inside Scoop,** 395 S. Moapa Valley Blvd. (☎ **702-397-2055**), open Monday through Saturday from 10 a.m. to 8 p.m. and Sunday from 11 a.m. to 7 p.m. It's an old-fashioned ice-cream parlor run by extremely friendly people. In addition to the much-needed ice cream, classic sandwiches, and the like, the menu features some surprising choices — for example, a vegetarian sandwich and a fish salad with crab and shrimp.

Day Trip No. 2: Red Rock Canyon and Bonnie Springs Ranch

If you're craving a temporary escape from Vegas but you don't want such an ambitious trip as Day Trip No. 1, head over to **Red Rock Canyon.** Like Valley of Fire, it's a surreal and lovely landscape of outer-space-like rock formations, perfect for hiking or even just driving through while emitting cries of "Oooooo!!!" It's a fine way to recharge your batteries — and it's only 19 miles west of Vegas.

Getting there

Just drive west on Charleston Boulevard, which becomes Nev. 159. Virtually as soon as you leave the city, the red rocks begin to loom around you. The **visitor center** will appear on your right.

You can also go by **bike.** Charleston Boulevard has a bike path that starts at Rainbow Boulevard and continues for about 11 miles to the visitor center/scenic drive. The path is hilly, but it isn't difficult if you're in reasonable shape.

However, you should explore Red Rock Canyon by bike only if you're an exceptionally fit and experienced biker.

Taking a tour

You also can take an **organized tour** of the canyon. **Gray Line** (☎ 800-634-6579 or 702-384-1234; www.grayline.com), among other companies, runs bus tours to the canyon. Inquire at your hotel tour desk.

Seeing the sights

Just off Nev. 159, you see the **Red Rock Canyon Visitor Center** (☎ 702-515-5350), which marks the actual entrance to the park. There you can pick up information on trails and view history exhibits on the canyon. The center is open daily from 8:30 a.m. to 4:30 p.m.

The easiest thing to do is to drive the **13-mile scenic loop.** It really is a loop, and it only goes one way, so after you start, you're committed to drive the whole thing. You can stop the car to admire any number of fabulous views and sights along the way, have a picnic, or take a walk or hike. In fact, we can't stress enough that the way to really see the canyon is by **hiking,** if you're up to it. Every trail is incredible, with mini-caves and rock formations to scramble over.

You can begin from the visitor center or drive into the loop, park, and start from points therein. Hiking trails range from a ¾-mile-loop stroll to a waterfall (its flow varying seasonally) at **Lost Creek,** to much longer and more strenuous treks. Actually, all the hikes involve a certain amount of effort, because you have to scramble over rocks on even the shorter hikes. The unfit or the ungraceful should be cautious. Be sure to wear good shoes (the rocks can be slippery) and bring a map. As you hike, keep your eyes peeled for lizards, the occasional desert tortoise, flocks of bighorn sheep, birds, and other critters.

On the way to or fro, if you feel the need for some munchies, stop at the fancy **Red Rock Resort,** 11011 W. Charleston Rd. (☎ 866-767-7773). It's worth an ogle on its own (good star-spotting, so early reports say), but within its food court is an outlet of our beloved submarine sandwich place, **Capriotti's,** which is perfect for a bargain meal or even a picnic to take with you while you go explore the canyon.

After Red Rock, you can keep going another 5 miles west to **Bonnie Springs Ranch** and **Old Nevada.** The latter is a kind of Wild West theme park (complete with shootouts and stunt shows) with accommodations and a restaurant — probably the best place to get a meal in this area. Okay, it's cheesy and touristy, but it's fun — honest. If you're traveling with kids, we recommend a day trip to Bonnie Springs — but it's surprisingly appealing to adults, too. It can even be a romantic getaway, offering horseback riding, gorgeous mountain vistas, proximity to **Red Rock Canyon,** and temperatures 5 to 10 degrees cooler than on the Strip.

For additional information, call **Bonnie Springs Ranch/Old Nevada** at
☎ 702-875-4191 or go to www.bonniesprings.com. Admission to Old
Nevada costs $20 per car (up to 6 people). Hours vary during summer
and winter, so call ahead, but it's generally open from 10:30 a.m. to
5 p.m.

Bonnie Springs Ranch (☎ 702-875-4191) is right next door to Old
Nevada, with additional activities, including a small and highly dated
zoo, and a less politically distressing aviary on the premises.

Riding stables offer guided trail rides into the mountain area on a contin-
uous basis throughout the day (10:30 a.m.–5 p.m. in winter, until 6 p.m.
in summer). Kids must be at least 6 years old to ride. It costs $55 per
hour.

Part V
Living It Up After Dark: Las Vegas Nightlife

The 5th Wave   By Rich Tennant

FAILED LAS VEGAS ACT

"And now ladies and gentlemen, the Del Mar Hotel and Casino presents, 'Angels in Corduroy!'"

In this part . . .

*L*as Vegas is a nonstop town, and when the sun goes down, the city really lights up. Although Vegas has a sophisticated side, it's not exactly known for symphony or ballet. Nightlife in Vegas means dropping some of your hard-earned gambling dough on big, splashy production shows and checking out the hippest clubs and bars. This part of the book helps you plan your Vegas nights.

Chapter 16

It's Showtime!

In This Chapter

▶ Getting show tickets and information
▶ Uncovering the facts about Las Vegas showrooms
▶ Checking out the best Las Vegas productions
▶ Visiting the hottest headliner showrooms

*L*as Vegas has a lot more to offer these days than the magic shows and showgirls that helped build its reputation. Thanks to the wildly successful (and quite avant-garde) Canadian circus troupe **Cirque du Soleil,** you now have a wide variety of similar big-budget shows to tickle your fancy. These days, the trend in major production shows is toward bigger, louder, brighter, and more expensive creations — just the right speed for Vegas audiences.

But never fear, this is still the town of illusionists and showgirls (creatures of illusion themselves). If you want to see big-time magic acts or topless-dancer revues, you won't go home disappointed. This chapter walks you through your options.

What's On and Getting Tickets

Unless you're a pampered high roller, a reservation is a must if you want to see a show. Some shows — especially those going on during peak periods — sell out weeks in advance. You often can get last-minute tickets for a weekday performance, but Lady Luck will have to be on your side to get them on weekends. You won't have such luck for major concerts, boxing matches, and other big-ticket performances, so reserve your tickets to these events as soon as possible. Order tickets through **Ticketmaster** (☎ **702-474-4000;** www.ticketmaster.com).

Keep your itinerary in mind when making show reservations so that you're not racing through your meal to make your show of choice. If the show you want to see is on the Strip, plan for the extra time en route. You don't want backed-up traffic to bring down your good time.

The best way to find out what is happening in town when you're visiting is to contact the **Las Vegas Visitor Information Center** (☎ **877-847-4858;** www.visitlasvegas.com) and ask them to send you their *Showguide*.

Shows on the Strip

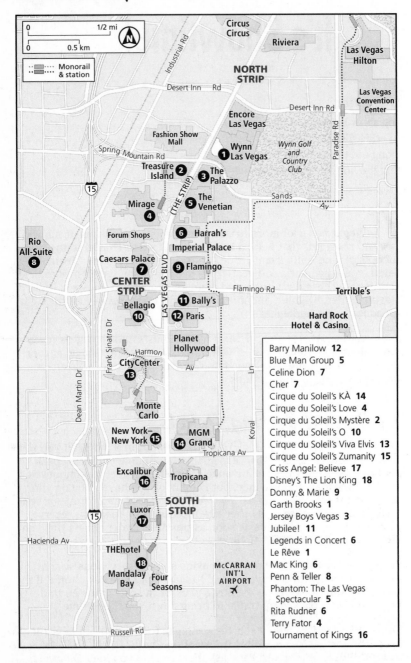

0	1/2 mi
0	0.5 km

Monorail & station

Industrial Rd

Circus Circus

Riviera

Las Vegas Hilton

NORTH STRIP

Desert Inn Rd

Desert Inn Rd

Las Vegas Convention Center

Encore Las Vegas

Fashion Show Mall

Spring Mountain Rd

Wynn Las Vegas ❶

Wynn Golf and Country Club

Treasure Island ❷

The Palazzo ❸

(THE STRIP)

Paradise Rd

Mirage ❹

The Venetian ❺

Sands Av

Forum Shops

Harrah's ❻

Imperial Palace

Rio All-Suite ❽

Caesars Palace ❼

Flamingo ❾

CENTER STRIP

Terrible's

Flamingo Rd

Bellagio ❿

Bally's ⓫

Paris ⓬

Hard Rock Hotel & Casino

Frank Sinatra Dr

LAS VEGAS BLVD

Planet Hollywood

Harmon

CityCenter ⓭

Av

Dean Martin Dr

Monte Carlo

Koval Ln

New York–New York ⓯

MGM Grand ⓮

Tropicana Av

Excalibur ⓰

Tropicana

SOUTH STRIP

Hacienda Av

Luxor ⓱

THEhotel

Mc CARRAN INT'L AIRPORT ✈

Mandalay Bay ⓲

Four Seasons

Russell Rd

Barry Manilow **12**
Blue Man Group **5**
Celine Dion **7**
Cher **7**
Cirque du Soleil's KÀ **14**
Cirque du Soleil's Love **4**
Cirque du Soleil's Mystère **2**
Cirque du Soleil's O **10**
Cirque du Soleil's Viva Elvis **13**
Cirque du Soleil's Zumanity **15**
Criss Angel: Believe **17**
Disney's The Lion King **18**
Donny & Marie **9**
Garth Brooks **1**
Jersey Boys Vegas **3**
Jubilee! **11**
Legends in Concert **6**
Le Rêve **1**
Mac King **6**
Penn & Teller **8**
Phantom: The Las Vegas Spectacular **5**
Rita Rudner **6**
Terry Fator **4**
Tournament of Kings **16**

Check the Web site for a calendar of Las Vegas events; you can search for shows, sporting events, and more by date.

Other recommended resources:

- ✔ **Vegas4Visitors.com**, run by the author of this book, is a comprehensive online resource packed with unbiased reviews of hotels, attractions, shows, dining, and more — plus a weekly column on the latest happenings around town, gaming tips, and travel advice.

- ✔ *What's On, The Las Vegas Guide* (www.whats-on.com) is a free weekly publication found everywhere around Las Vegas. It's chock-full of all the latest information on shows, attractions, hotels, and restaurants. One note of caution: It's not precisely unbiased journalism. It's all paid advertising — but at least it tells you, up to the minute, what's happening where. Browse this magazine to find lots of coupons and specials in the advertisements.

- ✔ *Las Vegas Weekly* (www.lasvegasweekly.com) and *Las Vegas City Life* (www.lasvegascitylife.com) are free weekly publications that you can find at local newsstands and stores. They're the place for the hip to find tips on alternative culture and the like, but they're also more detailed than other publications when it comes to listing who can be found at what club or lounge that week. Did we mention that both are free? The Friday edition of the local newspaper, the *Las Vegas Review-Journal* (www.lvrj.com) is another good resource.

- ✔ The **Las Vegas Chamber of Commerce** (☎ 702-735-1616; www.lvchamber.com) will send you a packet of information about what to do and where to go.

- ✔ **Reservations agents** at Las Vegas hotels can tell you what's going on during your stay. They can fill you in on all the hotel's restaurants and give you details and times for any resident shows or upcoming concerts. They may even be able to offer you a discount on reservations. Sure, they tell you only about their specific property, but they know their stuff!

We include **admission prices** on every listing in the following section, but use them only as guidelines. Recent show changes or special promotions may result in slightly different prices than those listed here. Tickets generally cost $40 to $250 per person. Be sure to check to see if your hotel offers discounts on shows (especially shows staged on the premises). If you're gambling, ask about discounted admission or even free passes to shows and nightspots.

Some shows may not necessarily be obscene, but they may include **adult themes** or **skimpy costumes.** It used to be that you could tell the difference at a glance by looking for shows that offered discount admission for kids, but very few of them do these days, even those that may be good for a family audience. Double-check the content before taking the young 'uns to any show.

The Inside Scoop on Las Vegas Showrooms

Most showrooms these days are nonsmoking and have preassigned seating. And most shows take place in the large hotels, so you'll find free self-parking or valet parking unless otherwise noted.

If the show you're going to see has maitre d' seating, it's likely that "Old Vegas" rules apply; you may be able to haul out some extra cash to tip for a better seat. If you decide to take this route, plan to part with $5 to $20 per couple, depending on the original price of your ticket. One method you can try is to tip the captain who shows you to your seat rather than the maitre d'. This way, if you're led to a satisfactory seat, you don't have to tip anything. But if you want something better, discreetly show the captain what you're prepared to tip. What can we say? Money talks.

If the venue charges extra for drinks, and you plan to have a few while you enjoy the show, you may want to reconsider. These shows usually charge very high prices for even the most modest cocktails. A better option may be to have a couple of drinks beforehand and then a night-cap later at a more reasonably priced bar.

Las Vegas Productions A to Z

Given the spectrum of nightlife in Las Vegas, ranging all the way from glitz to sleaze, choosing what to do at night is a highly personal matter. The shows listed here are the most noteworthy of the pack. You can find other big shows in the major hotels, but we've seen them all so you don't have to. Why waste your time and money? That's why we're here!

Most productions rearrange their showtimes every so often, and many go dark for a week or two here or there throughout the year. Be sure to call in advance to ensure a production is playing when you think it is.

Wow, look at those prices! They are . . . well, excuse us while we go lie down, as we feel a little faint. ($255 for Donny and Marie? Dearie me.) Thank goodness for the multiple locations of **Tix4Tonight** (☎ **877-849-4868;** www.tix4tonight.com). Each day at 2 p.m., these outlets put unsold seats for that evening on sale for half-price. Are they going to have front-row seats for Cher the night you're in town? Unlikely. But you may get a shot at decent seats for Cirque and who knows? Maybe there's a pair in the back for Ms. Sarkisian, too. Or just play a wild card and see what comes up. Naturally, this service is popular, so you probably have to get in line a couple of hours before it opens.

Barry Manilow
Center Strip

You don't have to be one of the almost obsessive "Fanilows" to be totally won over by Barry Manilow's latest Vegas show at Paris Las Vegas. His voice is still crystal clear and his songs can now safely be viewed as the pop gems they are, without the irony or eye-rolling that has accompanied them for most of the years since they were actually popular. From the sway-along "Daybreak" to the powerful "Weekend in New England" to such megahits as "Mandy," "I Write the Songs," and (of course) "Copacabana," the show is a retro wonder made all the more enjoyable by Manilow's natural charm.

3655 Las Vegas Blvd. S. (in Paris Las Vegas). ☎ *800-745-3000. Admission: $95–$250 (plus tax and fees). Showtimes: Fri–Sun 7:30 p.m. at intervals throughout the year. Showroom policy: Nonsmoking with preassigned seating.*

Blue Man Group
Center Strip

Yes, there are men in this show, and yes, they are blue — not emotionally but literally, having been dipped in azure paint. This is not a typical Vegas show. It originated in New York City, where it's a still-running, highly successful performance-art show for the masses. Cheese is involved, as are marshmallows, paint, and a whole lot of crepe paper, not to mention printed and electronic non sequiturs, and some exquisite and unusual percussion music. So, what's it about? Nothing. Call it slapstick Dada. It's every bit as pointless as the many revues playing around Vegas, and it's also about 1,000 times smarter. You'll laugh yourself silly.

3355 Las Vegas Blvd. S. (in the Venetian). ☎ *866-641-7469. Reservations accepted up to 30 days in advance. Admission: $54–$143 (plus tax and fees). Showtimes: Nightly 7 p.m. and 10 p.m. Showroom policy: Nonsmoking with preassigned seating. Children 4 and younger not allowed.*

Celine Dion
Center Strip

The Colosseum at Caesars Palace was built for Celine Dion, and after five years of performing here, she left for other pastures, turning the keys over to the likes of Elton John, Cher, and Bette Midler. But Dion is coming back, kicking off a new three-year residency scheduled to begin in March 2011. Meant to "capture the romance of classic Hollywood movies," she will be backed by a full orchestra and the production will feature big-scale sets and visuals effects. Dion will perform roughly 70 shows per year.

3570 Las Vegas Blvd. S. (in Caesars Palace). ☎ *877-423-5463. Admission: $55–$255 (plus tax and fees). Showtimes had not been set at press time. Showroom policy: Nonsmoking with preassigned seating.*

Cher
Center Strip

Is it possible that all of evolution, all the history of civilization has led to . . . Cher with her own show at Caesars Palace? Hey, don't laugh! There is something truly momentous about her rags-to-gaudy-riches tale, overcoming adversity and reaching new heights in music, television, film and . . . oh, heck. She's got Bob Mackie outdoing himself for her outfits (which she changes more than frequently), she tells self-deprecating tales, she swears like a sailor, she sings her 40-plus years of hits from "The Beat Goes On" through "Believe" with fabulous choreography and visual spectacle. Maybe she'll even do "Half Breed"! If it's after February, you may be wishing you could turn back time — Cher's run ends on February 5, 2011.

3570 Las Vegas Blvd. S. (in Caesars Palace). ☎ *866-510-2437. Admission: $95–$250 (plus tax and fees). Showtimes: Tues, Wed, Sat, Sun 7:30 p.m. at intervals throughout the year. Showroom policy: Nonsmoking with preassigned seating.*

Cirque du Soleil's KÀ
South Strip

"No, not *another* Cirque show!" we cried. But then we went to see this glorious production, and "Yes, another Cirque show, please," we said. First of all, unlike most Cirque shows, it has a real plot: an epic saga of royal siblings separated by betrayal, battling their way back to each other. Second, it has an extraordinary stage, a hydraulic masterpiece that moves and shifts in order to provide any number of different settings (a ship, a mountainside, and much more) for the magical-realism martial-arts action. Think *Crouching Tiger, Hidden Dragon* and similar movies as a stage show, and you almost have the idea. It's gorgeous, it's touching, it's smart, it's Cirque. Wow. Again. And some more, please.

3799 Las Vegas Blvd. S. (in the MGM Grand). ☎ *866-774-7117. Reservations accepted up to 90 days in advance. Admission: $69–$150 (plus tax). Showtimes: Tues–Sat 7 p.m. and 9:30 p.m. Showroom policy: Nonsmoking with preassigned seating. Children 4 and under not allowed.*

Cirque du Soleil's Love
Center Strip

You could make a case that this particular Cirque production, conceived with the help of Fifth Beatle/producer Sir George Martin and with the official stamp of the surviving members and their families, is best enjoyed if you're a Beatles fan. Given their record sales, of course, you could reasonably wonder if anyone isn't, but never mind. Still, so many mop-top pop-culture references spun through the avant-garde Cirque machine may make those without that particular knowledge feel a bit left out. Plus, there aren't any big centerpiece numbers, with the emphasis instead on dance and scenic interpretations of Beatles tunes. It's still a delight, but there may be other Cirque productions you could choose first.

3400 Las Vegas Blvd. S. (in the Mirage). ☎ *800-963-9637. Reservations accepted up to 90 days in advance. Admission: $94–$150 (plus tax). Showtimes: Thurs–Mon 7 p.m. and 9:30 p.m. Showroom policy: Nonsmoking with preassigned seating. Children 4 and under not allowed.*

Cirque du Thriller

For years, there had been rumors of a possible collaboration between Cirque du Soleil and Michael Jackson, but it took the singer's untimely death in 2009 to make the dream a reality. A new Cirque production featuring Jackson's music will debut in a permanent home in Las Vegas sometime in 2012. At press time, details of where, when, and exactly what were not being released, but it will most likely be at one of the MGM Mirage hotels and will be accompanied by a Michael Jackson–themed nightclub. For updates, visit www.cirquedusoleil.com.

Cirque du Soleil's Mystère
Center Strip

This was the show that really changed the long-stagnant Vegas entertainment scene, an innovative spectacle and an experience like no other in Las Vegas. Of course, now there are (as we write this) seven Cirque shows on the Strip, not to mention Cirque-influenced shows, so it's hardly unique. But it's still a great lot of enigmatic and gorgeous fun. If you're expecting a traditional circus performance, forget it. There are no animals in this entrancing show. Instead, a human troupe of acrobats, dancers, gymnasts, and clowns perform highly choreographed, imaginative acrobatics and hypnotic feats of human strength. It's surreal, engaging, whimsical, dreamlike, and, occasionally, bewildering. It may be a bit too sophisticated and arty for smaller kids' tastes, however. The show is presented in a huge customized showroom with state-of-the-art hydraulics, and the performers use every inch of it. Arrive early, because the high jinks usually start about 15 minutes before the actual show begins.

3300 Las Vegas Blvd. S. (in Treasure Island). ☎ *800-392-1999. Reservations accepted up to 90 days in advance. Admission: $60–$95 (plus tax). Showtimes: Sat–Wed 7 p.m. and 9:30 p.m. Showroom policy: Nonsmoking with preassigned seating.*

Cirque du Soleil's O
Center Strip

At some point, when writing something like this, you run out of adjectives and superlatives, particularly when you have to describe a show that's difficult to describe to begin with. (If we could describe it, it wouldn't be Cirque.) But this is the one high-priced ticket where we can look you straight in the eye — and wallet — and earnestly say, "But it's worth it."

How do we figure? Let's say this: Read the preceding review for *Mystère* and understand that everything said there applies here, except that this show takes place in, on, above, and around a 1.5-million-gallon pool (*Eau* — pronounced *O* — is French for water), housed in an $80-million theater that puts the *Mystère* one to shame. To say much more than that would be to ruin many a visual surprise. Don't expect a linear narrative, but do expect to get whiplash as you suddenly realize something else marvelous has quietly begun taking place on another part of the stage. And don't be surprised if the sheer beauty of this extraordinary production makes you weep a little.

3600 Las Vegas Blvd. S. (in the Bellagio). ☎ *888-488-7111 or 702-693-7722. Admission: $94–$150 (tax included). Showtimes: Wed–Sun 7:30 p.m. and 10 p.m. Showroom policy: Nonsmoking with preassigned seating. Children 4 and under not allowed.*

Cirque du Soleil's Viva Elvis
South Strip

It's surprising that it took this long for two of Vegas's biggest entertainment icons — Elvis Presley and Cirque du Soleil — to come together. The pairing is more successful here than with Cirque du Soleil's Beatles show *Love,* with a nice balance of Cirque magic and Elvis-style showmanship. Essentially telling his life story (up to his big comeback in Vegas), Presley's music is reinterpreted with multimedia displays, big sets, dancers, acrobats, gymnasts, aerialists, and more than few Elvis impersonators, while the King's music (originals, remixes, and covers) propels the action forward. It's lightweight in comparison to other Cirque shows — the darkest moment is his breakup with Priscilla, told with a stunning lyrical dance *pas de deux* to "Caught in a Trap" — but it's also the most genuinely fun. Forty years after his final comeback in Vegas, Elvis is having another one.

3720 Las Vegas Blvd. S. (in Aria Las Vegas). ☎ *877-253-5847. Admission: $99–$175 (plus tax and fees). Showtimes: Fri–Tues 7 p.m. and 9:30 p.m. Showroom policy: Nonsmoking with preassigned seating. Children 4 and under not allowed.*

Cirque du Soleil's Zumanity
South Strip

Into every life, a little rain must fall. And onto every reviewer must fall the task of describing a venture that, though by a company one previously has thoroughly admired, one doesn't love. And so, Zumanity. It's the Cirque du Soleil adults-only show. Oh, it sounds good — all those taut bodies writhing and contorting — but in reality, not only is it not erotic, but it kind of has the opposite effect. It's like every other Cirque show, except with the contortions and acrobatics done naked (or appearing naked). See . . . Vegas isn't for families anymore. Even the circus has gone NC-17. Oh, and it has even less cohesion and plot. In its other shows, Cirque has succeeded by assuming its audience is smart; here it fails by assuming the opposite. Be honest, not to mention fiscally savvy — just go to a strip club, and tip the girls well.

3790 Las Vegas Blvd. S. (in New York–New York). ☎ *866-606-7111. Admission: $69–$142 (tax included). Showtimes: Tues–Wed and Fri–Sun 7:30 p.m. and 10:30 p.m. Showroom policy: Nonsmoking with preassigned seating. Children 17 and under not allowed.*

Criss Angel: Believe
South Strip

The eclectic magician, illusionist, and escapologist has teamed up with the ubiquitous Cirque du Soleil — man, you've read a lot about Cirque as these listings have gone on, haven't you? — for a less-than-inspired pairing. Angel's visuals are striking, while Cirque is nothing if not eye-catching, but the two don't form a cohesive whole, disappointing those who are fans of one or the other and not satisfying those who are fans of both.

3900 Las Vegas Blvd. S. (in New York–New York). ☎ *800-557-7428. Admission: $70–$181 (plus tax and fees). Showtimes: Tues–Sat 7 p.m. and 9:30 p.m. Showroom policy: Nonsmoking with preassigned seating. Children 4 and under not allowed.*

Disney's The Lion King
South Strip

A family-friendly show like this one seems like a strange fit for a decidedly un-family-friendly Las Vegas casino but it seems to be working both from a creative level and an audience-attendance one. Unlike many other Broadway transplants, there are only minor trims to the Tony Award–winning musical, so if you haven't caught it on the Great White Way or any of the places it toured, no need to worry about a less-than-faithful adaptation. The story about a lion cub struggling to find his rightful place in the wild kingdom is told with human actors in costumes that evoke, rather than imitate, the animals they're portraying, along with some amazing puppetry and special effects that dazzle. The music is kind of blah but does include crowd favorites like "Circle of Life" and "Can You Feel the Love Tonight." It's worth noting that some of the scenes (especially a stampede that closes the first act) may be a bit too intense for younger viewers.

3950 Las Vegas Blvd. S. (in Mandalay Bay). ☎ *877-623-7400. Admission: $53–$169 (plus tax and fees). Showtimes: Mon–Thurs 7:30 p.m., Sat–Sun 4 p.m. and 8 p.m. Showroom policy: Nonsmoking with preassigned seating.*

Donny & Marie
Center Strip

She's a little bit country, he's a little bit . . . well, you know the rest. Yes, your favorite toothy Osmonds are back on the Las Vegas stage, and no matter how much you may want to, it's virtually impossible not to like them. Their show is a throwback of the highest order, presenting the same sibling rivalry schtick and some of the same music they did on their variety show in the 1970s ("Puppy Love," "Paper Roses"). It's harmless kitsch mixed with saucy fluff, and you'll find yourself smiling almost as widely as they do through the whole thing.

3555 Las Vegas Blvd. S. (in Flamingo Las Vegas). ☎ *702-733-3333. Admission: $90–$255 (plus tax and fees). Showtimes: Tues–Sat 7:30 p.m. Showroom policy: Nonsmoking with preassigned seating. Children 4 and under not allowed.*

Garth Brooks
North Strip

Winston Churchill once said "All of the great things are simple." Although historians may have a different answer, we choose to believe he was talking about the Garth Brooks show, a master class in how to be great by being simple. Brooks takes the stage casually in dress, demeanor, and accompaniment — no band, staging, or fancy light tricks — looking and acting like he's your down-home best friend who just happened to bring along his guitar in case he felt like singing a song or two. And he does, although few of his greatest hits. Instead he looks back at his life, playing songs by artists his parents loved (Merle Haggard and Simon & Garfunkel), artists he loved as a teenager and young adult (Bob Seger and James Taylor), and his own contemporaries (Randy Travis and George Strait); then he shows how their music influenced his own. With just Brooks and a guitar, it's hard to believe that he could rivet your attention for two hours, but he does, presenting a thrillingly off-the-cuff experience for music fans of all genres, not just country-western.

3121 Las Vegas Blvd. S. (in Encore Las Vegas). ☎ **702-770-7469.** *Admission: $125 (plus tax and fees). Showtimes: Fri–Sun 8 p.m., with an additional show Sat at 10:30 p.m., at intervals throughout the year. Showroom policy: Nonsmoking with pre-assigned seating. Children 4 and under not allowed.*

Jersey Boys Vegas
Center Strip

Although Broadway shows aren't usually long-term successes here, *Jersey Boys,* like *Mamma Mia!* (which ran for years) before it, has the benefit of being stuffed with recognizable, and in many cases much-beloved, hit songs. This slightly truncated (there is no intermission) version of the Tony Award–winning musical tells the story of the rise to fame of Frankie Valli and the Four Seasons; it's as much drama as it is musical and, thus, more than just an exercise in tribute bands. Still, the format means that this is a solid combo of concert and theater, and the quality means it's far more than just a pleasant diversion from gambling. The subject matter, apart from some Joisey-style cussing, is suitable for families, though, of course, kids may not care about a group whose heyday was four decades ago. But the lively nature of the staging may draw them in anyway.

3325 Las Vegas Blvd S. (in the Palazzo). ☎ **866-641-7469.** *Admission: $64–$235 (plus tax and fees). Showtimes: Mon, Thurs, Fri, and Sun 7 p.m.; Tues and Sat at 6:30 p.m. and 9:30 p.m. Children 4 and under not allowed.*

Jubilee!
Center Strip

This is what you envision when you think of a Las Vegas topless extravaganza. The show includes lots of singing, dancing, fantastic costumes, elaborate sets, and variety acts. And, oh yeah, bare breasts. Lot's of 'em. It's a huge show, with more than 100 dancers and over-the-top sets, and we don't even know how many bosoms. Wild production numbers abound, including "Samson and Delilah" and a musical re-creation of the *Titanic* sinking (which prompted at least one recent attendee to comment, "The effects are better here than in the movie"). We're not saying that it's good theater, but we are saying that it's mighty good entertainment — in an utterly camp way. If you want to see a classic out-there Vegas show, this is the one. Heck, even if you never thought that you wanted to see such a production, trust us, you'll want to see this.

3645 Las Vegas Blvd. S. (in Bally's Las Vegas). ☎ *800-237-7469. Reservations accepted up to 6 weeks in advance. Admission: $53–$113 (plus tax). Showtimes: Sat–Thurs at 7:30 p.m. and 10:30 p.m. Showroom policy: Nonsmoking with preas-signed seating. Children 12 and under not allowed to covered shows; children 17 and under 18 not allowed to topless shows.*

Legends in Concert
Center Strip

Celebrity impersonations used to be the rage in Vegas, but these days there are only a handful of the shows and *Legends* is the granddaddy of them all. In business for more than 25 years, the show's move to Harrah's a couple of years ago hasn't done anything to either diminish what makes it fun (when the impersonators are good) or enhance what doesn't (when the impersonators aren't so good). Which fake celebrity you see depends on the day you visit, but figure on seeing folks like Britney, Dolly, Cher, and, of course, Elvis. (It may be a law in Vegas that impersonator shows have to have an Elvis, but we're still checking local statutes.) If this is your cup of faux tea, you can't get a better cup of the stuff in this town.

3475 Las Vegas Blvd. S. (in Harrah's). ☎ *702-369-5111. Admission: $48–$58 (plus tax and fees). Showtimes: Sun–Fri 7:30 p.m. and 10 p.m. Showroom policy: Nonsmoking with preassigned seating.*

Le Rêve
North Strip

Truth be told — and we always tell you the truth — *Le Rêve* will always suffer from Cirque comparisons. It's hard not to make them, since this, like *O,* is set in and around a large body of water and features gifted per-formers doing hypnotic dance moves and acrobatics. It helped that they brought in Momix choreographer/resident genius Moses Pendleton to give it an overhaul, but this is still second choice after all those Cirque productions listed earlier. (Well, it's a lot better than *Zumanity!*)

3131 Las Vegas Blvd S. (in Wynn Las Vegas). ☎ *888-320-7110. Admission: $99–$179 (plus tax and fees). Showtimes: Fri–Tues 7 p.m. and 9:30 p.m. Showroom policy: Nonsmoking with preassigned seating. Children 4 and under not allowed.*

Mac King
Center Strip

Sure, this isn't cheap like going to a movie matinee, but given the increasingly high double-digit (and frequently triple-digit) prices of most Vegas shows and the undeniable quality of the show, this ranks as a great value. A favorite of local performers himself, King does clever, close-up magic, in a most hilarious and original way — and he's an utter charmer. One of the rare shows that's suitable for the kids, it's timed just right for an afternoon break for anyone.

3475 Las Vegas Blvd. S. (in Harrah's). ☎ **800-427-7247.** *Showtimes: Tues–Sat 1 and 3 p.m. Admission: $25 (plus tax and fees). Showroom policy: Nonsmoking with maitre d' seating. Children 4 and under not allowed.*

Penn & Teller
Center Strip

Magicians Penn & Teller wear boring gray suits; loudmouth Penn does all the talking and yammering, while poor silent Teller slinks around like a demented Seuss character, as they expose all the terrible, awful tricks magicians play on audiences. Then they go ahead and play even more terrible, awful tricks on their own audience — who love every minute of it. This is, by far, the most intelligent show in Vegas. They're wicked geniuses, the two of them — and we don't deserve them.

3700 W. Flamingo Rd. (in the Rio Suites Hotel). ☎ **888-746-7784.** *Admission: $75–85. (plus tax and fees). Showtimes: Sat–Wed 9 p.m. Showroom policy: Nonsmoking with preassigned seating. Children 4 and under not allowed.*

Phantom: The Las Vegas Spectacular
Center Strip

Peculiar title notwithstanding, this is a 90-minute, intermission-free, heavy-on-the-special-effects, costly staging of Andrew Lloyd Webber's ubiquitous musical *The Phantom of the Opera.* Those who know and love the show may be delighted, despite the truncated length and additional presence of pyrotechnics; those who don't may find themselves less moved than befuddled. (Okay, so there's this guy who lives under an opera house and hides his face 'cause he's ugly, and he loves a girl who may love him back or may love another guy instead, and there's singing. There you go.) The "spectacular" part may be Vegas's attempt at greater success with the current Broadway-import experiment, which has already seen the premature demise of otherwise charming and worthy award winners such as *Avenue Q* and *Hairspray.*

3355 Las Vegas Blvd. S. (in the Venetian). ☎ **888-641-7469.** *Admission: $69–$165 (plus tax). Showtimes: Tues–Fri 7 p.m., Mon and Sat 7 p.m. and 9:30 p.m. Showroom policy: Nonsmoking with preassigned seating. Children 4 and under not allowed.*

Rita Rudner
Center Strip

Rudner doesn't break new ground or push boundaries with her stand-up comedy, but her keenly off-kilter observations on the mundane, day-to-day realities of relationships, parenthood, childhood, and other G-rated topics are hilarity-inducing anyway. The joke to out-loud-laugh ratio is high here, with the vast majority of the material safe but still funny — like comedy comfort food. Edgy Kathy Griffin fans may be shocked to hear an f-bomb-free set, but all of it is relatable, even if you don't have a man in your life who doesn't understand you or kids who say the darndest things.

3475 Las Vegas Blvd. S. (in Harrah's). ☎ 702-369-5222. Admission: $54–$90 (plus tax and fees). Showtimes: Mon–Sat 8:30 p.m. Showroom policy: Nonsmoking with preassigned seating. Children 4 and under not allowed.

Terry Fator
Center Strip

Winning *America's Got Talent* is apparently good enough to get you a headlining gig on the Strip, or at least it was for ventriloquist/impersonator Fator. This is an odd hybrid of a show, with the puppeteer making his charges not only talk but impersonate famous singers. Familiar faces from the TV show include Walter the Cowboy and Winston the Turtle sending up everyone from Brooks & Dunn to James Blunt. The ventriloquism part is spot-on, while the impressions range from just okay to spookily similar. Fator needs to work on his stage presence, which can be a bit too laid-back, but the show is an entertaining bit of fluff (or perhaps felt).

3400 Las Vegas Blvd. S. (in the Mirage). ☎ 800-963-9634. Admission: $59–$129 (plus tax). Showtimes: Tues–Sat 7:30 p.m. Showroom policy: Nonsmoking with preassigned seating. Children 4 and under not allowed.

Tournament of Kings
South Strip

Kings in various distant lands gather together to compete in a highly choreographed tournament — and all the while, you eat dinner with your hands. Sound like fun? Well, it kind of is — we even got some too-cool teenagers to acknowledge that they had a good time, and you know how hard that can be. The show is full-blown medieval tournament fare, with audience participation encouraged to the point of overkill. There's a whole lot of hooting and hollering going on. Think of it as dinner theater mixed with professional wrestling. If you're into the WWE or Renaissance fairs, or you're just a child at heart (underneath your armor), you may find it entertaining. But actual children are the ones who most enjoy this show; their parents usually look like they'd prefer to be at *Jubilee!*

3850 Las Vegas Blvd. S. (in Excalibur). ☎ 800-933-1334. Admission: $55. Dinner, drinks, tax, and gratuity included. Showtimes: Mon–Thurs 6 p.m., Fri–Sun 6 p.m. and 8:30 p.m. Showroom policy: Nonsmoking with preassigned seating.

Headliner Showrooms

It used to be that Vegas's nightlife was dominated by showroom headliners — heard of the Rat Pack? — but although they're no longer the major players in town, headliner showrooms still offer great entertainment (especially in the rock-music genre).

Describing the venues is really a waste of time — you're not going for the décor. Policies, prices, and showtimes vary by performer and venue, so call the showroom for information. We give a few examples of the performers who have played in each place in order to give you a sense of the type and caliber of performers that management tends to book. Here's a list of the best of the bunch:

- The **Joint,** in the Hard Rock Hotel & Casino, 4455 Paradise Rd. (☎ 800-693-7625), is the place to see rock headliners (or those who rock hard), including Santana, Puddle of Mud, the Black Eyed Peas, Norah Jones, and even Bob Dylan. Bigger but not necessarily better than it used to be, the revamped Joint is still a big barn of a space with uncomfortable folding chairs and terrible sightlines but the acoustics are top-notch.

- The main competition for the Joint is the **House of Blues** in Mandalay Bay, 3950 Las Vegas Blvd. S. (☎ 877-632-7400). Both target the same kind of rock acts — the Psychedelic Furs, Collective Soul, and Cyndi Lauper were a few on the upcoming list at press time. During the summer, the **Mandalay Bay Beach** hosts outdoor concerts with performers playing on a stage in the wave pool while the audience relaxes on the sandy shore. Recent performers have included the Barenaked Ladies and One Republic. **Mandalay Bay's Events Center** is a 12,000-seat arena for big touring shows, such as those put on by Rhianna and Kelly Clarkson.

- The 15,225-seat **MGM Grand Garden,** in the MGM Grand, 3799 Las Vegas Blvd. S. (☎ 800-929-1111), offers sporting events and the biggest pop concerts: Lady Gaga, Paul McCartney, Britney Spears, the Rolling Stones, Janet Jackson, and U2. Tickets are available through **Ticketmaster** (☎ 702-474-4000; www.ticketmaster.com). The 650-seat **MGM Grand Hollywood Theatre** is located in the same hotel. Here, you can see smaller shows in a more intimate setting.

- The 450-seat **Orleans Showroom,** in the Orleans, 4500 W. Tropicana Ave. (☎ 800-675-3267), hosts such acts as Trisha Yearwood, Clint Black, Gladys Knight, and Michael Bolton. It also has the new 9,000-seat **Orleans Arena,** featuring sporting and concert events.

- The state-of-the-art **Pearl** at the Palms, 4321 W. Flamingo Rd. (☎ 702-942-7777), has 2,500 seats but, because of its layout (three levels of theater seating), feels more intimate. Recent acts include Erykah Badu, the Goo Goo Dolls, 50 Cent, and Norah Jones.

Chapter 17

Bars, Stars, and Gee-tars: Las Vegas at Night

*L*as Vegas is a 24-hour town, so it goes without saying that the night-time is the right time. This chapter explores some of your nightlife alternatives. Whether you're a *Swinger* or a Ring-a-Ding-Dinger, Vegas has something for you — and we try to list it (or a portion of it) here. Pry yourself away from the slot machines or the roulette wheel, if only to give your wallet (and wrists) a rest. It won't even cost you anything, if you choose; it's fun just wandering around, checking out the neon spectacle, and barhopping from hotel to hotel.

Insomniacs rejoice! This city is the answer to your prayers. If you find yourself with a sudden burst of party energy late at night, you're in luck in Las Vegas. You can legally buy liquor 24 hours a day, and many joints take advantage of that fact by never closing. Because of the late-night mentality that prevails in this city, you may find that most bars and nightclubs don't really start jumping until late.

 A word to the wise: Nevada has extremely tough laws regarding drinking and driving, public intoxication, and disorderly conduct. It's fine to go out and have a good time, but don't think that absolutely *anything* goes. There are boundaries (and they are enforced), despite the hedonistic, party-zone atmosphere.

Laughing the Night Away: Comedy Clubs

A haven for stand-up comedians, Vegas has several hotel-based comedy clubs; many prominent comics have paid their dues on the Vegas stage.

Las Vegas Nightlife

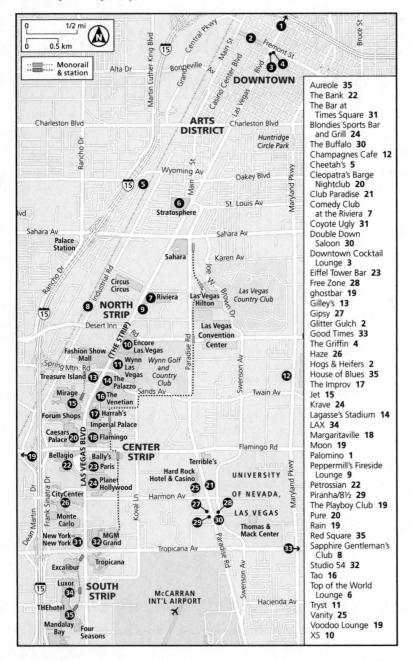

0 — 1/2 mi
0 — 0.5 km

Monorail & station

DOWNTOWN

ARTS DISTRICT

Alta Dr
Bonneville Av
Central Pkwy
Grangeville Av
Martin Luther King Blvd
Main St
Casino Center Blvd
Las Vegas Blvd
Fremont St
Bruce St

Charleston Blvd
Charleston Blvd
Rancho Dr
Wyoming Av
Main St
Oakey Blvd
St. Louis Av
Huntridge Circle Park
Maryland Pkwy

Stratosphere

Sahara Av
Palace Station
Rancho Dr
Industrial Rd
Circus Circus
Sahara
Joe W.
Brown Dr
Sahara Av
Karen Av
Las Vegas Country Club
Las Vegas Hilton

NORTH STRIP
Riviera
Desert Inn
(THE STRIP) Rd
Encore Las Vegas
Wynn Las Vegas
Fashion Show Mall
Spring Mtn. Rd
Treasure Island
Mirage
Forum Shops
Caesars Palace
Bellagio
Wynn Golf and Country Club
The Palazzo
Sands Av
The Venetian
Harrah's
Imperial Palace
Flamingo
Las Vegas Convention Center
Paradise Rd
Swenson Av
Twain Av

CENTER STRIP
Bally's
Paris
Planet Hollywood
CityCenter
Monte Carlo
Frank Sinatra Dr
LAS VEGAS BLVD
Terrible's
Hard Rock Hotel & Casino
Harmon Av
Koval Ln
Flamingo Rd
UNIVERSITY OF NEVADA, LAS VEGAS
Thomas & Mack Center
Maryland Pkwy

Dean Martin Dr
New York-New York
MGM Grand
Tropicana
Excalibur
Luxor
SOUTH STRIP
THEhotel
Mandalay Bay
Four Seasons
Tropicana Av
McCARRAN INT'L AIRPORT
Paradise Rd
Swenson Av
Hacienda Av

Aureole **35**
The Bank **22**
The Bar at Times Square **31**
Blondies Sports Bar and Grill **24**
The Buffalo **30**
Champagnes Cafe **12**
Cheetah's **5**
Cleopatra's Barge Nightclub **20**
Club Paradise **21**
Comedy Club at the Riviera **7**
Coyote Ugly **31**
Double Down Saloon **30**
Downtown Cocktail Lounge **3**
Eiffel Tower Bar **23**
Free Zone **28**
ghostbar **19**
Gilley's **13**
Gipsy **27**
Glitter Gulch **2**
Good Times **33**
The Griffin **4**
Haze **26**
Hogs & Heifers **2**
House of Blues **35**
The Improv **17**
Jet **15**
Krave **24**
Lagasse's Stadium **14**
LAX **34**
Margaritaville **18**
Moon **19**
Palomino **1**
Peppermill's Fireside Lounge **9**
Petrossian **22**
Piranha/8½ **29**
The Playboy Club **19**
Pure **20**
Rain **19**
Red Square **35**
Sapphire Gentleman's Club **8**
Studio 54 **32**
Tao **16**
Top of the World Lounge **6**
Tryst **11**
Vanity **25**
Voodoo Lounge **19**
XS **10**

Up-and-coming comics frequently perform in the Vegas clubs, so the performer you see may be that next sitcom star. Show times and prices vary, but we list the latest pricing information throughout this section.

Here's something cool to consider: Some big-name comedians are known to put in special unannounced appearances at Las Vegas comedy clubs to test out new material. In fact, many of the jokes you hear from Jay Leno on *The Tonight Show* were told to Vegas audiences beforehand. The clubs don't tell you in advance, so you can't plan to see these "previews"; but you may be in for a pleasant surprise.

- ✔ The **Comedy Club,** in the **Riviera Hotel & Casino,** 2901 Las Vegas Blvd. S. (☎ **800-634-6753** or 702-734-9433), features comics, hypnotists, and occasional theme shows (shock comics, X-rated, all gay, and so on) nightly at 8:30 p.m. and 10:30 p.m. The price is $25 and includes one drink and tax. You can't call ahead and charge over the phone, so plan to buy your tickets at the box office. Oh, and it even includes maitre d' seating.

- ✔ An offshoot of the famous New York City club, the **Improv,** in **Harrah's,** 3475 Las Vegas Blvd. S. (☎ **800-392-9002** or 702-369-5111), has a 400-seat showroom that often books the top comics on the comedy-club circuit. You can catch shows every day, except Monday, at 8:30 p.m. and 10:30 p.m. for $40 (tax and drinks extra). Call ahead to charge tickets. Seating is pre-assigned.

Live from Las Vegas

The next section covers the rooms where you can scream "Hey, Mr. DJ, put a record on," but what if you want to hear real live music? For brand names, check what's happening at the major arenas and venues in town — we provide information on the biggest and best in Chapter 16. It'll probably cost you a small fortune to see Rhianna or Gaga, but you were expecting that, weren't you?

Looking for lounge lizards

If you're looking for lounge acts, you don't have to go far: Just about every hotel has a lounge with some sort of live, nightly entertainment. There was a time when you could find a flood of top-drawer acts in hotel lounges; but these days, expect stand-up comedy or impersonator shows. Some are good, some are comedic, and many are just plain campy. If you're looking for the latter, keep your eyes peeled for the dreaded — and delightful — **Cook E. Jarr** (www.cookejarr.com), a cult figure currently lauded as the worst, yet most special, lounge act in Vegas. (At this writing, he was performing at Harrah's Carnival Court Fri–Sat 6–8 p.m.)

If you want good music for low prices (often free!), your best bet is to check out the hotel lounges. Although some lounges are better than others, and you can say the same about the quality of the acts they book, you'll usually find some sort of cover band playing someone's greatest hits — maybe even Rhianna or Gaga's! Because there is usually no cover charge at these lounges, you lose nothing by going to check it out. Hotel lounges are also great for those folks who want to dance but feel out of place among the young and pretty crowd that populates most nightclubs.

Shaking Your Groove Thang: The Best Dance Clubs

You can find plenty of places to dance the night away. In contrast to Las Vegas's normally casual atmosphere, the hot clubs have dress codes — some more strict than others. You also encounter a number of steep cover charges and more than a little attitude. Call ahead to get the scoop on the details (although you may not find out about the attitude factor until it's too late!).

If you don't want to break the bank to have a good time at the local nightclubs, go earlier in the evening, before cover charges go into effect. Yes, you may get there before the hoards of partygoers arrive, but you also can consider the lack of huge crowds on the dance floor to be a bonus.

The scoop on Vegas's hottest clubs

A note of warning to the ladies: These places are major meat markets, so if you're not obviously with a date, you may be hit on endlessly. But, hey, you may be up for that sort of game! (If you want to avoid that and you're just into dancing, you may want to check out **Krave,** a predominantly gay nightspot listed later in this chapter.) A piece of good news for the ladies: You tend to pay considerably less in cover charges than the men — sometimes nothing at all.

✔ Everything about the **Bank,** in Bellagio (3600 Las Vegas Blvd. S. (☎ 702-797-7517), is geared toward the high-end clubbing crowd — the 500 bottles of Cristal that line the entrance, the gold crocodile skin on the bar, the couture suits for the staff, and, of course, the often hefty cover charges. And that's before you realize that most of the room is dedicated to ludicrously expensive "bottle tables." But the dance floor is hot, the snow machines are cool, and it sure is top of the line. Open Thursday through Sunday, 10:30 p.m. to 4 a.m. Cover can vary but is usually $50 for men and free for women.

✔ Done by the same people who brought you the Bank, **Haze,** in Aria Las Vegas, 3730 Las Vegas Blvd. S. (☎ 702-693-8300), is one of the hottest of hot spots right now (although by the time you read this, it could be passé — that's how Vegas works). Dark to the point of needing a flashlight, the multilevel club serves up plenty of high-energy partying with a crowd that looks like it stepped out of a fashion show. Lines can be insanely long, so make sure those heels are comfy. The club is open Thursday through Saturday from 10:30 p.m. to 4 a.m. and the cover is usually around $40.

✔ Hard Rock's old club Body English was in the basement but their new one, **Vanity,** 4455 Paradise Rd. (☎ 702-693-5555), has moved up, literally. Overlooking the pool area, Vanity is an indoor/outdoor space with a slamming dance floor under a cool LED crystal chandelier. Expect fierce competition to get inside and very little personal space once you do. It's open Thursday through Saturday from 10 p.m. to 4 a.m. Cover varies but is usually around $40.

✔ Want to dance on a boat but can't help but notice that you're in the desert? No fear — Caesars Palace has provided **Cleopatra's Barge Nightclub,** 3570 Las Vegas Blvd. S. (☎ 702-731-7110). Yes, the dance floor (a small one) is on an actual floating barge. No, you won't get seasick (although it can be an odd sensation if everyone is groovin' at once). It's pretty nifty. There's no cover charge, but there is a two-drink minimum. It's open nightly from 10:30 p.m. to 3 a.m.

✔ **Jet,** in the Mirage, 3400 Las Vegas Blvd. S. (☎ 702-632-7600), is another sibling of the Bank and Haze, even bigger (Three dance floors! Four bars! Multiple levels!), and, if a tad less fabulous, it's also more accessible. Open Thursday through Saturday and Monday from 10:30 p.m. until 4 a.m. Cover varies, but it's usually at least $30.

✔ Speaking of big, nothing is as big as the 40,000-square-foot **Pure,** in Caesars Palace, 3570 Las Vegas Blvd. S. (☎ 702-731-7873). Caesars Palace took a space that used to house a combination magic club and theater and turned it into the largest nightclub on the Strip. It's all white — get it? — and styled in such a way that, size notwithstanding, all the action is sort of right in your face. Escape how big and loud it is by heading to the rooftop club with amazing views of the Strip. Open Thursday through Sunday and Tuesday from 10 p.m. to dawn. Cover varies, but expect to pay at least $30.

✔ Not quite as huge as Pure but still awfully big, **LAX,** at the Luxor, 3900 Las Vegas Blvd. S. (☎ 702-242-4529), is an explosive combo of red and dark, confined and spacious, Gothic and electric. Also, Christina Aguilera is one of the investors. If it's good enough for her. . . . Open Friday through Monday from 10 p.m. to dawn. Cover varies but figure it starts at $30 and goes up from there.

✔ **Tao,** in the Venetian, 3355 Las Vegas Blvd. S. (☎ 702-388-8588), is styled as a Buddhist temple — because nothing says serenity and nirvana like a big, loud, multilevel club with a really high cover charge — and it's where all the celebrity entourages are heading. Open Thursday and Friday from 10 p.m. to dawn and Saturday from 9:30 p.m. until dawn. Cover varies but it isn't any cheaper than anything else in this section.

✔ **Rain,** in the Palms Casino Resort, 4321 W. Flamingo Rd. (☎ 702-942-6832), used to be the single hottest club in Vegas, but it has been outshone lately by the bigger and newer. It's still a great place to dance the night away. Rain has everything such a club needs (smoke, light and fire effects, a booming sound system, go-go dancers in stripper boots, various floors and levels). It's open Friday and Saturday from 10 p.m. until 5 a.m. Cover varies, but it's usually $25 and up.

✔ At the top of one of the hotel towers, high above the ground-floor Rain, is the other dance club at the Palms, **Moon,** 4321 W. Flamingo Rd. (☎ 702-942-6832). The outdoor patio serves up amazing views (and a really disturbing glass floor looking down about 40 stories). If the weather is nice, they open the roof over the dance floor. It's open Tuesday and Thursday through Sunday from 11 p.m. until the sun replaces the moon. Expect a cover in the $40 range, but that includes admission to the Playboy Club.

✔ The first incarnation of Wynn Las Vegas's own nightclub didn't work out, so here's the second attempt. **Tryst,** 3131 Las Vegas Blvd. S. (☎ 702-770-3375), is definitely better, with a brighter-than-usual atmosphere, a great dance floor, and a big outdoor patio with a giant waterfall. Look for a more subtle crowd than at some of the other over-the-top venues listed here — after all, this is called Tryst, not "Hook-up!" Open Thursday through Sunday from 10 p.m. to 4 a.m. You'll usually get inside for $30 to $40.

✔ You may experience déjà vu if you go from Tryst to **XS,** in Encore Las Vegas, 3121 Las Vegas Blvd. S. (☎ 702-770-0097). It's basically the same layout but bigger, including the outdoor patio that has its own pool. Although it's impossible to describe any Vegas nightclub as "grown-up," this one probably comes closest with a slightly more mature crowd — and we mean attitude, not age. Open Friday through Monday from 10 p.m. until 4 a.m. Expect to pay around $40 to enter.

✔ You've read the book and seen the movie — now come to the re-creation of New York's legendary **Studio 54** in the **MGM Grand,** 3799 Las Vegas Blvd. S. (☎ 702-891-1111). Strangely, although Las Vegas is known as Sin City, this is a downright tame, strictly-for-tourists kind of place (but if you want to pretend, that's all right with us). Tennis shoes, baggy or ripped jeans, and hats (for men or women) are not allowed. Cover ranges from free for women on certain nights to upwards of $40 or more depending on what's happening. It's open Tuesday through Saturday from 10 p.m. to dawn.

Hanging Out: Las Vegas's Best Bars

There's no shortage of places to drink in Las Vegas, whether you're looking for a sophisticated cocktail or a pitcher of beer. Here are some of our favorites.

Hip watering holes to hoist a few

If you want your bars to come with personality, you may have to leave your hotel (in most cases) to search out spots that aren't generic watering holes. Your reward will be a glimpse of that rapidly vanishing true Vegas vibe.

✔ You can start at **Champagnes Cafe**, 3557 S. Maryland Pkwy. (☎ 702-737-1699). This is the sort of place those hip guys who made the movie *Swingers* just worship. It's so outmoded that it's hip again — they just don't know it (or, worse, think they never lost it) — and it serves ice-cream shakes spiked with booze. You don't get this in a hotel bar.

✔ On the other hand, the **Double Down Saloon**, 4640 Paradise Rd., at Naples (☎ 702-791-5775), knows it's hip, but it's too hip to let on (if you follow). There's no flashy décor (unless you count the you puke, you clean sign and the arty graffiti on the walls). Instead, the Double Down lets its jukebox — from the Germs and Zappa to Dick Dale and Reverend Horton Heat — do the talking.

✔ Back to dated views of hip: At **Peppermill's Fireside Lounge,** inside the **Peppermill Coffee Shop**, 2985 Las Vegas Blvd. S. (☎ 702-735-4177), romance is provided by a water and fire pit, a piece of kitsch that you probably thought had gone the way of the dodo bird. Those basketball-size drinks will put you into a stupor, after which the plush, cozy booths support you in womblike comfort until you feel (if you ever do) like moving on. Many don't — this is one of the last places that feels like genuine Vegas, as opposed to a prefab nightclub.

✔ Our snippy comment about generic hotel bars notwithstanding, a few hotel bars are worth seeking out — heck, even the locals do! Some actually are housed in restaurants, including a few in the **Mandalay Bay,** 3950 Las Vegas Blvd. S. (☎ 877-632-7000 or 702-632-7000). **Aureole** has a four-story glass wine tower, and bottles are fetched by comely young ladies wearing *Peter Pan*–style harnesses that whisk them up and down as they fetch the bottle of a patron's choosing. The bar in the front facing the wine tower has become a nighttime hangout, with people ordering obscure wines just to send the damsels as high up as they can. You can keep your drink nicely chilled all night long on the ice bar, created by water freshly poured and frozen daily at **Red Square.** Or join the locals who feel the blues late at night at the small, bottle-cap-bedecked bar in the corner of the **House of Blues** restaurant.

✔ The downtown Las Vegas scene used to be pretty nonexistent, but it features a few bright spots these days, including at the **Downtown Cocktail Lounge,** 111 Las Vegas Blvd. S., at Fremont St. (☎ 702-880-3696). This small, cool ultralounge is a perfect spot for a low-attitude crowd to sip a cosmopolitan or three.

✔ Right around the corner is the **Griffin,** 511 E. Fremont St., just east of Las Vegas Boulevard (☎ 702-382-0577), less loungey and more funky, with fire pits; intimate conversation areas; and a cool, low-pressure vibe that draws a lot of off-duty performers.

✔ One of the other few good options for downtown nightlife, the rowdy **Hogs & Heifers Saloon,** 201 N. Third St., between Ogden and Stewart, one block from the Fremont Street Experience (☎ 702-676-1457; no cover), is a prefab version of the NYC bar that started the whole dancing-waitresses-on-the-bar gimmick. Bikers and beer — a reliable combination that explains why this place is often such a fun scene.

✔ Hogs & Heifers was the inspiration for the movie and bar **Coyote Ugly,** in New York–New York, 3790 Las Vegas Blvd. S. (☎ 702-740-6969). Nubile bartenders stuffed into tight-fitting garments strut their stuff on bar tops, whipping the crowd into a hootin', hollerin' frenzy and dousing them with liquids if they begin to have too much fun. We really, really want to look down on this sort of behavior, but we're too busy whooping it up. Open Sunday through Thursday from 6 p.m. until 2 a.m. and Friday and Saturday from 6 p.m. until 3 a.m. Cover varies, usually $10 and up on weekends.

✔ Moving from coyotes to bunnies, the **Playboy Club,** in the Palms, 4321 W. Flamingo Rd. (☎ 702-942-6832), is back with this combo lounge and boutique casino. The ambience is distinctly Hef (think wingback chairs and fireplaces) but with a modern twist. And yes, the drinks are served by the famous Playboy Bunnies.

✔ Also at the Palms, the terrifyingly chic **ghostbar,** 4321 W. Flamingo Rd. (☎ 702-942-6832), attracts the young and the beautiful, who gaze out at the less blessed with cool indifference. Witness it for yourself or read about their antics in the next day's gossip columns. Cover varies, but it's usually $10 and up.

✔ If all that standing and posing has worn you out and what you really need is a raucous pick-me-up, head over to the **Bar at Times Square,** in New York–New York, 3790 Las Vegas Blvd. S. (☎ 702-740-6969), where dueling pianos and drunken singalongs will get your blood pumping again. Shows are nightly from 8 p.m. until 2:15 a.m.

Cool clubs for the special-interest set

Not everyone wants to spend the night bumping and grinding to the latest in hip-hop, and if you fall into that category, don't worry. Some Vegas clubs cater to specific groups, including college students, businessmen, cowboys (and those who love them), and people looking for a less frenetic atmosphere than the average club offers.

✔ All the dance clubs play pop, dance, and hip-hop, but if you need something to two-step to, mosey on over to **Gilley's,** in Treasure Island, 3300 Las Vegas Blvd. S. (☎ 702-894-7111). The dance floor isn't that big but there's plenty of room for line dancing (lessons are offered on some nights), and, if you need to rest, you can always take a seat on the mechanical bull. Open nightly from 8 p.m. until 2 a.m. and later on the weekends. There is no cover except for special events.

✔ Parrot Heads, you aren't forgotten. Your avatar, Jimmy Buffett, has opened up a branch of his **Margaritaville** bar and restaurant, in the Flamingo, 3555 Las Vegas Blvd. S. (☎ 702-733-3302). Live music, booze, and merchandise are the key components here. It's open daily from 11 a.m. to 2 a.m.; no cover except for special events.

✔ Looking for a bar that's a *bar* — as in, a place with bartenders who know how to pour a real cocktail? And by *real cocktail,* you don't mean some liquor with a shot of Red Bull in it? The answer is **Petrossian,** in Bellagio, 3600 Las Vegas Blvd. S. (☎ 702-693-7111), where the bartenders know that martinis are made with vermouth and that grown-ups are happy to drink them and have some grown-up snacks (we're talking Beluga caviar and the like) along with them — and, it must be admitted, pay grown-up prices for the privilege. No one said educated sophistication comes cheap.

A view to kill for

Few cities have a skyline as unique and beautiful as Vegas's, especially when night falls. Paris may be called the City of Lights, but nowadays, it has nothing on Vegas. For a perfect end to a day in Sin City, nothing beats a nightcap at a lounge that provides a panoramic view of the city.

✔ Ready to test your vertigo? The most memorable view in town is the nighttime vista from the **Top of the World Lounge** on the 107th floor of the Stratosphere Tower, 2000 Las Vegas Blvd. S. (☎ 702-380-7711). It costs $9 to get up there, and drinks can be pricey, but sipping a martini while gazing down at the sea of neon spread out before you is an undeniable thrill. The lounge, like the restaurant directly below, revolves slowly; give yourself an hour to make a 360-degree trip around the city. Live entertainment plays nightly and a DJ takes over at midnight on Fridays and Saturdays. It's open daily, 4 p.m. until the wee hours.

✔ If you want to look down on the rest of the world, like a true Parisian, try the **Eiffel Tower Bar** in Paris Las Vegas, 3655 Las Vegas Blvd. S. (☎ 702-948-6937). The bar is located in the restaurant on the 11th floor of the hotel's half-size replica of the most famous landmark in the City of Lights. It's cool and sophisticated. Bar hours are daily from 11 a.m. to 11:30 p.m. No cover or minimum.

✔ **Voodoo Lounge,** on the top of the Rio, 3700 W. Flamingo Rd. (☎ 702-252-7777), offers a different view perspective because it's located a short distance off the Strip. It's also a fun and funky place, with touches of juju here and there, plus a grand, multilevel outdoor patio for true view gazing. It's open daily from 5 p.m. until 3 a.m., and the cover varies.

Root, root, root for the home team

The **Sports Books** at the major casinos are some of the best places to watch the latest sports action, but you also can find some other great places to catch a game. (If you think lap dancing is a sport, check out "Showing Some Skin: Sin City's Best Strip Joints," later in this chapter.)

✔ **Lagasse's Stadium,** in Palazzo Las Vegas, 3325 Las Vegas Blvd. S. (☎ **702-607-2665**), is a sports-bar concept from master of the "Bam!" Emeril Lagasse. It features more than 100 televisions on which to watch just about any sports you can think of (Israeli basketball? Check.), but the centerpiece is stadiumlike tiers of comfy couches facing a massive wall of monitors. It even has a sports book, if you feel like placing a little wager. It's open Monday through Friday from 11 a.m. to 10 p.m., Saturday from 7:30 a.m. to 10 p.m., and Sunday from 8 a.m. to 10 p.m. There is no cover, but there are table/couch minimums for food and drink ($25–$50).

✔ **Blondies Sports Bar and Grill,** in the Miracle Mile Shops, 3663 Las Vegas Blvd. S., No. 183 (☎ **702-737-0444;** www.blondieslas vegas.com), is a more traditional experience — and by that, we mean beer pong. Yes, in addition to lots of TVs on which to watch your game of choice, a wide-ranging menu of mostly fried things, and lots and lots of alcohol, you can relive your college glory days several nights a week for fun, bragging rights, or bar tabs as prizes for the best players. It's open daily from 11 a.m. until 2 a.m.

Stepping Out: The Gay and Lesbian Scene

Boys will be boys and girls will be girls, especially at the following places. *Note:* It doesn't matter which you prefer, as most of the gay bars in town are straight-friendly (some lesbians also frequent these bars due to the lack of lesbian bars in town). For straight people who like to dance but don't want to get hassled by the opposite sex all night, these are good spots for hanging out.

✔ The first gay bar on the Strip — can you believe it? **Krave** does pointedly style itself an "alternative" club, which brings in a slightly more mixed crowd than you may find at the other ones in this list. The high-rent address means a fancier interior, but with prices and other problems to match. Still, it's also considerably easier to get to than other boy bars, so it all works out. It's open Tuesday to Sunday from 8 p.m. until late, after hours until dawn Friday and Saturday. In the Planet Hollywood Resort & Casino, 3667 Las Vegas Blvd. S. (entrance on Harmon Ave.; ☎ **702-836-0830;** www.krave lasvegas.com). Cover varies.

✔ **Piranha/8½,** 4633 Paradise Rd., at Naples Drive (☎ **702-791-0100**), is one of the most popular clubs in town as of this writing. Piranha is the nightclub, with VIP booths and rooms overlooking the dance floor, and 8½ is the ultralounge, with comfy couches, TV monitors, and a fireplace. Lines can be long and cover and drink prices are high (at least $20). It's open nightly from 9 p.m. until dawn.

✔ Longtime favorite **Gipsy,** 4605 Paradise Rd. (☎ **702-731-1919**), is still packing them in on weekends with its tried-and-true combination of dancing, go-go boys, and shows. The interior sports plenty of glass and marble, and the dance floor has an odd Indiana Jones look. It's open Friday and Saturday from 10 p.m. until dawn, and the cover is usually around $20.

✔ Right across the street is **Free Zone,** 610 E. Naples St. (☎ **702-794-2300**), a neighborhood-style bar with videos and the like. The club sports a dance floor with a really loud sound system and a game room that features video poker and billiards. Weekly theme nights include karaoke, drag shows, and male strippers. There's no cover or drink minimum.

✔ The leather-and-Levis crowd can go to the **Buffalo,** 4640 Paradise Rd. (☎ **702-733-8355**), which is open 24 hours and often has beer busts and leather events. There's no cover, drinks are cheap, and you can try your hand at billiards, darts, and the ever-present video poker.

✔ If you're looking for something a little more cozy, try **Good Times,** 1775 E. Tropicana Ave. (☎ **702-736-9494**), a quiet neighborhood bar with a small dance floor. The 24-hour spot has no cover charge.

For more information on what's going on in gay Las Vegas during your visit, pick up a copy of *QVegas* (☎ **702-650-0636;** www.qvegas.com), a free gay-oriented magazine that's available at any of the places described in the preceding list and online. For online information on the gay nightlife scene, surf over to www.gayvegas.com.

Showing Some Skin: Sin City's Best Strip Joints

Welcome to Decadence Central. Sex is a major industry in Las Vegas — it isn't nicknamed Sin City for nothing — and on an evening's stroll down the Strip, you're likely to have dozens of flyers advertising a strip of a different sort shoved at you. If you have even the slightest interest in viewing naked or seminaked women dancing and prancing onstage, you've hit the jackpot. There are numerous topless or totally nude strip bars from which to choose. Some are actually clean, respectable establishments — if, of course, your idea of respectability includes half-naked women. The most prominent ones are generally the safest and nicest of the bunch. You can find seedier places in this town — but then you're on your own.

Keep in mind that in Las Vegas proper, topless bars can serve alcohol but all-nude clubs can't. Only the **Palomino,** an all-nude joint in North Las Vegas, is allowed to serve stiff drinks (the exception due to a grandfather clause in the Clark County ban). The rules and regulations vary from club to club, so be sure to ask at the door if you want to stay out of trouble. In general, note that touching the dancers in a strip club is usually forbidden. Some clubs, however, allow a restrained bit of physical interaction between clients and dancers.

✔ Featured in that masterpiece of bad cinema, *Showgirls,* **Cheetah's,** 2112 Western Ave. (☎ 702-384-0074), is a clean, jovial place where many in the young party set hang out. Sure, it has a bit of a frat-house atmosphere, but you're likely to see some couples here having a bit of fun. Feel free to order up a table or couch dance. There's a $30 cover charge after 8 p.m., and the club is open 24 hours. (Go to Western Avenue just east of I-15, and the club is between Sahara and Charleston avenues.)

✔ One of the best of the strip joints, **Club Paradise,** 4416 Paradise Rd., just north of Flamingo Road (☎ 702-734-7990), is a glitzy spot that attracts an upscale white-collar crowd, with bright lighting, a plush interior, champagne, and cigars. Oh, and topless dancers. Can't forget that. The dancers, called "actual centerfolds," are more likely to be cosmetically enhanced than in the other establishments. Hours are Monday through Friday from 5 p.m. to 8 a.m., Saturday and Sunday from 6 p.m. to 8 a.m. There's a $30 cover charge.

✔ A perfect place for the merely curious, **Glitter Gulch,** 20 Fremont St. (☎ 702-385-4774), is something of a downtown landmark located smack-dab in the heart of the **Fremont Street Experience.** The club is open daily from 1 p.m. to 4 a.m. You don't have to pay a cover charge, but there is a two-drink minimum (drinks start at $7.75).

✔ The large, two-story **Palomino,** 1848 Las Vegas Blvd. N. (☎ 702-642-2984), boasts a bunch of stages, semiprivate rooms, and total nudity. Thanks to weekend male-stripper performances, it's gotten to be a hangout for women. It's a straight shot up Las Vegas Boulevard (the Strip) past downtown, but it takes 15 to 25 minutes, depending on traffic. It's open daily from 4 p.m. to 5 a.m., and there's a $15 to $30 cover charge depending on when you go.

✔ **Sapphire Gentleman's Club,** 3025 S. Industrial Rd. (☎ 702-796-0000), is the largest strip club in the world. Someone has to be. How big? 71,000 square feet. Four stages. Hundreds of girls. (Not all at once, of course!) It's too big to be intimate, which probably eliminates any hope of a serious thrill, but it's also a safe and well-designed exposure to some naughty Vegas fun. (The place looks suspiciously like the interior of Rain, but this club is actually quieter.) You must see it to believe it — at least, that's the excuse we'll give you. It's open 24 hours, and there's a $30 cover from 6 p.m. to 6 a.m.

Part VI

The Part of Tens

The 5th Wave   By Rich Tennant

"Hey you! Now I don't know if you're counting cards or not, but from now on, while I'm dealing at this table, you'll keep your hooves still!"

In this part . . .

*A*h, tradition. The Part of Tens is to *For Dummies* books what gambling is to Las Vegas — an integral part of the experience. This area of the book is where we feed you some fun information, just to give you some interesting topics of conversation, if nothing else. In the chapters of this part, you find out about some of Las Vegas's great claims to fame and also discover some interesting facts about institutions that went the way of the dinosaur. We fill you in on the top ten values to be had in Las Vegas, and we end by introducing you to ten denizens of the Nevada desert — just in case you venture beyond the reach of the neon lights.

Chapter 18

Ten Las Vegas Claims to Fame

In This Chapter

▶ Introducing Las Vegas's biggest boasts
▶ Discovering that some things truly need to be seen to be believed

Considering the city's reputation for doing things bigger — if not necessarily better — than anywhere else, it should come as no surprise that Vegas has secured a few spots in the *Guinness Book of World Records*. If this city loves anything, it's a challenge. Right now, some new project is probably in the works that eventually will end up on Vegas's roster of larger-than-life achievements.

Lighting Up the Sky

It used to be that the Great Wall of China was the only man-made structure that could be seen with the naked eye from outer space. Naturally, it was only a matter of time before Vegas aspired to reach such stellar heights (although one wonders how long it will be before they attempt to "do" the Great Wall as a theme hotel), and it succeeded. From the top of the pyramid of the **Luxor** shines the world's brightest beam of light — it's so bright, in fact, that you could use it to read a newspaper with your morning coffee 10 miles out in space. What a beam of light has to do with a pyramid we don't know, but you can see it from the space shuttle, so that's that. (Then again, it seems a recent Chinese astronaut said he couldn't actually see the Great Wall from space after all, and now China is going to delete that fun fact from the schoolbooks.)

Wide-Open Spaces

As if having the world's biggest light beam were not enough, the **Luxor** is also home to the planet's largest indoor atrium! Housed inside the hotel's 36-story pyramid, the atrium measures 29 million cubic feet. You could fit nine jumbo jets inside the pyramid — if you wanted to, that is.

Larger than Life

Following the bigger-is-better theory (a much cherished ideal in this town), it's only natural that Las Vegas is home to the second largest hotel in the world — at least in terms of number of rooms. The holder of this distinction is the appropriately named **MGM Grand.** It has 5,044 rooms, in case you're counting. And to put this number in perspective, think of this: It would take a person 13 years and 8 months to sleep one night in each of the hotel's rooms. If you stacked all the beds in those rooms up, the resulting tower would be ten times higher than the Empire State Building — the real one, not the one across the street.

No Room — Ha!

Okay, that may not be true — there have been numerous occasions where the odds of hitting it big on the craps tables were better than the odds of getting a room in Las Vegas, but that isn't due to lack of space. The city has more hotel rooms than any other — nearly 150,000 at last count. And in the next few years, you'll be able to tack on another 5,000 (or so) places to park yourself while resting up for the next round of blackjack.

Money Is No Object

You can't accuse Vegas of cheapening out on the luxury-hotel experience — okay, you can in some cases, but that's a totally different chapter — because it's home to the most expensive hotel ever built. **Wynn Las Vegas** cost an eye-popping $2.7 billion, and that's just for phase one — another $2 billion went toward its encore, named **Encore,** which opened in 2008. And yet, that all pales compared to MGM-Mirage's **CityCenter,** the most expensive privately funded construction project ever and the largest single development in Las Vegas history. It's a hotel/residential/entertainment complex that sprawls over more than 60 acres (requiring its own people mover!) and cost a reported $9 billion to build. That's a lot of quarters!

Reach for the Sky

Move over, Seattle Space Needle. Las Vegas is home to the tallest building west of the Mississippi. The **Stratosphere** checks in at 1,149 feet, which also makes it the tallest observation tower in the United States. It's also home to the world's highest thrill rides. Hope you don't have vertigo.

Going to the Chapel

Paris may have a better reputation for romance, but no city in the world hosts as many weddings as Las Vegas. Each year, more than 100,000 couples enter the bonds of holy matrimony here — and they call it Sin City! It doesn't get more romantic in Vegas than on Valentine's Day, when more people marry here than anywhere else on the planet.

Reeling in the Dough

Las Vegas makes really big bucks! More than 80 percent of all visitors to the city spend at least some time courting Lady Luck. The amount of money spent annually on gambling in Vegas totals more than the gross national product of several small countries combined. In 2009, visitors spent more than $38 billion in Vegas overall, more than $9 billion of it gambling — yes, that's *billion.* And that was considered a down year for the city. Imagine what it'll be like when the economy finally recovers.

Just Visiting

Those Super Bowl commercials may have you believing that everyone is heading for Walt Disney World (and we concede that they get more kids), but Vegas, the city that has been called an "adult's Disneyland," gets more visitors annually than all U.S. theme parks combined! More than 36 million souls made a pilgrimage here in 2009. And you wonder why there's no elbow room at the craps tables?

A Golden Moment

Forget about Fort Knox. Head to Las Vegas if you want to see the world's largest gold nugget on display. The Hand of Faith nugget was discovered in Australia in 1980. The nugget currently resides at the **Golden Nugget** (where else?) in downtown Vegas, weighing in at 61 pounds, 11 ounces.

Chapter 19

Ten (Or So) Las Vegas Institutions That Are No More

In This Chapter

▶ Disappearing hotels
▶ A legend lives on

*I*t would be hard to imagine New York City ever razing the Plaza (entirely redoing the inside, sure), or Paris tearing down the Ritz, but Las Vegas has brought down many of its historic landmarks without so much as a toodle-oo. Heck, by the 1990s, the city was promoting the destruction as a tourist attraction — at least if they had to go, they went out in style. Here's a list of just a few of the oldies but goodies that have been lost during the Strip's endless makeover.

El Rancho Vegas

Built in 1941, **El Rancho** was the first hotel resort ever built on the Strip — not Bugsy Siegel's **Flamingo,** as many people mistakenly assume. Its success launched a building boom on the Strip, a movement that is still going strong today. Alas, the hotel was destroyed by a fire in 1960 and was never rebuilt; all that's left of it is a big vacant lot at the corner of Sahara and Las Vegas Boulevard South.

The Other El Rancho Hotel

Not to be confused with **El Rancho Vegas,** this place actually started out in the 1940s as the **Thunderbird** hotel before being renamed El Rancho in 1982 after a series of ownership changes. Standing right across from **Circus Circus,** it closed in 1992 and remained empty and decaying until 2000, when it was purchased by Turnberry Place, the new $600-million condo development right behind it (just opposite the **Las Vegas Hilton**).

The company says that it will probably partner with a casino developer and build something there, but for now, it just wants to demolish the graffiti-covered buildings.

Dunes

A Strip fixture since the 1950s, the **Dunes'** claim to fame is that it was first to host that most Vegas of art forms, the topless showgirl review (in 1957). Purchased by former **Mirage** owner Steve Wynn in 1992, the Dunes at least got a proper Vegas sendoff. In 1993, more than 200,000 spectators watched as the Dunes imploded and its famous neon sign exploded amid a fireworks display that set Wynn back more than a million dollars. Wynn then spent more than a billion dollars putting up the Bellagio in its place.

Sands

This legendary spot made its debut on the Strip in 1952, but it's most famous for hosting the "Summit Meeting" of the Rat Pack (Frank Sinatra, Dean Martin, Peter Lawford, and Sammy Davis, Jr.) in 1960. No show ticket since has been as hard to come by. Renowned for its entertainment, the **Sands** helped boost Las Vegas's reputation as a happening town. The hotel was reduced to a 30-foot-high pile of rubble in 1996 to make way for the **Venetian,** which memorialized the Sands by naming its convention center for it.

Hacienda

Another old-timer that went out with a bang, the Hacienda opened in 1956 and quickly became a Strip favorite. Known for its friendly service and old-style character, it simply couldn't compete with the mega-resorts that sprang up along the Strip in the 1990s. Hundreds of thousands came out to say goodbye to the hotel when it was blown up on New Year's Eve 1997 to make way for **Mandalay Bay.**

The Old Aladdin

Following the tradition of the **Hacienda** and the **Sands,** the **Aladdin** went up (or down, if you want to be picky) in smoke in 1998. Built in 1963, the Aladdin had major history behind it — Elvis married Priscilla here in 1967. Caught up in financial problems, management finally decided to ditch the old resort and replace it with a new and improved — and more expensive — version. The new **Aladdin** opened on the site of the old one in August 2000, promptly went bankrupt, and was redone as **Planet Hollywood.**

Vegas World

More notorious than famous, **Vegas World** sprang from the imagination of the casino maverick Bob Stupak, a PR master determined to take guests for every dollar he could — he was eventually fined by the casino commission for false advertising. Calling the hotel a money pit would have been kind. As a marketing ploy, Stupak started building a large tower next to the hotel as a tourist attraction, but it went bankrupt and was forced to sell out to Grand Casinos. Cutting his losses, the new owner stuck with the tower — today's Stratosphere hotel — and demolished Vegas World.

Desert Inn

When Mirage Resorts was acquired by **MGM Grand** in the spring of 2000, Steve Wynn went looking for a new hotel to revamp. He settled on the **Desert Inn.** The venerable Strip contender had been losing money for a while, but, unlike many of its megaresort competitors, it had class. With more than 50 years on the Strip, the historic hotel was home to Howard Hughes for most of the '60s. It gained major fame as the main setting for the '70s television show *Vega$*. On October 23, 2001, the hotel's Augusta Tower was spectacularly imploded to make way for the Wynn Las Vegas luxury resort, which cost an unprecedented $2.7 billion to construct.

Elvis

Okay, he wasn't a hotel — but with all due respect to the King, he was a Las Vegas institution that did blow up there toward the end. And, like the Strip hotels that continue to re-create major landmarks and themes, Vegas is awash in Elvis impersonators and a *Cirque du Soleil* show ensuring that his legacy lives on in some form or another. From his marriage to Priscilla in 1967 to his sold-out stints at the **Las Vegas Hilton,** Elvis did as much to promote the city as any hotel did. Elvis may have left the building, but his presence is very much alive in Sin City.

Chapter 20

Top Ten Vegas Values

by Anthony Curtis

● ●

In This Chapter

▶ Getting tips from a budget guru

▶ Finding the best meal deals on steak, shrimp, buffets, and more

▶ Enjoying entertainment on the cheap

● ●

*W*ith literally hundreds of options to choose from, Las Vegas visitors often find themselves struggling to distinguish between the real deals and the come-ons. Many great values are available in Bargain City, but a few stand out above the others.

Anthony Curtis, publisher of the highly recommended *Las Vegas Advisor* newsletter, has long been considered the leading consumer advocate for Las Vegas visitors. Visit his Web site at www.lasvegasadvisor.com to find current information on Las Vegas shows, buffets, coupons, and good deals; you'll also want to check out the free Las Vegas Question of the Day and the current Top Ten, updated monthly.

 The deals that follow have all stood the test of time and have a good chance of being there when you are. However, there's never any guarantee in Vegas — and that's not just with gambling — so it's possible that some of the following bargains will no longer be available by the time you get to Sin City. Call first to avoid disappointment (and check the Las Vegas Advisor Web site for alternatives).

Steak Dinner, Ellis Island, $6.95

Carrying on the tradition of the legendary Las Vegas bargain steak dinners is the 10-ounce "filet-cut" sirloin at **Ellis Island Casino & Brewery**, 4178 Koval Lane (☎ 702-733-8901; www.ellisislandcasino.com). This complete dinner comes with choice of soup or salad, baked potato, vegetable, dinner rolls, and an Ellis Island microbrewed beer for just $6.95. Though it's available in the cafe 24 hours a day, seven days a week, you won't see this great dinner listed on the menu — you have to ask for it.

Shrimp Cocktail, Golden Gate, 99¢–$1.99

Downtown's **Golden Gate Hotel & Casino,** 1 E. Freemont St. (☎ 702-385-1906; www.goldengatecasino.com), has been home to the best shrimp cocktail in Las Vegas since 1959. Its price was 50¢ for more than 30 years, until it was raised to 99¢. The Golden Gate recently raised the price again, this time to $1.99, but it also upgraded the size of the shrimp. And here's the good news: You can get the 99¢ price simply by joining the casino's players club, which is free. The Golden Gate serves nearly 2 tons of shrimp per week in an old-fashioned sundae glass (not plastic).

No cost-reducing lettuce or celery fillers here — just shrimp (cold-water Bay variety) and the Golden Gate's "secret" cocktail sauce. It's available seven days a week, from 11 a.m. to 2 a.m., in the deli at the rear of the casino.

Fremont Street Experience, Free

It's a close call for the town's best free spectacle, and in a huge survey of nearly 3,000 voters at LasVegasAdvisor.com, the Fountains of Bellagio nudged out the **Fremont Street Experience,** Fremont Street between Las Vegas Boulevard and Main Street (☎ 702-678-5777; www.vegas experience.com), with 46 percent of the vote to 45 percent. But don't think that means you should skip the downtown light show. With 12.5 million light-emitting diodes supplying the overhead images, the crooning-canopy show runs five times per night, beginning when it gets dark.

Harrah's Entertainment Buffets, $29.95

Although you'd have to be kind of crazy to eat this much food, it's impossible to deny the bargain of all you can eat, all day long, at every buffet in a Harrah's Entertainment hotel (for the record, that would be **Caesars Palace, Flamingo, Harrah's, Paris Las Vegas, Planet Hollywood,** and **Rio Suites**). For the math challenged, that's roughly $10 per meal — an almost impossible price to beat.

Pizza and Pitcher, Binion's, $10

Benny's Bullpen at **Binion's Gambling Hall,** 128 E. Fremont St. (☎ 702-382-1600; www.binions.com), serves up a large pizza and pitcher of beer, both big enough to satisfy four people (if you aren't really hungry or thirsty) for $10. This is another example of how downtown Las Vegas really is the place to go for bargain hunters, especially when it comes to food.

Ham and Eggs, Arizona Charlie's Decatur, $3.99

The giant ham-and-eggs breakfast at **Arizona Charlie's Decatur,** 740 S. Decatur Blvd. (☎ **702-258-5200;** www.arizonacharliesdecatur. com), comes with a cover-the-plate ham steak, two eggs, hash browns, and toast. It's served 24 hours a day, 7 days week, and has been for more than a decade. If you don't feel like standing in the usual long line, check the 20-seat counter, where seats turn over quickly.

Hot Dog, South Point, 75¢

The best hot dog in Las Vegas is served from a cart near the sports book at the **South Point Hotel, Casino & Spa,** 9777 Las Vegas Blvd. S. (☎ **702-796-7111;** www.southpointcasino.com). This all-beef dog is a good one, but it's the free extras that set it apart. Load your dog with mustard, onions, relish, and sauerkraut, all for the base price of 75¢.

Dollar Days, Sahara, $1

What does a buck get you in Vegas these days? At the **Sahara,** 2535 Las Vegas Blvd. S. (☎ **702-737-2111;** www.saharavegas.com), quite a bit it seems. One thin dollar will buy you a beer at all casino bars, a shot with a souvenir glass, a hot dog, or a hand of blackjack. The alcohol may not be top shelf and the hot dog is not Pink's, but what do you want for a dollar?

Steak and Shrimp, California, $7.95

The **Market Street Cafe** in downtown's California Hotel and Casino, 12 E. Ogden Ave. (☎ **702-385-1222;** www.thecal.com), has other daily specials, but this one runs every day from 5 to 11 p.m. The entree comes with a vegetable, potato, and roll. If the lines are long, look for a seat at the big counter.

Fontana Bar, Bellagio, $7 cover

Walk into the **Fontana Bar** at **Bellagio,** 3600 Las Vegas Blvd. S. (☎ **702-693-7111;** www.bellagio.com/nightlife/fontana-bar.aspx), and for a mere $7 (cost of a beer to satisfy the one-drink minimum), you're in the middle of one of the swankiest lounges in town, ready for an evening of live music, plush surroundings, and the best view possible of the Bellagio fountain show outside.

Bonus Bargains

Excellent alternatives not quite making the top ten include the **Mac King Comedy Magic Show** at **Harrah's,** 3475 Las Vegas Blvd S., which is priced well at $25 but also offers entry with a coupon for $9.95; the $7.77 off-the-menu steak and shrimp in **Mr. Lucky's 24-7** at the **Hard Rock,** 4455 Paradise Rd.; 24-hour $1.25 draft beer and $2 bottled imports at **Slots-A-Fun,** 2890 Las Vegas Blvd. S. (☎ **800-354-1232** or 702-734-0410); and, of course, room rates citywide in July and December. Finally, one of our favorite restaurants, **Todd English P.U.B.,** 3720 Las Vegas Blvd. S., in Crystals at CityCenter (☎ **702-489-8080;** see Chapter 10 for a full review), is rapidly becoming famous — or infamous depending on your viewpoint — for its Nickel Beer Night. Tuesdays you get draft Pabst Blue Ribbon for only 5¢.

Chapter 21

Nevada's Top Ten Desert Denizens

In This Chapter

▶ Discovering Nevada's desert dwellers

▶ Getting to know the good, the bad, the ugly, and the creepy-crawly

---

*T*he Great Basin Desert and the Mojave Desert, both of which spread across Nevada, are home to all kinds of creatures that love the dry climate or have adapted over the years to live here. This chapter presents ten of the more exotic critters you're likely to encounter — although not necessarily up close and personally and almost definitely not in your hotel room.

Want to know more? One of the best places to learn about local animal life is **Valley of Fire State Park** (55 miles northeast of Las Vegas at exit 75 on I-15; see Chapter 15 for details), where you can view the desert — and if you're lucky — some of the creatures described here in their habitats.

Coyotes

The coyote — a type of wild dog roughly the size of a German shepherd — is the speedster of the *canid* species: It can sprint up to 40 mph and cover several hundred miles in a single night. Coyotes are social, often traveling in packs, and they're domestic: They mate for life, and the pups often hang out with their folks for more than a year. In addition, the coyote is very intelligent and has a larger, more sophisticated vocabulary than that of any other type of dog, communicating through growls, whines, yips, barks, and howls, as well as such body language as tail wagging, lip curling, and mock fighting. The most distinctive of the coyote's calls — a series of barks and yelps followed by a drawn-out howl and a few short, sharp yaps — is used to gather group members together before or after a hunt. Its verbal nature has earned the coyote the name "song dog" in several Native American languages.

These animals keep to themselves during the day, so you may not see any, but you're very likely to hear them at night. And, no, coyotes don't wear bandanas.

Desert Tortoise

At just 10 to 14 inches long, these guys are surprisingly hard-core. They can live 80 to 100 years, all the while surviving temperatures ranging from freezing to more than 140°F by digging burrows into the desert floor. They can go more than a year without water, getting all the moisture they need from the plants they eat. Despite their long lives, it is thought that they rarely venture more than 2 miles from where they were born.

 Touching, harming, or collecting wild desert tortoises is illegal.

Hummingbirds

These adorable birds flit and hover, helicopter-like, around flowers — but what they're actually doing is pigging out. With the highest metabolic rate of any warm-blooded vertebrate, hummingbirds eat all day long to keep from starving.

Jackrabbits and Desert Cottontails

You're most likely to see jackrabbits and their cousins, desert cottontails (the latter's ears are smaller, and they have cute, fluffy tails), hopping around at dawn or dusk. Both types are constant noshers — they nibble voraciously on a variety of plants, including cacti.

Lizards

Small, pinkish, and delicate geckos are notable for the round pads on their fingers and toes — helpful in climbing the walls, literally. These lizards are far more common — you may be relieved to hear — than the 2-foot-long, black-and-orange-striped Gila monster. The largest native lizard in the United States, the Gila monster is the only venomous animal protected by state law.

 Don't be deceived by its placid, sluggish demeanor; Gila monsters can bite with a viselike grip. Pick one up, and you may need to pry it off with a screwdriver — and then head for the nearest emergency room. Gila monsters aren't considered deadly to humans, but you don't really want to test that theory.

Quails

These chubby, plumed birds tend to cross the road together in family groups called *coveys*. The mother quail shepherds her babies on outings. These birds also may turn up on your dinner plate — but I won't discuss that here.

Rattlesnakes

Public-relations people throughout the Southwest like to point out that rattlers are present in nearly every state in the United States. However, said PR people aren't likely to mention the fact that the Southwest has more species of rattlesnakes than does any other single region in the Americas. The good news: Rattlers don't really want to tussle with you — that rattling sound means "go away." Nor do they want to waste venom on you — you're too large to kill and eat. If you do get bitten, chances are 50/50 that the bite is dry (nonpoisonous). ***The bottom line:*** Watch where you step in the wild, but don't make yourself miserable with worry. You're 20 times more likely to be struck by lightning than to be bitten by a rattlesnake.

Roadrunners

Members of the cuckoo family, these 2-foot-long crested birds live throughout the Southwest. Although they prefer sprinting (at 15 mph) to flying, they will take flight to avoid fast predators, such as coyotes. Roadrunners eat insects, lizards, and snakes. They'll even devour rattlesnakes whole.

Scorpions

These miniature lobsters like to hang out in dark, dry spots. All varieties are nearly invisible in the dark (although they glow under ultraviolet light). The scorpion's bite is painful, but not dangerous. Their sting is venomous, but they sting humans only in self-defense, and most species' stings just cause a painful swelling.

 If your shoes have been under your bed all night, shake them out before sticking your feet back into them.

Spiders

Big, hairy tarantulas are the most conspicuous of the desert spiders, but they're harmless — honest. Some people even keep them as pets.

The spiders you really want to give a wide berth are the much smaller, but far more poisonous, black widows. A black widow spider's bite can be deadly, but, fortunately, black widows aren't aggressive — just don't go poking your fingers in their faces or into dark corners. You can recognize the venomous females by the bright red, hourglass-shaped markings on their chests.

Appendix

Quick Concierge

*T*his handy section is where we condense all the practical and pertinent information — from airline phone numbers to mailbox locations — you need to make sure that you have a successful and stress-free Las Vegas vacation. And in case you believe in being really prepared, we also give you some additional resources to check out.

Fast Facts

AAA

The nearest regional office for the nationwide auto club is located at 3312 W. Charleston Blvd. (☎ 702-415-2200).

American Express

If you lose your American Express Travelers Cheques, dial ☎ 800-221-7282 anytime, 24 hours a day. There's an American Express Travel Services office at the Fashion Show Mall (☎ 702-739-8474).

Area Code

The area code for Las Vegas is 702.

ATMs

ATMs are everywhere, because casinos want you to have easy access to your money. Remember that each ATM will charge you a fee, as will your bank (probably), adding up to as much as a $5 surcharge on your withdrawal.

Baby Sitters

Most major hotels can provide you with referrals to licensed and bonded baby sitters or child-care specialists. Around the

Clock Babysitters (☎ 800-798-6768 or 702-365-1040) have been in business for 30 years and not only screen all their sitters with the sheriff and the FBI, but also check references. Office hours are 10 a.m. to 3 p.m., and sitters are available 24 hours a day, seven days a week.

Camera Repair

You can find photo and camera service in the main gift shop of most major hotels. Check with your hotel's concierge or guest-services desk.

Convention Centers

Las Vegas is one of America's top convention destinations. Much of the action takes place at the Las Vegas Convention Center, 3150 Paradise Rd. (☎ 877-847-4858 or 702-892-0711), which is the largest single-level convention center in the world. Its 3.2 million square feet includes 144 meeting rooms. This immense facility is augmented by the Cashman Field Center, 850 Las Vegas Blvd. N. (☎ 702-892-0711). Under the same auspices, Cashman provides another 483,000 square feet of convention space.

Credit Cards

If your credit card is lost or stolen, call these emergency numbers: Citicorp Visa (☎ 800-847-2911), American Express (☎ 800-221-7282), or MasterCard (☎ 800-622-7747).

Doctors and Dentists

Most major hotels have physician-referral services, but you also can call the free service at Desert Springs Hospital (☎ 702-388-4888) Monday through Friday 8 a.m. to 8 p.m. and Saturday 9 a.m. to 3 p.m. For a dental referral, call the Southern Nevada Dental Society (☎ 702-733-8700) weekdays 9 a.m. to noon and 1 to 5 p.m., or visit its Web site at www.sndsonline.org.

Dry Cleaners

Most major hotels offer laundry and dry-cleaning services or can direct you to the nearest cleaners, if you don't want to pay the sometimes exorbitant rates they charge.

Emergencies

Dial ☎ 911 to contact the police or paramedics. You can get emergency service at any time, day or night, at Sunrise Hospital and Medical Center, 3186 Maryland Pkwy., between Desert Inn Road and Sahara Avenue (☎ 702-731-8057). For less-critical emergencies, try the Harmon Medical Center, 150 E. Harmon Ave. (☎ 702-796-1116), the closest urgent-care facility to the Strip. It's open 24 hours a day.

Gambling Laws

You must be 21 years old to enter a casino area.

Highway Conditions

For recorded local information, call ☎ 702-486-3116.

Hospitals

See "Emergencies," earlier in this section.

Hot Lines

In a crisis, you can contact the Rape Crisis Center (☎ 702-366-1640), the Suicide Prevention Hot Line (☎ 702-731-2990), or Poison Emergencies (☎ 800-446-6179).

Information

All the major hotels have tour and show desks, but you can get additional information from the Las Vegas Visitor Information Center, 3150 Paradise Rd. (☎ 877-847-4858 or 702-892-7575), or from the Las Vegas Chamber of Commerce, 6671 Las Vegas Blvd. S. (☎ 702-735-1616). The LVCVA is open daily from 7 a.m. to 7 p.m.; the LVCC is open Monday through Friday 8 a.m. to 5 p.m.

See also "Where to Get More Information," later in this chapter.

Liquor Laws

You must be 21 to buy alcohol — period. You can buy liquor at bars and stores 24 hours a day, including Sunday. You can even drink from open containers as long as you're on the Strip or at the Fremont Street Experience — a practice that is banned in most other cities — but don't try it anywhere else in town.

Maps

All major hotels have basic city maps available to hotel guests. You can buy more-detailed maps at any hotel gift shop.

Newspapers/Magazines

Las Vegas has two major newspapers that you can buy in the city: The *Las Vegas Review-Journal* and the *Las Vegas Sun*. Both are available at almost every hotel gift shop. In addition, a variety of free local publications have information on local happenings. The most prominent is *What's On, The Las Vegas Guide,* available in hotels and restaurants throughout the city. For a totally unbiased and more hip, alternative opinion, try the free weekly papers *Las Vegas Weekly* and *Las Vegas City Life,* both of which are available at various record and used-clothing stores and the like around town.

Pharmacies

CVS, 1360 E. Flamingo Rd. at Maryland Parkway (☎ 702-731-5373), is part of a large national pharmacy chain and is open 24 hours. You can find a Walgreens at 3339 Las Vegas Blvd. S., next to the Venetian (☎ 702-369-8166). If you want to patronize an independent store that's not part of a chain, try White Cross Drugs, 1700 Las Vegas Blvd. S., just north of the Stratosphere Tower (☎ 702-382-1733); it will deliver to your hotel if you so desire.

Police

For emergencies, dial ☎ **911;** for non-emergencies, dial ☎ 702-795-3111.

Post Office

The most convenient post office is near Circus Circus, at 3100 Industrial Rd., between Sahara Avenue and Spring Mountain Road (☎ 800-297-5543). It's open Monday through Friday 8:30 a.m. to 5 p.m. You can mail letters and packages at your hotel, and there's a full-service post office in the Forum Shops in Caesars Palace.

Restrooms

All the major hotels have public restroom facilities. They are, for the most part, clean and safe. Remember not to leave your children unattended.

Safety

As long as you stick to well-lit tourist areas, crime usually isn't a major concern. However, pickpockets who target people coming out of casinos (or people in the casinos who are entranced by gambling) can be a problem. Men should keep wallets well concealed, and women should keep purses in sight and secure at all times. Be warned — thieves tend to be particularly bold during outdoor shows such as the Volcano at the Mirage or the Fountains of Bellagio. Many hotel rooms have safes for cash or valuables. If yours does not, the front desk can offer you a safe-deposit box.

Smoking

Smoking is permitted only in designated areas, which is limited to the gambling areas of casinos, bars that don't serve food, and some hotel rooms. Smoking is not permitted in any other indoor public place including malls, restaurants, theaters, or hallways.

Taxes

Clark County hotel room tax is 12 percent to 13 percent, and sales tax is 8.1 percent.

Taxis

Basic fare is $3.30 at the meter drop and $2.40 for each additional mile, with time penalties for sitting still and additional charges for airport runs. Major operators include Ace (☎ 702-736-8383), Checker (☎ 702-873-2000), Desert (☎ 702-386-9102), Henderson (☎ 702-384-6111), Star (☎ 702-873-2000), Western (☎ 702-736-8000), Whittlesea (☎ 702-384-6111), and Yellow (☎ 702-873-2000).

Time Zone

Las Vegas is in the Pacific time zone, three hours earlier than the East Coast (New York, Florida), two hours earlier than the Midwest (Iowa, Texas), and one hour earlier than the Mountain states (Colorado, Wyoming).

Transit Information

Call Citizen's Area Transit (CAT) at ☎ 702-228-7433.

Weddings

If you want to get hitched in the state of Nevada, you don't need a blood test, and you don't have to withstand a waiting period. Get your license downtown at Clark County Marriage License Bureau, 201 Clark Ave. (☎ 702-671-0600), for $60. It's open 8 a.m. to midnight daily. For more information, see Chapter 12.

Toll-Free Numbers and Web Sites

Airlines

Aeromexico
☎ 800-237-6639
www.aeromexico.com

Air Canada
☎ 888-247-2262
www.aircanada.com

Alaska Airlines
☎ 800-426-0333
www.alaskaair.com

Allegiant
☎ 702-505-8888
www.allegiantair.com

American
☎ 800-433-7300
www.aa.com

British Airways
☎ 800-247-9297
www.britishairways.com

Continental
☎ 800-525-0280
www.continental.com

Delta
☎ 800-221-1212
www.delta.com

Frontier
☎ 800-432-1359
www.frontierairlines.com

Hawaiian Airlines
☎ 800-367-5320
www.hawaiianair.com

JetBlue
☎ 800-538-2583
www.jetblue.com

Mexicana
☎ 800-531-7921
www.mexicana.com

Midwest Airlines
☎ 800-452-2022
www.midwestexpress.com

Southwest
☎ 800-435-9792
www.southwest.com

Sun Country
☎ 866-359-6786
www.suncountry.com

United
☎ 800-241-6522
www.united.com

US Airways
☎ 800-428-4322
www.usairways.com

Virgin Atlantic
☎ 800-862-8621
www.virgin-atlantic.com

Car-rental agencies

Advantage
☎ 800-777-9377
www.advantage.com

Alamo
☎ 877-227-8367
www.alamo.com

Avis
☎ 800-230-4898 in continental United States
☎ 800-272-5871 in Canada
www.avis.com

Budget
☎ 800-527-0700
www.budget.com

Dollar
☎ 800-800-3665
www.dollar.com

Enterprise
☎ 800-736-8227
www.enterprise.com

Hertz
☎ 800-654-3131
www.hertz.com

National
☎ 800-227-7368
www.nationalcar.com

Payless
☎ 800-729-5377
www.paylesscar.com

Thrifty
☎ 800-847-4389
www.thrifty.com

Major hotel and motel chains

Best Western
☎ 800-780-7234
www.bestwestern.com

Clarion
☎ 877-424-6423
www.clarionhotel.com

Comfort Inn
☎ 877-424-6423
www.comfortinn.com

Courtyard by Marriott
☎ 800-321-2211
www.courtyard.com

Days Inn
☎ 800-329-7466
www.daysinn.com

DoubleTree
☎ 800-222-8733
www.doubletree.com

EconoLodge
☎ 877-424-6423
www.econolodge.com

Fairfield Inn by Marriott
☎ 800-228-2800
www.fairfieldinn.com

Hampton
☎ 800-426-7866
www.hamptoninn.com

Hilton
☎ 800-445-8667
www.hilton.com

Holiday Inn
☎ 800-465-4329
www.holidayinn.com

Howard Johnson
☎ 800-446-4656
www.hojo.com

Hyatt
☎ 800-233-1234
www.hyatt.com

La Quinta
☎ 866-725-1661
www.laquinta.com

Marriott
☎ 888-236-2427
www.marriott.com

Motel 6
☎ 800-466-8356
www.motel6.com

Quality
☎ 877-424-6423
www.qualityinn.com

Radisson
☎ 888-201-1718
www.radisson.com

Ramada
☎ 800-272-6232
www.ramada.com

Red Carpet Inn
☎ 800-251-1962
www.bookroomsnow.com

Red Lion Hotel
☎ 800-733-5466
www.redlion.com

Red Roof Inn
☎ 800-733-7663
www.redroof.com

Residence Inn by Marriott
☎ 800-331-3131
www.residenceinn.com

Rodeway Inn
☎ 877-424-6423
www.rodewayinn.com

Sheraton
☎ 888-625-5144
www.sheraton.com

Super 8 Motel
☎ 800-800-8000
www.super8.com

Travelodge
☎ 800-578-7878
www.travelodge.com

Vagabond Inn
☎ 800-522-1555
www.vagabondinn.com

Where to Get More Information

If you want more detailed information on attractions, accommodations, or just about anything else in Las Vegas, you won't find it difficult to come by. Check out the following list for some excellent sources for tourist information, maps, and brochures:

✔ The **Las Vegas Visitor Information Center,** 3150 Paradise Rd. (☎ **877-847-4858** or 702-892-7575; www.visitlasvegas.com), can answer any questions you have and send you a comprehensive packet of brochures, a map, a show guide, an events calendar, and an attractions list. It also can help you find a hotel that suits your needs and assist you in making a reservation.

✔ The **Las Vegas Chamber of Commerce,** 6671 Las Vegas Blvd. S. (☎ **702-735-1616;** www.lvchamber.com), another great source of local information, offers the *Visitor's Guide,* which contains extensive information about accommodations, attractions, excursions, children's activities, and more. The Chamber of Commerce can answer all your Las Vegas questions, including those about weddings and divorces.

✔ The *Las Vegas Review-Journal* (www.lvrj.com) is the largest paper in town. Its Neon section has numerous listings for entertainment, dining, and nightlife. Head to its Web site for detailed descriptions of places of interest, such as the best romantic restaurant, best blackjack tables, best wedding chapel, and best roller coaster. The Best of the Worst section features such notables as the slowest stoplight in town and the worst place to take visitors.

✔ Another helpful paper, the ***Las Vegas Weekly*** (`www.lasvegas weekly.com`), can be picked up in local shops and restaurants around town. The Web site for this alternative weekly offers reviews of bars, cafes, nightclubs, restaurants, bookstores, amusement parks, and shops. The dining listings are especially good if you're looking for an alternative to the touristy restaurants at the hotels.

✔ The Web site **A2Z Las Vegas** (`www.a2zlasvegas.com`) lives up to its name. It's chock-full of information on everything from hotels and guided tours to shows and getting married in Las Vegas. It even keeps tabs on the status of progressive slot-machine jackpots in Nevada. The hotel and dining reviews feature objective comments and ratings by fellow visitors.

✔ Get more information on Las Vegas from these **Frommer's guidebooks** (published by Wiley): *Frommer's Las Vegas, Frommer's Portable Las Vegas, The Unofficial Guide to Las Vegas, Frommer's Las Vegas with Kids,* and *Frommer's Portable Las Vegas for Non-Gamblers.*

Index

See also separate Accommodations and Restaurant indexes at the end of this index.

Accommodations Index

Restaurant Index

Notes

Notes